TESTIMONIALS FROM ATHLETES AND JOURNALISTS

"I was inspired by Robert's motivation and energy—he has a real passion for sports....They say there are three types of people, some make things happen, some watch things happen, and others wonder what happened. Robert truly makes things happen."

—WALT FRAZIER, Basketball Legend and NBA Hall of Famer

"Robert's drive, passion, and energy for EVERYTHING is a real source of inspiration in my everyday life....His vision, dedication, persistence, and professionalism are just some of the reasons why he will always be a great champion. We all owe Robert a major debt of gratitude for his endless contributions toward making this world a better place."

—BILL WALTON, Basketball Legend and NBA Hall of Famer

"Robert Tuchman brings a tremendous amount of energy and enthusiasm....He did not need a 'miracle'...just a tremendous work ethic and passion for what he does. He is someone we all can learn from."

—MIKE ERUZIONE, Captain of the 1980 Olympic Champion
U.S. Hockey Team

"Some people are really into sports. Then there's Robert Tuchman."

—MICHAEL KANE, *New York Post*

"Robert Tuchman has made a living out of giving people inside access to athletes, celebrities, and sporting events."

—ASHLEY JUDE COLLIE, Southwest Airlines' *Spirit* Magazine

"Want to reward your employees with a trip to the World Series or the Daytona 500, or perhaps the Maui Film Festival or the Daytime Emmy Awards? If so, then Robert Tuchman is the man to know."

—*Incentive Magazine*

THE
100 SPORTING
EVENTS

YOU MUST SEE LIVE

An Insider's Guide to Creating
the Sports Experience of a Lifetime

Robert Tuchman

BENBELLA BOOKS, INC.
Dallas, Texas

BenBella Books, Inc.
6440 N. Central Expressway, Suite 503
Dallas, TX 75206
www.benbellabooks.com
Send feedback to feedback@benbellabooks.com

Printed in the United States of America
10 9 8 7 6 5 4 3 2

Library of Congress Cataloging-in-Publication Data

Tuchman, Robert.
    The 100 sporting events you must see live : an insider's guide to creating the sports experience of a lifetime / Robert Tuchman.
        p. cm.
    ISBN 978-1-933771-45-8
    1. Sports—United States—Anecdotes. I. Title. II. Title: Hundred sporting events you must live to see.

  GV583.T73 2009
  796.0973—dc22

                                                                    2008045905

Proofreading by Emily Chauvier and Stacia Seaman
Cover design by Laura Watkins
Text design and composition by John Reinhardt Book Design
Printed by Bang Printing

Distributed by Perseus Distribution:
perseusdistribution.com

To place orders through Perseus Distribution:
Tel: 800-343-4499
Fax: 800-351-5073
E-mail: orderentry@perseusbooks.com

I dedicate this book to my daughter Mia, who I hope will experience all that life has to offer. To my parents Kenneth and Esther, who allowed me to do just that. And of course to my beautiful wife Amy, who continues to allow me to do so.

ACKNOWLEDGMENTS

I would like to acknowledge:

Amy Mirer Tuchman, my love, my soul mate, and my rock of support.

Mia Tuchman, my baby girl forever. Daddy loves you more than you will ever know.

My parents, Esther Tuchman and Kenneth Tuchman. Thank you for all the love and support you have given me throughout my life.

Mark, Julie, Julia, Adam, Paula, Steve, Mitch, Michelle, Anna, Sam, and Arlene, thank you for all your love.

Brett Sklar. Thank you for being my business partner and my friend, and for really making this book possible with all your hard work and dedication over the years.

My research team Vanessa Vera, Emily Clare Fenn, Kimberly Nathan, Jonathan Jacobs, and Allie Gropp, and all the others who assisted with this book.

My agent and friend, Frank Weimann, who really made this happen.

Carl Koerner and Ivan Kronenfeld, who believed in me and who set the wheels in motion for this book.

Andy Robb and Jennifer Amini, without whom there would be no TSE Sports & Entertainment.

Scott Jernigan and Brian Wilder. Sorry I couldn't get any NC State stuff on the list but your support has always been appreciated.

Michael Kahan, for that computer you gave me and Sklar ten years ago. No computer = no company = no book.

Glenn, Jeff, Leah, Yara, and the team at BenBella Books.

The old time TSE Sports & Entertainment crew: Adam Rauch, Willie Steinberg, Chris Shammas, Jay Palmer, Brendan McCallion, Sal Parikh, Hope Newman, Dave Sowers, Bob Masura, Nick Roos, Freddie Etsiakoh, Jayne Wise, Lauren Levy, Keith Creegan, and the Webs.

All the current PCE, Dodd's, GO, and PST employees.

The Pfingsten Partners team.

Joel Solomon, thanks for the checklist idea.

The Little Reds.

To my close friends whom I have gone to so many games with, thanks for all the great times and the special memories: JH, BZ, AR, GS, CS, BA, JK, SG, PE, and MK.

Thanks to several longtime clients who always had faith in me to deliver: BJ Zellers (Edy's Grand Ice Cream), Maryann Matteo (Eastman Kodak), Ernie De La Torre (Eastman Kodak), Art Niosi (Ocean Spray), Tom Joyce (Hershey's), Nicole Moran (CapitalOne), Dan Martinez (ESPN), Janet Abbazia (Turner), and Pam Griggs (AT&T).

I would also like to acknowledge
those who helped me with insight about specific events:

Jonathan Scher and the Krautdogs
Greg Marius (Rucker Park)
Chuck Mycoff (Chicago Cubs)
The Cincy crew: Jeff Weber, Nick Roos, Jerry Weber, and Cadi Schultz (Reds
    Opening Day)
Amy Prunty (Backyard Brawl)
Fred Schoch and Ben Hamilton (Head of the Charles)
Laurence Goldstein (Montreal Canadiens vs. Toronto Maple Leafs)
Stacy Grill (Montreal Canadiens vs. Toronto Maple Leafs and Harvard vs. Yale)
Richard Shea (Nathan's Hot Dog Eating Contest)
David Brewer (Rickwood baseball)
Kathryn Chapoton and Stefanie Gorder (Iditarod)
Krystal Bradnock (All Blacks Rugby)
Ethan Madson (Tour de France and Ironman)
Marie Johnson (Alabama vs. Auburn)
Michael Dittelman (Harlem Globetrotters)
Robin Jerstad and Andrea Davis (Indy 500 and Indiana High School Basketball)
Valarie Sakonoi (Ironman)
Chiara Trivella and Enza Valiante (Running of the Bulls)
Jimmy Delaney (Lady Vols)
Freddie Etsiakoh and Kevin Gray (Manchester United/Liverpool)
Tom Jordan (Prefontaine)
Daniel Holzhauer (Green Bay Packers game at Lambeau)
Cory Schouten (Little 500 and Indiana Hoops)
B Wilder and the Jern (NC/Duke)

CONTENTS

Introduction   1

Breakdown of the Event Sections   5

The Events
1   Masters   9
2   World Cup   12
3   Super Bowl   15
4   Summer Olympics   19
5   Army vs. Navy Football Game   21
6   New York City Marathon   25
7   World Series   28
8   Winter Olympics   31
9   Red Sox vs. Yankees at Yankee Stadium   33
10   UNC vs. Duke Basketball Game at Cameron Indoor Stadium   36
11   Wimbledon   40
12   Stanley Cup   44
13   Tour de France   46
14   Cubs Game at Wrigley Field   49
15   BCS National Championship Game in New Orleans   52
16   Liverpool vs. Manchester United at Old Trafford   56
17   Michigan vs. Ohio State at The Big House   60
18   NFL Conference Championships   63
19   Daytona 500   66
20   Final Four—NCAA Men's Basketball   70
21   Ryder Cup   72
22   Baseball Hall of Fame Induction Weekend   75
23   Harvard vs. Yale at Yale   78
24   Kentucky Derby   82
25   UEFA Champions League   85
26   Rose Bowl   88
27   British Open   91
28   Horse Racing at Saratoga   94
29   Late Season Green Bay Packers Game at Lambeau Field   97
30   Canadiens vs. Maple Leafs in Toronto   100

31	Indy 500	104
32	Professional Bull Riders World Finals	107
33	Dubai World Cup	111
34	Hong Kong Sevens	114
35	Monaco Grand Prix	117
36	Running of the Bulls	120
37	Rugby World Cup	124
38	Red River Shootout	126
39	Notre Dame Football Game	129
40	MLB All-Star Game	133
41	Iron Bowl at Alabama	136
42	Epsom Derby	139
43	Calgary Stampede	141
44	Koshien Baseball Tournament	145
45	Special Olympics	147
46	Soccer Game at Maracanã Stadium in Rio	151
47	Texas Football Friday Night Lights in Odessa	154
48	U.S. Open Tennis Tournament	156
49	USC vs. UCLA Basketball Game at Pauley Pavilion	161
50	Le Mans 24	163
51	Ironman World Championship	166
52	Iowa vs. Iowa State Wrestling Meet at Iowa	169
53	Golden Gloves at Madison Square Garden	171
54	French Open	174
55	Baseball Game at Fenway Park	177
56	Belmont Stakes	180
57	Kangaroos Australian Football Game	184
58	Heavyweight Title Fight at Madison Square Garden	187
59	All Blacks Rugby Game	190
60	ACC Basketball Tournament	194
61	Caribbean World Series	196
62	FA Cup	198
63	Indiana High School Basketball Tournament Finals	201
64	U.S. Open Golf Tournament	203
65	Midnight Madness at University of Kentucky	206
66	Preakness Stakes	209
67	NFL Draft	211
68	National Finals Rodeo	215
69	Basketball Game at Phog Allen Fieldhouse	218
70	Basketball Game at Madison Square Garden	221
71	Prefontaine Classic	224
72	MLB Opening Day in Cincinnati	227
73	Nathan's Hot Dog Eating Contest	231

74   Iditarod   234
75   Little 500   236
76   Basketball Game at Rucker Park, Harlem, NY   239
77   Boston Marathon   241
78   Cowboys Monday Night Football Game in Dallas   245
79   Head of the Charles Regatta   248
80   Florida vs. Georgia Football Game   251
81   Lady Vols Basketball Game   254
82   NBA All-Star Game   257
83   Pipeline Surfing   260
84   Australian Open Tennis Tournament   262
85   Baseball Game at Rickwood Field in Alabama   265
86   Harlem Globetrotters Performance   268
87   Spring Training Game at Tigertown   271
88   Backyard Brawl in Morgantown   274
89   London Marathon   277
90   Penn Relays   280
91   Presidents Cup   283
92   World Junior Hockey Championship   285
93   Westminster Dog Show   287
94   NFL Hall of Fame Induction   290
95   NCAA Men's Lacrosse Championship   293
96   College Baseball World Series   295
97   Beanpot Hockey Tournament   298
98   Bayou Classic   301
99   Little League World Series   305
100 UFC Title Fight   307

Honorable Mentions
     Frozen Four   311
     World Figure Skating Championships   313
     X Games   316
     Cheerleading Nationals   318
     Gym Dogs   321
     Japan Series   324

The Top Ten Cities for Hosting a Major Sporting Event   329

Your Checklist for the 100 Sporting Events You Must See Live   333

About the Author   337

INTRODUCTION

THE IDEA FOR THIS BOOK came to me while I was attending the 2006 World Cup in Germany. I witnessed hundreds of thousands of people who had traveled from around the world to experience this great sporting event. Passion could be seen in their eyes and heard through their cheers. I have seen many live sports events in my time, but few have been able to match the type of raw energy and enthusiasm that was evident that summer in Europe. The actual matches were only a part of the experience. The pride that countrymen felt toward their team, the parties and revelry in the streets in celebrating a victory, and the liveliness and enthusiasm provided a once-in-a-lifetime spectacle for me. I felt a need to share this type of live sports experience—not to mention ninety-nine others—in the very book you are reading.

When I first started researching this project, I found it amazing how people perceived the greatest sporting events to attend. No matter where they were from around the world, the discussion over great live sporting events would be filled with detailed recollections and fond memories. Lively debates ensued on the merits of what it would take to achieve a Top 100 recognition. "Why this one and not that one" or "You have to include this event; it's incredible" would invariably be the responses I received. I learned just how passionate sports fans are about individual events, and discussing the merits for a "Top 100" inclusion brought out that zeal.

Working in the sports travel industry over the past ten years, I have had the rare opportunity to attend many of the events you will read about. I have gained an understanding of the "must sees," "must stays," and "must eats." This list is not about my personal loyalties to any team or region of the world. Objectivity was paramount in determining each selection. In the end, it was about the energy of the event, not the number of people who attended it, the revenue it generated, or the television ratings it drew. One thing I am certain of is that you cannot quantify the experience of seeing any of these 100 events in person as opposed to from your couch.

This book is about going beyond the living room. What you see on television or read about in newspapers is nowhere close to the raw experience of actually being there. Today, the world is a smaller place and the opportunity to view these events via television and the Internet has never been easier. However, is the life of a sports fan lived in front of the television a life lived to its fullest? What about the experience of actually being there and seeing it all without the need for commentary or commercials? The sights. The sounds. The smells. The cultures that exist surrounding the event itself. Annual traditions, both formal and informal. There are so many nuances to a sporting event that occur away from the view of the camera or when the television is turned off.

Traveling to a sporting event makes the intangible tangible. People long for an interactive experience. What can be more exhilarating than inhaling the dust from the streets of Pamplona, Spain, while you frantically run from the bulls? You cannot get any more hands-on than walking the streets of Monaco immediately after the Grand Prix. How about being part of the electric crowd at Kentucky's Midnight Madness? It is a great way to relive your youthful days and be a part of something so special.

Have you ever imagined what it would have been like to be at the Final Four in Lexington, Kentucky, when Villanova stunned Georgetown to win the NCAA championship in 1985? Did you ever dream that you could go back in time and experience Jesse Owens's legendary performance at the 1936 Olympics in Berlin? My historical vantage point happened when the New York Rangers won the Stanley Cup at Madison Square Garden in 1994 after a fifty-four-year dry spell. I will never forget the sight of a man holding up a sign that summed up every long-suffering fan who has had the opportunity to watch their team win a major event after years of trying: "Now I can die in peace." The 100 events detailed in this book will provide you with a good start to your own personal bucket list.

Being at any one of these Top 100 sporting events is your chance to be a part of history. One day you might be able to tell your children and grandchildren, "I was there when..." You can boast to your friends about the event itself while offering insight about a certain restaurant, the amenities of a nearby hotel, or the over-the-top friendliness of the locals.

Now, attending the sporting event itself is many times only part of the experience. There are many surprises around every corner of the world to greet you. The cities, small towns, and villages that host these events have their own unique attributes. From the hotel you stay in to the food you eat to the residents that greet you with a hearty pat on the back, each event provides its own memorable moments for a die-hard sports fan and a casual observer. The revelry of the French Quarter when a BCS championship game finds its way to New Orleans. Augusta's small-town feel. A stroll through Krzyzewskiville prior to a Duke-UNC game. Feeling the bitter cold of Lambeau Field as you take your seat in the stands. Or something so simple as a young boy holding a basketball in one hand while taking his father's hand in the other as he attends his first Indiana high school basketball state finals.

Sports fans compose a brotherhood and sisterhood. There is no greater camaraderie than sitting in a section of fans that bleed the same team colors. The team does well and it's high-fives and hugs all around. When they lose, it's time to shed a tear and curse the officials in unison. For a brief moment in time, boundaries that separate members of society disappear. Cultural differences become meaningless. There are no differences in ethnicity, income level, or age. We are united in cheering, jeering, and just enjoying the sporting event. This is the greatest gift of sports, its ability to bring people together. Nowhere is this more evident than at live sporting events.

Generating a list of the Top 100 sporting events was a challenging task. The list of omissions is much longer, if not endless. However, there are events that some of us look forward to every year, regardless of if they make my or any other Top 100 list. There are some that you cannot take your eyes off because of the athletic prowess of an up-and-coming basketball player competing at Rucker Park. Others, you cannot look away because you will be afraid to miss the moment a champion of gastronomical proportions stuffs that record-setting Nathan's Famous hot dog down his (or her) gullet to take the mustard-colored title belt.

Today's sports fan may welcome the inclusion of the Super Bowl and the Kentucky Derby on the list. They may question the addition of a baseball game at Rickwood Field or a Harlem Globetrotters show. Traditionalists will likely turn up their nose at the Nathan's Hot Dog Eating Contest while harrumphing at the Westminster Dog Show.

The entire list will not please everyone, but reading about the event may very well whet the appetite of even the most avowed skeptic. Again, this list is about the entire experience and not just the sporting event itself. In this book, you can find out the significance of the sporting event and the history behind it. Highly recommended hotels and quality restaurants will give you options to rest and eat before and after whatever event or events you choose to attend.

Planning a trip around a sporting event may seem daunting. This book will provide you with the knowledge to make it simple. You can find out how to buy tickets, which airports to fly into, the best hotels to stay in, the perfect restaurants to enjoy a meal at, and all the attractions you will need to see while in town. This book focuses on getting you to the event, instead of just providing a bunch of "best of" lists and various opinions on the events and the amenities.

Let your friends see the Eiffel Tower while you watch the French Open. Family members can delight in visiting Radio City Music Hall while you are in New York City to see the Golden Gloves championships at The Garden or a baseball game at Yankee Stadium. In Las Vegas, your spouse can gamble to their heart's content. You have a UFC Match or the Pro Bull Riding Finals to attend.

London is for the London Marathon or Wimbledon. In Boston you should watch college hockey players battle for the Beanpot and stop off to see Paul Revere's house if you have time. Football in Wisconsin? It is meant to be played in the snow, Packer-style, so you can laugh at the warmer-weather teams as they try to adjust to the elements. The Great White North can be just that, as you watch the Iditarod mushers mush like no one else.

Now, before you leap from where you are sitting, let's define what it takes to make this exclusive list.

All the sporting competitions on the list were not created equal. Some are well funded while others struggle for sponsorship. Some have major network contracts so billions worldwide can watch the event on television while others cannot even make it to a public access station. Some enjoy fanatical followings with growing crowds attending every year while others attract a more niche market. Some require great athletic talent and skills while others require brute force. Some require a delicate touch while others mandate a strong stomach.

Some of the events were started on a wager while others were created based upon a rivalry. Some had to overcome financial problems and world wars to continue their honored tradition while others have enjoyed hundreds of successful and exciting years.

Yet, no matter the circumstances of their origins or the growth they have experienced, none of these sporting events ever fails to entertain and bring out the best in athletic competition.

As sports fans, we rabidly look forward to seeing the best and brightest battle it out. We roar in approval for the favorites as if they are family members or close friends. We boo the villains as if we were attending an old-time silent movie. With the advent of high-definition televisions and surround-sound systems, we can do all that while watching the event of our choice in the comfort of our home. We can invite friends and co-workers to join in on the happenings while enjoying fatty foods and libations. Yes, you can come close to the experience, but nothing can ever compare to simply being at one of these events. All of the events on this list in some way or another bring out a certain energy that makes for an experience that you just have to witness at least once in your lifetime.

Who wouldn't want to be a part of the crowd responding to the crack of the bat that signifies a World Series game-winning home run or the roar following a kicker's foot connecting with the pigskin of a football to complete a team's successful comeback? You could be fortunate enough to sit next to a longtime, grizzled fan of a team or resident of the area, listening to story after story. You may be standing in a concession line of fans filled with excitement, anticipation, and conversation about the competition. Haven't you ever wondered what goes on at an event before the cameras start rolling? There is so much more to each of these events than what you see on TV.

Now why wonder what might take place? Why not be there?

This book will give you the events you must go to and the means to get there.

Enjoy your experience.

BREAKDOWN OF THE EVENT SECTIONS

To make it easier to navigate this book, I have broken down each Top 100 listing into specific sections to help you understand the key elements associated with an event. There are innumerable ways to categorize what makes a great sporting event. Listed below, I detail the sections I have included and what each might entail. These categories include relevant factual information, historical perspectives, the "who's who" of attendees, ideal hotels and restaurants, and the best place to get that perfect view of all the action.

Where?
This section lists the city and the name of the venue where the event is located. With some events, the location changes every year or every few years and will be noted.

When?
The time of year or the day the event takes place. Most events usually occur around the same time each year or every few years. For example, the Kentucky Derby is always the first Saturday in May. Events that take place once every several years include the Ryder Cup, Olympics, and World Cup.

Significance:
What makes this event important enough to merit a Top 100 listing? In this section, I look at relevance of the event and the key factors associated with it.

Who attends?
A general look at crowd demographics and the faces you will see in attendance, from the man down the street to the famous celebrity.

History
Most of the Top 100 selections are steeped in history. This section will provide a more in-depth look into the past of many important and historic sporting events. How it started. How it came to be.

Notable Athletes/MVPs:
What would a sporting event be without the notable figures that have made it great? From high-profile athletes to heralded contributors, we name legendary names.

Records:
Historic milestones are noted. From who scored the most points to what team consistently appeared at the event, we reveal the best and the brightest of these impact players.

Things to know before you go:

Fuzzy on your hockey terminology? Confused about the buzzwords in lacrosse? We provide you with a primer so you can understand the hardcore fans' language spoken all around you.

How to get there?

You have arrived in the city of the event. Now you need to find it. From directions to recommended public transit, this section will show you how to get there.

Tickets:

This section reveals how to get your hands on the best tickets. When tickets are needed to get into the event, they are broken down into two categories:

Primary:

Tickets purchased from the original seller. Some events have an agency, like Ticketmaster, who handle their primary sales.

Secondary:

Tickets that are sold at the market rate. Reputable secondary sellers like GoTickets.com are listed in this section.

Accommodations:

If you have never visited a city where the sporting event is held, how do you know where to stay? This section offers not only contact information on many area hotels, but also brief notes on the benefits and amenities of being a guest. We cover everything from the luxurious to the more affordable options.

On-Site Hospitality:

When you get to the event, you want to know what to expect in the way of food, drink, and other amenities that the location has to offer. From where to get a good hot dog and beer to the luxury suites and executive seating for showing off to friends and impressing a client, we will let you know what that site offers.

Travel Packages:

This section lets you know where to purchase all-inclusive travel packages to the event. It also details information on reputable companies who can assist you in purchasing a travel package to the event. Those companies include Premiere Corporate Events (www.pcevents.com), Premiere Sports Travel (sportstravel. com), and Premiere College Sports (Powered by Dodd's Athletic Tours) (collegesportstravel.com), as well as others.

Dining:

From five-star restaurants to the popular area bar and grill, we will give you options for daily sustenance before and after the event. You can enjoy a multi-course meal with a classy atmosphere or find out about that place where all the locals congregate. Contact information is included.

Airports:

Not all airports are created equal. Nor are they all conveniently located. We provide options for the best place to take off and land. Contact information is included.

Sports Travel Insider's Edge:

Based on my extensive experience in the sports travel industry and a lot of help from many in the know, I will provide you with the following:

Best way to watch the action: If you are attending the event, you want the best vantage point possible. We will let you know about the premium seats and luxury suites that come at a price, but can be well worth the investment. However, we also note the "cheap seats" and student sections based on the experience, not the view.

Best way to get up close to the action: Getting up close could mean the floor seats or a ticket on the 50-yard line. It can also translate into a hard-to-find happening where you can rub shoulders with the heroes and legends of your favorite sporting event. We provide the details you need.

Best travel tip: Wherever there is a major sporting event, there are other things happening around town. We provide key insights to make your trip more enjoyable, including hot tips on other events to check out while you are in the area.

Notable Quotes:

From the significance of the event to the atmosphere of the stadium and fans, we let you know what others have said about all the Top 100 events.

Relevant Websites:

Learn more about the sporting event before you attend. Official websites of the event will provide you with more information on the ever-changing schedules as well as options for tickets and all-inclusive travel packages.

Some Companies Listed in This Book That I Highly Recommend for Travel and Ticket Needs:

Premiere College Sports
(Powered by Dodd's Athletic Tours)

Premiere College Sports (Powered by Dodd's Athletic Tours) specializes in developing official university sports tours for over forty leading schools from the Big Ten, Big 12, ACC, SEC, Pac-10, Big East, and other major conferences. Schools represented by PCS include University of Wisconsin, Ohio State University, University of Illinois, University of Tennessee, University of Kansas, University of Texas, Boston College, Florida State, and many others. Since 1963, PCS has excelled in providing travel and hospitality for the biggest events in college sports: BCS National Championship, Rose Bowl, Orange Bowl, Fiesta Bowl, Sugar Bowl, and the Final Four.

> Premiere College Sports
> (Powered by Dodd's Athletic Tours)
> 308 South Neil
> Champaign, IL 61820
> Phone: (217) 373-5067
> Fax: (217) 398-1313
> Toll-Free: 1-800-553-5527
> www.doddsathletictours.com
> www.collegesportstravel.com

Premiere Sports Travel

For almost a decade, Premiere has been committed to offering superior sports tours to events such as the Final Four, the Masters, Kentucky Derby, Super Bowl, World Series, BCS Bowl games, and the Daytona 500.

In addition to being the largest tour operator for NASCAR, Premiere Sports Travel operates first-class trips to most major events. In my opinion, Premiere is the best company out there when it comes to consumer travel for individuals and groups.

Premiere Sports Travel
201 Shannon Oaks Circle, Suite 205
Cary, NC 27511
Phone: (919) 481-9511
Fax: (919) 481-1337
Toll-Free: 1-800-924-9993
E-mail: sales@sportstravel.com
www.sportstravel.com

Premiere Corporate Events
(Formerly TSE Sports & Entertainment)

Premiere Corporate Events is definitely the industry leader in the world of corporate hospitality and event management. For over ten years, they have been taking people in luxury to major sporting and entertainment events.

PCE is able to design corporate and consumer travel programs to most sporting and entertainment events throughout the world. Although they work on consumer travel programs, they are best at the corporate side of the business.

Premiere Corporate Events
14 Penn Plaza, Suite 925
New York, NY 10122
Phone: (212) 695-9480
Fax: (212) 564-8098
Toll-Free: 1-877-621-5243
E-mail: requests@tseworld.com
www.tseworld.com
www.pcevents.com

GoTickets.com

GoTickets.com sells ticket packages and hotel packages for hard-to-find concert, sports, and theater tickets. They are a terrific trusted source for major, often sold-out sporting events like most of the events on the Top 100 list. They are extremely reliable and by far the best player in the secondary market.

GoTickets, Inc.
2345 Waukegan Road, Suite 140
Bannockburn, IL 60015-1552
Toll-Free: 1-800-775-1617
Fax: (919) 481-9101
E-mail: sales@gotickets.com
www.gotickets.com

All of the companies listed in this section are now part of the Premiere Global Sports family, a sports marketing firm headquartered in Illinois. You can access all of these companies at www.premieresports.com, or you can visit their individual websites listed above.

As you can see from my company selection, I might be a little biased, but I sure know a good company when I see one!

1

MASTERS

Where?
Augusta National Golf Course
2604 Washington Road
Augusta, GA 30904

When?
The Monday through Sunday annual event usually occurs during the second week of April with the first three days devoted to practice rounds and the remaining time featuring the tournament itself.

Significance:
If you can only go to one golf tournament in your lifetime, this is it. Heck, if you can only go to one event, this is the one I have selected, and I shall let you know I am not even a big golf fan!

How many golf fans have imitated *Caddyshack*'s Carl Spackler playing Augusta and shouted, "It's in the hole!" This is pure nirvana for players and watchers and akin to an All-Star game. Augusta National Golf Club is an exclusive association with immaculate landscaping. The most coveted of "Grand Slam" tournaments, the Masters is the only one that is played on the same course each year. The Green Jacket is the stuff of legend and the ultimate accomplishment for every professional golfer. There is not a more beautiful setting for an event than Augusta National.

Who attends?
Those lucky enough to get in are predominantly middle-aged men who likely dream of playing alongside their idols. Corporate executives are there with clients to get a peek at their favorite golfer. Private jets at Augusta Regional Airport are only outnumbered by the khaki pants and golf shirts embroidered with company logos.

How to get there?

From Atlanta (West):
Take I-20 East toward Augusta. Look for signs to Augusta National at Georgia Exits 195, 196B, and 199.

From Columbia, South Carolina (East):
Take I-20 West toward Augusta. Look for signs to Augusta National at South Carolina Exit 1, and Georgia Exits 200 and 199.

Tickets:
A ticket to the Masters is hard to come by and comes at a premium price. Tickets for the practice rounds and badges to get into the tournament are purchased in the secondary ticket market unless you are a member of "The National." Members and longtime homeowners in Augusta receive badges, along with broadcast partners and sponsors. For most of us, the only way to gain entrance is through a reliable secondary ticket provider.

For secondary market ticket access, consider:

GoTickets, Inc.
2345 Waukegan Road, Suite 140
Bannockburn, IL 60015-1552
Toll-Free: 1-800-775-1617
Fax: (919) 481-9101
E-mail: sales@gotickets.com
www.gotickets.com

A full-access tournament badge for all rounds will give you general access to the course and grounds. The practice rounds (Monday and Tuesday) and Par 3 Tournament (Wednesday) are sold as individual tickets and give you general access to the course and grounds. The best possible option for the actual tournament, but extremely scarce, are the Trophy Room Passes or Clubhouse Badges. These will offer you additional access to private areas at "The National." The Clubhouse Badges are the ultimate experience, offering an opportunity to mingle with actual members and professional golfers.

It's important to note that badges are not souvenirs and must be returned. Secondary ticket providers will ask for the badges back after the tournament and will usually ask for a credit card deposit. They must be returned to the original owner as they run the risk of losing their access for future years if not returned to Augusta National.

Accommodations:

Doubletree

2651 Perimeter Parkway
Augusta, GA 30909
Phone: (706) 855-8100
Fax: (706) 860-1720
www.doubletree.com

Note: Easy access to nearby restaurants and upscale shopping at Augusta Mall, and only minutes from the Augusta National Golf Club. Indoor and outdoor pool.

Best Western

2562 Center West Parkway
Augusta, GA 30909
Phone: (706) 736-9292
Fax: (706) 736-9234
www.bestwestern.com

Note: Personalized service from an attentive staff. Fifteen minutes from downtown Augusta.

The Partridge Inn

2110 Walton Way
Augusta, GA 30904
Toll-Free: 1-800-476-6888
Fax: (706) 731-0826
www.partridgeinn.com

Note: Established in 1836, this hotel provides 145 rooms, studios, and suites containing modern comforts and amenities. Award-winning, onsite restaurant.

Please know that during Masters week many hotels in Augusta establish a seven-night room requirement. The option of reserving fewer nights simply does not exist. Something to note is that travel providers who secure hotel inventory in advance will offer consumers options for fewer nights with their all-inclusive packages. They simply divide the hotel space into different packages for people interested in only attending a few days of the tournament. Private homes and mansions can also be rented out for the week. This is a desirable option for those looking for plush accommodations. Many travel providers will offer private home options for varying budgets. With the limited quality hotel space available in Augusta a private home package is a nice option. The companies that are listed as travel providers for this event specialize in securing these private homes. Amenities include maid service and even the opportunity to hire your own personal chef for the week. It is truly a unique experience and my favorite way to attend this event. Many of the homes in Augusta are absolutely beautiful.

On-Site Hospitality:

Off-site corporate hospitality is your only upscale option for this event. All of it is managed by private companies. An air-conditioned venue features premium bars and buffet-style catered meals. The closest high-profile hospitality areas can be found on Azalea Road right off of Washington Road. Stands providing reasonably priced food and beverages are located on the course. However, it does not boast the quality or the selection of the more private locations. The travel providers listed below are able to secure access to the better off-site hospitality venues.

Travel Packages:

If you are going to travel to this event, I would recommend using a reliable company to work with you on making the necessary arrangements. The suppliers listed in this book have solid references and are by far the most trusted in the business. Below are some of the organizations to try for this Top 100 Must See Sporting Event.

Premiere Corporate Events
14 Penn Plaza, Suite 925
New York, NY 10122
Phone: (212) 695-9480
Fax: (212) 564-8098
Toll-Free: 1-877-621-5243
E-mail: requests@tseworld.com
www.tseworld.com
www.pcevents.com

Premiere Sports Travel
201 Shannon Oaks Circle, Suite 205
Cary, NC 27511
Phone: (919) 481-9511
Fax: (919) 481-1337
Toll-Free: 1-800-924-9993
E-mail: sales@sportstravel.com
www.sportstravel.com

As the "filet mignon" of sports travel packages, the Masters is the most expensive. It is all about the coveted badge when it comes to cost. Ranging from $7,500 to $10,000 per person, the package should include all four days of the Masters experience, hotel or private home accommodations, private off-site hospitality, transportation, taxes, various amenities, and, oh yes, that badge.

Dining:
It is important to note that the Masters affects pricing at every area restaurant. Expect a 50 percent bump in prices during the tournament. There are many good dining options throughout Augusta.

TBonz Steakhouse
2856 Washington Road
Augusta, GA 30909
Phone: (706) 737-8325
Fax: (706) 737-8324
www.tbonz.com

Note: Good steaks and a lively atmosphere, but always crowded during Masters week.

Bistro 491
491 Highland Avenue
Augusta, GA 30909
Phone: (706) 738-6491
Fax: (706) 737-9795
www.bistro491.com

Note: An eclectic menu for a restaurant considered the best value in town for a quality meal.

The Public House
399 Highland Avenue
Augusta, GA 30909
Phone: (706) 364-2711

Note: Forget Augusta. This is one of the best meals in all of Georgia.

Stonecrest Steakhouse
601 North Belair Road
Evans, GA 30809
Phone: (706) 651-0123
www.stonecreststeakhouse.com

Note: Stonecrest Steakhouse opened in 2008 to rave reviews. The filet is the best in town.

Bonefish
2911 Washington Road
Augusta, GA 30909
Phone: (706) 737-2929
Fax: (706) 737-2733
www.bonefishgrill.com

Note: This is a great option right on Washington Road. Book early as the place fills up quickly during Masters week.

Airports:

Augusta Regional Airport
(fifteen-minute drive to most locations in Augusta)
1501 Aviation Way
Augusta, GA 30906
Phone: (706) 798-3236
Fax: (706) 798-1551
www.augustaregionalairport.com

Columbia Metropolitan Airport
(fifty- to sixty-minute drive to most
locations in Augusta)
3000 Aviation Way
West Columbia, SC 29170
Phone: (803) 822-5000
www.columbiaairport.com

**Atlanta Hartsfield-Jackson
International Airport**
(over a two-hour drive to Augusta)
Department of Aviation
6000 North Terminal Parkway
Atlanta, GA 30320
Toll-Free: 1-800-897-1910
www.atlanta-airport.com

Sports Travel Insider's Edge:

Best place to watch the action:
The best vantage point period is the grandstand on 13. That location gives you a vantage point where you can see the 2nd and
3rd shot on hole 13. You can also see the
drive on hole 14, the 2nd and 3rd shot on
hole 15, and the tee shot on hole 16.

Best place to get up close to the action:
The best amateur from the previous year's
Masters gets to stay in the "crow's nest," an
apartment at the top of the clubhouse with
a great view of the grounds. For most of us
sitting down in the grandstand, it gives you
a great view of players working on their
swings on the practice range behind the
clubhouse.

Best travel tip:
How can you turn two badges into four
when you have a quartet attending the event?
Easy. Buy two four-day badges, Thursday to
Sunday, for the entire tournament. That allows two members of your group to watch
one day while the other two can go golfing.
Everyone in your group will get to go to the
tournament for two full days and play golf
for the other two days.

Notable Quotes:

"If you asked golfers what tournament
they would rather win over all others, I
think every one of them...would say the
Masters."—SAM SNEAD, golfer

"The first time I played the Masters, I was
so nervous I drank a bottle of rum before
I teed off. I shot the happiest 83 of my
life."—CHI CHI RODRIGUEZ, golfer

"When people think of The Augusta
National Golf Club, usually they think of
its beauty, and when they picture its beauty, invariably they mean its appearance in
spring, at Masters time, with its flashes of
flowering crabapple and graceful dogwood
and blazing streaks of azalea. What attracts
us so irresistibly are those glorious patches
of color against a majestic green canvas of
turf and trees."—FRANK CHRISTIAN, writer of
Augusta National & The Masters

Relevant Websites:
www.themasters.com
www.augustaga.org
www.tseworld.com
www.pcevents.com
www.sportstravel.com
www.gotickets.com
www.premieresports.com

2

WORLD CUP

Where?
A different location every four years. Upcoming locations include South Africa in
2010 and Brazil in 2014.

When?
June and July, every four years.

Significance:
The whole world stops to watch this event,

with billions viewing on television and millions filling the stadiums, so you can imagine why it is so high on the list.

The FIFA World Cup is also known as the Football World Cup or the Soccer World Cup, depending on what country you reside in. The event is an international association football or soccer competition. Participants are men's national teams from the Fédération Internationale de Football Association (FIFA). Qualifying takes place over three years, with the best thirty-two teams competing in the finals for the Cup.

Who attends?

Whether you call it soccer or football, you should find a way to get to a FIFA World Cup. While soccer is hardly the most popular sport in the United States, football, as it is known in Europe, has an enormous following worldwide. Football/soccer fans from around the world attend the event, frenetically cheering on their favorite team to victory.

History

The event has its roots in the 1884 British Home Championship. Uruguay hosted the first FIFA World Cup and the event has gone on continuously every four years since 1930, save for a break during World War II.

The first two World Cup tournament matches took place simultaneously with France upending Mexico by a score of 4–1 and the United States claiming victory over Belgium, 3–0. France's Lucien Laurent claimed the first goal in World Cup history. Uruguay went on to win the inaugural World Cup when they beat Argentina 4–2 in front of 93,000 people in Montevideo.

Since 1958, the World Cup had alternated between Europe and the Americas until the Executive Committee decided to break tradition. Korea and Japan were named co-hosts in 1996 for the 2002 event. Seven different champions have been crowned throughout the history of the famed tournament. Brazil, Italy, and Germany have won multiple titles. No nation receives a permanent trophy, as they only retain it until the next tournament, with a replica given to them in its place. The coveted Cup will be retired when the name plaque has been filled.

Individual World Cup Awards

The Adidas Golden Shoe (Top goal scorer)
The Adidas Golden Ball (Best player)
The Yashin Award (Best goalkeeper)
The FIFA Fair Play Trophy (Team with the best record of fair play)
The Most Entertaining Team Award (Team that has entertained the public the most)
The Gillette Best Young Player Award (Best player aged twenty-one or younger at the start of the calendar year)

Notable Athletes:

Pelé (Brazil)
David Beckham (England)
Diego Maradona (Argentina)
Franz Beckenbauer (Germany)
Lothar Matthäus (Germany)
Ronaldo (Brazil)

Records:

Most appearances in tournaments (Tie): Antonio Carbajal (Mexico) and Lothar Matthäus (Germany), 5
Most matches: Lothar Matthäus (Germany), 25
Most winner's medals: Pelé (Brazil), 3
Most goals scored in a game: Oleg Salenko (Russia), 5
Most goals scored in a tournament: Just Fontaine (France), 13

Things to know before you go:

Give and Go: A player controlling the ball passes to a teammate and runs through an open field to get a possible return pass.
Hat Trick: Three goals scored in one game by one player.

Juggling: Keeping the ball off the ground by a player using their feet, thighs, chest, head, and the top of their shoulders.

Red Card: Shown by a referee to signify that a player has been sent off. The player who has been sent off must leave the field immediately and cannot be replaced during the game; their team must continue the game with one player fewer.

Yellow Card: A cautionary warning issued by the referee to a player for unsportsmanlike behavior for a variety of infractions.

Tickets:

FIFA offers select ticketing packages available approximately one year in advance.

Secondary ticket vendors will actually provide more of a selection based upon your specific budget. I would highly recommend using a reputable company such as GoTickets.com for this event, because they offer access to all of the games.

Tickets are usually sold in three specific categories classified as A, B, and C seating. The A seats are the premium locations in the stadium, while B and C offer lesser views.

Tickets for select games featuring premier teams with large followings always cost more on the secondary market. Some of these teams include England, Brazil, and France.

At recent World Cups, local organizers tried to prevent tickets from being transferred by having the buyer's name appear on the ticket. However, security at the stadiums was lax in enforcing this rule. It is advised that you check with the FIFA website prior to purchasing a ticket on the latest security measures that may affect seating.

For primary market ticket access, consider: www.fifa.com.

For secondary ticket market access, consider:

GoTickets, Inc.

2345 Waukegan Road, Suite 140
Bannockburn, IL 60015-1552
Toll-Free: 1-800-775-1617
Fax: (919) 481-9101
E-mail: sales@gotickets.com
www.gotickets.com

Travel Packages:

If you are going to travel to this event, I would recommend using a reliable company to work with you on making the necessary arrangements. The suppliers listed in this book have solid references and are by far the most trusted in the business. Below are some of the organizations to try for this Top 100 Must See Sporting Event.

Premiere Corporate Events

14 Penn Plaza, Suite 925
New York, NY 10122
Phone: (212) 695-9480
Fax: (212) 564-8098
Toll-Free: 1-877-621-5243
E-mail: requests@tseworld.com
www.tseworld.com
www.pcevents.com

Premiere Sports Travel

201 Shannon Oaks Circle, Suite 205
Cary, NC 27511
Phone: (919) 481-9511
Fax: (919) 481-1337
Toll-Free: 1-800-924-9993
E-mail: sales@sportstravel.com
www.sportstravel.com

Sports Travel Insider's Edge:

Best way to watch the action (Based on the host country):

If you love soccer, then any World Cup match will afford you the opportunity to enjoy the energy and excitement that only comes when this event is played. Purchase a ticket to see England or Brazil play and you will experience that feeling on another level. The passion and intensity of fans of these two teams will offer you an experience like no other in all of sports. If you are able to go to the final match, then you will realize what an incredible feeling it is to be at a game that the whole world is watching.

Best place to get up close (Based on the host country):

The nice thing about the host country organizing committee is that they make it very convenient for fans traveling to the World Cup who are not able to attend every match. Host countries will set up jumbo screens in local parks of tournament cities so fans who can't go to the game can watch their team with their fellow countrymen. If you are in town, you have to take in one of these matches this way. Make sure to get there early as people begin camping out hours in advance to get the best seats. The party usually starts hours before the game.

Best travel tip:

Whether South Africa in 2010 or Brazil in 2014, make sure to plan your trip carefully. Games are played in different cities throughout the country as there is not one area that hosts all the matches. This offers you the opportunity to see different cities and stadiums, but you will most likely have to move around a bit if you plan on seeing a lot of soccer. Tour companies are definitely recommended for this event as travel can quickly become a headache doing it on your own.

Notable Quote:

"These games feel like life or death. No, really. . . . You can see it on everyone's face. After Argentina's OT goal, the shell-shocked coach of Mexico looked as if he'd gotten a terminal diagnosis from his doctor. I half expected him to start hastily scribbling a will. For most of the countries involved, soccer is the equivalent of

baseball + football + basketball here, if those sports came around only one month every four years. You can feel the tension. It's suffocating. The winners are relieved, the losers decimated. There's no in-between."—BILL SIMMONS, writer for *ESPN Magazine*

Relevant Websites:

www.fifa.com
www.tseworld.com
www.pcevents.com
www.sportstravel.com
www.gotickets.com
www.premieresports.com

3

SUPER BOWL

When?

Every year, usually on the first Sunday of February, nicknamed "Super Bowl Sunday."

Future Locations:

2010–Dolphin Stadium,
    Miami Gardens, FL
2011–Cowboys New Stadium,
    Arlington, TX
2012–Lucas Oil Stadium, Indianapolis, IN

Significance:

It's the Super Bowl. Die-hard football fans look forward to the culmination of the pro football season. Parties are planned worldwide around the big event. Sportswriters analyze and break down the matchup. Oh, and those commercials. The Super Bowl is the National Football League's showcase as the National Football Conference (NFC) champion faces off against the American Football Conference (AFC) title holder for the coveted Vince Lombardi trophy.

The pageantry is as much of the show as the game itself. Pre-game and halftime shows feature high-profile musical performers, most recently Bruce Springsteen, Tom Petty, Prince, and Janet Jackson, complete with a wardrobe malfunction. Viewership approaches and breaks records as the Super Bowl ranks at the top of the Nielsen ratings. Even the commercials that companies pay a premium price to air are anticipated, analyzed, and reviewed.

The final game of the NFL playoffs can be dull or dramatic. While dynasties are born and continue, some Super Bowl champs become "one-hit wonders." This is the ultimate in sporting events and a defacto national holiday with one-day food consumption coming in a close second to Thanksgiving.

The NFL has turned the Super Bowl into a week-long series of events for host cities. Parties, benefits, and functions take place on a daily basis leading up to the game. With all the hoopla taking place, you can easily forget there is a game to be played on Sunday.

Who attends?

Casual and hardcore football fans, celebrities, athletes, dignitaries, corporate types, and anyone who wants to witness this much-anticipated championship event.

History

When the National Football League merged with the American Football League (AFL) on June 8, 1966, a condition was set. The two rival factions would meet in the AFL-NFL World Championship Game that would determine the "world champion of football." After seeing his children play with a Super Ball, Lamar Hunt, AFL founder and Kansas City Chiefs owner, jokingly referred to the game as the "Super Bowl." Needless to say, the name stuck and that very ball can be found in the Pro Football Hall of Fame.

The NFL's Green Bay Packers crushed their AFC counterpart in the first two Super Bowls. Fear set in that the AFL could not compete with the NFL. Along came Joe Namath guaranteeing a win, and the upstart New York Jets of the AFL beat the NFL's Baltimore Colts in Super Bowl III, the first championship to carry those famed Roman numerals.

The Vince Lombardi Trophy is something every NFL team covets. Named for the man who coached the Green Bay Packers to the first two Super Bowl victories, the award was first given to the Baltimore Colts at Super Bowl V in Miami, Florida.

Notable Athletes:

Joe Montana, quarterback, San Francisco 49ers

Jerry Rice, wide receiver, San Francisco 49ers

Troy Aikman, quarterback, Dallas Cowboys

Emmitt Smith, running back, Dallas Cowboys

Steve Young, quarterback, San Francisco 49ers

Desmond Howard, kick returner, Green Bay Packers

Kurt Warner, quarterback, St. Louis Rams

Tom Brady, quarterback, New England Patriots

Peyton Manning, quarterback, Indianapolis Colts

Eli Manning, quarterback, New York Giants

Lawrence Taylor, linebacker, New York Giants

Jim Kelly, quarterback, Buffalo Bills

Terry Bradshaw, quarterback, Pittsburgh Steelers

Doug Williams, quarterback, Washington Redskins

Marcus Allen, running back, Los Angeles/Oakland Raiders

Joe Namath, quarterback, New York Jets

Records:

Most rushing yards in a single game: Timmy Smith, 204, Washington vs. Denver, XXII

Longest run from scrimmage: Willie Parker, 75 yards, Pittsburgh vs. Seattle, XL

Most touchdowns (Tie): Roger Craig, San Francisco vs. Miami, XIX, 3 (1 run, 2 passes); Jerry Rice, San Francisco vs. Denver, XXIV, 3 (all passes), and San Francisco vs. San Diego, XXIX, 3 (all passes); Ricky Watters, San Francisco vs. San Diego, XXIX, 3 (1 run, 2 passes); Terrell Davis, Green Bay vs. Denver, XXXII, 3 (all runs)

Most points in a game: 55, San Francisco vs. Denver, XXIV

Traditions:

While television viewers tend to stay in their chairs and sofas during commercials, stick around for the halftime show and hold off on that bathroom break. One of the major events of the Super Bowl is the half-time show that serves as a bonus concert for free. Names such as Aerosmith, Michael Jackson, Prince, Tom Petty, and, of course, Janet Jackson and Justin Timberlake have displayed their wares, so to speak, for Super Bowl audiences.

Annual Events and Happenings:

Various parties and events that are held during Super Bowl Weekend:

Maxim Magazine Party: One of the best parties each year. It is usually on Friday or Saturday night. Strict guest list policy is followed.

Playboy Magazine Party: This was the first magazine to hold a major party at the Super Bowl. This party is usually on Friday or Saturday night and always contends for top party honors.

ESPN Party: Typically on Thursday or Friday night. Many ESPN sponsors and advertisers combine with sports celebrities.

Sports Illustrated Party: Most years this is a swimsuit issue themed event. This party most often takes place on Saturday night

and contends with Maxim and Playboy for premier Super Bowl party honors.

Taste of the NFL: Featuring relevant food from celebrity chefs and celebrity football players from every NFL city. This event usually happens early Saturday evening.

NFL Tailgate Party: The official tailgate party of the NFL. It usually kicks off a few hours before the game. It is always located right outside the host stadium or close by. Some years the NFL offers an option to come back after the game to party for an additional few hours.

PCE Celebrity Golf Tournament: Golf greats and NFL legends play with participants in this shootout. It most often takes place on Saturday afternoon. www.pcevents.com

PCE Chalk Talk: Pre-game event hosted by former and current NFL coaches. Takes place on Sunday morning prior to the game. www.pcevents.com

NFL Alumni Events: Pro football alums host a golf tournament and other onsite events each year.

For access to all the listed parties and events, your best bet is to consult with a travel package provider such as Premiere Corporate Events, www.pcevents.com; Premiere Sports Travel, www.sportstravel.com; or a secondary ticket source like GoTickets.com.

Tickets:

Only around 500 tickets are made available each year to the general public through a drawing conducted by the NFL. With the amount of people sending in applications, you have a better chance of winning your local lottery.

Secondary markets are usually the best source for a ticket to the Super Bowl. Prices fluctuate depending on the teams playing. Proceed with caution and choose a reputable secondary ticket provider. Participating teams will also have travel packages for their fans, so check out team websites for more information.

For secondary ticket market access, consider:

GoTickets, Inc.
2345 Waukegan Road, Suite 140
Bannockburn, IL 60015-1552
Toll-Free: 1-800-775-1617
Fax: (919) 481-9101
E-mail: sales@gotickets.com
www.gotickets.com

Travel Packages:
If you are going to the Super Bowl, I would recommend using a reliable company to work with you on making the necessary arrangements. The suppliers listed in this book have solid references and are by far the most trusted in the business. Below are some of the organizations to try for this Top 100 Must See Sporting Event.

Premiere Corporate Events
14 Penn Plaza, Suite 925
New York, NY 10122
Phone: (212) 695-9480
Fax: (212) 564-8098
Toll-Free: 1-877-621-5243
E-mail: requests@tseworld.com
www.tseworld.com
www.pcevents.com

Premiere Sports Travel
201 Shannon Oaks Circle, Suite 205
Cary, NC 27511
Phone: (919) 481-9511
Fax: (919) 481-1337
Toll-Free: 1-800-924-9993
E-mail: sales@sportstravel.com
www.sportstravel.com

Sports Travel Insider's Edge:

Best way to watch the action:
While a ticket anywhere in the stadium means you get to watch the Super Bowl live, you cannot beat a 50-yard line lower level sideline seat. You get the best view of the game and of course the halftime show. Make sure to note that sometimes the halftime show will face one sideline. Make sure you consult with your ticket provider before purchasing a seat if you want a good view of the show.

Best way to get up close:
Attending a Super Bowl themed celebrity event like the PCE Celebrity Golf Tournament will allow you to rub shoulders and get or give pointers to NFL legends. Remember that the game itself is only a part of Super Bowl weekend. There are many events that will allow you to get up close and personal with current and past NFL stars without paying a premium for a game ticket. With so many celebrities onsite each year at the Super Bowl, this is a great opportunity to get the inside scoop.

Best Travel Tip:
Plan ahead, preferably the minute you know what city is hosting the Super Bowl. Planes and hotels fill up at lightning speed. The NFL owns 90 percent of the rooms and the remainder are booked by travel providers years in advance. Don't worry about what teams are playing. After all, this is the Super Bowl.

Notable Quotes:
"As a player, it says everything about you if you made the Hall of Fame. But, then again, boy...there's something about winning a Super Bowl."—TERRY BRADSHAW, former quarterback, Pittsburgh Steelers, and current NFL announcer

"I've always said throughout the whole course of the week, when everyone says 'congratulations,' that we're happy to be here but this is not our final chapter. It's not what we set out to accomplish this year—to get to the Super Bowl. The main thing is to go out there and win a Super Bowl. That's more of a congratulations than anything, as opposed to just getting to the Super Bowl."—MARVIN HARRISON, wide receiver, Indianapolis Colts

"The Super Bowl is where corporate America comes to party."—ROBERT TUCHMAN, author

"It was just the excitement of seeing Ford Field filled to the absolute maximum capacity with screaming fans...it was absolutely thrilling."—DARLENE FERO, administrative assistant in Development, Budget, and Administration for the University of Michigan

Relevant Websites:
www.nfl.com
www.tseworld.com
www.pcevents.com
www.sportstravel.com
www.gotickets.com
www.premieresports.com

4
SUMMER OLYMPICS

When?
Every four years.

Future Locations:
2012–London, England
2016–TBD on October 9, 2009

Significance:
Over 10,000 athletes. Over 200 nations represented. More than twenty-five sports. Over 300 events. Only the Summer Olympic Games could contain that level of competition. With oversight by the International Olympic Committee, the Games of the Olympiad are played every four years in cities around the world. Even the bidding process to get an Olympics is as competitive as the Games themselves.

Athletes representing their sport and their country of citizenship compete for gold, silver, and bronze medals. It is a rare opportunity for countries to put their differences aside for a short time and come together in sportsmanlike competition. This is the closest we get to seeing people from across the world act in harmony.

Who attends?
Major sports fans make pilgrimages to the Olympics. Sports junkies will travel across the world to witness the Summer Games. Onsite fans marvel at knowing they are watching the absolute best-of-the-best compete.

Fun Facts

Australia, France, Great Britain, Greece, and Switzerland have sent teams to every Summer Olympic Games.

Great Britain also holds the distinction of winning at least one gold medal at every Summer Olympics.

Host Greece won the most medals (46) at the first Olympic Summer Games in 1896.

The United States has won more medals at the Summer Games than any other country.

The records for most gold medals in a single game and the most gold medals in an Olympic career were established by Michael Phelps at the 2008 Beijing Summer Olympics, with 8 gold medals and 14 gold medals respectively.

The five Olympic rings represent the major regions of the world, including Africa, the Americas, Asia, Europe, and Oceania.

Every national flag in the world includes one of the five colors of the Olympic rings: blue, yellow, black, green, and red.

The 1992 Barcelona Olympic Games were the first in three decades that were not boycotted by any country.

Up until 1992, the Olympics were held every four years. Since then, the Winter and Summer Games have alternated every two years.

The first Olympics covered by a broadcast network were the 1960 Summer Games in Rome by CBS.

197 countries competed in the 1996 Atlanta Olympic Summer Games.

History

The Games of the Olympiad is a sporting event that goes back to 776 B.C., celebrating the Greek god Zeus. In 393 A.D., the games ended over accusations that it was nothing more than a pagan festival. In 1896, the games returned when Baron Pierre de Coubertin proposed a revival of what is now the modern-day Summer Games. Out of those initial 245 competitors, 200 were Greek and only fourteen countries were represented. After a rough start, including the cancellation of the 1916 Berlin Olympics, the Games came into their own and grew both in prominence and in the number of athletes participating.

Summer Olympic Sports:

Archery, Badminton, Basketball, Beach Volleyball, Boxing, Cycling, Diving, Equestrian, Fencing, Field Hockey, Gymnastics, Judo, Mountain Biking, Rowing, Sailing, Shooting, Soccer, Swimming, Synchronized Swimming, Table Tennis, Tae Kwon Do, Tennis, Track and Field, Volleyball, Water Polo, Weightlifting, Wrestling, and the Triathlon (swimming, biking, and running).

Records:

Most career Olympic medals for a female:
  Larissa Latynina, USSR, 18
Most career Olympic medals for a male:
  Michael Phelps, USA, 16

Motto

Citius, Altius, Fortius, Latin for "faster, higher, stronger."

Traditions:

Opening Ceremonies

Receiving the Head of State of the Host
  Country
Parade of the Participants
Speech by the President of the Organizing
  Committee
Speech by the IOC President
Head of State Declares the Games Open
Playing of the Olympic Anthem and the
  Entry and Raising of the Olympic Flag
Last Stage of the Olympic Torch Relay and
  the Lighting of the Olympic Cauldron
Symbolic Release of the Pigeons
Taking of the Oath by a Competitor
Taking of the Oath by a Judge
National Anthem of the Host Country
Artistic Program

Flame and Torch

According to the ancient Greeks, Prometheus gave mankind fire, and it holds sacred qualities. The eternal flame comes from the flames that burned in front of the Greek temples lit using the sun's rays. The Olympic flame is lit in front of the ruins of the Temple of Hera. From there, runners pass the torch in relay fashion until it arrives at the site of the Games.

Release of Doves

Following the lighting of the cauldron, doves are released as a symbol of peace. The 1896 Olympics started that tradition and it is now an official part of the Summer Games' Opening Ceremony.

The Olympic Oath

One athlete and one judge from the home nation recite the Olympic Oath during the Opening Ceremony of every Olympics. The current form of the judges' oath is:

> "In the name of all the judges and officials, I promise that we shall officiate in these Olympic Games with complete impartiality, respecting and abiding by the rules which govern them, in the true spirit of sportsmanship."

The current form of the athletes' oath is:

> "In the name of all the competitors I promise that we shall take part in these Olympic Games, respecting and abiding by the rules which govern them, committing ourselves to a sport without doping and without drugs, in the true spirit of sportsmanship, for the glory of sport and the honor of our teams."

Tickets:

For primary ticket options, check with the official Olympic movement website, www.olympic.org, for information.

Travel Packages:

If you are going to travel to the Olympics, I would recommend using a reliable company to work with you on making the necessary arrangements. The suppliers listed in this book have solid references and are by far the most trusted in the business. Below are some of the organizations to try for this Top 100 Must See Sporting Event.

Premiere Corporate Events

14 Penn Plaza, Suite 925
New York, NY 10122
Phone: (212) 695-9480
Fax: (212) 564-8098
Toll-Free: 1-877-621-5243
E-mail: requests@tseworld.com
www.tseworld.com
www.pcevents.com

Premiere Sports Travel

201 Shannon Oaks Circle, Suite 205
Cary, NC 27511
Phone: (919) 481-9511
Fax: (919) 481-1337
Toll-Free: 1-800-924-9993
E-mail: sales@sportstravel.com
www.sportstravel.com

Notable Quotes:

"For athletes, the Olympics are the ultimate test of their worth."—MARY LOU RETTON, 1984 Olympic gold medalist in the all-around, gymnastics

"When you win national titles, you're recognized by people in your sport. At the Olympics the recognition is not just from your sport…(but) from your country and the world."—PETER WESTBROOK, 1984 Olympic bronze medalist in fencing

Relevant Websites:

www.olympic.org
www.tseworld.com
www.pcevents.com
www.sportstravel.com
www.premieresports.com

5

ARMY VS. NAVY FOOTBALL GAME

Where?

Lincoln Financial Field
1020 Pattison Avenue
Philadelphia, PA 19148

Note: While 75 percent of the games have been played in Philadelphia, the game location is decided by Army and Navy. Other games have been played in Maryland and New Jersey.

When?

First weekend of December, usually the last weekend of the college football season.

Significance:

While some sports feuds see two teams with seething hatred for each other, the rivalry between Army and Navy football is considered friendly. Practical jokes replace the potential for brawling. However, that camaraderie does not belie the intensity when the two military mights battle on the football field. Sure, the Navy weight room has weight plates stamped with "Beat Army." Of course, every Army student has the phrase "Beat Navy" on the tip of their tongues. They play hard over the coveted Commander in Chief's Trophy. Even after that hard-fought victory, mutual respect closes out the event. Both teams stand together as both of their songs are played, the losing team first and then the winning one. The finale and the game preceding it takes on a particularly emotional element during wartimes when seniors are facing deployment.

CBS and other major networks have provided complete coverage of the game, but this is not a showcase for future NFL talent. The rigorous standards to enter the United States Military Academy or the United States Naval Academy have lessened the competitiveness of the teams among their peers in college football. Hall of Fame NFL players have competed at both schools, but the team accomplishments are minimal. However, this is a game steeped in too much tradition to let a perceived lack of talent diminish the event.

Who attends?

Army and Navy students, former service members, alumni, and college football enthusiasts.

How to get there?

Lincoln Financial Field is off of I-95 on Exits 17, 19, and 13. If you are taking I-76, take the 349 or 350 exit (Packer Avenue).

Public Transportation:

From New Jersey, you can take SEPTA's Broad Street Line (Orange Line) or PATCO's High-Speed line. For more information, log on to www.septa.org or www.ridepatco.org. Amtrak's historic 30th Street Station in Philadelphia provides service as well. For information, visit www.amtrak.com or call 1-800-872-7245.

Tickets:

For primary ticket access information, consider:

Army Athletics
1-877-TIX-ARMY
www.goarmysports.com

or

Navy Athletics
1-800-US4-NAVY
www.navysports.com

For secondary ticket access, consider:

GoTickets, Inc.
2345 Waukegan Road, Suite 140
Bannockburn, IL 60015-1552
Toll-Free: 1-800-775-1617
Fax: (919) 481-9101
E-mail: sales@gotickets.com
www.gotickets.com

Accommodations:

Sofitel Philadelphia
120 South 17th Street
Philadelphia, PA 19103
Phone: (215) 569-8300
Fax: (215) 564-7452
Toll-Free: 1-800-763-4835
www.accorhotels.com

Note: In the heart of the business district with many retail locations. A thirteen-minute trip to Lincoln Field.

Alexander Inn
301 South 12th Street
Philadelphia, PA 19107
Phone: (215) 923-3535
Toll-Free: 1-877-ALEX-INN
www.alexanderinn.com
Note: Restored seven-story hotel in a historic building. Fifteen minutes from Lincoln Field.

Sheraton University City Hotel (twelve minutes to Lincoln Field)
36th and Chestnut Streets
Philadelphia, PA 19104
Phone: (215) 387- 8000
Fax: (215) 387-7920
Toll-Free: 1-877-459-1146
www.philadelphiasheraton.com
Note: The official hotel of Navy, located twelve minutes from Lincoln Field.

The Inn at Penn - A Hilton Hotel
3600 Sansom Street
Philadelphia, PA 19104
Phone: (215) 222-0200
Fax: (215) 222-4600
Toll-Free: 1-800-231-4587
www.theinnatpenn.com
Note: AAA four-diamond-rated hotel in the heart of UPenn's campus with a thirteen-minute drive to Lincoln Field.

On-Site Hospitality:

For stadium fare, there is no mystery as to the signature menu item—the Philly cheesesteak. In addition, sample Chickie's & Pete's crab fries, a char-grilled Italian sausage, or a Johnny Brenda's roast pork Italian sandwich.

Travel Packages:

If you are going to travel to this event, I would recommend using a reliable company to work with you on making the necessary arrangements. The suppliers listed in this book have solid references and are by far the most trusted in the business. Below are some of the organizations to try for this Top 100 Must See Sporting Event.

Premiere Corporate Events
14 Penn Plaza, Suite 925
New York, NY 10122
Phone: (212) 695-9480
Fax: (212) 564-8098
Toll-Free: 1-877-621-5243
E-mail: requests@tseworld.com
www.tseworld.com
www.pcevents.com

Premiere Sports Travel
201 Shannon Oaks Circle, Suite 205
Cary, NC 27511
Phone: (919) 481-9511
Fax: (919) 481-1337
Toll-Free: 1-800-924-9993
E-mail: sales@sportstravel.com
www.sportstravel.com

Premiere College Sports (Powered by Dodd's Athletic Tours)
308 South Neil
Champaign, IL 61820
Phone: (217) 373-5067
Fax: (217) 398-1313
Toll-Free: 1-800-553-5527
www.doddsathletictours.com
www.collegesportstravel.com

Dining:

Alma de Cuba
1623 Walnut Street
Philadelphia, PA 19103
Phone: (215) 988-1799
Fax: (215) 988-0807
www.almadecubarestaurant.com
Note: Well-known for its modern Cuban cuisine.

Little Fish
600 Catharine Street
Philadelphia, PA 19147
Phone: (215) 413-3464
www.littlefishphilly.com
Note: Promising sophisticated seafood in a casual atmosphere. BYOB.

The Victor Café

1303 Dickinson Street
Philadelphia, PA 19147
Phone: (215) 468-3040
www.victorcafe.com

Note: Enjoy great music while you dine.

Jim's Steaks

400 South Street
Philadelphia, PA 19147
Phone: (215) 928-1911
www.jimssteaksphilly.com

*Note: Serving some of the best hoagies and
sandwiches in Philly since 1939.*

Chickie's & Pete's

1526 Packer Avenue
Philadelphia, PA 19145
Phone: (215) 218-0500
www.chickiesandpetes.com

*Note: Sports bar close to the stadium, offering
a "Taxi Crab," a drop-off and pickup service.
Crab Fries are a must.*

Airport:

Philadelphia International Airport

8000 Essington Avenue
Philadelphia, PA 19153
Phone: (215) 937-6937
www.phl.org

Sports Travel Insider's Edge:

Best way to watch the action:

First and foremost, make sure you sit on
the correct side, depending on your allegiance. The Club Seats at Lincoln Financial are a great option because of the
late-season, December chill. Seat holders
are invited to visit both of the exclusive
Club Lounges during the game. At 40,000
square feet each, there is plenty of room
for the full-service bars, concession stands,
and merchandise shops. Plus, you can stay
warm.

Best place to get up close:

The Army Navy Gala is a formal sit-down
dinner that attracts 1,500 attendees. Entertainment is provided by both schools and
season highlights are on display via a video
montage. Players, alums, administration,
and major donors are in attendance.

Best Travel Tip:

Is it possible to visit Philadelphia without
seeing one of the most famous statues in the
city? You have seen it in several movies, so
why not see it in person? The fictional Rocky
Balboa, immortalized in bronze in 1980, can
be found at the Art Museum steps.

Notable Quotes:

"When I got to Army, I just thought it was
another rivalry like Michigan-Ohio State,
teams that didn't really like each other.
But around campus, everywhere you
look there's a sign that says 'Beat Navy.'
Everything we do during the season, the
off-season, even in class, in the back of our
mind it's all about beating Navy."—JEREMY
TRIMBLE, Army senior receiver

"This is akin to almost like the Super Bowl
or some huge Major League event here in
our city."—MARTIN O'MALLEY, Maryland
governor on Baltimore hosting the Army-
Navy game

"It's explained as a nationwide game
because there's people all over the country
who have relatives, family members, broth-
ers, sisters, uncles, aunts, grandparents
that have been in the Army or Navy, and it
draws a lot of support."—Anonymous fan
at the Army/Navy Pep Rally

"This is a historical event. It is a great
atmosphere. We're concerned about the
actual outcome of the game, but it's a
celebration."—STEVE BOYKIN, Army Major

"It's just great to be here with so many great young men and women. Today I'm sitting on the Army side for the first half and then on the Navy side for the second. It's been kind of a fun week. I've got a lot of Army officers and a lot of Navy officers. In the end, we all serve together and there are a lot of special people on both sides."— ADMIRAL MIKE MULLEN, chairman of the Joint Chiefs of Staff

Relevant Websites:
www.lincolnfinancialfield.com
www.PhiladelphiaUSA.travel
www.phillylovesarmynavy.com
www.goarmysports.com
www.navysports.com
www.tseworld.com
www.pcevents.com
www.sportstravel.com
www.gotickets.com
www.premieresports.com

6

NEW YORK CITY MARATHON

Where?
New York City, the city that never sleeps, is also filled with runners who never take a break. From Staten Island at the Verrazano-Narrows Bridge through Brooklyn, Queens, Manhattan, and the Bronx and ending in Central Park.

When?
Annually at the beginning of November.

Significance:
It's an amazing display of support and sportsmanship that no other event can rival.

Considered one of the world's great road races and the premier event of the New York Road Runners Club, the ING New York City Marathon attracts an excess of 100,000 applicants. Many of those striving for a spot include world-class professional athletes. The stakes are high, with some of the most significant prize money in all of road racing. The opportunity to race on a grand stage and cross that finish line in Central Park is likely more valuable than a six-figure purse. Two million spectators cheer on the runners while 315 million watch from home. In 1970, 127 runners raced the 26.2 miles in laps around Central Park after paying a one-dollar entry fee. Only fifty-five runners made it to the end. Since then, it has grown in size, expanding to five boroughs and gaining media attention like no other marathon. In 2000, the official wheelchair division launched and grew to one of the most competitive races of that type in the world, boasting 200 wheelchair and hand-cycle athletes and a variety of ambulatory competitors with disabilities. The NYC Marathon is more than just a race. It is a much-heralded annual event that is just as much about competition as it is about community spirit throughout the greatest city in the world.

Who attends?
Friends and family of the runners come for support. New York City residents line the streets ten deep in all five boroughs looking forward to the annual event, as do fans of marathons.

How to get there?
Show up in any one of the five boroughs with a course map in hand. Find a spot on the side of the road and get ready to cheer.

Tickets:
This high-profile, historical event is free to the public. Private grandstand seating at the finish line in Central Park is made available to runner groups, charities, and sponsors. Check with the New York City Road Runners Club located in Manhattan for more information: www.nyrr.org.

Accommodations:

Park Central Hotel
870 7th Avenue at 56th Street
New York, NY 10019
Phone: (212) 247-8000
Fax: (212) 707-4500
Toll-Free: 1-866-850-0187
www.ParkCentralNY.com

Note: Simply put, this hotel is near the finish line and it is one of the better-priced ones.

Jumeirah Essex House
160 Central Park South
New York, NY 10019
Phone: (212) 247-0300
Fax: (212) 315-1839
Toll-Free: 1-888-645-5697
www.jumeirahessexhouse.com

Note: You'll find this hotel close to picturesque Central Park and bustling Broadway. Get a room with a view facing north and watch the race out your window.

Sherry-Netherland
781 5th Avenue
New York, NY 10022
Phone: (212) 355-2800
Fax: (212) 319-4306
Toll-Free: 1-877-743-7710
www.sherrynetherland.com

Note: A private setting is combined with excellent service from the staff.

Mandarin Oriental
80 Columbus Circle at 60th Street
New York City, NY 10023
Phone: (212) 805-8800
Fax: (212) 805-8888
Toll-Free: 1-866-801-8880
www.mandarinoriental.com

Note: Found mere blocks from the finish line, this hotel is considered one of the nicest in the city with one of the best spas for a runner's or a spectator's sore feet.

Pierre Hotel
2 East 61st Street
New York, NY 10021
Phone: (212) 940-8111
Fax: (212) 893-6042
www.tajhotels.com

Note: For those who are fans of finish-line action and fine hotels, this hotel is located right off the last mile on Fifth Avenue.

On-Site Hospitality:
Local street vendors are your best bet for some of New York City's finest cuisine.
A good old-fashioned New York hot dog cart or pretzel stand is ideal on this day.

Travel Packages:
If you are going to New York for this event, I would recommend using a reliable company to work with you on making the necessary arrangements. The suppliers listed in this book have solid references and are by far the most trusted in the business. Below are some of the organizations to try for this Top 100 Must See Sporting Event.

Premiere Corporate Events
14 Penn Plaza, Suite 925
New York, NY 10122
Phone: (212) 695-9480
Fax: (212) 564-8098
Toll-Free: 1-877-621-5243
E-mail: requests@tseworld.com
www.tseworld.com
www.pcevents.com

Premiere Sports Travel
201 Shannon Oaks Circle, Suite 205
Cary, NC 27511
Phone: (919) 481-9511
Fax: (919) 481-1337
Toll-Free: 1-800-924-9993
E-mail: sales@sportstravel.com
www.sportstravel.com

Dining:

Tavern on the Green
West 67th Street at Central Park West
New York, NY 10023
Phone: (212) 873-3200
Fax: (212) 875-8051
www.tavernonthegreen.com
*Note: This restaurant, located in the heart of
Central Park, hosts many pre-race pasta din-
ners that are perfect for carb-loading. Right at
the finish line so avoid on race day.*

The Central Park Boat House
East 72nd Street and Park Drive North (in-
side Central Park)
New York, NY 10028
Phone: (212) 517-2233
Fax: (212) 517-8821
www.thecentralparkboathouse.com
*Note: A legendary restaurant at the Loeb
Boathouse on the northeastern tip of the lake.
Will be packed on race day as it is right along
the route.*

Sambuca
20 West 72nd Street
New York, NY 10023
Phone: (212) 787-5656
www.sambucanyc.com
*Note: Southern Italian dining serving small
and family-sized portions. A perfect place to
carbo-load.*

Tony's Di Napoli
1606 2nd Avenue at 83rd Street
New York, NY 10028
Phone: (212) 861-8686
Fax: (212) 861-8889
www.tonysnyc.com
*Note: Cooking comes from Southern
Neapolitan traditions and served in family
style platters. A great place for a pre-race
meal or a victory dinner.*

Airports:

John F. Kennedy International Airport (JFK)
JFK Airport, Jamaica, NY 11430
Phone: (718) 244-4444
www.kennedyairport.com

LaGuardia Airport (LGA)
Ditmars Boulevard and 94th Street
Flushing, NY 11369
Phone: (718) 533-3400
www.panynj.gov

Newark Liberty International Airport (EWR)
North Avenue and Spring Street
Elizabeth, NJ 07201
Phone: (973) 961-6000
www.panynj.gov

Sports Travel Insider's Edge:

Best way to watch the action:
The place to watch is where spectators
crane their heads to see that first runner
coming off the 59th Street Bridge onto the
island of Manhattan. When those runners
are spotted, the party starts. The heavy celebration takes place at all the bars on 1st
Avenue from the bridge up to about 96th
Street. This area of 1st Avenue is where you
want to be if you are looking to enjoy the
race atmosphere but not necessarily to support a specific runner.

If you are more interested in seeing a
friend or family member and offering support, the best locations to do so are above
96th Street on 1st Avenue or in parts of the
Bronx. These are areas toward the end of
the race when runners need the most en-
couragement. They are also the least traf-
ficked, making it easy for a tired runner to
spot you.

Best place to get up close:
The New York City Marathon has a premier
running expo which takes place at Jacob

Javits Convention Center during the week of the race. Sponsors and organizers distribute information about the race and their respective products. First-timers get quite the introduction through this hands-on primer.

Best travel tip:

Even in a busy metropolis like New York City, the NYC Marathon clogs up the streets even more than usual. With many streets blocked off, walking and subways are your best modes of transportation to get you to the various viewing areas.

Notable Quotes:

"I love New York City and have always loved New York City and so I loved the experience of running the [ING] New York City Marathon. . . . I knew I wanted to debut there. I felt like it was the best thing for me. I had experience on the course. I knew the city really well. . . . I know it's not a fast course, but I like that it's a challenging course. I think that the bridges and the difficulty of the course make it a little bit more of a level playing field. . . . But I still have never run another marathon other than New York."—MATT DOWNIN, runner

"For the level of condition that I have now, that was without a doubt the hardest physical thing I have ever done. I never felt a point where I hit the wall, it was really a gradual progression of fatigue and soreness. . . . I think I bit off more than I could chew, I thought the marathon would be easier."—LANCE ARMSTRONG, cyclist and marathon runner

Relevant Websites:

www.nycmarathon.org
www.nycvisit.com
www.tseworld.com
www.pcevents.com
www.sportstravel.com
www.premieresports.com

7
WORLD SERIES

When?

It's not called the "October Classic" for nothing, though some games have been played on the first few days of November.

Significance:

Major League Baseball has taken its number of hits lately, and not from a bat. However, come October, any controversies from the regular season wash away as the best of the National and American leagues come together to determine their world champion. Dubbed the "Fall Classic" or the "October Classic," the World Series has become baseball's showcase since its inception in 1903, excluding the 1904 and 1994 seasons.

The World Series is a best-of-seven playoff (the Series in 1903, 1919, 1920, and 1921 were best-of-nine). Televised coverage began in 1947 when the New York Yankees took on the neighboring Brooklyn Dodgers in a "Subway Series." Today, the World Series is a sporting event that garners high ratings for any network owning the rights to broadcast the games. In front of that massive audience, the winning team makes history and each player takes home a World Series ring. Athletes have extended their careers and given up millions in contract restructurings just to have the chance at that coveted piece of jewelry.

Much to the chagrin of non-Yankee fans, the New York Yankees have taken home over a quarter of the championships from the over 100 World Series played. Dynasties such as the Yankees are created at the World Series. Superstars become legends. And, most recently, "curses" come to an end. In 2004, the Boston Red Sox finally won the big one after eighty-six years of coming up short, breaking the famous "Curse of the Bambino."

Now, about those Cubs....

Who attends?
This is an event for casual fans of all ages, as well as baseball fanatics who live for America's National Pastime.

History
Since the 1860s, baseball has had various forms of championship play. In 1903, the modern World Series took shape when the American League's Boston Americans (now Red Sox) defeated the National League's Pittsburgh Pirates, five games to three in a best-of-nine series. The following year, the New York Giants of the National League refused to play the Americans, claiming inferiority and almost ending the modern-day World Series before it got a chance to start. In response to those actions, baseball officials deemed the "Professional Baseball Championship" as a permanent institution in 1905.

In 1969, the Pennant Race was born. Instead of the teams with the best records in their respective leagues, each league was reorganized into two divisions, East and West. The winners of those divisions would face off in a best-of-five matchup. The victors would go on to the World Series. By 1994, Major League Baseball expansion necessitated the establishment of a Central Division for both leagues. With an odd number of champions, the "wild card" system was born with the best non-divisional winner making the playoffs. Ironically, that would be the year that the player's strike forced baseball fans to look for another October activity.

Notable World Series MVPs:
Sandy Koufax, Los Angeles Dodgers
Randy Johnson, Arizona Diamondbacks
  (co-MVP)

Curt Schilling, Arizona Diamondbacks
  (co-MVP)
Manny Ramirez, Boston Red Sox
Reggie Jackson, Oakland Athletics and
  New York Yankees
Derek Jeter, New York Yankees
Bob Gibson, St. Louis Cardinals
Brooks Robinson, Baltimore Orioles
Mariano Rivera, New York Yankees
Johnny Bench, Cincinnati Reds

Records:
Most home runs in a World Series: Reggie
  Jackson, 1977, 5 in 6 games
Most runs scored in a World Series: Reggie
  Jackson (1977) and Paul Molitor
  (1993), 10 in 6 games
Most hits in a World Series: Marty Barrett
  (1986), Lou Brock (1968), and Bobby
  Richardson (1964), 13 in 7 games
Best slugging average in a World Series: Lou
  Gehrig, 1928, 1.727 in 4 games
Most strikeouts by a pitcher in a World Series:
  Bob Gibson, 1968, 35
Most World Series sweeps: New York
  Yankees, 8

Things to know before you go:
Team's ace: A team's best starting pitcher.
Alley: The section of the outfield between
  the outfielders. Also known as the
  "gap."
Around the horn: A double play going from
  third base to second to first.
Backdoor slider: A pitch that appears to be
  out of the strike zone, but then breaks
  back over the plate.
Baltimore chop: A ground ball that hits in
  front of home plate and takes a large hop
  over the infielder's head.
Basket catch: When a fielder catches a ball
  with his glove near belt level.
Beanball: A pitch that is intentionally
  thrown at a batter.
Closer: Team's relief pitcher who finishes
  the game.

Cutter: A cut fastball (one with a late break to it).

Dinger: A home run.

Heat: A good fastball. Also "heater."

High and tight: Referring to a pitch that's up in the strike zone and inside on a hitter. Also known as "up and in."

Homer: A home run. Other terms include: blast, dinger, dong, four-bagger, four-base knock, moon shot, tape-measure blast, and tater.

Meatball: An easy pitch to hit, usually right down the middle of the plate.

Painting the black: When a pitcher throws the ball over the edge of the plate.

Pick: A good defensive play by an infielder on a ground ball. Also a shortened version of "pick-off."

Ribbie: Another way of saying RBI. Also "ribeye."

Sweet Spot: The part of the bat just a few inches from the barrel.

Twin Killing: A double play.

Wheels: A ballplayer's legs.

Whiff: Strikeout.

Yakker: Curve ball.

Tickets:

For primary ticket access information, consider the websites of the teams playing in the Series. Your best bet will be the secondary market as most tickets are made available only to season ticket holders.

For secondary ticket access, consider:

GoTickets, Inc.
2345 Waukegan Road, Suite 140
Bannockburn, IL 60015-1552
Toll-Free: 1-800-775-1617
Fax: (919) 481-9101
E-mail: sales@gotickets.com
www.gotickets.com

Travel Packages:

If you are going to travel to this event, I would recommend using a reliable company to work with you on making the necessary arrangements. The suppliers listed in this book have solid references and are by far the most trusted in the business. Below are some of the organizations to try for this Top 100 Must See Sporting Event.

Premiere Corporate Events
14 Penn Plaza, Suite 925
New York, NY 10122
Phone: (212) 695-9480
Fax: (212) 564-8098
Toll-Free: 1-877-621-5243
E-mail: requests@tseworld.com
www.tseworld.com
www.pcevents.com

Premiere Sports Travel
201 Shannon Oaks Circle, Suite 205
Cary, NC 27511
Phone: (919) 481-9511
Fax: (919) 481-1337
Toll-Free: 1-800-924-9993
E-mail: sales@sportstravel.com
www.sportstravel.com

Notable Quotes:

"This is the type of thing that as a kid you dream about. Something I've done in my backyard a hundred times. And you never know if you're going to get the opportunity to do it."—SCOTT BROSIUS, New York Yankee and World Series MVP

"The best possible thing in baseball is winning the World Series. The second best thing is losing the World Series."—TOMMY LASORDA, former Los Angeles Dodgers pitcher and manager

Relevant Websites:
www.mlb.com
www.tseworld.com
www.pcevents.com
www.sportstravel.com
www.gotickets.com
www.premieresports.com

8
WINTER OLYMPICS

When?
Every four years.

Future Locations:
2010–Vancouver, British Columbia,
   Canada
2014–Sochi, Russia

Significance:
The word *gymnasium* is derived from the Greek word *gymnos*, which means nude. Olympic athletes circa 776 B.C. preferred to practice and subsequently perform in the nude. That style of preparation would not quite work in today's Winter Olympic Games.

Athletic competitions that take place on the ice and snow are the featured attraction of the Winter Olympics. At first, they were combined with all other Olympic Games. Try as they might, combining sports that required drastically different climates did not work. A French town in the Haute-Savoie hosted the first Winter Olympics in 1924, spinning off their events from the now Summer Olympic Games.

The Winter Olympics enjoy a healthy following with fan attendance and international television broadcasts that draw billions of people, though the events may not have the same popularity as the Summer Games. Warmer countries closer to the equator simply do not have the training facilities to prepare properly for the Games. Yet, fans turn out and tune in to give a warm reception to the best and completely clothed athletes as they go for the gold.

Who attends?
From bobsledding to the biathlon, the Winter Olympics are a veritable smorgasbord of events for people from all walks of life from around the world to attend.

History
Following its establishment in 1894, the International Olympic Committee (IOC) was considering events for the first modern Olympics. When the subject of ice skating came up, the powers-that-be politely said, "Next." It would not be until the 1908 Olympics that four figure skating events would be added. Ten-time World Champion Ulrich Salchow took home the gold for the men, while Madge Syers nabbed the women's gold medal.

By 1911, Eugenio Brunetta d'Usseaux, an Italian count, suggested that a week of winter sports be made a part of the 1912 Summer Olympics in Stockholm, Sweden, similar to the Nordic Games. The idea was floated again, and the 1916 Olympics were set to debut the winter sports before World War I cancelled the event. At the 1920 Games in Antwerp, the winter games shared the stage and featured skating and ice hockey. The first actual games devoted solely to winter sports were the 1924 Games in Chamonix, retroactively designated by the IOC in 1926. It featured Charlie Jewtraw winning the 500-meter speed skating competition, making him the first official Olympic Winter Games champion.

Over the years, sports have been added, such as snowboarding and curling. While still not quite as popular as the Summer Games, the Winter Olympics have evolved into a high-profile display of the best winter sports athletes in the world.

Records:
Most decorated female Olympian: Raisa
   Smetanina (USSR/UT), 10 Medals,
   Cross Country
Most decorated male Olympian: Bjorn
   Daehlie (Norway), 12 Medals, Cross
   Country
Most gold medals–Male: Bjorn Daehlie
   (Norway), 8, Cross Country

Most gold medals–Female: Lyubov Egorova (USSR/UT), 6, Cross Country, and Lidia Skoblikova (USSR), 6, Speed Skating

Traditions:

The opening ceremonies are always the biggest draw at the Olympics.

Opening Ceremonies

Receiving the Head of State of the Host Country
Parade of the Participants
Speech by the President of the Organizing Committee
Speech by the IOC President
Head of State Declares the Games Open
Playing of the Olympic Anthem and the Entry and Raising of the Olympic Flag
Last Stage of the Olympic Torch Relay and the Lighting of the Olympic Cauldron
Symbolic Release of the Pigeons
Taking of the Oath by a Competitor
Taking of the Oath by a Judge
National Anthem of the Host Country
Artistic Program
Flame and Torch

According to the ancient Greeks, Prometheus gave mankind fire and it holds sacred qualities. The eternal flame comes from the flames that burned in front of the Greek temples lit using the sun's rays. The Olympic flame is lit in front of the ruins of the Temple of Hera. From there, runners pass the torch in relay fashion until it arrives to the site of the Games.

Release of Doves

Depending on the weather, doves are released as a symbol of peace following the lighting of the cauldron. If the temperature is too cold, balloons have been substituted. The 1896 Olympics started that tradition and it is now an official part of the Winter Games' Opening Ceremony.

The Olympic Oath

One athlete and one judge from the home nation recite the Olympic Oath during the Opening Ceremony of every Olympics. The current form of the judges' oath is:

> "In the name of all the judges and officials, I promise that we shall officiate in these Olympic Games with complete impartiality, respecting and abiding by the rules which govern them, in the true spirit of sportsmanship."

The current form of the athletes' oath is:

> "In the name of all the competitors I promise that we shall take part in these Olympic Games, respecting and abiding by the rules which govern them, committing ourselves to a sport without doping and without drugs, in the true spirit of sportsmanship, for the glory of sport and the honor of our teams."

Tickets:

For primary ticket options, check the Official movement website, www.olympic.org, for more information.

Travel Packages:

If you are going to travel to this event, I would recommend using a reliable company to work with you on making the necessary arrangements. The suppliers listed in this book have solid references and are by far the most trusted in the business. Below are some of the organizations to try for this Top 100 Must See Sporting Event.

Premiere Corporate Events

14 Penn Plaza, Suite 925
New York, NY 10122
Phone: (212) 695-9480
Fax: (212) 564-8098
Toll-Free: 1-877-621-5243
E-mail: requests@tseworld.com
www.tseworld.com
www.pcevents.com

Premiere Sports Travel
201 Shannon Oaks Circle, Suite 205
Cary, NC 27511
Phone: (919) 481-9511
Fax: (919) 481-1337
Toll-Free: 1-800-924-9993
E-mail: sales@sportstravel.com
www.sportstravel.com

Notable Quotes:

"I have to consider my greatest accomplishments winning the Olympics because everything that I've done after that is really because of the Olympics."—BRIAN BOITANO, 1988 Olympic gold medalist in figure skating

"So you wish to conquer in the Olympic games, my friend? And I too, by the Gods, and a fine thing it would be. But first mark the conditions and the consequences, and then set to work. You will have to put yourself under discipline; to eat by rule, to avoid cakes and sweetmeats; to take exercise at the appointed hour whether you like it or no, in cold and heat; to abstain from cold drinks and from wine at your will; in a word, to give yourself over to the trainer as to a physician. Then in the conflict itself you are likely enough to dislocate your wrist or twist your ankle, to swallow a great deal of dust, or to be severely thrashed, and, after all these things, to be defeated."—EPICTETUS, Greek Stoic philosopher

Relevant Websites:

www.olympic.org
www.tseworld.com
www.pcevents.com
www.sportstravel.com
www.premieresports.com

9

RED SOX VS. YANKEES AT YANKEE STADIUM

Where?
161st and 164th streets at River Avenue, parallel from the "old" Yankee Stadium.

When?
Any time the Yankees play the Red Sox at home. It can be during the regular baseball season, which starts anywhere in March or April and ends in late September. If you're lucky enough to see a Yankees/Red Sox playoff game in October at the Stadium, all the better.

Significance:
It's the best rivalry in pro sports, hands down.

The dislike that Boston and New York have for each other can be traced to the Revolutionary War. But nothing compares to the century-old rivalry between the Boston Red Sox and the New York Yankees. Wars have been waged. The U.S. presidency has changed hands several times. Mortal enemies have mended fences to become friends. Even the famed "Curse of the Bambino" has been broken. In an era where everything needs to change, there is one constant: the intense hatred between Boston and New York fans, not to mention a member or two of the organizations. While Yankee fans rabidly await the annual showdown at their stadium during the regular season, the Sox are anything but welcome on their hallowed grounds. Boos drown out the announcer's calls. Catcalls greet the Red Sox players. They have met before to decide the American League championship. However, in 2004, when the Red Sox defeated the Yankees in seven games, the feud continued, but at a breakneck speed.

Who attends?

Proud Yankee fans and an unexpected amount of brave Red Sox fans. No matter how these teams are doing in the standings, these games are as important as any championship matchup. Pride and bragging rights seem just as important as a pennant or ring.

How to get there?

The Yankee Stadium Subway stop is located at 161st Street and River Avenue, right outside the stadium. A trip from midtown Manhattan is around twenty-five minutes, accounting for crowds and rush hour. NY Waterways operates the Yankee Clipper from Manhattan and various points in New Jersey.

There are plans for a Metro-North station to serve commuters from Manhattan via Grand Central Terminal and 125th Street. Residents from New York's northern suburbs and Connecticut will have this option as well.

Tickets:

For primary ticket access information, consider: www.yankees.com.

For secondary ticket access, consider:

GoTickets, Inc.
2345 Waukegan Road, Suite 140
Bannockburn, IL 60015-1552
Toll-Free: 1-800-775-1617
Fax: (919) 481-9101
E-mail: sales@gotickets.com
www.gotickets.com

Accommodations:

W New York
541 Lexington Avenue at 49th Street
New York, NY 10022
Phone: (212) 755-1200
Fax: (212) 319-8344
www.whotels.com

Note: 652 rooms and sixty suites. Enjoy a drink at the Whiskey Blue, a great bar located off the lobby area.

Grand Hyatt
109 East 42nd Street at Grand Central
   Terminal
New York, NY 10017
Phone: (212) 883-1234
Fax: (212) 697-3772
www.hyatt.com

Note: 1,311 oversized and renovated guest-rooms with 24-hour room service, business center, and StayFit Gym. Easy access to the subway lines up to the Stadium.

Loews Regency Hotel
540 Park Avenue at 61st Street
New York, NY 10065
Phone: (212) 759-4100
Fax: (212) 826-5674
www.loewshotels.com

Note: 353 guest rooms encompass seventy-four suites and twelve specialty suites. Services include hairstyling, laundry, and even dog-walking. (Only in New York!)

On-Site Hospitality

(New Yankee Stadium):

The new Yankee Stadium (referred to as a "five-star hotel" with a "ball field in the middle") has luxury, outdoor, and party suites, a members-only restaurant, martini bar, conference space, and concierge services.

There is a "great hall" featuring over one million square feet of retail space. The famed Monument Park, featuring Yankee retired numbers, five freestanding monuments, and dozens of player and manager plaques, sits in center field under a restaurant covered in black tinted glass.

Keep in mind that Yankee stadium offers multiple concession fare available for those who just want to see the game.

Travel Packages:

If you are going to travel to this event, I would recommend using a reliable company to work with you on making the necessary arrangements. The suppliers listed in this book have solid references and are by far the most trusted in the business. Below are some of the organizations to try for this Top 100 Must See Sporting Event.

Premiere Corporate Events

14 Penn Plaza, Suite 925
New York, NY 10122
Phone: (212) 695-9480
Fax: (212) 564-8098
Toll-Free: 1-877-621-5243
E-mail: requests@tseworld.com
www.tseworld.com
www.pcevents.com

Premiere Sports Travel

201 Shannon Oaks Circle, Suite 205
Cary, NC 27511
Phone: (919) 481-9511
Fax: (919) 481-1337
Toll-Free: 1-800-924-9993
E-mail: sales@sportstravel.com
www.sportstravel.com

Dining/bars:

Yankee Tavern Bar

72 East 161 Street
Bronx, NY 10451
Phone: (718) 292-6130
Fax: (718) 292-9363
www.yankeetavern.com

Note: Yankee fans surround themselves with Bronx Bomber memorabilia while enjoying food and tipping back a cold beer. Right next to the stadium.

Stan's Sports Bar

836 River Avenue
Bronx, NY 10451
Phone: (718) 993-5548
www.stanssportsbar.com

Note: This place is legendary to the Yankee faithful. Since the 1970s, this "quintessential Bronx sports bar" has seen fans pouring beer while cheering on their heroes on the television screens.

Mickey Mantle's

42 Central Park South (59th Street between 5th and 6th Avenues)
New York, NY 10019
Phone: (212) 688-7777
Fax: (212) 751-5797
www.mickeymantles.com

Note: Opened in 1988, this has become a New York institution for tourists. Often the site of radio programs and sports and entertainment memorabilia auctions.

Aureole

34 East 61st Street (between Park Avenue and Madison Avenue)
New York, NY 10021
Phone: (212) 319-1660
Fax: (212) 750-8613
www.charliepalmer.com

Note: Close to the Lexington Street subway station at 59th Street for easy access up to the Stadium. A great place for pre- and post-game dinners.

Dominick's

2335 Arthur Avenue
Bronx, NY 10458
Phone: (718) 733-2807

Note: Family-style dining that does not require a menu, just a loud, commanding voice. New York accent optional. You've got it!

Mario's

2342 Arthur Avenue
Bronx, NY 10458
Phone: (718) 584-1188
Fax: (718) 584-1100
www.mariosrestarthurave.com

Note: Once upon a time this place was just a pizza shop in the 1940s. Today Mario's provides great Italian food within a baseball's throw of the stadium. An Arthur Avenue institution.

Airports:

John F. Kennedy International Airport (JFK)
JFK Airport, Jamaica, NY 11430
Phone: (718) 244-4444
www.kennedyairport.com

LaGuardia Airport (LGA)
Ditmars Boulevard and 94th Street
Flushing, NY 11369
Phone: (718) 533-3400
www.panynj.gov

Newark Liberty International Airport (EWR)
North Avenue and Spring Street
Elizabeth, NJ 07201
Phone: (973) 961-6000
www.panynj.gov

Sports Travel Insider's Edge:

Best way to watch the action:
Flock toward the "bleacher creatures" for the true Yankee experience. However, wearing red is not good for your health when interacting with the die-hard Yankee faithful. The least of your worries will be a Bronx cheer if they suspect you to be a Sox fan.

Best place to get up close:
Monument Park provides you with a bird's-eye view of Yankee history. Displays include retired uniform numbers and commemorative player plaques of legendary players, managers, and events. Perfect for the first-timer or the die-hard fan.

Best travel tip:
While the Yankees release tickets late on game day and make them available at the will call window, do not count on empty seats for the Sox game. You could get lucky, so it is worth a try.

Notable Quote:

"By now, even the casual sports fan has been flooded with Yankees–Red Sox arcana, including descriptions of the ghost that haunts Babe Ruth's old Boston hotel room—a room that (dum-dum) overlooks Fenway Park. There's lots of column inches and TV and sports-radio airtime to fill between the actual games, and a rivalry that's been raging for most of the past century provides a surplus of material."—CHRIS SMITH, *New York Magazine*

Relevant Websites:
www.yankees.com
www.nycvisit.com
www.gotickets.com
www.tickets.com
www.tseworld.com
www.pcevents.com
www.sportstravel.com
www.premieresports.com

10

UNC VS. DUKE BASKETBALL GAME AT CAMERON INDOOR STADIUM

Where?
Cameron Indoor Stadium
301 Whitford Drive
Durham, NC 27708

When?
Twice a year.

Significance:
Referred to as "The Battle of Tobacco Road" and "The Battle of the Blues," the rivalry between Duke University and neighboring University of North Carolina is considered one of the most intense in college basketball history and sports as a whole. Eight miles may separate the schools, but they are

considered worlds apart. Duke is a private university while North Carolina is a public state-supported school. To say this feud is intense is an understatement. Contempt, animosity, and hatred may be more appropriate terms. "Go to hell, Carolina, go to hell," can be heard from the Duke faithful and Carolina will reply in kind with just as colorful language. Since January 24, 1920, the two teams have done battle twice per year. Wins do not prove college basketball superiority as these teams are already the crème-de-la-crème, consistently ranking in the upper echelon. This is about North Carolina pride. UNC holds the advantage in number of wins, but Duke came on strong with consecutive wins in the 1990s and 2000s.

Who attends?
UNC faithful, Duke loyalists, and college basketball fans entertained by the blood feud. Celebrities have even gotten into the mix recently.

How to get there?
Easy to find from RDU Airport and all points east. From the north, take South I-85. Traveling from the south, take North I-85.

Public transportation is available via Go-Triangle, including:

Durham Area Transit Authority (DATA)
1907 Fay Street
Durham, NC 27704
Phone: (919) 485-RIDE
Fax: (919) 560-1534
www.durhamnc.gov

Triangle Transit Authority (TTA)
Phone: (919) 314-8888
www.ridetta.org

Tickets:
For primary ticket access information, consider:

Duke Athletic Ticket Office
107 Cameron Indoor Stadium
Durham, NC 27707
Phone: (919) 681-2583
Fax: (919) 681-8741
Toll-Free: 1-877-375-3853
www.goduke.com

North Carolina Athletic Ticket Office
Ernie Williamson Athletics Center
Skipper Bowles Drive
Chapel Hill, NC 27514
Phone: (919) 962-2296
Fax: (919) 962-5529
Toll-Free: 1-800-722-4335
www.tarheelblue.com

Even a large donation to the athletic departments will not guarantee you a ticket to this game. With students camping out for literally months in advance, your best bet is the secondary market.

For secondary ticket access, consider:

GoTickets, Inc.
2345 Waukegan Road, Suite 140
Bannockburn, IL 60015-1552
Toll-Free: 1-800-775-1617
Fax: (919) 481-9101
E-mail: sales@gotickets.com
www.gotickets.com

Accommodations:

Washington Duke Inn & Golf Club (0.6 miles from campus)
3001 Cameron Boulevard
Durham, NC 27705
Phone: (919) 490-0999
Fax: (919) 688-0105
Toll-Free: 1-800-443-3853
www.washingtondukeinn.com
Note: Luxury golf course named after Washington Duke and located less than a mile from campus.

Durham Courtyard

1815 Front Street
Durham, NC 27705
Phone: (919) 309-1500
Fax: (919) 383-8189
www.marriott.com

Note: Ten minutes from Duke. This non-smoking hotel provides reasonably priced breakfasts and a business center.

Homewood Suites by Hilton, Raleigh/ Durham

4603 Central Park Drive
Durham, NC 27703
Phone: (919) 474-9900
Fax: (919) 998-8804
Toll-Free: 1-800-CALLHOME
www.homewoodsuites.com

Note: Conveniently located in the Research Triangle district, this hotel provides convenient highway access to all local attractions and neighboring towns.

The Franklin

311 West Franklin Street
Chapel Hill, NC 27516
Phone: (919) 442-9000
Fax: (919) 442-4040
Toll-Free: 1-866-831-5999
www.franklinhotelnc.com

Note: This luxury boutique hotel on Franklin Street is non-smoking, pet-friendly, and close to the University of North Carolina.

On-Site Hospitality:

The setting is similar to a high school gym with pizza, popcorn, and soda sold at a premium price.

Travel Packages:

If you are going to travel to this event, I would recommend using a reliable company to work with you on making the necessary arrangements. The suppliers listed in this book have solid references and are by far the most trusted in the business. Below are some of the organizations to try for this Top 100 Must See Sporting Event.

Premiere Corporate Events

14 Penn Plaza, Suite 925
New York, NY 10122
Phone: (212) 695-9480
Fax: (212) 564-8098
Toll-Free: 1-877-621-5243
E-mail: requests@tseworld.com
www.tseworld.com
www.pcevents.com

Premiere Sports Travel

201 Shannon Oaks Circle, Suite 205
Cary, NC 27511
Phone: (919) 481-9511
Fax: (919) 481-1337
Toll-Free: 1-800-924-9993
E-mail: sales@sportstravel.com
www.sportstravel.com

Dining:

The Cosmic Cantina and Lounge

1920 Perry Street
Durham, NC 27705
Phone: (919) 286-1875

Note: Locally famous for great Mexican food.

Anotherthyme

109 North Gregson Street
Durham, NC 27701
Phone: (919) 682-5225
Fax: (919) 682 3826
www.anotherthyme.com

Note: Their philosophy is based on "rethinking seafood and vegetarian dishes as not being secondary to the meat and potatoes thing."

Bullock's Bar B Cue

3330 Quebec Drive
Durham, NC 27705
Phone: (919) 383-3211

Note: The name says it all—great Southern barbecue.

Pops Durham

810 West Peabody Street
Durham, NC 27701
Phone: (919) 956-7677
Fax: (919) 688-0098
www.pops-durham.com

Note: Committed to quality ingredients and support of local farmers, their menu changes with the seasons. My top choice in Durham.

Parizade

Erwin Square
2200 West Main Street
Durham, NC 27705
Phone: (919) 286-9712
Fax: (919) 416-9706
www.ghgrestaurants.com

Note: This restaurant touts "Mediterranean flavors at play."

Second Empire Restaurant and Tavern

The Historic Dodd-Hinsdale House
330 Hillsborough Street
Raleigh, NC 27603
Phone: (919) 829-3663
Fax: (919) 829-9519
www.second-empire.com

Note: Great private dining room downstairs for groups of ten or more. Terrific wine selection.

Airport:

Raleigh-Durham International Airport

2600 West Terminal Boulevard
Morrisville, NC 27623
Phone: (919) 840-7700
www.rdu.com

Sports Travel Insider's Edge:

Best way to watch the action:

Securing a premier center court middle section seat (Sections 6, 7, 14, or 15) will provide a great view of both the court and the student section. It is truly two shows in one.

Best place to get up close:

Get to know the Cameron Crazies in K-ville, a.k.a. Krzyzewskiville, by gaining access to the designated area where students stay in tents while waiting to get into Cameron for the game. You may even get a visit from Coach K himself, who has been known to bring a pizza to share or conduct an open-forum "team meeting" with the "campers."

Best travel tip:

A stay at the Washington Duke Inn on Duke's campus provides a five-star experience. While at the game, learn one of the many team-tailored taunting chants.

Notable Quotes:

"I'm biased, but I think this is the greatest rivalry, not just in college basketball, but in all of sports. . . . You believe this is just another game? Are you serious? Are you serious? There's no way you can tell these kids it's just another game."—DICK VITALE, ESPN broadcaster

"It's not about me vs. Dean, or me against Roy or Dean against Vic Bubas. Duke and Carolina will be here forever."—MIKE KRZYZEWSKI, Duke head basketball coach

Relevant Websites:

www.duke.edu
www.goduke.com
www.unc.edu
www.tarheelblue.com
www.durham-nc.com
www.tseworld.com
www.pcevents.com
www.sportstravel.com
www.gotickets.com
www.premieresports.com

11

WIMBLEDON

Where?
The All England Lawn Tennis and
Croquet Club
Church Road
Wimbledon, London, SW19 5AE, U.K.

When?
Six weeks before the first Monday in August and lasts approximately two weeks (or a fortnight, if you prefer) until all events are complete.

Significance:
In 1877, the Lawn Tennis Championships at Wimbledon were a mere garden party. The twenty-first century version of those championships—now called Wimbledon—attracts 500,000 tennis fans and players from over sixty countries. Millions watch worldwide via television, radio, and the Internet. Tournament winners gain acclaim for their accomplishment and become legends.

Wimbledon is the third Grand Slam event, preceded by the Australian Open and the French Open. It is recognized as the oldest major championship in tennis. For two weeks in June and July, players vie for titles in Gentlemen's Singles, Ladies' Singles, Gentlemen's Doubles, Ladies' Doubles, and Mixed Doubles. Youth tournaments include Boys' Singles, Girls' Singles, Boys' Doubles, and Girls' Doubles. Special invitational contests encompass 35 and over Gentlemen's Doubles, 45 and over Gentlemen's Doubles, 35 and over Ladies' Doubles, and wheelchair doubles.

Who attends?
People from all walks of life around the world. With the variety of seating and the various ways to secure tickets, the common folk and the well-to-do can rub elbows. If you are a fan of tennis or have uttered the phrase "Tennis anyone?" this is a showcase event to attend.

How to get there?
From Heathrow Airport (LHR), get on the Piccadilly Line at any of the terminals. Forty minutes later, you will arrive at Earls Court.

Tickets:
A public lottery that starts during the August before Wimbledon provides tickets for the main part of Centre, No. 1, and No. 2 Courts. The Lawn Tennis Association (LTA) holds their own exclusive lottery for LTA Advantage members on March 1st. The LTA also sells tickets to affiliated clubs, schools, and foreign tennis associations.

Debenture Tickets provide many perks to the lucky holders, including a Centre Court seat for every day of the Championships or a No. 1 Court seat for the first ten days of the Championships. Access to Debenture Holders' Lounges and exclusive dining facilities are provided as well. A lottery for a parking space is available for an additional fee.

The Debenture Office
The All England Lawn Tennis Club
Church Road, Wimbledon
London SW19 5AE

A Ground Admission ticket (out of 6,000 available) will get you into the No. 2 Court standing enclosure and unreserved seating and standing on Courts 3–19. Please note that you can only buy one ticket and it is cash only.

Approximately 500 tickets are available for Wimbledon fans on a daily basis for the Centre, No. 1, and No. 2 Courts, excluding the final four days.

For secondary ticket options, consider:

GoTickets, Inc.
2345 Waukegan Road, Suite 140
Bannockburn, IL 60015-1552
Toll-Free: 1-800-775-1617
Fax: (919) 481-9101
E-mail: sales@gotickets.com
www.gotickets.com

Accommodations:

Ann & Bernard's B & B
Bernard Gardens
London SW19 7BE, U.K.
Phone: +44 (0)20 8947 1866
www.walktowimbledonbandb.com
Note: This stylish B&B is close to the town center and a short train or tube ride to Wimbledon.

The Wimbledon Hotel
78 Worple Road
Wimbledon, London, SW19 4HZ, U.K.
Phone: +44 208 946 9265
Fax: +44 208 946 1581
www.wimbledonhotel.com
Note: Elegant boutique rooms with the latest multimedia facilities. Breakfasts include free-range eggs, fresh fruit, and organic yogurt.

Beaumont Apartments
24 Combemartin Road
London, SW18 5PR, U.K.
Phone: +44 (0)20 8789 2663
Fax: +44 (0)84 5638 4891
www.beaumont-london-apartments.co.uk
Note: Eighteen-minute walk to Wimbledon in a safe and quiet area with easy access to motorways, airports, and mainline stations.

The Phoenix Hotel
123-125 Merton Road
Wimbledon, London, SW19 1ED, U.K.
Phone: +44 (0)20 8542 0826
Fax: +44 (0)20 8540 9523
www.the-phoenix-hotel.co.uk
Note: In the heart of Wimbledon and close to central London. Accommodations include tea- and coffee-making facilities.

On-Site Hospitality and Events:

The Champions Lounge at Fairway Village: Not far from Centre and No. 1 Courts, guests can enjoy a private and tranquil garden setting that is temperature controlled. Seasoned, onsite staff provides full-service catering and hospitality that includes live television coverage updating the latest on Wimbledon, and Internet and e-mail terminals. All guests receive an official souvenir program and seat cushion.

Tea Lawn: 200 feet of counter space provide plenty of room for strawberries and cream, "Dutchees" (hot and spicy sausages in fresh rolls), pizzas, sandwiches, doughnuts, and baguettes. Tea, coffee, and soft drinks are provided, along with a champagne bar.

The Food Village: For those who want traditional English fare, the Village serves fish and chips. You can also find hot wok, pizza, and Southern-fried chicken.

Additional onsite venues include the Conservatory Buffet, Aorangi Food Court, Aorangi Café, and Renshaw Restaurant (for Debenture Holders only).

The Wimbledon Village Fair: For over 100 years, the Wimbledon Guild has organized this annual charity fundraising event that takes place prior to the tennis championships. Entry to the event is free.

Sights and Sounds of London (Luxury Premier Cruise): A four-course dinner cruise shows you London after dark.

The Wimbledon Lawn Tennis Museum: Get a taste of Wimbledon history with a guided ghost tour of the Gentleman's dressing rooms of 1980s by none other than John McEnroe. You can also see all men's and ladies' trophies. Adults get in for less than twenty dollars while children are usually charged about half of that.

Travel Packages:

If you are going to travel to this event, I would recommend using a reliable company to work with you on making the necessary arrangements. The suppliers listed in this book have solid references and are by far the most trusted in the business. Below are some of the organizations to try for this Top 100 Must See Sporting Event.

Premiere Corporate Events
14 Penn Plaza, Suite 925
New York, NY 10122
Phone: (212) 695-9480
Fax: (212) 564-8098
Toll-Free: 1-877-621-5243
E-mail: requests@tseworld.com
www.tseworld.com
www.pcevents.com

Premiere Sports Travel
201 Shannon Oaks Circle, Suite 205
Cary, NC 27511
Phone: (919) 481-9511
Fax: (919) 481-1337
Toll-Free: 1-800-924-9993
E-mail: sales@sportstravel.com
www.sportstravel.com

Dining:

Lighthouse
75-77 Ridgeway
Wimbledon, London, SW19 4ST, U.K.
Phone: +44 (0)20 8944 6338
www.lighthousewimbledon.com
Note: Unusual foods from various cultures are served: soy-braised duck leg with spiced apple and black bean ragout, bok choy, tamarind, and tuna carpaccio with crunchy vegetables and yuzu dressing.

San Lorenzo Fuoriporta
38 Wimbledon Hill Road
Wimbledon, London, SW19 7PA, U.K.

Phone: +44 (0)20 8946 8463
www.sanlorenzo.com
Note: Enjoy the crispy pizzas, fish, and grilled meats while viewing the pop-art paintings.

Est Est Est
38 High Street
Wimbledon, London, SW19 5BY, U.K.
Phone: +44 (0)20 8947 7700
Note: A restaurant chain serving modern Italian dishes and offering a variety of beers.

La Nonna
213-217 The Broadway
Wimbledon, London, SW19 1TB, U.K.
Phone: +44 (0)20 8542 3060
www.lanonna.co.uk
Note: Excellent cuisine served in warm traditional surroundings with a friendly atmosphere.

Villagio Italiano
25 High Street
Wimbledon Village
London, SW19 5DX, U.K.
Phone: +44 (0)20 8946 7779
www.villaggioitaliano.co.uk
Note: An authentic Italian family setting, with good food and entertaining, if not unpredictable service.

Lydon's Restaurant
67 High Street
Wimbledon Village, London, SW19 5EE, U.K.
Phone: +44 (0)20 8944 1031
www.lydonsrestaurant.co.uk
Note: This popular restaurant in Wimbledon village serves Italian wines and diverse items such as lobster, crab, tuna, swordfish, spicy marinated baby chicken, liver with bacon, and steak.

The Fire Stables
27-29 Church Road
Wimbledon Village, London, SW19 5DQ, U.K.

Phone: +44 (0)20 8946 3197

www.firestableswimbledon.co.uk

Note: No-nonsense, traditional pub food comes highly recommended.

Tootsies

48 High Street

Wimbledon Village, London, SW19 5AX, U.K.

Phone: +44 (0)20 8946 4135

www.tootsiesrestaurants.com

Note: Classic burgers served on a sourdough bun with fries, salad, and relishes. The exotic chicken and goat's cheese, or chorizo and red pepper are recommended.

Café Rouge

26 High Street

Wimbledon Village, London, SW19 5BY, U.K.

Phone: +44 (0)20 8944 5131

www.caferouge.co.uk

Note: A chain of Brasserie-style restaurants serves light meals, tea, and snacks.

Pizza Express

84 High Street

Wimbledon Village, London, SW19 5EG, U.K.

Phone: +44 (0)20 8946 6027

Note: Popular favorite for many locals. Revamped menu and brighter setting.

Strada

91 High Street

Wimbledon Village, London, SW19 5EG, U.K.

Phone: +44 (0)20 8946 4363

Note: A wide range of Italian dishes, including pizza, risotto, grilled meats, and fish.

Bayee Village

24 High Street

Wimbledon Village, London, SW19 5DX, U.K.

Phone: +44 (0)20 8947 3533

Note: The menu includes Peking and Szechwan food with an emphasis on fish and seafood.

Wagamama

46-48 Wimbledon Hill Road

Wimbledon Village, London, SW19 7PA, U.K.

Phone: +44 (0)20 8879 7280

www.wagamama.com

Note: Quick, cheap, and wholesome Oriental food, including noodle and rice dishes.

Thai Tho

20 High Street

Wimbledon Village, London, SW19 5DX, U.K.

Phone: +44 (0)20 8296 9034

www.thaitho.co.uk

Notes: Genuine Thai restaurant with friendly service.

Airport:

Heathrow Airport (LHR)

234 Bath Road

Hayes, Middlesex, UB3 5AP, U.K.

www.heathrowairport.com

London's major airport which is located fifteen miles west of central London.

Sports Travel Insider's Edge:

Best way to watch the action:

Wait in line every morning to grab one of the 500 seats located at Centre, No. 1, and No. 2 Courts or be selected as a member of the Lawn Tennis Association Advantage Ballot program. For information on the current system check lta.org.uk.

Best place to get up close:

Find a way to become a Debenture Holder, so you can be in a Centre Court seat every day. Centre Court and No. 1 Court Wimbledon debentures are issued roughly every five years to help fund capital expenditures like the retractable roof added in 2009. That does not even take into account the dining facilities and parking space provided to members as well.

Best travel tip:

Get a program for every day you are at Wimbledon, as a portion of it is updated on a daily basis. Plus, all that sitting mandates you rent or purchase a cushion.

Notable Quote:

"All in all, it's wonderful. But, I mean, the last time I won, it was a really outrageous way to win. I keep that trophy by my bed. That's the only one I keep close to me. I don't know if it can replace that trophy, but it's so wonderful."—VENUS WILLIAMS, former world numnber 1 professional tennis player

Relevant Websites:

www.wimbledonvisitor.com
www.tseworld.com
www.pcevents.com
www.sportstravel.com
www.gotickets.com
www.premieresports.com

12

STANLEY CUP

When?

The finals are played in June of every year. That's right. Hockey in hot weather.

Significance:

Called the Cup, the Holy Grail, and Lord Stanley's Mug, the Stanley Cup is what hockey players dream of hoisting high in the air. Baseball and football players can proudly wear their rings. The professional hockey lot prefers to drink from the Cup. The championship has been the sole property of the NHL since 1926 after various merges of now defunct hockey organizations.

For a sport that seemed exclusive to Canada and the northern regions of the United States, the Stanley Cup has been held by teams from California, North Carolina, Tampa Bay, and Dallas. Quite apropos considering the finals are played in the summer month of June. NHL hockey is no longer a sport exclusive to cold-weather areas, nor is its fans. It has experienced significant growth over the years, increasing the profile, importance, and fan following of the Stanley Cup tournament.

Who attends?

Fans of the teams playing mixed in with die-hard hockey fans from across the globe.

History

Frederick Stanley, 16th Earl of Derby and Lord Stanley of Victoria, shared an enthusiasm for hockey with his family. After watching a Montreal Victorias hockey game in 1888, he was hooked on the sport. With sons Arthur and Algernon forming the Ontario Hockey Association, their father felt that a challenge cup was necessary to determine a champion. Originally, the decorative bowl he purchased, engraved "Dominion Hockey Challenge Cup" on the outside rim with "From Stanley of Preston" on the other side, was to go to the top amateur hockey team in Canada.

The Montreal Hockey Club was the first Stanley Cup champion in 1893. The Cup eventually evolved into a trophy for professional hockey teams and became exclusive to the NHL in 1926 following several league mergers. Lord Stanley never saw a championship match that featured his name, nor did he receive the chance to present it. He was forced to return to England on July 15, 1893, to serve as the 16th Earl of Derby.

Cup Facts:

Crafted in Sheffield, England.
Purchased for ten guineas ($48.67) in 1892.
Weighs thirty-five pounds and stands less than three feet in height.

Stanley Cup Dynasties

Ottawa Senators
1919 to 1927 with four Stanley Cups
(1920, 1921, 1923, 1927)

Toronto Maple Leafs
1947 to 1951 with four Stanley Cups
(1947, 1948, 1949, 1951)
1962 to 1967 with four Stanley Cups
(1962, 1963, 1964, 1967)

Detroit Red Wings
1950 to 1955 with four Stanley Cups
(1950, 1952, 1954, 1955)

Montreal Canadiens
1956 to 1960 with five Stanley Cups
(1956, 1957, 1958, 1959, 1960)
1965 to 1969 with four Stanley Cups
(1965, 1966, 1968, 1969)
1976 to 1979 with four Stanley Cups
(1976, 1977, 1978, 1979)

New York Islanders
1980 to 1984 with four Stanley Cups
(1980, 1981, 1982, 1983)

Edmonton Oilers
1984 to 1990 with five Stanley Cups
(1984, 1985, 1987, 1988, 1990)

Notable Stanley Cup MVPs:
Patrick Roy, Montreal Canadiens and
Colorado Avalanche, 1993 and 2001
Mario Lemieux, Pittsburgh Penguins, 1991
and 1992
Wayne Gretzky, Edmonton Oilers, 1985
and 1988
Mark Messier, Edmonton Oilers, 1984
Bernie Parent, Philadelphia Flyers, 1974
and 1975
Bobby Orr, Boston Bruins, 1970 and 1972

Records:
Most Stanley Cup wins: Montreal, 24 (to date)
Most consecutive post-season appearances:
Boston Bruins, 29
Most years in the playoffs: Chris Chelios, 23

Most consecutive years in the playoffs: Larry
Robinson, 20
Most playoff games: Patrick Roy, 247
Most points in the playoffs: Wayne Gretzky,
382 (122 goals, 260 assists)
Most goals in the playoffs: Wayne Gretzky,
122
Most assists in the playoffs: Wayne Gretzky,
260
Most overtime goals in the playoffs: Joe Sakic,
8
Most power-play goals in the playoffs: Brett
Hull, 38
Most game-winning goals in the playoffs:
Wayne Gretzky and Brett Hull, 24
Most playoff wins by a goaltender: Patrick
Roy, 151
Most playoff shutouts by a goaltender: Patrick
Roy, 23

Things to know before you go:
Boards: Boards surrounding the ice.
Body Check: Legal hit where one player hits
another player on the opposite team
with either his shoulder or hip.
Center Line: Red line dividing the ice surface in half.
Checking: Poking the puck off the stick,
lifting your opponent's stick up and
taking the puck, or body checking off
the puck.
Chiclets: Teeth.
Goal: When a puck crosses over the goal
line.
Goon: Hockey-ese for a tough guy.
Hat Trick: Three goals by one player in a
single game.
Offside: A player from the attacking team
crossing over the defending team's blue
line before the puck crosses it.
Penalty: A foul that must be served in the
penalty box.
Penalty Box: The place to go to serve out a
penalty.
Period: Three of them at twenty minutes
each.

Power Play: Play continuing with one team having players in the penalty box, giving the other team more players on the ice.

Puck: Small black circular "biscuit" made of rubber.

Slap Shot: A shot made with a big back swing.

Zamboni: The large machine used to resurface the ice.

Tickets:

For primary ticket access information, consider: www.nhl.com.

For secondary ticket access, consider:

GoTickets, Inc.
2345 Waukegan Road, Suite 140
Bannockburn, IL 60015-1552
Toll-Free: 1-800-775-1617
Fax: (919) 481-9101
E-mail: sales@gotickets.com
www.gotickets.com

Travel Packages:

If you are going to travel to this event, I would recommend using a reliable company to work with you on making the necessary arrangements. The suppliers listed in this book have solid references and are by far the most trusted in the business. Below are some of the organizations to try for this Top 100 Must See Sporting Event.

Premiere Corporate Events
14 Penn Plaza, Suite 925
New York, NY 10122
Phone: (212) 695-9480
Fax: (212) 564-8098
Toll-Free: 1-877-621-5243
E-mail: requests@tseworld.com
www.tseworld.com
www.pcevents.com

Premiere Sports Travel
201 Shannon Oaks Circle, Suite 205
Cary, NC 27511
Phone: (919) 481-9511

Fax: (919) 481-1337
Toll-Free: 1-800-924-9993
E-mail: sales@sportstravel.com
www.sportstravel.com

Notable Quote:

"I couldn't breathe, and it wasn't because I was tired. It was just too much. I was trying to hold off the tears."—Ray Bourque, Hockey Hall of Famer and former Boston Bruins and Colorado Avalanche player on winning his first Stanley Cup

Relevant Websites:

www.nhl.com
www.tseworld.com
www.pcevents.com
www.sportstravel.com
www.gotickets.com
www.premieresports.com

13

TOUR DE FRANCE

Where?

The 2,200-mile course varies from year to year, but travels throughout France and neighboring border countries, always ending in Paris.

When?

Annually for twenty-three days in July.

Significance:

Only the best cycling teams from around the world are invited to participate in the Tour de France. Established in 1903, it is recognized as the world's largest cycling race and has grown in prominence and profile. Lance Armstrong has become a household name, primarily because of his success in the Tour de France. For twenty-three days, twenty to twenty-two cycling teams composed of nine riders each compete in twenty-one stages over 3,500 kilometers (2,200 miles). Each stage is considered an individual race and the time taken to complete each stage is added to a cumulative total for each rider. Adding to the drama, it is possible to win the overall race without winning a stage, as Greg LeMond did back in 1990. The terrain is unpredictable, ranging from flat to mountainous, but always ends at the Champs-Elysées in Paris (since 1975). The race is considered by many to be one of the most demanding athletic events, akin to running multiple marathons over three weeks or climbing three Mount Everests.

Who attends?

Seemingly increasing in popularity every year, the Tour de France attracts fans from throughout Europe. Cycling enthusiasts travel from all over the world for the race every July.

Tickets:

No ticket necessary. Find a spot along the lengthy route and get comfortable.

Accommodations (Paris):

Marriott Paris, Champs-Elysées Hotel
70 Avenue des Champs-Elysées
Paris, 75008, France
Phone: +33 (1)5393 5500
Fax: +33 (1)5393 5501
Toll-Free: 1-800-90-8333
www.marriott.com
Note: Classic Parisian atmosphere and the only hotel on the Champs-Elysées. Close to boutiques, businesses, and landmarks.

Hotel Raphael
17 Avenue Kléber
Paris, 75116, France
Phone: +33 (0)1 5364 3200
Fax: +33 (0)1 5364 3201
www.raphael-hotel.com
Note: Four-star hotel and a deluxe-class property with a personal touch similar to a

family-run hotel. Near to the Arc de Triomphe and the Champs-Elysées.

Elysées Union Hotel
44 Rue de l'Amiral Hamelin
Paris, 75116, France
Phone: +33 (0)1 4553 1495
Fax: +33 (0)1 4755 9479
www.elysees-paris-hotel.com
Note: In the heart of the Embassy District, it provides a sophisticated yet cozy atmosphere for guests.

Hotel Elysées Régencia
41 Avenue Marceau
Paris, 75116, France
Phone: +33 (0)1 4720 4265
www.hotelelyseesregencia.com
Note: This hotel offers charm, refinement, and tranquility with a great location. Close to businesses and tourist stops.

On-Site Hospitality:

The VIP zones are only available to those who buy an official Tour de France package or are invited by a sponsor. However, in the areas outside of Paris, hardcore followers camp out for days and have wine and cheese picnics while waiting for their favorite riders.

Travel Packages:

If you are going to travel to this event, I would recommend using a reliable company to work with you on making the necessary arrangements. The suppliers listed in this book have solid references and are by far the most trusted in the business. Below are some of the organizations to try for this Top 100 Must See Sporting Event.

Premiere Corporate Events
14 Penn Plaza, Suite 925
New York, NY 10122
Phone: (212) 695-9480
Fax: (212) 564-8098
Toll-Free: 1-877-621-5243

E-mail: requests@tseworld.com
www.tseworld.com
www.pcevents.com

Premiere Sports Travel
201 Shannon Oaks Circle, Suite 205
Cary, NC 27511
Phone: (919) 481-9511
Fax: (919) 481-1337
Toll-Free: 1-800-924-9993
E-mail: sales@sportstravel.com
www.sportstravel.com

Graham Baxter Sporting Tours
91 Walkden Road
Manchester, M28 7BQ, U.K.
Phone: +44 161 703 58 03
Fax: +44 161 703 85 47
E-mail: allan@sportstoursinternational.co.uk
www.sportingtours.co.uk

Dining:

Ratatouille
168 rue Montmartre
Paris, 75002, France
Phone: +33 (0)1 4013 0880
www.paris-restaurant-ratatouille.com
Note: Traditional and top-of-the-range French cuisine and the finest wines in an elegant atmosphere.

Le Vin dans les Voiles
8 rue Chapu
Paris, 75016, France
Phone: +33 (0)1 4647 8398
www.vindanslesvoiles.com
Note: One of the better wine restaurants in Paris.

La Grille Montorgueil
50 rue Montorgueil
Paris, 75002, France
Phone: +33 (0)1 4233 2121
www.paris-restaurant-grillemontorgueil.com
Note: Traditional French Bistro.

In addition to the fine local cuisine, you can make your own winner by picking up bread, cheese, and fruit from a local market. Bread is fresh and kept warm while the cheeses are top-notch. Grab a spot along the route and picnic.

Airport:

Paris Charles de Gaulle Airport
BP 20101
95711 Roissy Charles de Gaulle
France
Phone: +33 1 4862 2280
Fax: +33 1 4862 6389
www.airwise.com

Sports Travel Insider's Edge:

Best way to watch the action:
While the various stages take the riders through mountainous and rocky terrain, the final stage finishes with six laps on the Champs-Elysées and passes the beautiful Arc de Triomphe.

Best place to get up close:
Get up close and personal at the start of stages. The proximity allows spectators to interact with the athletes prior to the firing of the starting gun. The finishes also give you a unique perspective as well as a great view of the podium trophy and jersey presentations.

Best travel tip:
Secure a vacation package that exposes you to various aspects of the race, including mountain stages, time trials, starts, and finishes. In addition, prepare for crowds everywhere on the tour and in the local hotels, restaurants, and bars.

Notable Quote:

"This is a hell of a race. You should believe in these athletes, and you should believe in these people. I'll be a fan of the Tour de France for as long as I live. And there are no secrets—this is a hard sporting event and hard work wins it."—LANCE ARMSTRONG, cyclist and marathon runner

Relevant Websites:
www.sportingtours.co.uk
www.letour.fr
www.tseworld.com
www.pcevents.com
www.sportstravel.com
www.premieresports.com

14

CUBS GAME AT WRIGLEY FIELD

Where?
Wrigley Field
1060 West Addison
Chicago, Illinois

When?
Due to the longest dry spell between championships for a city that boasts teams in all four major United States sports leagues, do not count on attending Wrigley Field in October. Early April to late September has been the traditional Cubs season since 1908.

Significance:
It's the closest we can get today to how baseball was meant to be watched.

Wrigley Field, located in the North Side Lakeview neighborhood of Chicago called Wrigleyville, is more than the faux home of Elwood Blues. While 1060 West Addison is not a location that has hosted a World Series since 1908, it is still a building rich with history. The Cubs have their own history, as the only charter member of the National League, alongside the Atlanta Braves, and the sole remaining NL team that resides in their original city. However, they must share the affections of Chicagoans with their American League counterpart on the South Side, the White Sox.

Who attends?
Given the fanatical following the Cubs still enjoy on the North Side of Chicago, "Who doesn't attend?" is a more appropriate question. Local college-age fans and twenty-somethings can be seen throughout the park. Cubs hats of all sizes and conditions adorn the heads of fans, who usually don't mind if a wayward drink spills on it.

How to get there?
Public transportation, such as a cab or the CTA Red Line, is strongly encouraged when going to a Cubs game at Wrigley.

The Cubs operate a low-priced shuttle and parking service at the DeVry University campus off Addison and Western for weekend and night games.

For fans in the Northwest suburbs, take the Cubs Roundtripper bus. Park free at Pace's Northwest Transportation Center (NWTC) in Schaumburg and Yorktown Center in Lombard and climb aboard for less then ten dollars a person round-trip. Groups of six or more can purchase tickets and get individual tickets discounted even more.

Check out the RTA Trip Planner while planning your trip to Wrigley Field. They can be reached at (773) 836-7000.

Tickets:
For primary ticket access information, consider: www.chicago.cubs.mlb.

For secondary ticket access, consider:

GoTickets, Inc.
2345 Waukegan Road, Suite 140
Bannockburn, IL 60015-1552
Toll-Free: 1-800-775-1617
Fax: (919) 481-9101
E-mail: sales@gotickets.com
www.gotickets.com

Another great seating option are the multiple private rooftops, which put you literally on top of the action. While far away from the field, you can still enjoy a truly unique and traditional "Wrigley experience." Most rooftop locations offer one price for your seat and all you can eat and drink. It's best to consult with a travel package company for the best rooftop options.

Also note that during the spring and fall, the difference between sun and shade is similar to the difference between wearing short sleeves and wearing a sweatshirt. Seating along the third base line is the sunny side of Wrigley Field. The further down the line, the longer you will enjoy the warmth of the sun.

Accommodations:

The James
55 East Ontario Street
Chicago, IL 60611
Phone: (312) 337-1000
Fax: (312) 337-7217
www.jameshotels.com

Note: A boutique hotel located near Rush Street bars and restaurants. Top-rated David Burke's Primehouse steakhouse with the trendy JBar are located on the property as well.

Ritz Carlton
160 East Pearson Street
Chicago, IL 60611
Phone: (312) 266-1000
Fax: (312) 266-1194
www.fourseasons.com

Note: One of the only hotels in America to top Condé Nast Traveler magazine's Readers' Choice Awards seven times.

The Amalfi Hotel Chicago
River North
20 West Kinzie Street
Chicago, IL 60610
Phone: (312) 395-9000
Fax: (312) 395 9001
www.amalfihotelchicago.com

Note: Located across the street from Harry Caray's famed Chicago sports bar.

Hotel Sofitel Water Tower
20 East Chestnut Street
Chicago, IL 60611
Phone: (312) 324-4000
Fax: (312) 324-4026
www.sofitel.com

Note: Located in a great area known to local folks as "The Viagra Triangle."

Westin River North River
320 North Dearborn Street
Chicago, IL 60610
Phone: (312) 744-1900
Fax: (312) 527-2650
Toll-Free: 1-800-937-8461
www.westinrivernorth.com

Note: A solid choice for an upscale experience. Great views overlooking the River North.

On-Site Hospitality:
The Stadium Club, the Friendly Confines Café, and the Sheffield Grill offer food and drink for those in Wrigley Field. In addition, there are concession stands where you can buy "some peanuts and Cracker Jacks," along with Italian beef sandwiches, hot dogs, bratwursts, hamburgers, popcorn, and pretzels. In addition, it would not be Wrigley Field if the Old Style beer was not flowing freely.

A little-known outdoor party deck is located behind home plate on the second deck. While this secret spot does not provide a view of the field, it is ideal for tipping back a beer or two during a lull in the action.

Travel Packages:
If you are going to travel to a Cubs game, I would recommend using a reliable company to work with you on making the necessary arrangements. The suppliers listed in this book have solid references and are by far the most trusted in the business. Below are some of the organizations to try for this Top 100 Must See Sporting Event.

Premiere Corporate Events
14 Penn Plaza, Suite 925
New York, NY 10122
Phone: (212) 695-9480
Fax: (212) 564-8098
Toll-Free: 1-877-621-5243
E-mail: requests@tseworld.com
www.tseworld.com
www.pcevents.com

Premiere Sports Travel
201 Shannon Oaks Circle, Suite 205
Cary, NC 27511
Phone: (919) 481-9511
Fax: (919) 481-1337
Toll-Free: 1-800-924-9993
E-mail: sales@sportstravel.com
www.sportstravel.com

Dining:

Tuscany
1014 West Taylor Street
Chicago, IL 60607
Phone: (312) 829-1990
Fax: (312) 829-8023
Note: Known for their Northern Italian food and great game-day dining.

The Cubby Bear
1059 West Addison Street (across the street
   from Wrigley Field)
Chicago, IL 60613
Phone: (773) 327-1662
Fax: (773) 472-7736
Note: Serves bar fare such as Cubby Burgers, Chicago Dogs, fries, and calamari. Tap beer includes Bud and Miller products.

Murphy's Bleachers
3655 North Sheffield
Chicago, IL 60613
Phone: (773) 281-5356
Fax: (773) 477-4751
www.murphysbleachers.com
Note: The place to hang out on game day, or for any day for that matter.

Casey Morans
3660 North Clark Street
Chicago, IL 60613
Phone: (773) 755-4444
www.caseymorans.com
Note: Since the 1930s, hot dogs by the pound and beer by the pail have been sold. While undergoing multiple facelifts, the former Ernie's Bleachers remains a long-standing tradition.

The Goose Island Brew Pub
3535 North Clark Street
Chicago, IL 60657
Phone: (773) 832-9040
Fax: (773) 832-9053
www.gooseisland.com
Note: Heaping portions of burgers, fries, and other traditional pub food are available. Wash it all down with top of the line of Goose Island beers, including seasonal specialties like Hefeweizen and Summertime Kolsch.

Airports:

O'Hare International Airport
10000 West O'Hare
Chicago, IL 60666
Phone: (773) 686-3700
www.ohare.com

Midway International Airport
5600 South Cicero Avenue
Chicago, IL 60638
Phone: (773) 838-0756
www.chicago-mdw.com

Sports Travel Insider's Edge:

Best way to watch the action or get up close:
Many Chicago baseball enthusiasts will tell you that Wrigley is not about where you sit, it's about the overall experience. This park will take you back in time regardless of where you're seated. Enjoy the minimal in-stadium advertising and the proximity that most seats offer to the field.

Best way to get up close to the action:
Arrive early and stand on Waveland Avenue. There you can do battle with the "Ball Hawks" who scramble for a home run hit out of the park during batting practice. It's a Wrigley tradition.

Best travel tip:
Wrigley Field is famous for the seventh-inning stretch where the late Harry Caray led the fans in a rousing rendition of "Take Me Out to the Ball Game." Famed Chicagoans have now taken over that hallowed duty. While it is a reason to stay until the seventh inning, don't leave so quickly after the game ends. A chorus of "Go Cubs Go" fills the stadium before everyone leaves for a post-game meal or libation.

Notable Quotes:

"While baseball's oldest ballparks close their gates one after another, their proud structures humbled by the years, their nostalgia outdone by luxury boxes, Wrigley Field remains a time capsule of the game. It looks the same as it did on that day in 1932, when Babe Ruth called his famous home run, and will stay that way well into the next century."—from an Associated Press article called "Glorious Wrigley"

"Every player should be accorded the privilege of at least one season with the Chicago Cubs. That's baseball as it should be played—in God's own sunshine. And that's really living."—ALVIN DARK, former Boston Braves shortstop

"What does a mama bear on the pill have in common with the World Series? No cubs."—HARRY CARAY, former Chicago Cubs radio and television broadcaster

Relevant Websites:
www.chicago.cubs.mlb.com
www.choosechicago.com
www.tseworld.com

www.pcevents.com
www.sportstravel.com
www.gotickets.com
www.premieresports.com

15

BCS NATIONAL CHAMPIONSHIP GAME IN NEW ORLEANS

Where?
The Louisiana Superdome
1500 Sugar Bowl Drive
New Orleans, LA 70112

When?
First weekend in January. Under the current BCS championship game rotation this event will take place next in New Orleans in 2012, then again in 2016 and every four years thereafter.

Significance:
The BCS (Bowl Championship Series) National Championship Game was created to downplay the controversy of who was truly best in college football. Little has been done to quell that controversy since the BCS title game's inception in 1998. Big Ten, Pac-10, and the Rose Bowl Game joined members of the ex-Bowl Alliance to form the BCS. The current group replaces the now-defunct Bowl Coalition, who hosted championship games from 1992 to 1997. In 2006, the National Championship Game became a separate event from the host bowl played at the same site as the host on the Monday following New Year's Day. The game's location still rotates between the sites of the BCS bowls; note that the date of the game occurs in the calendar year following the corresponding NCAA football season. The formula for selecting the participants is constantly under fire, among many other

rousing discussions regarding the overall process. Nonetheless, the USA Today Coaches Poll is contractually obligated to name the winner of the BCS title as their national champion in its final poll of the season. That means that the winner receives the AFCA National Championship Trophy and the National Football Foundation's MacArthur Bowl national championship trophy. With three trophies going to one team, one would think that the fans and experts would accept the outcome and recognize the champ. Think again.

Who attends?
Fans of the competing teams and college football fans from all walks of life.

How to get there?
All you need to do is get on I-10 to downtown New Orleans and look for the Superdome exits.

Tickets:
For primary ticket access information, check the websites of the participating teams.

For secondary ticket access, consider:

GoTickets, Inc.
2345 Waukegan Road, Suite 140
Bannockburn, IL 60015-1552
Toll-Free: 1-800-775-1617
Fax: (919) 481-9101
E-mail: sales@gotickets.com
www.gotickets.com

Accommodations:

New Orleans Marriott
555 Canal Street
New Orleans, LA 70130
Phone: (504) 581-1000
Fax: (504) 553-2171
Toll-Free: 1-800-228-9290
www.neworleansmarriott.com
Note: Conveniently located a little over one mile from the stadium.

Hotel Le Cirque
936 St. Charles Avenue
New Orleans, LA 70130
Phone: (504) 962-0900
Fax: (504) 962-0901
Toll-Free: 1-800-684-9525
www.hotellecirqueneworleans.com
Note: Touted as "New Orleans's hottest and hippest property." Conveniently located in the Arts District and close to the Convention Center and the French Quarter.

Holiday Inn Express at Historic Cotton Exchange
221 Carondelet Street
New Orleans, LA 70130
Phone: (504) 962-0800
Fax: (504) 962-0701
Toll-Free: 1-800-972-2791
www.ichotelsgroup.com
Note: Located in the heart of New Orleans's French Quarter, making it an exciting place to stay.

Hilton New Orleans Riverside
2 Poydras Street
New Orleans, LA 70140
Phone: (504) 561-0500
Fax: (504) 568-1721
www.hiltonfamilyneworleans.com
Note: This hotel often plays host to one of the BCS Championship teams.

Aster Crowne Plaza
739 Canal Street at Bourbon
New Orleans, LA 70130
Phone: (504) 962-0500
Fax: (504) 962-0501
Toll-Free: 1-888-696-4806
www.astorneworleans.com
Note: Perfect location right at the tip of the action on Bourbon. High story hotel is good for keeping out the noise of the French Quarter.

Hotel Monteleone
214 Royal Street

New Orleans, LA 70130
Phone: (504) 523 3341
Fax: (504) 681-4413
Toll-Free: 1-800-535-9595
www.hotelmonteleone.com

Note: A hotel full of history located on Royal Street in the French Quarter.

Royal Sonesta Hotel
300 Bourbon Street
New Orleans, LA 70130
Phone: (504) 586-0300
Fax: (5040 586-0335
Toll-Free: 1-800-SONESTA
www.sonesta.com

Note: Spacious rooms with great service from an attentive staff. Right smack in the middle of the action on Bourbon Street.

On-Site Hospitality:

The newly renovated Superdome Luxury Suites number 137 and cover the entire Superdome. Each suite has all the comforts of home, if not better. Watch the game on the field or via the plasma screen televisions while relaxing in plush, leather seating. In-house catering and reserved parking is part of the package. Please note that all suites are privately owned, but a number of suites on the 300 level are sometimes available for rent. There are also several private function area options inside the Superdome to rent out during the game for larger groups. These areas can host both pre-game and post-game parties. You will still need to secure tickets for your group if you select this option. To learn more about premium hospitality in the Superdome for this game check with the Sugar Bowl official website or with www.superdome.com.

Travel Packages:

If you are going to travel to this event, I would recommend using a reliable company to work with you on making the necessary arrangements. The suppliers listed in this book have solid references and are by far the most trusted in the business. Below are some of the organizations to try for this Top 100 Must See Sporting Event.

Premiere Corporate Events
14 Penn Plaza, Suite 925
New York, NY 10122
Phone: (212) 695-9480
Fax: (212) 564-8098
Toll-Free: 1-877-621-5243
E-mail: requests@tseworld.com
www.tseworld.com
www.pcevents.com

Premiere Sports Travel
201 Shannon Oaks Circle, Suite 205
Cary, NC 27511
Phone: (919) 481-9511
Fax: (919) 481-1337
Toll-Free: 1-800-924-9993
E-mail: sales@sportstravel.com
www.sportstravel.com

Premiere College Sports
(Powered by Dodd's Athletic Tours)
308 South Neil
Champaign, IL 61820
Phone: (217) 373-5067
Fax: (217) 398-1313
Toll-Free: 1-800-553-5527
www.doddsathletictours.com
www.collegesportstravel.com

Dining:

The Rib Room
621 St. Louis Street
New Orleans, LA 70140
Phone: (504) 529-5333
Fax: (504) 529-7089

Note: Located inside the French Quarter's Omni Royal Orleans Hotel. This place is known for its Prime Rib. A local hangout for lunch as it is right across from the courthouse.

Commander's Palace
1403 Washington Avenue

New Orleans, LA 70130
Phone: (504) 899-8221
Fax: (504) 891-3242
www.commanderspalace.com

Note: Reservations and proper dress will get you into this famed restaurant in the Garden District. Emeril Lagasse served as head chef from 1982 to 1990. Try the Lyonnaise Gulf Fish.

Allegro Bistro
1100 Poydras Street, Suite 100
  (Energy Center)
New Orleans, LA 70163
Phone: (504) 582-2350
Fax: (504) 582-2351

Note: Close to the Superdome, offering contemporary, Cajun, and Creole dishes. Usually hosts a great tailgate party outdoors before the big game.

Johnny White's Sports Bar
720 Bourbon Street
New Orleans, LA 70116
Phone: (504) 524-4909
www.johnnywhitesneverclosed.com

Note: Always open with nearby street performers. What else would you expect from a bar in the French Quarter? This bar did not even close during the Katrina disaster.

Acme Oyster House
724 Iberville Street
New Orleans, LA 70118
Phone: (504) 522-5973
Fax: (504) 524-1595
www.acmeoyster.com

Note: Serves raw oysters, jambalaya, and other entrées. The long wait is well worth it.

Mango Mango
201/236/333/400 Bourbon Street
New Orleans, LA
Phone: (504) 524-0114
www.mangodaiquiris.com

Note: Did you know that there are twelve different kinds of daiquiris? Only at Mango Mango.

Drago's
Hilton New Orleans Riverside
2 Poydras Street
New Orleans, LA 70140
Phone: (504) 584-3911
Fax: (504) 584-3937
www.dragosrestaurant.com

Note: Home of the first ever Charbroiled Oyster. Do not leave New Orleans before trying one. They are unreal.

Mother's Restaurant
401 Poydras Street
New Orleans, LA 70130
Phone: (504) 523-9656
Fax: (504) 525-9771
www.mothersrestaurant.net

Note: The world's best baked ham, which is one of many ingredients on their po'boy. Another New Orleans establishment where you will find the line worth the wait.

Pat O'Brien's Bar
718 Saint Peter Street
New Orleans, LA 70116
Phone: (504) 525-4823
Fax: (504) 582-6914
www.patobriens.com

Note: A great local place to grab a drink or something to eat at any time, day or night. The inventor of the Hurricane drink. Try one.

Airports:

Louis Armstrong New Orleans International Airport
900 Airline Drive
Kenner, LA 70062
Phone: (504) 464-0831
www.flymsy.com

New Orleans Lakefront Airport
6001 Stars and Stripes Boulevard
New Orleans, LA 70126
Phone: (504) 243-4010
www.lakefrontairport.com

Sports Travel Insider's Edge:

Best way to watch the action:
The Superdome is immense and was able to house thousands of families displaced during Hurricane Katrina. However, the second-level sideline seats give you the best view in the stadium, particularly the first several rows in the 200 level.

Best place to get up close:
Two words: French Quarter. It is an atmosphere like no other on any day but especially when the BCS is in town. Energy and excitement fill the streets and it is a great way to spend time before and after the game. It would not be a trip to New Orleans without visiting the historic French Quarter.

Best travel tip:
Be prepared to party or witness a great deal of partying. Sleep is a rare commodity in the Big Easy. The ideal refuge from the craziness of the French Quarter but still a place to enjoy the action would be Harrah's Casino for some gambling.

Notable Quotes:

"The city came together in a way that makes me truly proud. It was a challenge that was sent out to everybody top to bottom, from the shoeshine man to the person at the very top. Everybody met that challenge and I think exceeded expectations."—PAUL HOOLAHAN, Sugar Bowl chief executive

"It's an important statement to the country that New Orleans is back and ready to perform and put on the classic big-time college events that we're known for."—PAUL HOOLAHAN

Relevant Websites:
www.superdome.com
www.neworleanscvb.com
www.bcsfootball.org

www.tseworld.com
www.pcevents.com
www.sportstravel.com
www.gotickets.com
www.doddsathletictours.com
www.collegesportstravel.com
www.premieresports.com

16

LIVERPOOL VS. MANCHESTER UNITED AT OLD TRAFFORD

Where?
Old Trafford
Sir Matt Busby Way
Old Trafford, Manchester, M16 0RA, U.K.

When?
During football (a.k.a. soccer) season.

Significance:
The proximity of both clubs in the northwest of England makes the rivalry between Liverpool and Manchester. The origin of their feud can be traced back to their industrial roots. Manchester was well-known for manufacturing. Liverpool had a key port that was once used by their now rival. The construction of the Manchester Ship Canal allowed goods to be shipped directly to Manchester, bypassing their neighbor. In the 1970s, Liverpool joined Manchester in soccer dominance and the feud was born. They not only battle to improve their standings in the league, but also over the designation as "the Greatest English Football Club," a title both clubs claim. A heated rivalry may be an understatement. Not content with battling on the soccer field, in 2007 Manchester United blocked Gabriel Heinze from joining Liverpool via an appeal to the FA. Recognized as the most successful teams in English football history, Liverpool versus Manchester bian-

nual matchups are considered the biggest games of the season. Victories against each other are just as important as revenues and league standings.

Who attends?
Rabid football/soccer fans cheering on their favorite team and jeering their rival.

How to get there?
Travel onto the M60 by the most appropriate route and then leave at the nearest junction to you. Select from Junctions 7, 9, and 12 as follows:

From Clockwise M60 (increasing junction numbers): Take the Motorway at Junction 7 to join the A56 Manchester bound. Stay on the A56 following the signs for Manchester United. Turn left into Sir Matt Busby Way. Parking is located on the right in front of the stadium.

From Anti-Clockwise M60 (decreasing junction numbers): Take the M60 at Junction 9 and merge onto Parkway (A5081) toward Trafford Park. At the first island, take the 3rd exit onto Village Way and remain on this road until the next island (traffic lights). Take the second exit and then merge onto Wharfside Way. Turn right at the junction with Sir Matt Busby Way. Parking is on the left in front of the stadium.

Alternative route from Anti-Clockwise M60 (decreasing junction numbers): Take the M60 at Junction 12 for M602 (Salford/Manchester). At the end of the M602 (Junction 3), follow signs for Salford Quays and Trafford Park. At the roundabout, turn right into Trafford Road (A5063). You will go over the bridge over the Manchester Ship Canal. Stay in the right hand lane to turn right at the next set of lights and follow the road to Trafford Wharf Road. Turn left at the next set of lights onto Waters Reach. The Golden Tulip Hotel will be on your left. Continue through the lights onto Sir Matt Busby Way.

NOTE: Please seek alternative on match days when Sir Matt Busby Way is closed.

Tickets:
For primary ticket access information, consider: www.manutd.com.

For secondary ticket access, consider:

GoTickets, Inc.
2345 Waukegan Road, Suite 140
Bannockburn, IL 60015-1552
Toll-Free: 1-800-775-1617
Fax: (919) 481-9101
E-mail: sales@gotickets.com
www.gotickets.com

Accommodations:

The Lowry Hotel
50 Dearmans Place
Chapel Wharf
Manchester, M3 5LH, U.K.
Phone: +44 161 827 4000
Fax: +44 161 876 4001
Toll-Free: 1-888-667-9477
www.thelowryhotel.com
Note: Established in April of 2000, this has become a popular place to stay.

The Midland Hotel
Peter Street
Manchester, M60 2DS, U.K.
Phone: +44 161 236 3333
Fax: +44 161 932 4100
www.qhotels.co.uk
Note: Located on the south side of St Peter's Square, this is a celebrated luxury hotel and a grade II-listed architectural treasure.

Palace Hotel Manchester
Oxford Street
Manchester, M60 7HA, U.K.
Phone: +44 161 288 1111
Fax: +44 161 228 7792
www.palace-hotel-manchester.co.uk
Note: Friendly staff and quality service in a carefree and relaxing environment.

The Britannia Sachas Hotel

12 Tib Street
Manchester, M4 1SH,U.K.
Phone: +44 (0)871 222 0018
Fax: +44 (0)871 222 7705
www.britanniahotels.com

Note: Several health and beauty facilities, including the Spindles Health & Leisure Club, allow you to calm your nerves and improve your health.

Hotel Ibis Manchester City Centre

96 Portland Street
Manchester, M1 4GX, U.K.
Phone: +44 161 234 0600
www.accorhotels.com

Note: This hotel is a great value for those on a budget.

Travelodge

9 Peter Street
Manchester, M3 5AL, U.K.
Phone: +44 871 984 6159
www.travelodge.co.uk

Note: Another economical option for those coming to see the game.

On-Site Hospitality:

Old Trafford offers suites, boxes, and private restaurants for people who are entertaining others or for those who just want to enjoy the game. All hospitality packages include tickets, food, and drink. Phone: +44 (0)870 442 1994, e-mail: hospitality@manutd.co.uk.

Travel Packages:

If you are going to travel to this event, I would recommend using a reliable company to work with you on making the necessary arrangements. The suppliers listed in this book have solid references and are by far the most trusted in the business. Below are some of the organizations to try for this Top 100 Must See Sporting Event.

Premiere Corporate Events

14 Penn Plaza, Suite 925
New York, NY 10122
Phone: (212) 695-9480
Fax: (212) 564-8098
Toll-Free: 1-877-621-5243
E-mail: requests@tseworld.com
www.tseworld.com
www.pcevents.com

Premiere Sports Travel

201 Shannon Oaks Circle, Suite 205
Cary, NC 27511
Phone: (919) 481-9511
Fax: (919) 481-1337
Toll-Free: 1-800-924-9993
E-mail: sales@sportstravel.com
www.sportstravel.com

Dining:

Pre-match:

Bishops Blaize

Chester Road
Stretford, Manchester, M32 0SF, U.K.
Phone: +44 (0)161 873 8845

Note: Closest pub to the ground and one of the nosiest if you want a pre-match sing song.

The Trafford

699 Chester Road
Manchester, M16 0GW, U.K.
Phone: +44 (0)161 848 0736

Note: Another great pre-game option that is much like Bishops Blaize.

The Tollgate

Seymore Grove
Trafford, Manchester, M16 0TG, U.K.
Phone: +44 (0)161 873 8213

Note: A bit further away (right outside the Trafford Bar tram station) and more sedate! No singing, just drinking!

Post-match:

Gaucho Grill
2a St. Marys Street
Manchester, M3 2LB, U.K.
Phone: +44 (0)161 833 4333
www.gauchorestaurants.co.uk
Note: Generous portions served at this
Argentinean steakhouse. Bring your appetite.

Yang Sing
34 Princess Street
Manchester, M1 4JY, U.K.
Phone: +44 (0)161 236 2200
www.yang-sing.com
Note: This Cantonese restaurant has set the
standard both in and out of the city.

The Olive Press
4 Lloyd Street
Manchester, M2 5AB, U.K.
Phone: +44 (0)161 832 9090
www.heathcotes.co.uk
Note: A taste of Italy in jolly old England with
rustic, cozy surroundings.

The Restaurant Bar and Grill
14 John Dalton Street
Manchester, M2 6JR, U.K.
Phone: +44 (0)161 839 1999
www.therestaurantbarandgrill.co.uk
Note: Known locally and nationally for great,
simple dishes in a modern and stylish environ-
ment.

Shimla Pinks
Dolefield
Manchester, M3 3HA, U.K.
Phone: +44 (0)161 839 1999
www.shimlapinksmanchester.com
Note: A welcoming area venue where you can
just relax and have fun.

Cloud 23
The Hilton-23rd floor
Beetham Tower
303 Deansgate, Manchester, M3 4LQ, U.K.

Phone: +44 (0)161 870 1688
Note: Manchester's answer to the world
famous Rainbow Room in NYC.

Panacea
14 John Dalton Street
Manchester, M2 6JR, U.K.
Phone: +44 (0)161 833 0000
www.panaceamanchester.co.uk
Note: Pricey drinks, but you may catch a
glimpse of a celebrity.

Ampersand
244 Deansgate
Manchester, M3 4BQ, U.K.
Phone: +44 (0)161 832 3038
www.theampersand.co.uk
Note: A good place to go, but a bit upscale for
most game-day fans.

Mulligans
12 Southgate
Manchester, M3 2RB, U.K.
Phone: +44 (0)161 288 0006
Note: One of the better Irish bars in the area.

Airport:

Manchester International Airport
Manchester, M90 1QX, U.K.
Phone: +44 (0)8712 710 711
Fax: +44 (0)161 489 3813
www.manchesterairport.co.uk

Sports Travel Insider's Edge:

Best way to watch the action:
The best place to watch this game is at the
West End of the stadium, formerly known
as the Stretford End. This is the area with
the best game atmosphere in a stadium
filled with it.

Best place to get up close:
If you want the best local experience and
to rub shoulders with the Brits, check out
any of the pre-match dining options. You
will not be disappointed as you will be sure

to have someone talking or singing in your face about football. It's much more enjoyable with a few in you.

Best travel tip:
Deansgate provides the ultimate Manchester experience with many local dining and shopping options. Authentic cuisine and souvenirs aplenty.

Notable Quote:
"This is definitely the game which rises above all others.... You can't escape the history of a Manchester United–Liverpool game and how much it means to the fans of each club."—SIR ALEXANDER CHAPMAN FERGUSON, Manchester United F.C. manager

Relevant Websites:
www.manchesteronline.co.uk
www.manutd.com
www.liverpoolfc.tv
www.tseworld.com
www.pcevents.com
www.sportstravel.com
www.gotickets.com
www.premieresports.com

17

MICHIGAN VS. OHIO STATE AT THE BIG HOUSE

Where?
Michigan Stadium, a.k.a. "The Big House"
South Main Street and East Stadium Boulevard
Ann Arbor, MI 48104

When?
Every other year at Michigan.

Significance:
From 1897 to 1919, the University of Michigan dominated Ohio State University in their annual matchup, planting the seeds

for a century-long college football rivalry. The two college powerhouses choose the last game of the regular college football season to compete. Many times, the Big Ten championship and an invitation to the Rose Bowl are on the line, but winning is also about pride and bragging rights for the Wolverine and Buckeye faithful. While the feud is considered one of the greatest of all time (ESPN ranks it first), "Ohio State/Michigan Week" takes a charitable turn with blood donations to the Red Cross and collections for local food banks. Since 1927, Michigan Stadium, nicknamed "The Big House," has hosted the big game and consistent sellout every other year. Well over 100,000 Wolverine and Buckeye students, alums, and fans are in attendance. Many times, the size of the crowd matches the population of Ann Arbor.

Who attends?
This one is all Wolverine and Buckeye fans as it's hard to find any of them giving up their tickets.

Tickets:
For primary ticket access information, consider: www.mgoblue.com.

For secondary ticket access, consider:

GoTickets, Inc.
2345 Waukegan Road, Suite 140
Bannockburn, IL 60015-1552
Toll-Free: 1-800-775-1617
Fax: (919) 481-9101
E-mail: sales@gotickets.com
www.gotickets.com
Note: If tickets are bought from students, those students need to make sure they are validated at the ticket office before 5:00 P.M. on the Friday before the game. A Student ID is needed to enter with an unvalidated student ticket. Your best bet is the secondary market, as this game is always sold out.

Accommodations:

The Bell Tower
300 South Thayer Street
Ann Arbor, MI 48104
Phone: (734) 769-3010
www.belltowerhotel.com
Note: Located on campus near State Street. A ten-minute walk to "The Big House."

The Campus Inn
615 East Huron Street
Ann Arbor, MI 48104
Phone: (734) 769-2200
www.campusinn.com
Note: This is the hotel where the football team is known to stay before games, so it may be a challenge to get a room on the weekend of the event. Roughly a ten-minute walk to the stadium.

Holiday Inn Express Hotel & Suites
600 Briarwood Circle
Ann Arbor, MI 48108
Phone: (734) 761-2929
www.ichotelsgroup.com
Note: Five-minute drive to the campus and stadium, not accounting for the heavy traffic on game day.

Travel Packages:
If you are going to travel to this event, I would recommend using a reliable company to work with you on making the necessary arrangements. The suppliers listed in this book have solid references and are by far the most trusted in the business. Below are some of the organizations to try for this Top 100 Must See Sporting Event.

Premiere Corporate Events
14 Penn Plaza, Suite 925
New York, NY 10122
Phone: (212) 695-9480
Fax: (212) 564-8098
Toll-Free: 1-877-621-5243
E-mail: requests@tseworld.com
www.tseworld.com
www.pcevents.com

Premiere Sports Travel
201 Shannon Oaks Circle, Suite 205
Cary, NC 27511
Phone: (919) 481-9511
Fax: (919) 481-1337
Toll-Free: 1-800-924-9993
E-mail: sales@sportstravel.com
www.sportstravel.com

Premiere College Sports (Powered by Dodd's Athletic Tours), official travel partner for Ohio State University
308 South Neil
Champaign, IL 61820
Phone: (217) 373-5067
Fax: (217) 398-1313
Toll-Free: 1-800-553-5527
www.doddsathletictours.com
www.collegesportstravel.com

Dining:

The West End Grill
120 West Liberty
Ann Arbor, MI 48104
Phone: (734) 747-6260
Note: Make reservations in advance to dine at this very small, locally-run restaurant. The cost for entrées are on the high side, but worth the extra money.

Zingerman's Delicatessen
422 Detroit Street
Ann Arbor, MI 48104
Phone: (734) 663-3354
www.zingermansdeli.com
Note: Long lines will greet you, but massive sandwiches await those who are patient. You'll also have the time to choose a sandwich out of the sixty-seven combinations offered.

Afternoon Delight
251 East Liberty Street
Ann Arbor, MI 48104
Phone: (734) 665-7513

www.afternoondelightcafe.com

Note: Homemade muffins (warmed and topped with soft-serve yogurt) and omelets are but two of the many breakfast offerings.

The Gandy Dancer

401 Depot Street
Ann Arbor, MI 48104
Phone: (734) 769-0592

Note: This local favorite of former Michigan football coach Lloyd Carr provides excellent seafood, steaks, and pasta along with the biggest and best Sunday brunch in town.

Pizza Bobs

814 South State Street
Ann Arbor, MI 48104
Phone: (734) 665-4517
www.pizzabobs.net

Note: Yes, you can get pizza, but those who have a sweet tooth can enjoy extra thick milkshakes. Over ten flavors to choose from.

Airports:

Detroit Metropolitan Wayne County Airport

Detroit, MI 48242
Phone: (734) AIRPORT
www.metroairport.com

Willow Run Airport (for corporate and private jet use)

801 Willow Run Airport
Ypsilanti, MI 48198-0899
Phone: (734) 485-6666
www.willowrunairport.com

Sports Travel Insider's Edge:

Best way to watch the action:

For a fully immersive experience, sit in the student section. Actually, sitting is not an option as they tend to stand for the entire game. The top row will provide a great view of the game. If you sit too low you will most likely be staring at the back of someone's head instead of the game.

Best place to get up close:

A chilly walk up and down State Street or attending a team pep rally the night before the game allows you to see the players and coaches gearing up for "the game."

Best travel tip:

Parking in Ann Arbor comes at a premium, so scope out a willing college student on State Street for the cheapest spot. You can park in the main athletic campus parking lot, but good luck getting out after the game.

Notable Quotes:

"The Ohio State–Michigan game is always the biggest game. It doesn't matter what the records are or what's on the table for the outcome. The fact that it's 1 vs. 2, we think that's the way it should be."—JIM TRESSEL, Ohio State football coach

"When Ohio Stadium opened in 1922, Michigan spoiled the party with a 22-0 victory. The rivalry was heated in the early days as both have been long-time college football powers. But it got even hotter in 1969, when Bo Schembechler took over as Michigan's coach and upset Woody Hayes' No. 1-ranked, undefeated Buckeyes. Four times in the next six years, both teams were ranked in the top five when they met. In 1970 and 1973, both were undefeated (they tied 10-10 in '73). From 1970 through 1975, Michigan entered without a loss every year. The Wolverines won just once. Ohio State was 9-0-1 in 1993, 11-0 in 1995, and 10-0 in 1996. The Buckeyes lost each time. *That* is rivalry."—ESPN.com

"The Ohio State–Michigan rivalry can be traced back to the earliest days of college football. A simple look at the rotunda at Ohio Stadium reveals the age of the rivalry. In 1922, the doors to Ohio Field opened, but it was not until the third game, against Michigan, that the stadium was dedicated."—MIKE FURLAN, Author of *The Five Greatest Traditions of Ohio State*

"As the story goes, the flowers adorning the top of the rotunda were to be painted in the colors of the school that won the dedication game. To this day the flowers bear the very same urine color as a Michigan helmet, for the Buckeyes fell in defeat to Michigan 19-0."—MIKE FURLAN

"(Woody) Hayes supposedly could not bring himself to speak the name of "that school up north" and (Bo) Schembechler, who played for Hayes at Miami of Ohio and was an Ohio State assistant coach, savored nothing more than putting it to his old mentor."—Excerpt from bentley. umich.edu

Relevant Websites:
www.mgoblue.com
www.annarbor.org
www.tseworld.com
www.pcevents.com
www.sportstravel.com
www.gotickets.com
www.premieresports.com

18

NFL CONFERENCE CHAMPIONSHIPS

When?
End of January.

Significance:
Football's regular season is a grueling seventeen weeks with one bye week in each team's schedule. The bumps, bruises, and pure physicality of the sport test the mettle of a team and its players. The teams that persevere put up impressive numbers, particularly in the win column. By the season's end, those teams from the National Football Conference (NFC) and the American Football Conference (AFC) who make it through the playoffs vie for the right to represent their respective conference in the biggest football game under the brightest spotlight of the year—the Super Bowl.

The NFC Championship Game is usually played two weeks before the Super Bowl. The winning team receives the George Halas Trophy and advances to the Super Bowl to face the AFC's champ. That weekend, the AFC is also on the gridiron to determine their representative in the Super Bowl. The winning team receives the Lamar Hunt Trophy.

Outside of the Super Bowl itself, the penultimate weekend of football action is a fan's dream come true and a seminal event in the football season. Sure, there are parties organized around the Super Bowl. Yes, there is hype and pageantry associated with that February clash. But the NFC and the AFC championships make for a marathon day of football where the elite teams are determined to play for it all. For sheer emotion and excitement of the crowd, these games bring more energy than the Super Bowl itself.

Who attends?
Unlike the corporate crowd at the Super Bowl, this one is mostly the hardcore football fans of the teams doing battle.

History
The American Football League (AFL) was coming into its own in 1966, creating bidding wars for NFL players. This caught the attention of the NFL and they were more than willing to come to the table to discuss a merger of the leagues. The alliance was announced on June 8, 1966, and was effective by the 1970 season. Since the merger was going forward, but not official, the NFL and the AFL champs were truly playing interleague games in Super Bowl I through IV.

The NFL's sixteen teams were split into two conferences that contained two divisions each. Capital and Century were in the Eastern Conference. Coastal and Central composed the Western Conference. Four divisional champions participated in the tournament to determine who would go to the NFL Championship game.

Initially, the AFL took their nine teams and maintained the one-game playoff format except when they needed to break a divisional tie. Adding the Cincinnati Bengals in 1969 forced the AFL to adopt their own four-team playoff.

Following the 1969 season, the merger was official and the NFL was realigned into the National Football Conference (NFC) and the American Football Conference (AFC). Each conference split into three divisions. The league designed an eight-team playoff tournament with the division winners and two wild card teams selected from the second-place finishers with the best records in each conference.

Today, the NFC and the AFC are aligned into eight divisions of four teams per conference. Four division winners and two wild-card teams make up each conference in the twelve-team tournament. The first round for the NFC and AFC championship is the Wild Card Playoff, the second round is the Divisional Playoff, and the final round prior to the Super Bowl is the Conference Championship. It is a conference championship that brings out an experience like no other in football.

Notable Athletes:

Tom Brady, quarterback, New England Patriots

Peyton Manning, quarterback, Indianapolis Colts

Eli Manning, quarterback, New York Giants

Brett Favre, quarterback, Green Bay Packers

LaDainian Tomlinson, running back, San Diego Chargers

Steve Young, quarterback, San Francisco 49ers

Lawrence Taylor, linebacker, New York Giants

Karl Mecklenburg, linebacker, Denver Broncos

Dan Marino, quarterback, Miami Dolphins

Reggie White, defensive end, Green Bay Packers

Terry Bradshaw, quarterback, Pittsburgh Steelers

Records:

NFC Records:
Most victories: Dallas Cowboys, 8
Most appearances: Dallas Cowboys, 14
Most points scored in one game (Tie): Washington Redskins and New York Giants, 41

AFC Records:
Most victories: Denver Broncos, 6
Most appearances: Pittsburgh Steelers, 13
Most points scored in one game: Buffalo Bills, 51

Things to know before you go:

Blitz: Defensive players rushing through the offensive line into the backfield to "sack" the quarterback.

Blocking: Offensive players using their bodies and arms to prevent defenders from making tackles and move them away from the ball carrier.

Bomb: A very long forward pass.

Down: The offensive sequence of plays starting from the line of scrimmage that begins with the center's snap and ends when the ball is dead.

Extra Point: A place-kick through the goal posts, scoring a point after a touchdown.

Fair Catch: A punt receiver signals by waving his hand in the air that he will not advance on a ball that has just been punted, preventing him from being tackled.

Field Goal: A place-kick from the line of scrimmage that goes over the crossbar between the uprights of the opponent's goal post, giving a team three points.

Forward Pass: A throw made from behind the line of scrimmage. If the ball is not caught, it is an incomplete pass. If the player passes the line of scrimmage, a forward pass is not permitted.

Fumble: A ball carrier dropping the ball on the field. The team first to recover the ball gains possession.

Intentional Grounding: The quarterback throws the ball down on the field to avoid a sack.

Interception: When a forward pass is caught by a defender and results in a turnover.

Kickoff: Starting each half or after each score, a place-kick in which one team kicks the ball to the other.

Lateral: A player with the ball is ahead of the line of scrimmage and tosses the ball to a teammate beside or behind him, but not in front of him.

Line of Scrimmage: The line along which both teams set up on each down. The offensive team must have at least seven players on or within a foot of this line.

Neutral Zone: The one-yard area encompassing the line of scrimmage that separates the offense from the defense.

Onside Kick: An attempt for a team to regain possession of the ball by kicking it only a short distance forward, allowing its players a chance to recover the ball. The ball must travel at least ten yards before the kicking team can recover it.

Pass Rush: The defensive team rushing the quarterback in an attempt to tackle or pressure him before he passes.

Punt: A kick taken from behind the line of scrimmage in which the ball is dropped from the kicker's hands and kicked before it touches the ground.

Rushing: The use of running plays by the offensive team to move the ball downfield.

Sack: Defensive players tackling the quarterback behind the line of scrimmage, resulting in a loss of yards for the offense.

Safety: Two points awarded to the defensive team when a ball carrier is tackled within or runs out of the backside of his team's end zone.

Sweep: A rushing play in which the ball carrier runs around one end, rather than through the middle of the offensive line.

Touchback: When the ball is caught in the end zone, the receiving team does not run it out, or the ball goes through the end zone after a kickoff. To signal a touchback, the receiving player kneels on one knee in the end zone. The next offensive play begins from the twenty-yard line.

Touchdown: When a player carries the ball across the opposing goal line, catches the ball in the end zone, or recovers a fumble in the end zone. Worth six points.

Tickets:

For primary ticket access information, consider: www.nfl.com or the individual websites of the teams in the game.

For secondary ticket access, consider:

GoTickets, Inc.

2345 Waukegan Road, Suite 140
Bannockburn, IL 60015-1552
Toll-Free: 1-800-775-1617
Fax: (919) 481-9101
E-mail: sales@gotickets.com
www.gotickets.com

Travel Packages:

If you are going to travel to this event, I would recommend using a reliable company to work with you on making the necessary arrangements. The suppliers listed in this book have solid references and are by far the most trusted in the business. Below are some of the organizations to try for this Top 100 Must See Sporting Event.

Premiere Corporate Events

14 Penn Plaza, Suite 925
New York, NY 10122
Phone: (212) 695-9480
Fax: (212) 564-8098
Toll-Free: 1-877-621-5243
E-mail: requests@tseworld.com
www.tseworld.com
www.pcevents.com

Premiere Sports Travel

201 Shannon Oaks Circle, Suite 205
Cary, NC 27511
Phone: (919) 481-9511
Fax: (919) 481-1337
Toll-Free: 1-800-924-9993
E-mail: sales@sportstravel.com
www.sportstravel.com

Notable Quotes:

"Super Bowl Sunday is 85 percent hype, 10 percent Aunt Sally's secret-recipe bean dip and 5 percent football. Conference championship day is 85 or 95 percent football, 5 percent bean dip and—in the best years—10 percent horrendous weather."— KING KAUFMAN, Salon.com

"It's definitely special. I've been in the league for like 12 years, and I've been in this situation twice. It's one of those things that you never really can take for granted because it might be everybody's last time doing this no matter what year it is for you. If I heard anybody in the locker room that thought, 'Oh, this is going to happen every year,' I would tell them that there's only one team a year that goes this far in our conference and the percentages of getting back here are pretty small. So they

better take this like I take it. You can't take it for granted."—AMANI TOOMER, New York Giants veteran wide receiver

Relevant Websites:

www.nfl.com
www.tseworld.com
www.pcevents.com
www.sportstravel.com
www.gotickets.com
www.premieresports.com

19

DAYTONA 500

Where?

Daytona International Speedway
1801 West International Speedway
    Boulevard
Daytona Beach, FL 32114

When?

The second or third Sunday in February.

Significance:

It brings in the highest television ratings. It pays out the biggest purses. And it comes first. The Daytona 500, while serving as the inaugural race of the season, is considered key in the overall NASCAR Spring Cup Series. The prestige for the driver who wins is equal to the momentum they have after such a big win. No championship is at stake, unless you count the prestigious Harley J. Earl Trophy presented to the winner in Victory Lane. Every driver is starting at Daytona with zero points. Yet, it is the highest-rated NASCAR event on television and always in the Top 10 of sporting events of the year aired on television.

The "Great American Race" is one of four restrictor plate races on NASCAR's schedule. It takes place at the Daytona International Speedway in Daytona Beach, Florida, and lasts for 200 2.5-mile laps stretching out over 500 miles. Daytona is a super speedway that houses 168,000 screaming NASCAR fans. The inaugural Daytona 500 was on February 22, 1959. Fifty-nine drivers vied for $67,760 while 41,000 fans cheered them on over the roar of the engines. No winner was announced right away, as the race was too close to call. In the end, Lee Petty was eventually declared the winner, even though Johnny Beauchamp visited Victory Lane immediately after his car crossed the finish line.

Who attends?
Who else but NASCAR fans?

How to get there?

From the North:
I-95 South to US-1 (Exit 273)
South on US-1 to S.R. 40 (Granada
    Boulevard)
West on S.R. 40 to Clyde Morris Boulevard
Clyde Morris Boulevard. South to Parking
    Lot 7

From the South:
I-95 to LPGA Boulevard (Exit 265)
LPGA Boulevard East to Clyde Morris
    Boulevard
Clyde Morris Boulevard. South to Parking
    Lot 7

From the East:
From A1A, take any one of the bridges to US-1
US-1 to Mason Avenue
West Mason Avenue to Clyde Morris
    Boulevard
North on Clyde Morris to Lot 7

From the West:
I-4 East to S.R. 44 (Exit 118)
S.R. 44 East to US-1
US-1 North to S.R. 400/Beville Road
S.R. 400 West to Clyde Morris Boulevard
Clyde Morris Boulevard. North to Parking
    Lot 7

Free speedway parking and shuttle are available.

Tickets:
For primary market ticket access, consider:
www.daytona500.com

For secondary ticket market access, consider:

GoTickets, Inc.
2345 Waukegan Road, Suite 140
Bannockburn, IL 60015-1552
Toll-Free: 1-800-775-1617
Fax: (919) 481-9101
E-mail: sales@gotickets.com
www.gotickets.com

Accommodations:

Hilton Oceanfront Resort
100 North Atlantic Avenue
Daytona Beach, FL 32118
Phone: (386) 254-8200
Fax: (386) 253-0275
www.daytonahilton.com
Note: Right on the Atlantic Ocean, this hotel is considered by many to be Daytona's premier resort destination. Close to everything, right in the middle of all the action.

Hilton Garden Inn
189 Midway Avenue
Daytona Beach, FL 32114
Phone: (386) 944-4000
Fax: (386) 944-4001
www.daytonaairport.gardeninn.com
Note: Perfect location with only a half-mile distance between you and the International Speedway. Located at the airport for a quick easy escape after the Daytona 500.

Bahama House
2001 South Atlantic Avenue
Daytona Beach, FL 32118
Phone: (386) 248-2001
Fax: (386) 248-0991
www.daytonabahamahouse.com
Note: Located on the beach and a fifteen-

minute drive to the International Speedway. Reasonably priced hotel.

Homewood Suites Daytona Beach-Speedway
165 Bill France Boulevard
Daytona Beach, FL 32114
Phone: (386) 258-2828
Fax: (386) 258-2281
www.homewooddaytona.com
Note: So close to the track that you can hear the roar of the engines from your room.

On-Site Hospitality:

Fan Zone: As interactive as it gets. You can walk the track surface to the grassy Tri-Oval area, past Pit Road and into the Spring Fan Zone.

Rolex Executive Suites: Luxury seating and a perfect view of the course in the Spring Tower Suites. Great hospitality for you and your friends or co-workers.

Green Flag Club/Superstretch Terrace Club: Climate-controlled pavilion to keep you comfortable on a hot Florida day. A variety of pre-race activities are sometimes included.

Daytona Club Pavilion: Celebrate racing history behind the Spring Tower, a one-of-a- kind pavilion. Racing aficionados will "ooh" and "ah" when they relive memorable moments and view nostalgic images of Daytona's storied history.

Travel Packages:

If you are going to travel to this event, I would recommend using a reliable company to work with you on making the necessary arrangements. The suppliers listed in this book have solid references and are by far the most trusted in the business. Below are some of the organizations to try for this Top 100 Must See Sporting Event.

Premiere Corporate Events
14 Penn Plaza, Suite 925
New York, NY 10122
Phone: (212) 695-9480
Fax: (212) 564-8098
Toll-Free: 1-877-621-5243
E-mail: requests@tseworld.com
www.tseworld.com
www.pcevents.com

Premiere Sports Travel
201 Shannon Oaks Circle, Suite 205
Cary, NC 27511
Phone: (919) 481-9511
Fax: (919) 481-1337
Toll-Free: 1-800-924-9993
E-mail: sales@sportstravel.com
www.sportstravel.com

This is one of Premiere Sports Travel's largest events as they send thousands of NASCAR fans each year to the Daytona 500 and other key races.

Dining:

Daytona Beach Chart House
1100 Marina Point Drive
Daytona Beach, FL 32114
Phone: (386) 255-9022
Fax: (386) 255-5362
www.chart-house.com
Note: Fill up on Snapper Hemingway or Prime Rib and end your meal with a decadent Hot Chocolate Lava Cake.

Fresh
1130 South Ridgewood Avenue
Daytona Beach, FL 32114
Phone: (386) 947-9736
Fax: (386) 947-9739
www.freshatasteofitaly.com
Note: Fresh Italian food with excellent service. A little something for everybody.

Pasha Café
919 West International Speedway Boulevard
Daytona Beach, FL 32114

Phone: (386) 257-7753
Fax: (386) 255-3421

Note: Great Indian cuisine close to the Speedway.

Ocean Deck Restaurant & Beach Club

127 South Ocean Avenue
Daytona Beach, FL 32118
Phone: (386) 253-5224
Fax: (386) 253-7226
www.oceandeck.com

Note: A combination of great American and seafood dishes to choose from while on the beach.

Robbie O'Connell's Pub

530 Seabreeze Boulevard
Daytona Beach, FL 32118
Phone: (386) 252-6003
www.robbieoconnellspub.com

Note: You can find great food and a wide variety of beers at this friendly local pub.

Airports:

Daytona Beach International Airport

700 Catalina Drive
Daytona Beach, FL 32114
Phone: (386) 248-8030
www.flydaytonafirst.com

Orlando International Airport

(about sixty miles from Daytona Beach)
1 Airport Boulevard
Orlando, FL 32827
Phone: (407) 825-2001
www.orlandoairports.net

Sports Travel Insider's Edge:

Best way to watch the action:

If you can get your hands on tickets in the Sprint Tower seating area, you will get the best view of all the Daytona 500 action.

Best place to get up close:

Get intimate with racing history. The Daytona Club Pavilion is a shrine to all that is the famed Daytona 500. Memorable mo-ments are on display as racing fans honor the past. Unforgettable imagery surrounds the pavilion and takes you back in NASCAR time. If you book a package through Premiere Sports Travel, they offer many terrific onsite hospitality options.

Best travel tip:

NASCAR racing was meant to be watched outdoors. The open-air Pit Patio area gives you the opportunity to experience the Daytona 500, and all the elements that come with it, while living with a bit of luxury at the same time.

Notable Quotes:

"It's the ultimate race. There's just no better place to win at than Daytona. You know the sport's getting more competitive. It's getting bigger and it's just one of those races if you pick one, this is the one you want to win."—JEFF GORDON, NASCAR driver and winner of multiple Daytona 500s

"When you've got the Daytona 500 out there at stake and everything riding on the line, guys go for it, and the guys that go for it are the ones that are either going to win or they're going to wreck. I know in just about every one of the Daytona 500s that I've ever won you had to take some risk and make some bold moves that could have worked for you or might not."—JEFF GORDON

Relevant Websites:

www.daytona500.com
www.daytonaintlspeedway.com
www.daytonabeach.com
www.tseworld.com
www.pcevents.com
www.sportstravel.com
www.gotickets.com
www.racetickets.com
www.premieresports.com

20

FINAL FOUR—
NCAA MEN'S BASKETBALL

When?
Every year in the beginning of April.

Future Locations:
2009–Ford Field in Detroit, MI
2010–Lucas Oil Stadium in Indianapolis, IN
2011–Reliant Stadium in Houston, TX

Significance:
March is a significant month for not only college basketball fans, but also office betting pool participants. "March Madness" sees sixty-five teams compete in a single elimination tournament throughout the country to crown the NCAA Men's Division I basketball champion. Throughout the season all teams vie for one thing: a chance to appear at the "Big Dance." The last four teams standing then move on to the Final Four national semifinals to determine the NCAA champion. Locations vary from year to year.

While wagering is on the rise in office complexes across the country during March Madness, productivity tends to dim. With broadcasts throughout what seems like all hours of the day, many of those games occur during times where viewers should be attending to work-related matters. CBS is the current home of the NCAA basketball tournament, composed of conference tournament champions from each Division I conference. They receive automatic bids with the remaining slots chosen and seeded by the NCAA selection committee based on various criteria. The two lowest seeds play for the opportunity to enter the first round, called the "play-in-game," a tradition started in 2001.

The Final Four is just that, a surviving quartet of the best teams that have won their regional brackets. Winners advance to the finals. This is a seminal event in college basketball history, with March being one of the most anticipated months for sports fans overall. It's the chance to see the best play the best, and the underdogs upset the favorites. There is so much "hoopla" that takes place onsite at this event as thousands of ardent college basketball fans take over a host city. Look out for well-known coaches as the National Association of Basketball Coaches holds its annual conference each year during Final Four weekend.

Who attends?
Die-hard college basketball fans and loyalists of the schools competing in the Final Four.

History
According to the NCAA, the term "Final Four" was originated in a 1975 newspaper article by Ed Chay, a sportswriter for the *Cleveland Plain Dealer*, in reference to the NCAA basketball semifinals. The name grew in popularity and the NCAA owned the trademark by the early eighties.

H. V. Porter of the Illinois High School Association (IHSA) was the first to coin the phrase "March Madness" in a 1939 essay titled the same. Television announcer Brent Musburger popularized it in the early eighties while calling the NCAA tournament games. Today the IHSA and the NCAA share the trademark, but that did not come without a legal tussle that saw the IHSA buying the trademark from a resourceful television production company called Intersport, Inc. After much legal wrangling, a dual-trademark was granted by the United States Court of Appeals for the Seventh Circuit, allowing the NCAA to share ownership.

Notable Athletes:
Patrick Ewing, Georgetown University
Isiah Thomas, Indiana University
Bill Walton, UCLA
Carmelo Anthony, Syracuse University
Richard Hamilton, University of
    Connecticut
Michael Jordan, University of
    North Carolina
Chris Webber, University of Michigan
Pervis Ellison, University of Louisville
Ed Pinckney, Villanova University
Larry Johnson, UNLV
Chris Mullin, St. Johns University
Danny Manning, University of Kansas
Christian Laettner, Duke University

Records:

Team:
Most titles: UCLA, 11
Final Four appearances (Tie): University of
North Carolina and UCLA, 17
Most Final Four wins: UCLA, 24

Individual:
Points: Bill Bradley, 58, Princeton vs.
    Wichita State, 1965
Three-Point field goals: Freddie Banks, 10,
    UNLV vs. Indiana, 1987
Rebounds: Bill Russell, 27, San Francisco
    vs. Iowa, 1956
Assists: Mark Wade, 18, UNLV vs. Indiana,
    1987
Blocked Shots (Tie): Danny Manning, 6,
    Kansas vs. Duke, 1988; Marcus Camby,
    6, Massachusetts vs. Kentucky, 1996;
    Joakim Noah, 6, Florida vs. UCLA,
    2006

Traditions:
At the event itself, the NCAA Fan Experience is a hands-on, interactive event that gets fans in the mood for great college basketball, if they're not already. Fans can participate in various activities, see the history of NCAA basketball and even have the chance to bump into the NBA stars of tomorrow. The Fan Experience runs all week leading up to the Championship game and usually takes place at the host city's convention center.

Tickets:
For primary ticket access information, consider contacting the NCAA for rules on the lottery system. A minimal number of upper-level seats are offered via the lottery each year. Your best bet, though, for this event is to use the secondary market as odds are against getting seats through the lottery. In addition, the seats made available in the lottery are always upper level.

For secondary ticket access, consider:

GoTickets, Inc.
2345 Waukegan Road, Suite 140
Bannockburn, IL 60015-1552
Toll-Free: 1-800-775-1617
Fax: (919) 481-9101
E-mail: sales@gotickets.com
www.gotickets.com

Travel Packages:
If you are going to travel to this event, I would recommend using a reliable company to work with you on making the necessary arrangements. The suppliers listed in this book have solid references and are by far the most trusted in the business. Below are some of the organizations to try for this Top 100 Must See Sporting Event.

Premiere Corporate Events
14 Penn Plaza, Suite 925
New York, NY 10122
Phone: (212) 695-9480
Fax: (212) 564-8098
Toll-Free: 1-877-621-5243
E-mail: requests@tseworld.com
www.tseworld.com
www.pcevents.com

Premiere Sports Travel
201 Shannon Oaks Circle, Suite 205

Cary, NC 27511
Phone: (919) 481-9511
Fax: (919) 481-1337
Toll-Free: 1-800-924-9993
E-mail: sales@sportstravel.com

Best place to watch the action:

It is important to note that the tickets for the NCAA championship game are not as pricey as seats to the Final Four semifinals. If you do not hold allegiance to one particular team, then wait until the Monday of the title match. By then, the losing teams and their die-hard fans go home after the semifinals. You have a chance to score some great seats at below-market prices from a devastated loyalist whose team let them down. Join the masses lining the corridors as these fans exit for your chance to get a ticket or upgrade to a better seat for the second game after the first of the two games on Saturday. An easier option is to arrange for tickets to the championship game through a secondary ticket provider such as GoTickets.com.

Best place to get up close:

Take in the College All-Star basketball game on Friday night. Usually, the host city will hold one prior to the start of the Final Four. While you will not see players from the semifinals, you will have an opportunity to see some of the best that college basketball has to offer. Compared to the price of Final Four and championship tickets, this is a bargain.

Best Travel Tip:

Prepare to take in the sights of the host city. While Final Four weekend is never-ending excitement, there is downtime between Saturday's games and Monday's title tilt. Find out the local haunts or high-profile tourist spots to attend to fill that time.

Notable Quotes:

"The drama and the magic relate to the nature of the event itself, to the fact that these are college students. They are still young. They are well trained and well coached in most cases. But in every Final Four the human factor looms large: who rises to the occasion; who makes mistakes."—SENATOR BILL BRADLEY, 1965 Most Valuable Player of the Final Four

"It's the best sporting event that I've ever attended. I feel fortunate to be able to have been a part of that. But I'm also looking forward to going to a Super Bowl one day. Or a World Series. An Indianapolis 500. Or the Kentucky Derby. But as of right now, that's the most enjoyable sporting event that I've ever experienced."—DANNY MANNING, former University of Kansas basketball star

Relevant Websites:

www.tseworld.com
www.pcevents.com
www.sportstravel.com
www.gotickets.com
www.ticketmaster.com
www.premieresports.com

21
RYDER CUP

When?
September, every other year.

Future Locations:
2010—Celtic Manor Resort, Newport, Wales
2012–Medinah Country Club, Medinah, Illinois
2014–Gleneagles Hotel, Auchterarder, Perth & Kinross, Scotland
2016–Hazeltine National Golf Club, Chaska, Minnesota
2018–TBA, in Europe
2020–Whistling Straits, Sheboygan, Wisconsin

Significance:

Many golfing aficionados claim the Ryder Cup is one of the last sporting events about prestige and not money. While the origin of the event is the subject of dispute, no one can deny that golf history is made in some form every two years. Golfing teams from the United States and Europe meet at various places throughout the globe for the Ryder Cup, a tournament sanctioned by the PGA of America and the PGA European Tour. In the current format, players selected from two teams of twelve engage in match play over three days. Those matches include:

Eight foursome matches: Two teams of two golfers each take alternate shots with the same ball.

Eight fourball matches: Two teams with two golfers where everyone plays their own ball.

Twelve singles matches: Standard competition between two golfers.

Winners score points for their team with half-points assigned for any match tied after eighteen holes. Players are paired up by the team captain, who submits the order of play to an official of the tournament. Pairings are final when the match starts; modifications are only allowed if a player becomes sick or injured.

The United States has dominated the Ryder Cup since its inception in 1927. By 1979, that domination prompted a change to expand the British-Irish alliance and allow players from Denmark, France, Germany, Italy, Sweden, and Spain. Matches became more competitive and Team Europe began winning their fair share of Ryder Cups, including a "hat trick of sorts" in 2002, 2004, and 2006. The U.S. reclaimed the title in 2008.

Who attends?

Golf fans who like to watch their country or continent team up and take on some of the world's best golf courses for charity.

History

Seed merchant Samuel Ryder was not a young man when he decided that he wanted to play golf. To learn the fundamentals, he hired Abe Mitchell as his private tutor and paid him £1,000 annually for six days a week of work. Mitchell taught Ryder the basics of driving, pitching, and putting. By the age of fifty-one, Ryder was a member of the Verulam Golf Club in St. Albans and boasted a handicap of six. One year later, in 1921, he was captain of the golf club. He returned to that capacity in 1926 and 1927. Quite a meteoric rise for a middle-aged golfer.

While informal tournaments were played in the years prior to the tournament's inception, the Ryder Cup was born in 1927. Samuel Ryder donated a gold trophy and paid £5 to each member of the winning team. A Ryder Cup has been held every two years since that time. There were interruptions in 1939 and 1945 for World War II. The matches in 2001 were delayed one year due to the events of 9/11. From that point on, the Ryder Cup would be played on even-numbered years.

Walter Hagen, considered by many to be one of the greatest golfers of all time, captained the first U.S. Ryder Cup Team. On his team were Leo Diegel, Johnny Farrell, Johnny Golden, Bill Mehlhorn, Gene Sarazen, Joe Turnesa, and Al Watrous. The alternates were Mike Brady and Al Espinosa.

Abe Mitchell was scheduled to head up the first British PGA team, but suffered a bout of appendicitis that took him out of the competition. Ted Ray captained a team composed of Aubrey Boomer, Archie Compston, George Duncan, George Gadd, Arthur Havers, Herbert Jolly, Fred Robson, and C. A. (Charles) Whitcombe.

Notable Athletes:

Fred Funk
Jim Furyk

Phil Mickelson
Jack Nicklaus
Arnold Palmer
Tiger Woods
Nick Faldo
Sergio Garcia

Records:

Most appearances: Nick Faldo, 11, 1977–1997
Most points: Nick Faldo, 25, 1977–1997
Youngest player: Sergio Garcia, 19 years and 258 days, 1999
Oldest player: Raymond Floyd, 51 years and 20 days, 1993

Ryder Cup, Holes-in-one:

Peter Butler, 1973, Muirfield
Nick Faldo, 1993, The Belfry Constantino Rocca, 1995, Oak Hill
Howard Clark, 1995, Oak Hill
Paul Casey, 2006, K Club
Scott Verplank, 2006, K Club

Traditions:

The Ryder Cup

Originally commissioned for £250 by Samuel A. Ryder, the Ryder Cup weighs four pounds, stands seventeen inches high, and measures nine inches from handle to handle. Ryder presented the self-named trophy to the Professional Golfer's Association of Great Britain as a prize to the winner of a competition between British and American golfers. The image of Ryder's gardener, friend, and instructor Abe Mitchell stands atop the trophy.

Things to know before you go:

Ace: A hole-in-one.
Front nine: The first half of a round of golf.
Back nine: The second half of a round of golf.
Fore: A warning cry to other players that your ball is headed in their direction.
Par: A certain number of shots needed to hole your ball depending on the hole's distance and difficulty.
Birdie: One under par.
Eagle: Two under par.
Albatross: Three under par.
Bogey: One over par. Double and triple bogeys are self-explanatory.

Tickets:

For the organizers of the Ryder Cup, the crowd is more about quality viewing than the quantity of the people attending. While it is one of the most popular events in sports, a limited number of tickets are sold to the public because of the format of this spirited international event. Demand always exceeds availability. Your best bet here is the secondary market.

The PGA of America sells tickets via a random draw. Odds of landing tickets are not high but it's worth a shot. For an application, call 1-800-PGA-GOLF.

For primary ticket access information consider: www.rydercup.com.

For secondary ticket access, consider:

GoTickets, Inc.
2345 Waukegan Road, Suite 140
Bannockburn, IL 60015-1552
Toll-Free: 1-800-775-1617
Fax: (919) 481-9101
E-mail: sales@gotickets.com
www.gotickets.com

Travel Packages:

If you are going to travel to this event, I would recommend using a reliable company to work with you on making the necessary arrangements. The suppliers listed in this book have solid references and are by far the most trusted in the business. Below are some of the organizations to try for this Top 100 Must See Sporting Event.

Premiere Corporate Events
14 Penn Plaza, Suite 925
New York, NY 10122
Phone: (212) 695-9480
Fax: (212) 564-8098

Toll-Free: 1-877-621-5243
E-mail: requests@tseworld.com
www.tseworld.com
www.pcevents.com

Premiere Sports Travel
201 Shannon Oaks Circle, Suite 205
Cary, NC 27511
Phone: (919) 481-9511
Fax: (919) 481-1337
Toll-Free: 1-800-924-9993
E-mail: sales@sportstravel.com
www.sportstravel.com

Notable Quote:

"Very proud. Very proud. Apart from my marriage and the birth of my children, without a doubt this is the proudest moment of my life."—SAM TORRANCE, European Team Captain on his team's victory

Relevant Websites:

www.rydercup.com
www.tseworld.com
www.pcevents.com
www.sportstravel.com
www.gotickets.com
www.premieresports.com

22

BASEBALL HALL OF FAME INDUCTION WEEKEND

Where?

The Clark Sports Center
124 Susquehanna Avenue
Cooperstown, NY

When?

Usually the last weekend in July.

Significance:

Considered sacred ground by many, Cooperstown is one place that you will hear most people say they need to visit before they leave this world. While the National Pastime has taken a drubbing in the media, the annual induction ceremony hearkens back to the days of old where Congress was not investigating the pharmaceutical choices of players. Each event has its own history and gives fans the chance to view baseball legends up close. Those legends include managers, players, umpires, and announcers. Babe Ruth started the tradition as part of the first induction ceremony in 1936, and that tradition continues every July.

Who attends?

Hardcore baseball fans, wannabe pro baseball players, and family members and former teammates of the inductees come together to honor baseball's finest. For the fans, it is best to keep an autograph book and pen accessible with former players, coaches, and managers milling all about Cooperstown.

How to get there?

Just ninety minutes from Albany, Cooperstown is a short and scenic drive away.

Tickets:

No tickets are necessary as this event is open to the public and free of charge. The ceremony takes place in the large grassy area next to the Clark Sports Center.

Additional Information on admission can be found at www.baseballhalloffame.org.

Accommodations:

The Inn at Cooperstown
16 Chestnut Street
Cooperstown, NY 13326
Phone: (607) 547-5756
Fax: (607) 547-8779
Toll-Free: 1-800-437-6303
www.innatcooperstown.com

Note: This award-winning historic Inn offers clean comfortable lodging just a short walk from the Baseball Hall of Fame. Built as a ho-

tel in 1874, and fully restored in 1985, the Inn is Cooperstow's only hotel in the distinguished Select Registry of Inns of North America.

Best Western Cobleskill/Cooperstown
121 Burgin Drive
Cobleskill, NY 12043
Phone: (518) 234-4321
Fax: (518) 234-3869
Toll-Free: 1-800-WESTERN
www.bestwesterncobleskill.com
Note: A great value option close to the action.

The Otesaga Resort Hotel
60 Lake Street
Cooperstown, NY 13326
Phone: (607) 547-9931
Fax: (607) 547-9675
Toll-Free: 1-800-348-6222
www.otesaga.com
Note: A member of the Historic Hotels of America by the National Trust for Historic Preservation, the Otesaga is a grand federal style hotel situated on the shores of Lake Otsego. It features a heated outdoor swimming pool, the Leatherstocking Golf Course, a fitness center, tennis courts, an onsite restaurant, and canoe rentals, among other amenities.

On-Site Hospitality and Events:
Food is sold onsite, but it can get expensive and the lines are long. Bringing your own food and drink (non-alcoholic) is recommended.

Play Ball With Ozzie Smith and Special Guests:
This annual event raises funds for the Museum's educational programs. The "Wizard" is joined by other baseball luminaries. Fans are welcomed on the field and receive souvenirs to commemorate the event. This event does have a fee to attend, so be sure to check for pricing. Make sure to ask, as fans booking for two or more participants will usually receive a discount. Phone: (607) 547-0329.
Website: www.baseballhalloffame.org

Legends for Youth Skills Clinic:
Children ages five to twelve can work on their baseball skills with the help of former major league players in historic Doubleday Field. The event is free, but pre-registration is usually required. Phone: (607) 547-0329.
Website: www.baseballhalloffame.org

New York Penn League Game:
Most years the Oneonta Tigers face the Aberdeen Iron Birds on Doubleday Field. The ball game is free and open to the public. Check with the Hall of Fame for specific game information. Toll-Free: 1-888-HALL-OF-FAME.
Website: www.baseballhalloffame.org

Travel Packages:
If you are going to travel to this event, I would recommend using a reliable company to work with you on making the necessary arrangements. The suppliers listed in this book have solid references and are by far the most trusted in the business. Below are some of the organizations to try for this Top 100 Must See Sporting Event.

Premiere Corporate Events
14 Penn Plaza, Suite 925
New York, NY 10122
Phone: (212) 695-9480
Fax: (212) 564-8098
Toll-Free: 1-877-621-5243
E-mail: requests@tseworld.com
www.tseworld.com
www.pcevents.com

Premiere Sports Travel
201 Shannon Oaks Circle, Suite 205
Cary, NC 27511
Phone: (919) 481-9511
Fax: (919) 481-1337
Toll-Free: 1-800-924-9993
E-mail: sales@sportstravel.com
www.sportstravel.com

Dining:

The Doubleday Café
93 Main Street
Cooperstown, NY 13326
Phone: (607) 547-5468

Note: The Doubleday offers burgers, sand-
wiches, and American cuisine in a great
atmosphere at a decent price.

Cooperstown Diner
136 ½ Main Street
Cooperstown, NY 13326
Phone: (607) 547-9201
www.cooperstowndiner.com

Note: The Cooperstown Diner is home to the
"Jumbo" burger and other great diner selections.

Alex and Ika
149 Main Street
Cooperstown, NY 13326
Phone: (607) 547-4070
www.alexandika.com

Note: It was ranked as one of Frommer's "Top
Ten Restaurants in New York State" in 2006.

Airport:
With limited options for air travel, your best
bet is flying into the Albany International
Airport. Cooperstown is a one-and-a-half
hour drive by car from AIA.

Albany International Airport
737 Albany-Shaker Road
Albany, NY 12211
Phone: (518) 242-2200
www.albanyairport.com

Sports Travel Insider's Edge:

Best place to watch the action:
Being that it is an outdoor event in the summer, lawn chairs and blankets are your best
option for comfortable viewing of the ceremony. You probably won't have a front row
seat, so bring binoculars. Water is provided,
but a picnic would help pass the time with
food and beverages (alcohol is not allowed).

Best way to get up close to the action:
While you cannot get too close to your favorite baseball players during the ceremony,
the "Red Carpet Arrivals" event, which takes
place the night before the ceremony, provides an opportunity to see them up close
and personal. Arrive early to get yourself a
good vantage point. Players are dropped off
by trolleys and participate in live interviews
on the red carpet before heading into a private gala.

Best travel tip:
Free seating in an outdoor event mandates
an early arrival to claim your space, and do
not forget your sunscreen. The main road
leading into Cooperstown is mostly one lane
so be prepared for delays all weekend. Also,
driving once in town is not recommended
as parking is limited in the village. Free
shuttles are available from most hotels.

Notable Quote:
"The feeling I've had since I got the call is
a feeling I suspect will never go away. I'm
told it never does. It's the highest high you
can imagine. I wish you all could feel what
I feel standing here. This is my last big
game. This is my last big at-bat. This is my
last time catching the final out. I dreamed
of this as a child but I had too much
respect for baseball to think this was ever
possible."—RYNE SANDBERG, former Chicago
Cubs second baseman, at his Hall of Fame
induction

Relevant Websites:
www.baseballhalloffame.org
www.thisiscooperstown.com
www.tseworld.com
www.pcevents.com
www.sportstravel.com
www.premieresports.com

23

HARVARD VS. YALE AT YALE

Where?
Yale Bowl
276 Derby Avenue
West Haven, CT 06516

When?
November every other year.

Significance:
The prestige of attending Harvard or Yale is a designation that few receive. The institutions are two of the oldest colleges in the country. Their football teams are very much a different story. The Harvard Crimson and Yale Bulldogs are not considered dominant Division 1 programs, nor will you see them in BCS post-season competition anytime soon. However, Harvard and Yale football do have their own "Rose Bowl" when they play each other. They simply call it "The Game" and it alternates between Harvard Stadium and the Yale Bowl. Since 1875 (interrupted only by World Wars I and II), future statesmen and captains of industry compete for pride and, less frequently, the Ivy League title. The prim and proper stereotype of both schools goes out the window as ribald cheers and dirty pranks have become as much of a tradition as the game itself. Harvard vs. Yale is the oldest college football rivalry, with students and alums bringing grills to cook food and kegs to drink beer. Not to worry, tents are constructed with buffets that serve shrimp cocktail and champagne. This is Harvard and Yale, after all.

Who attends?
Students and alums of both Ivy League institutions.

How to get there?
New Haven has excellent train services. Union Station is serviced by Amtrak high-speed trains that run from New York's Penn Station and Boston or Vermont.

MTA Metro North also has trains that run from New York's Grand Central Terminal.

Bus Service:
Dattco Bus Company
Toll-Free: 1-800-229-4879

Greyhound Bus from Union Station
Phone: (203) 772-2470

Peter Pan from Greyhound Terminal
Toll-Free: 1-800-237-8747

Tickets:
For primary ticket access information, consider:

Yale Ticket Office
20 Tower Parkway
New Haven, CT 06511
Phone: (203) 432-1400
www.yalebulldogs.com

Harvard Athletic Ticket Office
Murr Center
65 North Harvard Street
Cambridge, MA 02165
Phone: (617) 496-2222
www.gocrimson.com

For secondary ticket access, consider:

GoTickets, Inc.
2345 Waukegan Road, Suite 140
Bannockburn, IL 60015-1552
Toll-Free: 1-800-775-1617
Fax: (919) 481-9101
E-mail: sales@gotickets.com
www.gotickets.com

Accommodations:

Clarion Hotel & Suites
2260 Whitney Avenue
Hamden, CT 06518

Phone: (203) 288-3831
Fax: (203) 281-6032
Toll-Free: 1-800-4-CHOICE
www.clarionhotels.com

Note: Non-smoking property with an onsite coffee lounge. Located minutes from Yale.

New Haven Hotel
229 George Street
New Haven, CT 06510
Phone: (203) 498-3100
Fax: (203) 498-0911
Toll-Free:1-800-644-6835
www.newhavenhotel.com

Note: Close to Yale, the Shubert Theater, and other downtown attractions.

Courtyard New Haven at Yale
30 Whalley Avenue
New Haven, CT 06511
Phone: (203) 777-6221
Fax: (203) 772-1089
Toll-Free: 1-800-MARRIOTT
www.marriott.com

Note: Surrounded by the Yale campus and close to quaint shops and fine dining.

Courtyard Shelton
780 Bridgeport Avenue
Shelton, CT 06484
Phone: (203) 929-1500
Fax: (203) 929-6711
Toll-Free: 1-800-MARRIOTT
www.marriott.com

Note: Full-service hotel minutes off Route 8 and I-95. Twelve minutes from Yale.

Hampton Inn
129 Plains Road
Milford, CT 06460
Phone: (203) 874-4400
Fax: (203) 874-5348
Toll-Free: 1-800-HAMPTON
www.hampton-inn.com

Note: Touted as "an inlet for culture, history, and entertainment." Located at I-95 on Exit 36 (Plains Road).

Crown Plaza
1284 Strongtown Road
Southbury, CT 06488
Phone: (203) 598-7600
Fax: (203) 598-7541
Toll-Free: 1-800-227-6963
www.hilton.com

Note: Conveniently located right off of I-84.

Hilton Garden Inn
25 Old Stratford Road
Shelton, CT 06484
Phone: (203) 447-1000
Fax: (203) 447-1050
Toll-Free: 1-800-HILTONS
www.hiltongardeninn.com

Note: After the game, check out the nearby P. T. Barnum Circus Museum.

Holiday Inn
201 Washington Avenue
North Haven, CT 06473
Phone: (203) 239-6700
Fax: (203) 234-1247
Toll-Free: 1-800-HOLIDAY
www.ichotelsgroup.com

Note: Off I-91 at Exit 12. Eight miles north of downtown New Haven.

Homewood Suites by Hilton
6905 Main Street
Stratford, CT 06614
Phone: (203) 377-3322
Fax: (203) 378-6677
Toll-Free: 1-800-HILTONS
www.homewoodsuites.com

Note: Studio and two-bedroom suites. Beautiful view of the Housatonic River and easy access to major highways.

La Quinta Inn and Suites
400 Sargent Drive
New Haven, CT 06511
Phone: (203) 562-1111
Fax: (203) 865-7440
Toll-Free: 1-800-531-5900
www.laquinta.com

Note: Perfect for the business type and leisure traveler. Continental breakfast bar and nearby restaurants.

Courtyard New Haven Orange
136 Marsh Hill Road
Orange, CT 06477
Phone: (203) 799-2200
Fax: (203) 799-2626
Toll-Free: 1-800-894-8733
www.marriott.com

Note: Many conveniences, including a swimming pool and hot tub.

Marriott Fairfield Inn
111 Schoolhouse Road
Milford, CT 06460
Phone: (203) 877-8588
Fax: (203) 874-3121
Toll-Free: 1-800-228-2800
www.marriott.com

Note: Take Exit 35 off I-95. Located strategically between Stamford and New Haven.

Premiere Hotel and Suites
3 Long Wharf Drive
New Haven, CT 06511
Phone: (203) 777-5337
Fax: (203) 777-2808
Toll-Free: 1-866-458-0232
www.newhavensuites.com

Note: An ideal hotel for extended stays. All the comforts of home and the benefits of hotel life. Free breakfast buffet and nightly social events.

Omni Hotel
155 Temple Street
New Haven, CT 06510
Phone: (203) 772-6664
Fax: (203) 974-6780
Toll-Free: 1-800-843-6664
www.omnihotels.com

Note: Four-diamond hotel with the convenience of boutique shopping.

Touch of Ireland Guest House
670 Whitney Avenue
New Haven, CT 06511
Phone: (203) 787-7997
Fax: (203) 787-7999
Toll-Free: 1-866-787-7990
www.touchofirelandguesthouse.com

Note: Award-winning bed and breakfast combining old traditions with new technologies.

On-Site Hospitality:
The Yale Football Hospitality Program creates memorable and custom-made tailgate experiences. Their staff does the work for you, partnering with tenting companies and two of the state's premier caterers. Phone: (203) 436-1256.

A Yale Bowl Skybox comes with a private tent that holds twenty-five people. Official caterers provide the food and drink. Seasonal packages are available. Single-game skybox packages include the private tent, forty skybox passes, signage in the Yale Bowl, and a public welcome over the public address system during the game. Phone: (203) 432-2205.

The Yale Football Hospitality Village offers a private tent as well. Various options are available based on your budget. Choose from their official caterers, La Cuisine or Culinary Concerts. Phone: (203) 436-1256.

Travel Packages:
If you are going to travel to this event, I would recommend using a reliable company to work with you on making the necessary arrangements. The suppliers listed in this book have solid references and are by far the most trusted in the business. Below are some of the organizations to try for this Top 100 Must See Sporting Event.

Premiere Corporate Events
14 Penn Plaza, Suite 925
New York, NY 10122
Phone: (212) 695-9480
Fax: (212) 564-8098

Toll-Free: 1-877-621-5243
E-mail: requests@tseworld.com
www.tseworld.com
www.pcevents.com

Premiere Sports Travel
201 Shannon Oaks Circle, Suite 205
Cary, NC 27511
Phone: (919) 481-9511
Fax: (919) 481-1337
Toll-Free: 1-800-924-9993
E-mail: sales@sportstravel.com
www.sportstravel.com

Dining:

Au Bon Pain
1 Broadway
New Haven, CT 06511
Phone: (203) 865-5554
www.aubonpain.com
Note: Serving soups, pasta, and bakery items.

Patricia's
18 Whalley Avenue
New Haven, CT 06511
Phone: (203) 787-4500
Note: Don't let the looks of the place deter you from eating here. The food is delicious!

Copper Kitchen
1008 Chapel Street
New Haven, CT 06510
Phone: (203) 777-8010
Note: Great pastrami sandwiches and Reubens.

Poppy's Deli
153 Saw Mill Road
West Haven, CT 06516
Phone: (203) 937-SUBS
Note: Excellent breakfast sandwiches, deli food, and homemade entrées.

Modern Apizza Palace
874 State Street
New Haven, CT 06511
Phone: (203) 776-5306
www.modernapizza.com

Note: Considered by many to be the city's best pizza place.

Pizza Empire
16 Whalley Avenue
New Haven, CT 06511
Phone: (203) 562-5500
Note: This "hole-in-the wall" looking place is great for Greek-style pizza and subs.

Yorkside Pizza
288 York Street
New Haven, CT 06511
Phone: (203) 787-7471
www.yorksidepizza.com
Note: Everything is made from scratch, even the salad dressing.

A-One on Broadway
21 Broadway
New Haven, CT 06510
Phone: (203) 865-8888
Note: A pizza place that serves omelets and other items for breakfast.

Pasta Fair
262 Boston Post Road
Orange, CT 06477
Phone: (203) 799-9601
www.pastafair.com
Note: Generous portions of pasta to fill you up after the big game.

Airports:

Tweed New Haven Regional Airport
155 Burr Street
New Haven, CT, 06512
Phone: (203) 466-8833
Fax: (203) 466-1199
www.flytweed.com

Hartford/Bradley International Airport
Schoephoester Road and Terminal
Windsor Locks, CT 06096
Phone: (860) 292-2000
www.bradleyairport.com

White Plains Airport
(fifty-four miles from the Yale Bowl)
240 Airport Road
White Plains, NY 10604
Phone: (914) 995-4850
www.whiteplainsairport.com

Sports Travel Insider's Edge:

Best way to watch the action:
Once inside the stadium you're immediately engulfed in the complete Yale vs. Harvard experience. This is the game you want to invite all the boys from the firm to attend. You won't even need to use the company expense account to purchase a single-game skybox for this one. Contact the hospitality department for more information. Phone: (203) 432-2205.

Best place to get up close:
Is it the game on the inside or the action on the outside that is more exciting? For many, the main event is the tailgating in the parking lot. It starts at 9 A.M. and allows visitors the opportunity to witness some great interactions between Harvard and Yale alums.

Best travel tip:
If you find yourself on the Yale campus, try to stay close to the school. Downtown New Haven is just like any other city, not the safest place to roam around late at night.

Notable Quote:
"Gentlemen, you are now going out to play football against Harvard. Never again in your whole life will you do anything so important."—T. A. D. JONES, former Yale head football coach

Relevant Websites:
www.the-game.org
www.yalebulldogs.com
www.gocrimson.com
www.cityofnewhaven.com
www.tseworld.com

www.pcevents.com
www.sportstravel.com
www.gotickets.com
www.premieresports.com

24
KENTUCKY DERBY

Where?
Churchill Downs
Louisville, KY

When?
The first Saturday in May.

Significance:
At two minutes, the race itself is likely shorter than your travel time. Parking, walking to the track, and finding your seat will take longer. However, size isn't everything. This is an event rife with tradition of pricey hat-wearing horse-race aficionados sipping mint juleps while placing their wager on their favorite horse. This is truly an all-day event and the race itself promises excitement and drama. Yes, there are other races, but the Kentucky Derby is the main event of the day and the racing season. Whether you are a casual equine enthusiast or a hardcore fan of the sport of kings, this is a premier sporting event to attend.

Who attends?
Fashion is not what it used to be at the Kentucky Derby. From well-dressed to nattily attired, the crowd can resemble a fashion show. There are those who forsake tradition and choose the t-shirt and shorts route. Some decide a bare-chested au naturel look is for them. The free flow of alcohol and money for gambling makes this an adult gathering. Even with Churchill Downs's capacity of 51,000, Derby crowds can reach 165,000. Even though the annual event is always a

sellout, don't lose hope, infield tickets are often available on race day. VIPs are in the clubhouse while fans on a more limited budget fill the infield and grandstand.

Tickets:

It is possible to attend the Kentucky Derby by general admission on race day. Those tickets (approximately forty dollars per person) are unlimited and only sold on Derby Day. No advance sales are available. Seating is unlikely as the tickets are for Standing Room Only.

For secondary ticket access, and your best bet (no pun intended) for this event, consider:

GoTickets, Inc.
2345 Waukegan Road, Suite 140
Bannockburn, IL 60015-1552
Toll-Free: 1-800-775-1617
Fax: (919) 481-9101
E-mail: sales@gotickets.com
www.gotickets.com

If you choose to live the life of a Churchill Downs VIP, third-floor clubhouse seats, a few sections off the finish line in Sections 315 and 318, are available for a couple thousand dollars on the secondary ticket market. The best value for a ticket, simply put, are the first-floor grandstand seats. If you want the best ticket period, no pun intended, get ready to "pony" up the dough. Millionaires Row (4th, 5th, and 6th level clubhouse on the finish line) will set you back several thousand dollars. For the best deals check with a GoTickets representative.

Accommodations:

Horseshoe Casino Hotel Southern Indiana
11999 Casino Center Drive Southeast
Elizabeth, IN 47117
Fax: (812) 969-6780

Toll-Free: 1-866-676-SHOE
www.harrahs.com
Note: Right over the border in Indiana, it is only about a half hour from the track. With a casino on site, it offers those who don't get enough gambling at the track some more opportunities.

Holiday Inn Louisville Downtown
120 West Broadway
Louisville, KY 40202
Phone: (502) 582-2241
Fax: (502) 584-8591
Toll-Free: 1-877-863-4780
www.ichotelsgroup.com
Note: A good value for Derby week. Nothing too fancy with this standard Holiday Inn located downtown.

Galt House Hotel
140 North 4th Street
Louisville, KY 40202
Phone: (502) 589-5200
Fax: (502) 585-9029
Toll-Free: 1-800-THE-GALT
www.galthouse.com
Note: This historic hotel is the official host hotel of Churchill Downs. A lot of history has taken place at this hotel, including the original meeting to form the Kentucky Derby.

On-Site Hospitality:

Churchill Downs does not rest on its historical laurels when it comes to hospitality. Every year, more impressive options crop up for fans.

Marquee Village: Spacious chalets, available in varying sizes, will accommodate larger groups, offering private patios with umbrella tables for open-air dining. Each chalet includes reserved grandstand seating on Churchill Downs' first turn. Marquee Village is literally a mini village of corporate tents set up in a private area. It is not for everyone. You need a pass to get in. There is also a betting area in the village that is less crowded than the public lines in other sections. A short walk to the grandstand is another perk.

Infield Suites: Glass-enclosed suites down the homestretch provide a unique viewing perspective of the track. Sitting in this area, you actually face the grandstand and clubhouse sections, giving you the feeling of being right on top of the action.

Section 111 Suite: These are double-decked suites on Churchill Downs' famous first turn. The best suite option for the price, although it provides the worst view of all the suites.

Finish Line Suites: Leave your binoculars at home. Positioned between the winner's circle and the finish line, this area provides an incomparable view of the Kentucky Derby. Located right on the finish line, not only does it give you a great view of the race, but an up-close seat to watch the winning horse receive the coveted garland of roses in the winner's circle.

Trackside Village: Spacious accommodations for large groups of people. This provides the best option for groups of over 100. Each glass-enclosed unit features two floors and a sizeable patio with a panoramic view of the track and grandstand. Upscale style and comfort with lavish buffets, a premium bar, closed-circuit TVs, patio or rooftop decks, and exclusive access to pari-mutuel windows or self-betting machines.

Travel Packages:

If you are going to travel to this event, I would recommend using a reliable company to work with you on making the necessary arrangements. The suppliers listed in this book have solid references and are by far the most trusted in the business. Below are some of the organizations to try for this Top 100 Must See Sporting Event.

Premiere Corporate Events

14 Penn Plaza, Suite 925
New York, NY 10122
Phone: (212) 695-9480
Fax: (212) 564-8098
Toll-Free: 1-877-621-5243
E-mail: requests@tseworld.com
www.tseworld.com
www.pcevents.com

Premiere Sports Travel

201 Shannon Oaks Circle, Suite 205
Cary, NC 27511
Phone: (919) 481-9511
Fax: (919) 481-1337
Toll-Free: 1-800-924-9993
E-mail: sales@sportstravel.com
www.sportstravel.com

Premiere Sports Travel has a terrific assortment of hospitality options available with their Kentucky Derby packages. Both of these companies offer individual hospitality options for consumers as well as add-on options like horse farm tours and private meet and greets with celebrity jockeys, trainers, and handicappers.

Dining:

Irish Rover

2319 Frankfort Avenue
Louisville, KY 40206
Phone: (502) 899-3544
Fax: (502) 899-7977
www.theirishroverky.com

Note: True to its Irish roots of raising community and relaxation to an art form. This "social center" is a place for friends and family to meet, talk over the issues of the day, and enjoy authentic Irish food and homemade wine. Great atmosphere and a great place to meet people.

Vincenzo's Italian Restaurant

150 South 5th Street
Louisville, KY 40202
Phone: (502) 580-1350
Fax: (502) 580-1355
www.vincenzositalianrestaurant.com

Note: Best value in town for a quality meal.

Mark's Feed Store BBQ
1514 Bardstown Road
Louisville, KY 40205
Phone: (502) 458-1570
Fax: (502) 458-9492
www.marksfeedstore.com

Note: Do not let the name fool you. This is a very high-quality meal. The ribs are their specialty.

Airport:

Louisville International Airport (just ten minutes from downtown Louisville)
600 Terminal Drive
Louisville, KY 40209
Phone: (502) 367-4636
www.flylouisville.com

Sports Travel Insider's Edge:

Best way to watch the action:
All totaled the horse races last less than a half-hour. You have another six hours to keep yourself occupied. Without the luxury of a hospitality suite, you may want to find an individual spot in the Marquis Village hospitability tents. Those can be purchased through private hospitality companies. Add to that the option of a seat in the third floor clubhouse sections (315 to 318) to watch the race. No money for seats? The 100 level is on the first turn. It is close to the Marquis Village and provides a unique view of the race.

Best place to get up close:
The paddock area will show you the horses before they are led out to the track. There is a special viewing section roped off to get an up-close view of the jockeys, horses, and trainers. Crowds tend to gather there, so make sure you get out of there early enough so that you do not miss the race.

Best travel tip:
Leaving right after the Kentucky Derby race is unwise at best. Approximately 75 percent of the crowd is looking for the exit. Patience is key. Let the crowd thin out and you will find it much easier to leave Churchill Downs after all the races have been run. Maybe even place a wager on a post-Derby race to make up for any money you lost on the main race.

Notable Quotes:

"Until you go to Kentucky and with your own eyes behold the Derby, you ain't never been nowheres and you ain't never seen nothin'!"—Irvin S. Cobb, American author and columnist

"It's the sport of kings, it's the greatest two minutes in sports, and it's the greatest horse race in the world."—Steve Nunn, former Kentucky state representative

"This is the aspiration of anybody and everybody in the horse business. It's just overwhelming."—Jim Tafel, horse owner and breeder

Relevant Websites:
www.gotolouisville.com
www.tseworld.com
www.pcevents.com
www.sportstravel.com
www.gotickets.com
www.premieresports.com

25

UEFA CHAMPIONS LEAGUE

When?
Annually, starting in mid-July.

Future Locations of Finals:
2009–Rome, Italy (subject to change)
2010–Santiago Bernabeu Stadium in Madrid, Spain

Significance:
In Europe, they call it football and it does not get more exciting than the chase for the

European Champion Clubs' Cup in a ten-month tournament. Every year, the most successful football/soccer clubs vie for the most prestigious club trophy in the sport. The UEFA Champions League is open to member associations and clubs that finish first to fourth in the strongest leagues. For a soccer team to compete in the league shows that they are the best of the best, with or without a title.

Rabid soccer fans from around the world follow each match closely to see which team will emerge as a potential champion. They attend their team's league matches, cheering on their home country heroes. Fantasy leagues are even set up through the UEFA website, further whetting the appetite of the fanatical followers who build their rosters and compete against each other.

Who attends?
Soccer fanatics who want to watch some of the world's best teams compete against each other.

History
French sports writing journalist Gabriel Hanot had an idea back in the 1950s that would change European soccer/football history forever. Those football teams recognized as winners of European national football leagues should come together in a continental competition to determine the European Cup champion. In the 1955/1956 season, the first tournament commenced for the then-European Cup, which became the UEFA Champions League Cup in the 1992/1993 season.

At that time, only national league champions were allowed into the tournament. Today, those title-holders compete with runners-up for UEFA Champions League superiority, a significant change that was implemented in the 1997/1998 season. Qualifying for the tournament starts in July with three preliminary knockout rounds that winnow the competition down to thirty-two teams. Further changes in 2007 resulted in twenty-two teams receiving automatic qualifying berths to the group stage, an increase from sixteen. The remaining ten teams qualify based on elaborate champion and non-champion rankings. The objective of the change was to enable champions from low-ranked associations access to the main tournament by competing against non-champions from higher-ranked associations that did not qualify for the group stage.

From there, eight group winners and eight runners-up compete in the final knockout rounds. The two teams that are left over compete in the final match for the Cup in May.

Notable Athletes:
Cristiano Ronaldo, Manchester United
Steven Gerrard, Liverpool
Lionel Messi, Barcelona
Fernando Torres, Liverpool
Raúl González, Real Madrid
Zlatan Ibrahimović, Inter Milan
Deivid, Fenerbahçe
Frédéric Kanouté, Sevilla

Records:
All-Time top goal scorer: Raúl, 63 goals in 120 games, Real Madrid
Nation with most championship teams: 11 (Tie), Spain, Italy, and England

Things to know before you go:
Hat Trick: Three goals scored in one game by one player.
Give and Go: A player controlling the ball passes to a teammate and runs through an open field to get a possible return pass.
Juggling: Keeping the ball off the ground by a player using their feet, thighs, chest, head, and the top of their shoulders.
Red Card: Shown by a referee to signify

that a player has been sent off. The player who has been sent off must leave the field immediately and cannot be replaced during the game; their team must continue the game with one player fewer.

Yellow Card: A cautionary warning issued by the referee to a player for unsports-manlike behavior or a variety of other infractions.

Tickets:

For primary ticket access information, consider: www.uefa.com.

Note: Applications are vetted to identify anyone banned from football games. No tickets are distributed to ticket agencies or secondary sources.

Lottery: Tickets are decided by a lottery held by UEFA. Fans fill out an application/ballot and those are accepted for a set amount of time. Each person selected is entitled to a maximum of two tickets.

Finalist Tickets: Three-quarters of all the tickets are reserved for the general public and fans of the two teams competing in the finals. Each finalist can take up to roughly 21,000 tickets and distribute them.

Tickets for the Public: About 10,500 tickets remain for sale to fans on a worldwide basis through UEFA.

For secondary ticket access, consider:

GoTickets, Inc.
2345 Waukegan Road, Suite 140
Bannockburn, IL 60015-1552
Toll-Free: 1-800-775-1617
Fax: (919) 481-9101
E-mail: sales@gotickets.com
www.gotickets.com

Travel Packages:
If you are going to travel to this event, I would recommend using a reliable company to work with you on making the neces-

sary arrangements. The suppliers listed in this book have solid references and are by far the most trusted in the business. Below are some of the organizations to try for this Top 100 Must See Sporting Event.

Premiere Corporate Events
14 Penn Plaza, Suite 925
New York, NY 10122
Phone: (212) 695-9480
Fax: (212) 564-8098
Toll-Free: 1-877-621-5243
E-mail: requests@tseworld.com
www.tseworld.com
www.pcevents.com

Premiere Sports Travel
201 Shannon Oaks Circle, Suite 205
Cary, NC 27511
Phone: (919) 481-9511
Fax: (919) 481-1337
Toll-Free: 1-800-924-9993
E-mail: sales@sportstravel.com
www.sportstravel.com

Notable Quotes:

"This tour is setting new standards in regards to its size, the technologies used, and the ability to offer thousands of football fans an unforgettable football experience."—MICHEL PLATINI, UEFA President

"You can imagine the fan frenzy at the higher-up levels of the championship—a UEFA Champions League game is absolutely amazing to watch live! With fans, sponsors, and world-renowned football players in the mix, watching live UEFA Champions League games is an unreal experience not only in person but on television as well."—*Live Football Online*'s website

Relevant Websites:
www.uefa.com
www.tseworld.com

www.pcevents.com
www.sportstravel.com
www.gotickets.com
www.premieresports.com

26
ROSE BOWL

Where?
Rose Bowl
1001 Rose Bowl Drive
Pasadena, CA 91103-2813

When?
January

Significance:
Twelve years after the first Tournament of Roses in 1890, the organizers decided to add something new to the mix. During the early years, the Pasadena-based festival added marching bands and motorized floats to their showcase. Athletic competitions were composed of bronco busting and races between various animals, including ostrich versus ostrich and camel versus elephant. In 1902, they added a more human touch with their first college football game. Stanford University stomped the University of Michigan 49–0 before Michigan surrendered in the third quarter. The lopsided victory ended that "experiment" in favor of Roman chariot races.

Football returned in 1916. By 1923, a stadium was built to host the New Year's football game, now called "The Rose Bowl." Since 1947, the year Big Ten and Pac-10 became exclusive to the event, "The Granddaddy of Them All" has been a solid sellout with a current capacity of over 90,000. During that time, floats in the Tournament of Roses parade have taken on a high-tech feel and sometimes take a year to construct. In fact, professional float-building companies have replaced the volunteers.

With the addition of the Bowl Championship Series, the Rose Bowl plays home to the National Championship Game every four years.

Who attends?
College football fans who want to see the best that the gridiron has to offer, whether the teams are playing for the National Championship or not.

How to get there?
If you are in the Los Angeles area, take Interstate 405 (North) to the 605 Freeway (North) from Long Beach. Take the 210 Freeway toward San Fernando. Exit at Mountain/Seco, Lincoln, Arroyo Boulevard/Windsor. Follow the signs.

Parking:
Parking is first-come, first-serve, except the pass-required lots. Overnight parking is only allowed in the designated RV lot. Rain may open up some golf course lots. Street parking is available as well.

Park at Parsons at the corner of Fair Oaks Avenue and Holly Street. From there, you can take a free city shuttle bus, which usually runs from 10 A.M. until two hours after the game's end. Parking at Parsons is around thirty dollars unless you purchase in advance at a lower rate. Phone: (626) 440-2844 or go to www.ParPark.com.

Tickets:
As a contractual sellout, most of the tickets are distributed by the participating teams and conferences. Everyone, including children, needs a ticket to gain entrance.

For secondary ticket access, consider:

GoTickets, Inc.
2345 Waukegan Road, Suite 140
Bannockburn, IL 60015-1552
Toll-Free: 1-800-775-1617

Fax: (919) 481-9101
E-mail: sales@gotickets.com
www.gotickets.com

Accommodations:

The Langham Huntington Hotel and Spa Pasadena
1401 South Oak Knoll Avenue
Pasadena, CA 91106
Phone: (626) 568-3900
Pasadena.langhamhotels.com

Note: Located in a prestigious residential area, this 380-room (including thirty-eight suites) hotel is a historic Pasadena landmark.

Pasadena Inn
400 South Arroyo Parkway
Pasadena, CA 91105
Phone: (626) 795-8401
www.pasadenainn.net

Note: Contemporary low-rise property located three miles from the stadium, fifteen miles from Universal Studios, and thirty-five miles from Disneyland.

The Westin Pasadena
191 North Los Robles Avenue
Pasadena, CA 91101
Phone: (626) 792-2727
Fax: (626) 795-7669
www.westin.com

Note: Close to historic Old Town, museums, restaurants, and the Pasadena Conference Center.

On-Site Hospitality:

The Rose Bowl has a Hospitality Village area onsite where groups are able to lease private tents and order premium food and beverages. In addition, individuals have the opportunity to buy into existing pre-game hospitality options in the village. For access consider travel packages.

Premiere Sports Travel and Dodd's Athletic Tours have official travel relationships with many universities. Check their web-sites to see who their partners are and if they are playing in the Rose Bowl.

Travel Packages:

If you are going to travel to this event, I would recommend using a reliable company to work with you on making the necessary arrangements. The suppliers listed in this book have solid references and are by far the most trusted in the business. Below are some of the organizations to try for this Top 100 Must See Sporting Event.

Premiere Corporate Events
14 Penn Plaza, Suite 925
New York, NY 10122
Phone: (212) 695-9480
Fax: (212) 564-8098
Toll-Free: 1-877-621-5243
E-mail: requests@tseworld.com
www.tseworld.com
www.pcevents.com

Premiere Sports Travel
201 Shannon Oaks Circle, Suite 205
Cary, NC 27511
Phone: (919) 481-9511
Fax: (919) 481-1337
Toll-Free: 1-800-924-9993
E-mail: sales@sportstravel.com
www.sportstravel.com

Premiere College Sports
(Powered by Dodd's Athletic Tours)
308 South Neil
Champaign, IL 61820
Phone: (217) 373-5067
Fax: (217) 398-1313
Toll-Free: 1-800-553-5527
www.doddsathletictours.com
www.collegesportstravel.com

Dining:

Dong II Jang
3455 West 8th Street
Los Angeles, CA 90005
Phone: (213) 383-5757

Note: Located in Korea town, Korean and Japanese food is served. The Korean barbecue, katsu, or kalbi is recommended.

JJ's Steakhouse
88 West Colorado Boulevard
Pasadena, CA 91105
Phone: (626) 844-8889
www.jjsteakhouse.net

Note: Juicy steaks seared at a high temperature. Great seafood served as well. Choose an after-dinner smoke from the diverse cigar menu.

Old Towne Pub
66 North Fair Oaks Avenue
Pasadena, CA 91103
Phone: (626) 577-6583
www.lochnesspub.com

Note: Rustic atmosphere with weathered wood walls. Live music every night with people and their dogs hanging out in the outdoor courtyard.

Fred 62
1850 North Vermont Avenue
Los Angeles, CA 90027
Phone: (323) 667-0062
www.fred62.com

Note: "Eat now, dine later" is their motto. Open twenty-four hours, this classic American coffee shop is often a place where you will see a celebrity grabbing a bite.

Tarantino's Pizzeria
784 East Green Street
Pasadena, CA 91101
Phone: (626) 796-7836

Note: Known for great Italian food and even greater prices.

Big Mama's Rib Shack
1453 North Lake Avenue
Pasadena, CA 91104
Phone: (626) 797-1792
www.bigmamas-ribshack.com

Note: Southern menu with tender ribs and all the trimmings.

Beckham Grill
77 West Walnut Street
Pasadena, CA 91103
Phone: (626) 796-3399
www.beckhamgrill.com

Note: Reserve the Knight's Table Room that seats eight in privacy just off the main dining room.

Bistro 45
45 South Mentor Avenue
Pasadena, CA 91106
Phone: (626) 795-2478
Fax: (626) 792-2676
www.bistro45.com

Note: Pricey, but worth every penny.

Yard House
330 East Colorado Blvd.
Pasadena, CA 91101
Phone: (626) 577-9273
www.yardhouse.com

Note: Upscale, yet casual, with an extensive menu and over 125 brews on tap.

Freddie 35er Bar
12 East Colorado Boulevard
Pasadena, CA 91105
Phone: (626) 356-9315
www.the35er.com

Note: Family owned and operated since 1962, great place to play pool or pinball, watch television, or listen to some music.

Tom Bergin's Tavern
840 South Fairfax Avenue
Los Angeles, CA 90036
Phone: (323) 936-7151
Fax: (323) 936-7871
www.tombergins.com

Note: Established in 1936, the horseshoe bar is often credited as the inspiration for the sitcom "Cheers."

Airports:

Burbank/Bob Hope Airport
2627 North Hollywood Way

Burbank, CA 91505
Phone: (818) 840-8840
www.burbankairport.com

LAX
1 World Way
Los Angeles, CA 90045
Phone: (310) 646-5252
www.lawa.org

Sports Travel Insider's Edge:

Best way to watch the action:
All seats provide a good view due to the design of the open bowl with no columns. Some lower seats are not as good as you think and provide obstructions. Corner sections, particularly 22 to 24, 27 to 1, 8 to 10, and 13 to 15 provide the best bang for your buck.

Best place to get up close:
For over five miles, the Rose Bowl Parade provides the best up-close view of the events. Many attendees consider the parade, at times, to be better than the Rose Bowl game itself. Lasting about two hours and thirty minutes at any given place, you can see the pageantry of the entire event and the hard work that goes into making this the most famous parade of all. Prepare to camp out starting at noon the day before if you want to get up close.

Best travel tip:
The Rose Bowl is not the only act in town. Remember, you're near Hollywood. The Lakers or Clippers may be in town at the Staples Center. Place a bet on the ponies at Santa Anita Park. Grab a Warner Bros. Studio Tour. Visit the Getty Museum, the Santa Monica Pier, or Grauman's Chinese Theater.

Notable Quotes:

"In New York, people are buried in snow. Here our flowers are blooming and our oranges are about to bear. Let's hold a festival to tell the world about our paradise."
—PROFESSOR CHARLES F. HOLDER, Pasadena Hunt Club

"The Rose Bowl is hard to get to. There's a reason why they call it 'The Granddaddy of them all.'"—RON ZOOK, Illinois Head Coach

Relevant Websites:
www.tournamentofroses.com
www.rosebowlstadium.com
www.pasadenacal.com
www.ParPark.com
www.SharpSeating.com
www.tseworld.com
www.pcevents.com
www.sportstravel.com
www.gotickets.com
www.doddsathletictours.com
www.collegesportstravel.com
www.premieresports.com

27

BRITISH OPEN

When?
Annually on the weekend after the third Friday in July.

Future Locations:
Ailsa Course, Turnberry, Ayrshire, July 16–19, 2009
www.turnberry.co.uk

Old Course, St. Andrews, Fife, July 15–18, 2010
www.standrews.org.uk

Royal St. George's, 2011
www.royalstgeorges.com

Royal Lytham & St Annes, 2012
www.royallytham.org

Significance:

Winning the British Open carries a prestige that comes with few golf tournaments. It is also the oldest of the four major golf championships with its roots dating back to 1860. The Open Championship, as it is called in the United Kingdom, is the third event following the Masters Tournament and the U.S. Open, and preceding the PGA Championship.

With oversight by the Royal and Ancient Golf Club of St. Andrews (R&A), the British Open is played on the weekend following the third Friday in July. While the PGA European Tour always recognized the Open as an official event, it recently became part of the PGA Tour in 1995. Past British Open victories are now retroactively considered PGA Tour wins. Nine historic courses located throughout the United Kingdom rotate hosting duties every year.

Unlike other tournaments, professionals and amateurs must qualify to play on the beautifully maintained, yet challenging courses. While the links are pretty to look at, the weather combined with the unique surfaces are the professional golfers' true adversary at the British Open.

Some rules at the British Open are as unique as the topography. Golfers tied at the end of regulation play a four-hole playoff starting with the 1st hole and then move to the 16th, 17th, and 18th holes. If a deadlock is still in effect, play on the 18th hole is repeated until there is a winner. However, victory is well worth it, as is raising the Claret Jug (the Golf Champion Trophy) high in the air.

Who attends?

Golfing fans from around the world come to watch the world's best golfers navigate some of the world's most difficult courses.

History

When the first Open Championship was played on October 17, 1860, at the Prestwick Golf Club, only professionals were allowed. That rule would change the following year. Eight pro golfers played three 12-hole rounds. Willie Park, Sr., (Junior would eventually play too) beat the just-as-aptly-named Old Tom Morris (yes, there was a Young Tom Morris who golfed) by two strokes. No prize money for the first three years went to the winner and the Claret Jug had yet to be created. Instead, Park was presented with a Champion's Belt made of red leather and a silver buckle with various emblems adorning the strap. Most winners in those formative years were Scottish professionals who made their livings as greens keepers, club makers, and caddies.

With the Royal and Ancient Golf Club of St Andrews and The Honourable Company of Edinburgh Golfers (until 1920) taking over the administration of the tournament in 1871, more golfers were flocking to the Open. By 1898, two rounds of qualifications were implemented to winnow down the number of participants.

After nearly a century of ups and downs that included the cancellation of the 1871 Open due to a championship committee in disarray, the British Open was added to the PGA Tour's official schedule in 1995. The British Open is a place of history, most recently with the famous wave goodbye by Jack Nicklaus in 2000 while Tiger Woods looked on. A passing of the torch, of sorts. At least it wasn't a red belt.

Notable Athletes:

Tiger Woods
Ernie Els
Todd Hamilton
Tom Lehman
John Daly
Jack Nicklaus

Tom Watson
Lee Trevino
Bobby Jones
Peter Thomson
Greg Norman

Records:

Oldest winner: Old Tom Morris (46 years, 99 days), 1867
Youngest winner: Young Tom Morris (17 years, 181 days), 1868
Nation with most titles: United Kingdom, 70

Multiple Winners:

Six wins: Harry Vardon
Five wins: James Braid, J. H. Taylor, Peter Thomson, and Tom Watson
Four wins: Walter Hagen, Bobby Locke, Old Tom Morris, Young Tom Morris, and Willie Park, Sr.
Three wins: Jamie Anderson, Seve Ballesteros, Henry Cotton, Nick Faldo, Bob Ferguson, Bobby Jones, Jack Nicklaus, Gary Player, and Tiger Woods
Two wins: Pádraig Harrington, Harold Hilton, Bob Martin, Greg Norman, Arnold Palmer, Willie Park, Jr., and Lee Trevino

Things to know before you go:

Ace: A hole-in-one.
Front nine: The first half of a round of golf.
Back nine: The second half of a round of golf.
Fore: A warning cry to other players that your ball is headed in their direction.
Par: A certain number of shots needed to hole your ball depending on the hole's distance and difficulty.
Birdie: One under par.
Eagle: Two under par.
Albatross: Three under par.
Bogey: One over par. Double and triple bogeys are self-explanatory.

Tickets:

For primary ticket access information, consider: www.opengolf.com.

For secondary ticket access, consider:

GoTickets, Inc.
2345 Waukegan Road, Suite 140
Bannockburn, IL 60015-1552
Toll-Free: 1-800-775-1617
Fax: (919) 481-9101
E-mail: sales@gotickets.com
www.gotickets.com

Travel Packages:

If you are going to travel to this event, I would recommend using a reliable company to work with you on making the necessary arrangements. The suppliers listed in this book have solid references and are by far the most trusted in the business. Below are some of the organizations to try for this Top 100 Must See Sporting Event.

Premiere Corporate Events
14 Penn Plaza, Suite 925
New York, NY 10122
Phone: (212) 695-9480
Fax: (212) 564-8098
Toll-Free: 1-877-621-5243
E-mail: requests@tseworld.com
www.tseworld.com
www.pcevents.com

Premiere Sports Travel
201 Shannon Oaks Circle, Suite 205
Cary, NC 27511
Phone: (919) 481-9511
Fax: (919) 481-1337
Toll-Free: 1-800-924-9993
E-mail: sales@sportstravel.com
www.sportstravel.com

Sports Travel Insider's Edge:

Best way to watch the action:
The best action and drama will most often take place on the 18th hole. Grab a seat in the grandstand if available and await history to be made. Get there early because the area fills up fast. Note that smoking and alcohol are not permitted on most courses.

Best place to get up close:

One specific area is usually designated for autograph seekers. This helps to create a more orderly, non-*Happy Gilmore* environment as opposed to spectators approaching golfers for a quick signature between holes. Check with the course to find out the exact location.

Best travel tip:

While the British Open is played on a specific course, other links close by and throughout the country are perfect for a quick golfing excursion during off times. England boasts many British Open–style venues. Scotland offers some of the finest courses in the world. Play where golf history has been made. For golfing packages where you can play some of these great courses try www.tseworldgolf.com.

Notable Quotes:

"Any golfer worth his salt has to cross the sea and try to win the British Open."—JACK NICKLAUS, renowned professional golfer

"It is incredibly gratifying to sit here and know my name is on this trophy. If you look at the names of the players who have won the Open championship and the golf courses they've won it on, it's a tremendous honor."—MARK O'MEARA, professional golfer

Relevant Websites:

www.opengolf.com
www.turnberry.co.uk
www.standrews.org.uk
www.royalstgeorges.com
www.royallytham.org
www.tseworld.com
www.pcevents.com
www.sportstravel.com
www.gotickets.com
www.premieresports.com
www.tseworldgolf.com

28

HORSE RACING AT SARATOGA

Where?

Saratoga Race Course
267 Union Avenue
Saratoga Springs, NY 12866

When?

Annual events held from late July to Labor Day weekend.

Significance:

The perfect sporting event for a midsummer afternoon. The Saratoga Race Course is also known as "The Spa" for the mineral springs located near the track. Also referred to as the Graveyard of Favorites, in honor of the many upsets that have happened here. Notably, Man o' War suffered his one and only loss in twenty-one starts, Onion upset Secretariat, and Jim Dandy (100-1 long shot) defeated Gallant Fox. Launching on August 3, 1863, as a four-day event, the Saratoga Meet is recognized as the oldest organized sporting event in the history of the United States. The Travers Stakes that takes place during the event is the oldest thoroughbred horse race in United States history. Now six weeks in duration, it is often the place where you can see some of the biggest upsets of the horse-racing season.

Who attends?

While horse-racing fans come from all walks of life, Saratoga maintains a strict dress code. From neat casual attire to collared shirts, this is not an event for the haute couture–challenged.

Tickets:

For primary ticket access information, consider: www.saratogaraceway.com.

Reserved seating is the proverbial hot ticket as reservations for upcoming seasons are made after the previous season ends. General admission can be had for a few dollars and Clubhouse admission is not much more. Children under twelve are admitted free with a parent or guardian. It is important to note that some clubhouse seats offer television viewing and electronic access for placing a wager.

For secondary ticket access, consider:

GoTickets, Inc.
2345 Waukegan Road, Suite 140
Bannockburn, IL 60015-1552
Toll-Free: 1-800-775-1617
Fax: (919) 481-9101
E-mail: sales@gotickets.com
www.gotickets.com

Accommodations:

Holiday Inn
232 Broadway
Saratoga Springs, NY 12866
Phone: (518) 584-4550
Fax: (518) 554-4417
Toll-Free: 1-888-465-4329
www.spa-hi.com
Note: Within walking distance of the track, this hotel is the most conveniently located.

Gideon Putnam Resort
24 Gideon Putnam Road
Saratoga Springs, NY 12866
Phone: (518) 584-3000
Fax: (518) 584-1354
Toll-Free: 1-866-890-1171
www.gideonputnam.com
Note: Surrounded by Saratoga Spa State Park, this hotel provides excellent service and modern facilities.

Saratoga Arms
497 Broadway
Saratoga Springs, NY 12866
Phone: (518) 584-1775
Fax: (518) 581-4064
www.saratogaarms.com
Note: Award-winning, family-owned and

operated hotel in historic Saratoga with an unmatched intimate charm.

The Inn at Saratoga
231 Broadway
Saratoga Springs, NY 12866
Phone: (518) 583-1890
Fax: (518) 583-2543
Toll-Free: 1-800-274-3573
www.theinnatsaratoga.com
Note: For families and businesses, this has been a popular destination for 150 years. Enjoy a drink in the cocktail lounge overlooking Broadway.

On-Site Hospitality and Events:

The Turf Terrace Dining Room: Multilevel trackside dining area with a view of the racing and several television screens. Strict dress code (no jeans or shorts). Reservations are required.

The Club Terrace: Races can be viewed on any one of many television monitors while you enjoy your meal. Reservations required.

The At The Rail Pavilion: An upscale luncheon in a tent. This track-level buffet restaurant is a favorite.

Additional onsite restaurants include The Carousel Restaurant, The Porch, The Paddock Tent, and The Travers Bar.

Breakfast at Saratoga: A race-day tradition at The Porch from 7 to 9:30 A.M. Enjoy your meal while the thoroughbreds prepare for races. The extremely popular and free tram will take you to the famed stable area.

Travel Packages:

If you are going to travel to this event, I would recommend using a reliable company to work with you on making the necessary arrangements. The suppliers listed in this book have solid references and are by far the most trusted in the business. Below are some of the organizations to try for this Top 100 Must See Sporting Event.

Premiere Corporate Events
14 Penn Plaza, Suite 925
New York, NY 10122
Phone: (212) 695-9480
Fax: (212) 564-8098
Toll-Free: 1-877-621-5243
E-mail: requests@tseworld.com
www.tseworld.com
www.pcevents.com

Premiere Sports Travel
201 Shannon Oaks Circle, Suite 205
Cary, NC 27511
Phone: (919) 481-9511
Fax: (919) 481-1337
Toll-Free: 1-800-924-9993
E-mail: sales@sportstravel.com
www.sportstravel.com

Dining:

Sperry's
30½ Caroline Street
Saratoga Springs, NY 12866
Phone: (518) 584-9618
Note: A favorite destination for both residents and fans who visit "The Spa" annually.

Brindisis
390 Broadway
Saratoga Springs, NY 12866
Phone: (518) 587-6262
Fax: (518) 587-6358
www.brindisis.com
Note: A focus on quality of ingredients, preparation, and presentation helps this restaurant stand out. The lamb comes highly recommended.

Pennells
284 Jefferson Street
Saratoga Springs, NY 12866
Phone: (518) 583-2423
Note: Solid reputation for consistently good meals and exceptional service.

Putnam Market
435 Broadway
Saratoga Springs, NY 12866
Phone: (518) 587-3663
www.putnammarket.com
Note: A specialty food store with a dedicated staff who maintains strict attention to detail in the food they serve.

Airport:

Albany International Airport
737 Albany-Shaker Road
Albany, NY 12211
Phone: (518) 242-2200
www.albanyairport.com

Sports Travel Insider's Edge:

Best way to watch the action:
There is no better way to watch this race than in one of the reserved sections that offer wagering at your seat. You will need to purchase a basic NYTRA debit card onsite and load money into it. This type of seating will allow you to stay in your seat and wager on each race without having to go back to the betting booth all the time. Unless of course you run out of money on your card. On a hot day, and there are many in Saratoga, this is a nice convenience since most of the reserved seating is without air-conditioning.

Best place to get up close:
You need to spend time walking the beautiful grounds and checking out the tailgating scene that goes on outside the main track area. People make this an all-day affair after setting up their own little camps on the main grounds. This is where you will find folks eating, drinking, hanging out with friends, and of course watching the races on the multiple screens.

Best travel tip:
If you are in the clubhouse area, dress well and leave the mesh tank top and short shorts

at home. Also, if you have not reserved your seats the year before, unsold same-day seat and "Sun Seat" tickets are available at 8 A.M. at Gate A or the night before at the Holiday Inn on Broadway. Cash only and admission is not included.

It is important to note that everyone has to pay a small admission charge in addition to having a ticket to the races.

Notable Quote:

"Saratoga was always special because it was world-class racing in a country fair like atmosphere."—JERRY BAILEY, Hall of Fame jockey

Relevant Websites:

www.saratoga.com
www.saratogagamingandraceway.com
www.tseworld.com
www.pcevents.com
www.sportstravel.com
www.gotickets.com
www.premieresports.com

29

LATE SEASON GREEN BAY PACKERS GAME AT LAMBEAU FIELD

Where?

Lambeau Field
1265 Lombardi Avenue
Green Bay, WI 54304

When?

A Packer game sometime during the late part of the NFL season when the snow is most likely to fall and it's freezing outside.

Significance:

Grab your winter coat and get your hat. In this day and age of temperature-controlled and retractable dome stadiums, Lambeau Field seems downright archaic. What it lacks in a cover and a heat source, it makes up for with fanatical Cheeseheads cheering on their beloved Packers while risking frostbite. They thrive on the falling snow and the sub-zero temperatures. The more, the better. Opposing teams often look lost and frozen as they slip-and-slide around the field.

Who attends?

Cheeseheads, young and old, defy Old Man Winter for a glimpse of their boys in green and gold. Lambeau is filled with season ticket holders, selling out the famed stadium for nearly half a century. The fanatical Packer lot makes it nearly impossible for fans of opposing teams to attend. Many are adorned in Packer paraphernalia or defying the elements by putting their painted bodies on display. Win or lose, Green Bay and the entire state of Wisconsin are dedicated to their Pack.

Tickets:

For primary ticket access information, consider: www.nfl.com.

It is nearly impossible to score a ticket from a primary source. Since 1960, Lambeau Field has been sold out to devoted season ticket holders. Those treasured tickets are passed down from generation to generation. Probate courts have heard disputes over season tickets inherited by beneficiaries. Getting a ticket is akin to an act of God, or Vince Lombardi (a god to Packer fans). No matter where you sit, you will be surrounded by the Packer faithful. The closer to the action, the better. However, just getting through the doors is a miracle in and of itself. Your best bet, outside of a secondary ticket seller, is to buddy up to or marry a longtime Green Bay Packer fan. The good tickets to get up close are closely guarded and handed down from generation to generation.

For secondary ticket access, consider:

GoTickets, Inc.
2345 Waukegan Road, Suite 140
Bannockburn, IL 60015-1552
Toll-Free: 1-800-775-1617
Fax: (919) 481-9101
E-mail: sales@gotickets.com
www.gotickets.com

Accommodations:

Tundra Lodge
865 Lombardi Avenue
Green Bay, WI 54304
Phone: (920) 405-8700
Fax: (920) 405-1997
Toll-Free: 1-877-886-3725
www.tundralodge.com
Note: Warm up in this lodge on game day with their forty-five-foot stone fireplace.

Radisson Hotel & Conference Center Green Bay
2040 Airport Drive
Green Bay, WI 54313
Phone: (920) 494-7300
Fax: (920) 494-9599
Toll-Free: 1-800-333-3333
www.radisson.com/greenbaywi
Note: Close to the airport and an opportunity for a little gaming while in town.

Hilton Garden Inn
1015 Lombardi Avenue
Green Bay, WI 54304
Phone: (920) 405-0400
Fax: (920) 405-0512
Toll-Free: 1-800-445-8667
www.hiltongardeninn.com
Note: Two blocks from Lambeau. This is the perfect hotel to stay at if you are in town for the game festivities and nothing more.

On-Site Hospitality:

At Brett Favre's Steakhouse, there is a tailgate party three hours prior to kickoff. Located just two blocks from Lambeau on Brett Favre Pass. Approximately twenty-five dollars gets you all the food you can eat and all the beverages you can consume. Phone: (920) 438-1640 or Toll-Free: 1-800-851-7225.

The best in beer, brats, and other Packer delicacies can be found throughout Lambeau Field, including locations such as:

Curly's Pub
Curly's Game Zone
Green Bay Packers Hall of Fame Grill
Frozen in Time
Brett Favre's Two Minute Grill
Chili John's
Goin' Deep Pizza
Meat Packing Company

Travel Packages:

If you are going to travel to this event, I would recommend using a reliable company to work with you on making the necessary arrangements. The suppliers listed in this book have solid references and are by far the most trusted in the business. Below are some of the organizations to try for this Top 100 Must See Sporting Event.

Premiere Corporate Events
14 Penn Plaza, Suite 925
New York, NY 10122
Phone: (212) 695-9480
Fax: (212) 564-8098
Toll-Free: 1-877-621-5243
E-mail: requests@tseworld.com
www.tseworld.com
www.pcevents.com

Premiere Sports Travel
201 Shannon Oaks Circle, Suite 205
Cary, NC 27511
Phone: (919) 481-9511
Fax: (919) 481-1337
Toll-Free: 1-800-924-9993
E-mail: sales@sportstravel.com
www.sportstravel.com

Dining:

Kroll's
1990 South Ridge Road
Green Bay, WI 54304
Phone: (420) 947-1111
www.krollswest.com

Note: Offers an outside tailgate party with burgers, grilling, and chili cooking. Expect to see a live band playing on most, if not all, game days. Serving usually starts a few hours before kickoff.

Brett Favre's Steakhouse
1004 Brett Favre Pass
Green Bay, WI 54304
Phone: (420) 499-6874
Fax: (420) 405-6896
www.brettfavressteakhouse.com

Note: Two blocks from Lambeau is the namesake restaurant of Green Bay's legendary quarterback. Also plays host to a pre-game tailgate party.

Stadium View Bar & Grill
1963 Holmgren Way
Green Bay, WI 54304
Phone: (420) 498-1989
www.thestadiumview.com

Note: Live music, outdoor tailgating, and general fun had by all Cheeseheads is a mere football throw from Lambeau. Open Sunday to Thursday from 10 A.M. to 2 A.M., and Friday and Saturday from 10 A.M. to 2:30 A.M.

Sideline Sports Bar and Grill
1049 Lombardi Access Road
Green Bay, WI 54304
Phone: (920) 496-5857
www.sideline-sportsbar.com

Note: As with any other establishment in the shadows of Lambeau, good food, cold beer, and lots of tailgating.

Champion's Sports Bar
1007 Tony Canadeo Run
Green Bay, WI 54304
Phone: (920) 544-8367

Note: Although it is a chain, this is another great area sports bar and restaurant on game day.

Airports:

Austin Straubel International Airport
2077 Airport Drive
Green Bay, WI 54313
Phone: (920) 498-4800
www.greenbayairport.org

General Mitchell International Airport (Milwaukee—consider it a second option)
5300 South Howell Avenue
Milwaukee, WI 53207
Phone: (414) 747-5300
www.mitchellairport.com

Sports Travel Insider's Edge:

Best way to watch the action:
In the lower rows of the end zone. The end zone is the place where a successful Packer touchdown is celebrated with the famed "Lambeau Leap." The player carrying the ball will vault himself into the Cheesehead faithful, who join in the celebration with public displays of affection and spilled beer.

Best place to get up close:
Try hanging out on Saturday night at Vince Lombardi's Steakhouse in the Radisson Paper Valley Hotel in Appleton. Former players, and even certain Lombardi family members, have been known to eat there the night before the game. It is also a favorite hotel amongst visiting teams.

Best travel tip:
Take a stadium tour or visit the Hall of Fame right inside the Packer Atrium at Lambeau Field. While outside watching the game, dress extremely warm. Don't forget to watch out for snowballs.

Notable Quotes:

"I think it was pretty close to 20-below. It was snowing—you could barely see past

15 yards. All you knew is coming out of the mist of the snow and the white mist, you would see the ball come out of the white. You knew what the route was and you knew the direction of the ball."—PRESTON DENNARD, former Green Bay Packers wide receiver

"Like the city of Green Bay (population 100,353), Lambeau Field appears far too small to house so much historical significance. There are no towering upper decks, just the original seating bowl surrounded by the red-brick veneer of a renovated exterior. A stadium this intimate can't possibly hold 72,615 fans, 12 NFL titles, and one of professional sports' most unique game-day experiences."—DOUG WARD, Special to ESPN SportsTravel

Relevant Websites:

www.ci.green-bay.wi.us
www.packers.com
www.packerfantours.com
www.tseworld.com
www.pcevents.com
www.sportstravel.com
www.gotickets.com
www.premieresports.com

30

CANADIENS VS. MAPLE LEAFS IN TORONTO

Where?

Air Canada Centre
40 Bay Street
Toronto, ON M5J 2X2, Canada

When?

Scheduled times during the NHL season, October to June.

Significance:

It's safe to say that the Montreal Canadiens and the Toronto Maple Leafs share the af-

fections of Canada's hockey fans. That following has translated into success for both teams. The Canadiens have the honor of having won the most Stanley Cups. Who is second? The Maple Leafs. However, the love for the teams does not translate into the teams loving each other. Their rivalry is as lengthy as it is bitter. Their battle is steeped in hatred and a spin-off of the rift between the English (Toronto) and the French-Canadians (Montreal).

In 1917, the NHL was formed and the Maple Leafs and Canadiens were born. The blood feud between cities could now be played out on the ice. Throughout the sixties, the teams traded Stanley Cups, except for 1961 and 1970. In 1967, they met in the Stanley Cup Finals. Toronto won in an upset. Realignment in the following season brought new NHL teams to Canada, slightly cooling the heat between the two rivals. They were reunited in the Eastern Conference's Northeast Division in 1998, which again fanned the flames of this heated rivalry. No matter whom they play, the Maple Leafs still enjoy a large national following in English Canada and reign as the top draw on Canadian sports television.

Who attends?

Fans of both teams who are hardly fans of each other. The tension is not just on the ice. Toronto has a large population of ex-Montreal residents due to the influx of English-speaking Quebec citizens who migrated to Toronto during the threatened Quebec separation.

How to get there?

From the (East): Highway 401 West to DVP South to Gardiner Expressway to Yonge Street exit. Go West on Lakeshore to York Street.

From the (West): QEW East to Gardiner Expressway toYork Street North.

If you are taking the subway, get off at Union Station.

Tickets:

For primary ticket access information, consider: mapleleafs.nhl.com.

For secondary ticket access, consider:

GoTickets, Inc.
2345 Waukegan Road, Suite 140
Bannockburn, IL 60015-1552
Toll-Free: 1-800-775-1617
Fax: (919) 481-9101
E-mail: sales@gotickets.com
www.gotickets.com

Accommodations:

Residence Inn Toronto Downtown/ Entertainment District
255 Wellington Street West
Toronto, ON M5V 3P9, Canada
Phone: (416) 581-1800
Fax: (416) 581-0255
Toll-Free: 1-800-MARRIOTT
www.marriott.com

Note: A short, three-minute drive to the Air Canada Centre.

SoHo Metropolitan Hotel
318 Wellington Street West
Toronto, ON M5V 3T4, Canada
Phone: (416) 599-8800
Fax: (416) 599-8801
Toll-Free: 1-866-SOHO-MET
www.metropolitan.com

Note: Touted on their website as "Toronto's finest, whether you call it a luxury, boutique, or designer hotel."

Suites at 1 King West
1 King Street West
Toronto, ON M5H 1A1, Canada
Phone: (416) 548-8100
Fax: (416) 548-8101
Toll-Free: 1-866-470-5464
www.onekingwest.com

Note: Walking distance to the arena, saving you a drive home if you had too many beers at the game. Reasonably priced.

Four Seasons Hotel
21 Avenue Road
Toronto, ON M5R 2G1, Canada
Phone: (416) 964-0411
Fax: (416) 964-2301
Toll-Free: 1-800-332-3442
www.fourseasons.com

Note: Offering some of the most luxurious guest rooms you will find in Toronto. Close to shopping, entertainment, and dining.

Park Hyatt Toronto
4 Avenue Road
Toronto, ON M5R 2E8, Canada
Phone: (416) 925-1234
Fax: (416) 924-4933
Toll-Free: 1-800-233-1234
www.parktoronto.hyatt.com

Note: Surrounded by high-end retail shops and five-star restaurants. Complimentary services include everything from free Internet to car service. Onsite, bistro-style restaurant.

Hazelton Toronto
118 Yorkville Avenue
Toronto, ON M5R 1C2, Canada
Phone: (416) 963-6300
Fax: (416) 963-6339
Toll-Free: 1-866-473-6301
www.thehazeltonhotel.com

Note: Considered one of the most exclusive five-star hotels in Toronto. Dine at ONE, the onsite restaurant by Mark McEwan.

On-Site Hospitality:

For business purposes and gatherings of family and friends, the Air Canada Centre Suites offer a great setting to watch the game and literally stay above the fray of the intense rivalry. Count on convenience, comfort, and exceptional service. Suites include theater-style seating, gourmet catering services, and an opportunity for a Maple Leaf alumni visit, even for Canadiens fans.

Fifty concession stands and bars fill the Air Canada Centre. A wide variety of food includes the traditional fare of pizza, hot dogs, popcorn, nachos, and pretzels. You can also enjoy hot-carved sandwiches, fresh cut fries, deluxe hamburgers, beef and chicken stir-fry, house-smoked barbecue pork sandwiches, and a variety of kosher foods. Healthier options include sushi, vegetarian paninis and stir-fry, salads, and pita with hummus and crudité.

In stadium dining:

Platinum Club
Phone: (416) 814-2582

Note: Fine dining with a professional trained staff waiting on you. Also, a 500-label wine list with Sommeliers to help you select the best.

Air Canada Club
Phone: (416) 814-2582

Note: Newly renovated with a design that features light oak tables and plush leather chairs for a classy dining experience.

Hot Stove Club
Phone: (416) 814-2582

Note: For dining and socializing, there are few better places for Hot Stove Club members.

Travel Packages:

If you are going to travel to this event, I would recommend using a reliable company to work with you on making the necessary arrangements. The suppliers listed in this book have solid references and are by far the most trusted in the business. Below are some of the organizations to try for this Top 100 Must See Sporting Event.

Premiere Corporate Events
14 Penn Plaza, Suite 925
New York, NY 10122
Phone: (212) 695-9480
Fax: (212) 564-8098
Toll-Free: 1-877-621-5243
E-mail: requests@tseworld.com
www.tseworld.com
www.pcevents.com

Premiere Sports Travel
201 Shannon Oaks Circle, Suite 205
Cary, NC 27511
Phone: (919) 481-9511
Fax: (919) 481-1337
Toll-Free: 1-800-924-9993
E-mail: sales@sportstravel.com
www.sportstravel.com

Dining:

Le Papillon On Front
69 Front Street East
Toronto, ON M5E 1M1, Canada
Phone: (416) 367-0303
www.lepapillon.ca

Note: Toronto Sun readers have voted Le Papillon as the most popular French restaurant for over eight consecutive years.

Tutti Matti
364 Adelaide Street West
Toronto, ON M5V 1R3, Canada
Phone: (416) 597-8839
www.tuttimatti.com

Note: Tuscan-style Italian restaurant that makes its own fresh breads and pastas on a daily basis.

Barberian's Steakhouse and Tavern
7 Elm Street
Toronto, ON M5G 1H1, Canada
Phone: (416) 597-0335
www.barberians.com

Note: Wood-paneled emporium where lots of steaks are served and martinis get poured.

Harbour 60
60 Harbour Street
Toronto, ON M5J 1B7, Canada
Phone: (416) 777-2111
www.harboursixty.com

Note: This fabulous steakhouse is located right next to the arena.

Ruth's Chris Steak House
145 Richmond Street West
Toronto, ON M5H 2L2, Canada

Phone: (416) 955-1455

www.ruthschris.com

Note: Enjoy appetizers, desserts, seafood, and, of course, USDA prime steaks broiled to perfection. Reservations can be made online.

Wayne Gretzky's

99 Blue Jays Way

Toronto, ON M5V 9G9, Canada

Phone: (416) 979-7825

www.gretzky.com

Note: While in Canada, why wouldn't you dine at the restaurant of one of the most famous hockey players in history? This museum-like restaurant caters to all sports fans!

Airport:

Toronto Pearson International Airport

P.O. Box 6031

3111 Convair Drive

Toronto AMF, ON L5P 1B2, Canada

www.torontoairport.com

Sports Travel Insider's Edge:

Best way to watch the action:

Real hockey fans in Toronto sit in the nosebleed seats in the upper levels. Enthusiasm reigns with fans draped in the Blue and White, as they cheer on their heroes and jeer opponents. Lower-level seats? You will get a great view but it will never match the energy of upstairs.

Best place to get up close:

See if you can get into the Platinum area close to the Platinum suites. There you can greet the players with high-fives, as they go on and off the ice to and from the dressing room area.

Best travel tip:

What kind of hockey fan would you be without a visit to the Hockey Hall of Fame? After watching history, relive even more

history of this great sport. In addition, it is only a three-minute walk from the ACC.

Notable Quotes:

"I've always liked playing in Toronto. It's a fun building. With Toronto, any night you play in their building, anything can happen. It could be close, a blowout, a tough fighting night, a skill night. It could be anything, so you have to always be ready for whatever game comes at you. In that building, in that atmosphere, I've played some teams in Toronto that were just flying out there because of the electricity."—MARTIN BIRON, Philadelphia Flyers goaltender

"In terms of overall history, it doesn't get any richer than the rivalry between the Montreal Canadiens and Toronto Maple Leafs. Back in the day, it meant much more than just the sweaters on the players' backs. It represented the duality of Canada's cultures—French and English—and the hopes of two great cities. Their regular season games were intense and passionate and their playoff games were—in a word—monumental."
—www.tsn.ca

Relevant Websites:

mapleleafs.nhl.com

www.theaircanadacentre.com

www.torontotourism.com

www.ticketmaster.com

www.tseworld.com

www.pcevents.com

www.sportstravel.com

www.gotickets.com

www.premieresports.com

31

INDY 500

Where?

Indianapolis Motor Speedway
4790 West 16th Street
Indianapolis, IN 46222

When?

Held annually on Memorial Day weekend.

Significance:

"The Greatest Spectacle in Racing" carries with it a rich history in the venue of motor sport events. The Indianapolis 500 boasts one of the largest attendances and highest television and radio ratings of any single-day sporting event on a nationwide basis. While it is televised live throughout the nation on ABC, local residents must attend the event to see it as the network blacks it out in the immediate area. The Indy 500 attracts well over a quarter-million casual fans and race enthusiasts each year. It has enjoyed over ninety runnings for the coveted Borg-Warner Trophy.

Who attends?

While national in its scope, with fans attending from around the country, the Indianapolis 500 is truly a community event for the residents of Indianapolis. Families from throughout the area attend, as there is something for all ages. Kids see their favorite costumed cartoon characters and adults cheer on their favorite Indy racers. There is nothing like actually being there for this event.

How to get there?

Located just minutes from the Indianapolis International Airport, the Indianapolis Motor Speedway can be found on the West Side of Indianapolis. I-465 to Crawfordsville Road will get you to 4790 West 16th Street.

Tickets:

For primary ticket access information, consider: www.indy500.com.

For secondary ticket access, consider:

GoTickets, Inc.
2345 Waukegan Road, Suite 140
Bannockburn, IL 60015-1552
Toll-Free: 1-800-775-1617
Fax: (919) 481-9101
E-mail: sales@gotickets.com
www.gotickets.com

Accommodations:

Hilton Indianapolis

120 West Market Street
Indianapolis, IN 46204
Phone: (317) 972-0600
Fax: (317) 972-0660
www.hilton.com

Note: AAA 3-star property is pet friendly with 332 rooms. Conveniently located near major attractions throughout Indianapolis. Onsite eateries include McCormick & Schmick's and 120 West Market Restaurant.

Sheraton Indianapolis Hotel and Suites

8787 Keystone Crossing
Indianapolis, IN 46240
Phone: (317) 846-2700
Fax: (317) 574-6775
www.starwoodhotels.com

Note: Two twelve-story towers with 560 rooms close to sporting attractions, cultural events, and the Fashion Mall.

Conrad Indianapolis

50 West Washington Street
Indianapolis, IN 46204
Phone: (317) 713-5000
Fax: (317) 638-3687
Toll-Free: 1-800-HHONORS
www.conradindianapolis.com

Note: At one of the city's prominent intersec-

tions at Washington and Illinois. Conrad Indianapolis provides access by walkway to the Artsgarden and Circle Centre Mall. Twenty-three stories house 241 guest rooms.

Canterbury Hotel
123 South Illinois Street
Indianapolis, IN 46225
Phone: (317) 634-3000
Fax: (317) 685-2519
Toll-Free: 1-800-538-8186
www.canterburyhotel.com
Note: European, boutique-style hotel located in downtown Indianapolis. The ninety-nine guest suites include five bi-level penthouse suites and one Presidential suite. Look for your chocolate truffle left on your pillow when available.

On-Site Hospitality and Events:
There is food aplenty at the Indy 500. Hot dogs, shish kabob, funnel cakes, turkey legs, polish sausage, and barbecue will fill you up. A bucket of fried chicken remains a popular and economic choice as well. Soda and beer (from Busch Light to Fosters) is available to wash down the edibles. Do not be surprised to see grills in the infield where people cook burgers and even entire lambs. Local grocery stores as well as the Speedway itself have box lunches available.

Corporate Hospitality accommodations are available at:

The Pavilion
North Chalet
East Chalet
Legends Row
Gasoline Alley Suites

The Indy 500 also has annual traditions within its own annual tradition, including:

The IPL 500 Festival Parade:
An Indianapolis 500 mainstay that has launched the festivities for over fifty years, the parade will attract 300,000 racing fans.

With the thirty-three starting drivers serving as honorary grand marshals, floats, marching bands, giant helium-filled balloons, and famed costumed characters fill the streets. Don't forget the Character Breakfast for your kids that starts prior to the event.

Breakfast at the Brickyard, a.k.a. Mayors Breakfast:
The mayor of Indianapolis joins the public in honoring past mayors of the Hoosier city. In addition, the Festival Princesses find out which one of them will be crowned the 500 Festival Queen. The event also features a notable keynote speaker. Individual reserved seating is around sixty dollars with tables of ten seated together available for a little more per person.

American Family Insurance 500 Festival Community Day:
All-access day means access to the Indianapolis Motor Speedway. Suite and race control tours will take you throughout the Speedway, including the legendary Gasoline Alley and the Hall of Fame Museum. With your very own vehicle, your family can drive the actual 2.5-mile oval track. Admission is under ten dollars with children six and under usually admitted for free.

Additional events include *Carb Day* (the last practice on the Friday before the race), the *Pro Series* (100-mile race), and an annual impromptu party along Georgetown Road.

Travel Packages:
If you are going to travel to the race, I would recommend using a reliable company to work with you on making the necessary arrangements. The suppliers listed in this book have solid references and are by far the most trusted in the business. Below are some of the organizations to try for this 100 Must See Sporting Event.

Premiere Corporate Events
14 Penn Plaza, Suite 925
New York, NY 10122
Phone: (212) 695-9480
Fax: (212) 564-8098
Toll-Free: 1-877-621-5243
E-mail: requests@tseworld.com
www.tseworld.com
www.pcevents.com

Premiere Sports Travel
201 Shannon Oaks Circle, Suite 205
Cary, NC 27511
Phone: (919) 481-9511
Fax: (919) 481-1337
Toll-Free: 1-800-924-9993
E-mail: sales@sportstravel.com
www.sportstravel.com

Dining:

St. Elmo's Steak House
127 South Illinois Street
Indianapolis, IN 46225
Phone: (317) 635-0636
Fax: (317) 687-9162
www.stelmos.com

Note: As a downtown landmark since 1902, this steakhouse has earned national praise for its steaks, seafood, chops, and high level of service. The first restaurant anyone mentions when discussing Indianapolis dining.

Harry and Izzy's
153 South Illinois Street
Indianapolis, IN 46225
Phone: (317) 635-9594
Fax: (317) 635-9599
www.harryandizzys.com

Note: The founders of St. Elmo's established a restaurant with a more casual environment for their customers while maintaining the quality of the food and service.

Oceanaire
30 South Meridian Street
Indianapolis, IN 46204

Phone: (317) 955-2277
Fax: (317) 955-2278
www.theoceanaire.com

Note: Fresh seafood is flown in daily from around the world. New menus are printed for lunch and dinner every day to accommodate those different choices.

Six Lounge & Restaurant
247 South Meridian Street
Indianapolis, IN 46204
Phone: (317) 638-6660
www.6indy.com

Note: Ideal for private parties. Food is provided by Chef Tyler and music is provided by their resident DJ, which made this lounge and restaurant a unique and exciting experience. Open seven days a week.

Capital Grille, The Conrad Hotel
50 West Washington Street
Indianapolis, IN 46204
Phone: (317) 423-8790
Fax: (317) 423-8797
www.thecapitalgrille.com

Note: The place to go for dry-aged steaks and fresh seafood that is flown in daily. Choose from their award-winning collection of over 400 wines.

Mikado
148 South Illinois Street
Indianapolis, IN 46225
Phone: (317) 972-4180
Fax: (317) 972-4191
www.mikadoindy.com

Note: Well-known for their sushi and other great Japanese cuisine.

Dunaway's
351 South East Street
Indianapolis, IN 46204
Phone: (317) 638-7663
Fax: (317) 638-7677
www.dunaways.com

Note: Enjoy rooftop dining when the weather allows for it.

Mug-N-Bun Drive-In

5211 West 10th Street
Indianapolis, IN 46224
Phone: (317) 244-5669
www.mug-n-bun.com

Note: Classic drive-in atmosphere and old-school diner food. Root beer is brewed onsite.

Union Jack Pub

924 Broad Ripple Avenue
Indianapolis, IN 46220
Phone: (317) 257-4343
www.unionjackpub-broadripple.com

Note: Many of the drivers, crews, and officials hang out here. The highlight is the hundreds of driver's helmets that adorn the wall. Definitely try the pizza that they're known for.

Airport:

Indianapolis International Airport

2500 South High School Road
Indianapolis, IN 46241
(317) 487-7243
www.indianapolisairport.com

Sports Travel Insider's Edge:

Best way to watch the action:
No seat will provide you a full view of the entire track, so watching can be a struggle from time to time. JumboTron video screens will keep you up on the action. The "E" Penthouse is located at the entrance to turn one and provides a view of the entire straightaway. Hospitality suites are the way to go. They provide an infield vantage point of the front stretch, allowing fortunate spectators the best seat in the house. Then again, the event is about the overall experience and not just the race.

Best place to get up close:
Attend Carb Day the Friday before the Indianapolis 500. It's the last practice for the Indy cars before the race and always a blast.

Best travel tip:
With so many in attendance, get to the track early to beat the crowds and soak up the event's ambience. I would advise being in your seat about ninety minutes prior to the start of the event just to see all of the pageantry and pre-race events. And it would not be the Indy 500 if you did not purchase and wear an Indy 500 shirt customized with the name and number of your favorite driver.

Notable Quote:

"Stay tuned to the Greatest Spectacle in Racing."—ALICE GREENE, the copywriter who coined the famous phrase

Relevant Websites:

www.indy500.com
www.indy.com
www.tseworld.com
www.pcevents.com
www.sportstravel.com
www.gotickets.com
www.premieresports.com

32

PROFESSIONAL BULL RIDERS WORLD FINALS

Where?

Thomas & Mack Center
UNLV
4505 South Maryland Parkway
Las Vegas, NV 89154

When?

Every year from late October to early November.

Significance:

There are some exceptions to the oft-used phrase, "What happens in Vegas stays in Vegas." The annual Professional Bull Riders

World Finals event is one of them. Cowboys from PBR membership countries, the United States, Canada, Brazil, Australia, and Mexico, descend upon Sin City every year to take home the top prize.

In 1992, twenty professional bull riders put their "cattle heads" together and contributed $1,000 each to start the PBR. Today, the organization oversees 100 events in four tours annually with prize money valued at over $10 million. Quite a hike from the initial purse of $250,000. Over 16 million fans a year watch or attend a PBR event.

This is not your daddy's bull riding show. The current tour, Built Tough Ford Series, encompasses thirty-one events nationwide. Loud music, fireworks, and other special events kick off the show's riders. The goal of each rider is to stay on a snorting, bucking bull for eight seconds and show some technique while trying to stay on top of the animal. Points are given for the rider's and bull's performances and the highest point total wins. They go on to Vegas for bull riding supremacy.

Who attends?
Cowboys, cowboy-hopefuls, and people wearing cowboy hats from around the world.

How to get there?
On the corner of Tropicana and Swenson. Not far from the strip and easily accessible from I-15 (South), I-95 (South), and Las Vegas Boulevard.

Tickets:
For primary ticket access information, consider: www.pbrnow.com.

For secondary ticket access, consider:

GoTickets, Inc.
2345 Waukegan Road, Suite 140
Bannockburn, IL 60015-1552

Toll-Free: 1-800-775-1617
Fax: (919) 481-9101
E-mail: sales@gotickets.com
www.gotickets.com

Accommodations:

Mandalay Bay
3950 Las Vegas Boulevard South
Las Vegas, NV 89119
Phone: (702) 632-7777
Fax: (702) 632-7234
Toll-Free: 1-877-632-7800
www.mandalaybay.com

Note: Host hotel for the PBR World Finals. Touted as a hotel for the truly one-of-a-kind vacationer or business traveler. Add bull rider to that list.

Gold Coast Casino
4000 West Flamingo Road
Las Vegas, NV 89103
Phone: (702) 367-7111
Fax: (702) 367-8575
Toll-Free: 1-888-402-6278
www.goldcoastcasino.com

Note: A hotel with a Spanish flair located one mile from the Strip. Close to Chinatown and sister hotels, The Orleans and Bills Gamblin' Hall and Saloon (formerly Barbary Coast).

Golden Nugget
129 East Fremont Street
Las Vegas, NV 89101
Phone: (702) 385-7111
Fax: (702) 386-6970
Toll-Free: 1-800-846-5336
www.goldennugget.com

Note: A popular destination and old school Vegas hotel since 1977. This casino and high-rise hotel is just eight miles from the airport.

Luxor
3900 Las Vegas Boulevard South
Las Vegas, NV 89119
Phone: (702) 262-4444
Fax: (702) 262-0404

Toll-Free: 1-800-288-1000
www.luxor.com

Note: A unique, pyramid-shape design with a Sphinx replica that goes with the overall Egyptian theme.

The Mirage
3400 Las Vegas Boulevard South
Las Vegas, NV 89109
Phone: (702) 791-7111
Fax: (702) 791-7446
Toll-Free: 1-800-374-9000
www.themirage.com

Note: They boast a South Seas vibe combined with Strip excitement. A popular hotel and casino found in the heart of Las Vegas.

Excalibur Hotel and Casino
3850 Las Vegas Boulevard South
Las Vegas, NV 89109
Phone: (702) 597-7777
Fax: (702) 597-7009
Toll-Free: 1-877-750-5464
www.excalibur.com

Note: Medieval themes inspired by Camelot with four towers, castle gates, and spires of varying colors. I can't make this stuff up!

Las Vegas Hilton
3000 Paradise Road
Las Vegas, NV 89109
Phone: (702) 732-5111
Toll-Free: 1-888-732-7117
www.lvhilton.com

Note: Luxurious hotel with world-class entertainment options and a 40,000 square-foot casino. For the younger lot or the kid in all of us, they boast the city's best video arcade.

MGM Grand
3799 Las Vegas Boulevard South
Las Vegas, NV 89109
Phone: (702) 891-1111
Toll-Free: 1-877-880-0880
www.mgmgrand.com

Note: One of the best known Las Vegas hotels

and casinos. Iconic and part of Sin City history. The largest hotel in the world.

The Venetian Resort Hotel Casino
3355 Las Vegas Boulevard South
Las Vegas, NV 89109
Phone: (702) 414-1000
Fax: (702) 414-1100
Toll-Free: 1-877-883-6423
www.venetian.com

Note: An all-suite hotel providing luxury and comfort after a long day of bull riding. Canyon Ranch SpaClub onsite offers a great spa escape.

Treasure Island
3300 Las Vegas Boulevard South
Las Vegas, NV 89109
Phone: (702) 894-7111
Fax: (702) 894-7414
Toll-Free: 1-800-944-7444
www.treasureisland.com

Note: A More affordable Strip hotel with a little something for everyone.

On-Site Hospitality:
PBR Fan Zone and Marketplace: 180,000 square feet of live entertainment, interactive displays, and vendors selling Western merchandise. Open daily.

In addition, the week and weekend of the Bull Riders World Finals are chock-full of events that usually include:

Texas Hold'em Poker Tournament
The Founders Celebration
PBR After Party
PBR World Finals Awards Party
Autograph Sessions

Check out www.pbrnow.com for the most up-to-date list of fun and exciting onsite events and locations.

Travel Packages:
If you are going to travel to this event, I would recommend using a reliable compa-

ny to work with you on making the necessary arrangements. The suppliers listed in this book have solid references and are by far the most trusted in the business. Below are some of the organizations to try for this Top 100 Must See Sporting Event.

Premiere Corporate Events

14 Penn Plaza, Suite 925
New York, NY 10122
Phone: (212) 695-9480
Fax: (212) 564-8098
Toll-Free: 1-877-621-5243
E-mail: requests@tseworld.com
www.tseworld.com
www.pcevents.com

Premiere Sports Travel

201 Shannon Oaks Circle, Suite 205
Cary, NC 27511
Phone: (919) 481-9511
Fax: (919) 481-1337
Toll-Free: 1-800-924-9993
E-mail: sales@sportstravel.com
www.sportstravel.com

Dining:

Aqua Knox

3355 South Las Vegas Boulevard
Las Vegas, NV 89109
Phone: (702) 414-3772
Fax: (702) 414-3872
www.aquaknox.net

Note: Great place to get seafood if you don't mind paying a bit more.

Joe's

3500 South Las Vegas Boulevard
Las Vegas, NV 89109
Phone: (702) 792-9222
Fax: (702) 369-8384
www.icon.com/joes

Note: Seasonal seafood offerings from around the world with carry-out and children's menus.

Red Square

3950 Las Vegas Boulevard South
Las Vegas, NV 89119
Phone: (702) 632-7777
Fax: (702) 632-7234
Toll-Free: 1-877-632-7000
www.mandalaybay.com

Note: Pricey but great food, with a selection of over 100 different kinds of vodka.

Baja Beach Café

2400 North Rancho Drive
Las Vegas, NV 89130
Phone: (702) 631-7000
Toll-Free: 1-800-731-7333

Note: Great food with even greater values, including the Fiesta Burger and fries for only $2.99!

Blondie's Sports Bar & Grill at Miracle Mile Shops

Planet Hollywood Resort and Casino
3663 Las Vegas Boulevard
Las Vegas, NV 89109
Phone: (702) 737-0444

Note: Like most places in Las Vegas, a famous New York bar opens in the desert. Traditional bar menu with great appetizers and entrées.

Airport:

McCarran International Airport-Las Vegas

5757 Wayne Newton Boulevard
Las Vegas, NV 89119
Phone: (702) 261-5211
www.mccarran.com

Sports Travel Insider's Edge:

Best way to watch the action:
When you order your tickets, let the box office know that you want a seat close to the bucking chutes. Do the same if you use a travel package provider for an all-inclusive package. The chutes located at each end of the arena are where you will witness the

most action you've ever seen within two and a half hours.

Best place to get up close:
The Fan Zone gets you up close and personal with a meet and greet with all Team PBR members. In addition, you get the John Hancocks of forty-five riders competing in the World Finals at the autograph session. If you're not a member, call (719) 242-2800 ext. 3809, or visit www.teampbr.com for more information.

Best travel tip:
If you are a bull riding purist or are just not interested in seeing all the flash, wait for the second weekend of this two-weekend event. The finals and the crowning of the PBR champion are just two of this weekend's major events.

Notable Quotes:
"It's our job to find the very best bull riders in the world and let them showcase their sport to the fans."—RANDY BERNARD, PBR Chief Executive Officer

"To witness this event is to be able to say that you have seen one of the wonders of the modern world. This year's PBR World Finals saw the championship come down to the very final ride of the very last round and was not without some controversy."—RICK ROSEN, columnist

"For all those who've ever slowed to gawk at the sight of an automobile accident and then replayed it actually happening in their mind there is Pro Bull Riding."—RICK ROSEN

Relevant Websites:
www.pbrnow.com
www.unlvtickets.com
www.teampbr.com
www.lasvegas24hours.com
www.tseworld.com

www.pcevents.com
www.sportstravel.com
www.gotickets.com
www.premieresports.com

33
DUBAI WORLD CUP

Where?
Dubai Racing Club
Nad Al Sheba Racecourse
Dubai, United Arab Emirates

When?
Annually in late March.

Significance:
The annual, invitation-only, flat racing thoroughbred horse race spans a distance of 2,000 meters, 10 furlongs, on the state-of-the-art Nad Al-Sheba Racecourse. The Dubai World Cup was created by Sheikh Mohammed bin Rashid Al Maktoum. The Sheikh is not only the ruler of Dubai, but also the owner of the world's leading thoroughbred breeding and racing operation, Darley Stud & Godolphin Racing. Since its inception in 1996, the Dubai World Cup has become the world's richest horse race with runners competing from twelve different countries. Jockeys vie for a multi-million-dollar purse in a Group 1 flat race on dirt for Northern Hemisphere thoroughbred four-year-olds and up and for Southern Hemisphere thoroughbred three-year-olds and up. All totaled, the seven-race purse exceeds $21 million. The race is operated by the Emirates Horse Racing Authority (EHRA), whose chairman is Sheikh Mansour bin Zayed Al Nahyan, Dubai's Minister of Presidential Affairs.

Who attends?
Horse-racing aficionados meet fashion trendsetters. While the horses vie for the

Cup, the attendees compete in the BurJuman Style Stakes. Awards include "Best Dressed Lady," "Best Dressed Couple," and "Best Hat" events. Every year, the competitive spirit among the well-dressed rivals that of the jockeys. The competition grows more intense among style-conscious men, women, and couples.

Tickets:

For primary ticket access information, consider: www.dubairacingclub.com.

For secondary ticket access, consider:

GoTickets, Inc.
2345 Waukegan Road, Suite 140
Bannockburn, IL 60015-1552
Toll-Free: 1-800-775-1617
Fax: (919) 481-9101
E-mail: sales@gotickets.com
www.gotickets.com

Accommodations:

Madinat Jumeirahh
Al Sufouh Road
Dubai, United Arab Emirates
Phone: +971 (4) 366 8888
Fax: +971 (4) 366 7788
www.madinatjumeirah.com
Note: Provides a beautiful view of the Arabian Gulf, which complements the overall motif of the hotel.

Le Royal Méridien Beach Resort & Spa
Sheikh Zayed Road
Dubai, United Arab Emirates
Phone: +971 (4) 399 5555
www.leroyalmeridien-dubai.com
Note: Facing the Arabian Gulf on the Jumeirahh strip, this beachfront hotel is set in lush and beautiful tropical gardens.

Grosvenor House West Marina Beach by Le Méridien
Sheikh Zayed Road

Dubai, United Arab Emirates
Phone: +971 (4) 399 8888
www.grosvenorhouse-dubai.com
Note: Few locations provide a better view of a colorful Dubai sunset.

On-Site Hospitality:

Dubai Restaurant: With a glass front, this restaurant boasts an elevated view of the track and several television screens to watch the race. The pre-selected four-course table d'hôte (host table) menu provides multicourse meals charged at a fixed price. An array of soft drinks, beer, wine, and regular spirits is provided as well.

Millennium Views: A three-course international dinner buffet awaits patrons. Grandstand terrace seating is available, providing one of the best views of the race.

The Bubbly Lounge: Where else would you enjoy a glass of champagne while watching the horses?

International Village: A large garden area provides the best in Mexican, Japanese, Indian, and Italian cuisine for those attending the race.

Breakfast With the Stars: During morning track work, you can witness celebrity interviews with top guests and those in the equine field. A lavish breakfast buffet is served on the paddock lawns.

Oasis Village: Featuring open-fronted Arabic-style marquees with a bar for beverage service and a private garden, the Oasis Village provides informal facilities for groups of up to forty. Jebel Ali International Hotels offer afternoon tea and gourmet canapés.

Infield Pavilions: Private entrances and gardens with shaded seating are located at the entry of these air-conditioned pavilions furnished with dining tables and a private bar. Dining options include a buffet dinner, tea, and other beverages.

Travel Packages:

If you are going to travel to this event, I would recommend using a reliable company to work with you on making the necessary arrangements. The suppliers listed in this book have solid references and are by far the most trusted in the business. Below are some of the organizations to try for this Top 100 Must See Sporting Event.

Premiere Corporate Events
14 Penn Plaza, Suite 925
New York, NY 10122
Phone: (212) 695-9480
Fax: (212) 564-8098
Toll-Free: 1-877-621-5243
E-mail: requests@tseworld.com
www.tseworld.com
www.pcevents.com

Premiere Sports Travel
201 Shannon Oaks Circle, Suite 205
Cary, NC 27511
Phone: (919) 481-9511
Fax: (919) 481-1337
Toll-Free: 1-800-924-9993
E-mail: sales@sportstravel.com
www.sportstravel.com

Dining:

Shabestan
Radisson SAS Hotel, Dubai Deira Creek
Dubai, United Arab Emirates
Phone: +971 (4) 222 7171
Note: Classic Persian cuisine with freshly baked bread.

Fish Market
Radisson SAS Hotel, Dubai Deira Creek
Dubai, United Arab Emirates
Phone: +971 (4) 222 7171
Note: Dine on fresh seafood prepared by Southeast Asian chefs while enjoying a view of the Creek.

Al Mahara
Burj-al-Arab Hotel
Dubai, United Arab Emirates
Phone: +971 (4) 301 7600
www.burj-al-arab.com
Note: Known for their delicious seafood dishes.

Jules Bar
Le Meridien Hotel
Airport Road
Dubai, United Arab Emirates
Phone: +971 (4) 331 3555
Note: Enjoy tasty Mexican snacks.

The China Club
Dubai Inter Continental
Dubai, United Arab Emirates
Phone: +971 (4) 222 7171
www.dubai.intercontinental.com
Note: Fine food prepared by Chinese master chefs in a beautiful facility with great service.

Capri Grill
Hilton Trade Apartments
Dubai, United Arab Emirates
Phone: +971 (4) 331 4505
Note: Pasta, pizza, and lasagna are but a few Italian dishes served at this Italian eatery located at Hilton Trade Apartments.

Al Qasr Lebanese Restaurant
Dubai Marine Beach Club
Dubai, United Arab Emirates
Phone: +971 (4) 304 8101
Note: Food prepared by a chef before your eyes. Excellent service and plenty of seating.

Airport:

Dubai International Airport
P.O. Box 2525
Dubai, United Arab Emirates
Phone: + 971 (4) 216 2525
www.dubaiairport.com

Sports Travel Insider's Edge:

Best way to watch the action:
Watch the race from the Dubai Restaurant. You get an elevated view to see the race through the glass front and multiple tele-

visions screens for what you cannot see. Gorge on a four-course meal from a pre-selected menu charged at a fixed price.

Best place to get up close:
Get up close during the morning of the race. Professionals in the industry and celebrities are interviewed for their insight. You can see it all while enjoying the breakfast buffet on the paddock lawn.

Best travel tip:
Simply put, "dress to impress," and not just for the contest. National dress/lounge suits for men, and fashionable attire and extravagant hats for women. While casual dress is permitted in public enclosures, jeans and shorts are not allowed in hospitality areas.

Notable Quotes:
"It's extremely important, because not only is the purse so large, but they attract the best horses from all over the world."—RICHARD ENG, *Las Vegas Review Journal* horse racing columnist

"I think this is an extraordinary place. Every time I come here, the city changes and it's very interesting."—HIROYOSHI MATSUDA, trainer

"This is an unbelievable experience and I can't explain it. This is at the very top of the list."—ROBBY ALBARADO, jockey

Relevant Websites:
www.dubaiworldcup.com
www.dubairacingclub.com
www.tseworld.com
www.pcevents.com
www.sportstravel.com
www.gotickets.com
www.premieresports.com

34
HONG KONG SEVENS

Where?
Hong Kong Stadium, Hong Kong

When?
End of March every year.

Significance:
On March 28, 1976, Korea, Australia, New Zealand, Tonga, Japan, Sri Lanka, Malaysia, and Fiji descended upon Hong Kong for the first Hong Kong Sevens tournament. One year prior, it was merely a discussion topic over drinks between A. D. C. "Tokkie" Smith, the chairman of the Hong Kong Rugby Football Union, and Ian Gow, a tobacco company executive.

The Hong Kong Sevens is the premier rugby tournament and "jewel in the crown" in the IRB Sevens World Series. The tournament lasts two and a half days with the best rugby players facing off as their fans party until all hours. As the years went on, the Hong Kong Sevens tournament continued to grow in prominence and popularity. By 1994, the Hong Kong Government Stadium had to be rebuilt and now holds 40,000 enthusiastic and sometimes raucous rugby fans.

To say that the Hong Kong Sevens is a party atmosphere may be an understatement. Some contend that it resembles Mardi Gras in New Orleans. The party never ends with fans carousing everywhere from the bleachers in the stadiums to the streets of Hong Kong, chugging beer, throwing the pitchers, and perhaps getting in a bit of streaking. How ironic is it that the concept for this event was devised over drinks?

Who attends?
The games are major events on the Hong Kong sporting calendar. Well-dressed rugby fans crowd the South Stand and the party starts with dancing for most of the day. In

fact, the Hong Kong Sevens typically draws the largest crowd and is considered the biggest party on the IRB Sevens calendar.

How to get there?
The best way to get to Hong Kong Stadium is via public transportation. A bus, ferry, or train is an efficient way to get to the arena, not to mention inexpensive and user-friendly for all. Signs are posted in English and Chinese.

Tickets:
For primary ticket access information, consider: www.hksevens.com.

In addition, tickets are assigned to all Hong Kong Rugby Football Union (HKRFU) member clubs and HKRFU stakeholders first.

For secondary ticket access, consider:

GoTickets, Inc.
2345 Waukegan Road, Suite 140
Bannockburn, IL 60015-1552
Toll-Free: 1-800-775-1617
Fax: (919) 481-9101
E-mail: sales@gotickets.com
www.gotickets.com

Accommodations:

Lanson Place Hotel
133 Leighton Road
Causeway Bay, Hong Kong
Phone: +852 3477 6888
Fax: +852 3477 6999
www.lansonplace.com
Note: A popular hotel with fans and it's within walking/dancing distance from the stadium.

Metropark Hotel Caseway Bay, Hong Kong
148 Tung Lo Wan Road
Causeway Bay, Hong Kong
Phone: +852 2600 1000
Fax: +852 2600 1111
www.metroparkhotel.com
Note: Conveniently located in the commercial, shopping, and entertainment district.

Rosedale on the Park
8 Shelter Street
Causeway Bay, Hong Kong
Phone: +852 2127 8888
Fax: +852 2127 3333
www.rosedale.com.hk
Note: In the heart of Causeway Bay and walking distance to the Mass Transit Railway Station.

The Excelsior-Hong Kong
281 Gloucester Road
Causeway Bay, Hong Kong
Phone: +852 2894 8888
Fax: +852 2895 6459
www.excelsiorhongkong.com
Note: A historic hotel standing on Lot No. 1, the very first plot of land sold at auction when Hong Kong became a British Colony in 1841. Boasts a spectacular view of Victoria Harbour.

The Park Lane
310 Gloucester Road
Causeway Bay, Hong Kong
Phone: +852 2293 8888
Fax: +852 2576 7853
www.parklane.com.hk
Note: Touted as a luxurious and first-class hotel located five minutes from the stadium with spectacular views of Victoria Park and Hong Kong Harbour.

On-Site Hospitality:
Hospitality has been known to change from year to year. Go to www.hksevens.com for the latest in what the Hong Kong Rugby Football Union is offering onsite.

Travel Packages:
If you are going to travel to this event, I would recommend using a reliable company to work with you on making the necessary arrangements. The suppliers listed in this book have solid references and are by far the most trusted in the business. Below

are some of the organizations to try for this Top 100 Must See Sporting Event.

Premiere Corporate Events

14 Penn Plaza, Suite 925
New York, NY 10122
Phone: (212) 695-9480
Fax: (212) 564-8098
Toll-Free: 1-877-621-5243
E-mail: requests@tseworld.com
www.tseworld.com
www.pcevents.com

Premiere Sports Travel
201 Shannon Oaks Circle, Suite 205
Cary, NC 27511
Phone: (919) 481-9511
Fax: (919) 481-1337
Toll-Free: 1-800-924-9993
E-mail: sales@sportstravel.com
www.sportstravel.com

Dining:

Tsui Hang Village Restaurant
2/F, New World Tower
16-18 Queen's Road Central
Central, Hong Kong
Phone: +852 2524 2012
Fax: +852 2524 7020

Note: A Silver Award-winning restaurant for best all-around Chinese Food. Located about nine minutes from the stadium.

Jade Garden
1/F, 1 Hysan Avenue, Causeway Bay
Tsim Sha Tsui, Kowloon
Phone: +852 2577 9332

Note: Another Silver Award winner. Their menu includes Cantonese food in a restaurant two minutes from the stadium.

Star Seafood Restaurant
294-296 King's Road
North Point, Hong Kong
Phone: +852 2918 9828
Fax: +852 2918 9668

Note: Earned a Gold with Distinction Award for signature Hong Kong dishes. Ten minutes from the stadium.

Tai Woo Restaurant
G/F, 27 Percival Street
Causeway Bay, Hong Kong
Phone: +852 2893 0822
Fax: +852 2891 9564
www.taiwoorestaurant.com

Note: A Gold with Distinction Award was given for signature Hong Kong dishes.

Shanghai Garden
1/F, Hutchison House, 10 Harcourt Road
Central, Hong Kong
Phone: +852 2524 8181
Fax: +852 2596 0733

Note: Yet another Gold Award was given for their Shanghainese-style Chinese food.

Airport:

Hong Kong International Airport
HKIA Tower
1 Sky Plaza Road
Lantau, Hong Kong
Phone: +852 2181 8888
www.hongkongairport.com

Sports Travel Insider's Edge:

Best way to watch the action:
The legendary South Stand is not for those looking for a quiet and relaxing time while out and about in Hong Kong. They dress up and even wear costumes that honor everyone from cheerleaders to the Ghostbusters. Alcohol fuels the friendliness of many fans, but it can also create a rather raucous and boisterous environment. Just watch out for flying beer pitchers and the occasional streaker/naked Ghostbuster.

Best place to get up close:
You should note that while in town, based on the locale, expect England and Hong Kong to be the hometown favorites. China

will get a mixed reception. Because of the heavy British attendance, expect Australia and New Zealand to be treated like villains with boos and hisses, but not as much as France. Smaller nations such as Fiji and Samoa are popular, as are the underdogs from the United States and Canada.

Best travel tip:

While planning your trip to Hong Kong, definitely try to extend your stay and visit mainland China. If you can make it to Beijing, you can take in all the historic sites left over from the 2008 Olympic Games. Also, for some great gambling try Macau, which is just a short ferry ride away from Hong Kong. You can even make it a day trip.

Notable Quotes:

"It's unbelievable. I loved every minute of it. That is the best atmosphere I have ever experienced. The English support is fantastic."—BEN RUSSELL, Saracens

"Rugby is just a sideshow for the South Stand spectators, who concentrate on drinking, dancing, and throwing beer jugs at each other. Outrageous fancy-dress is virtually compulsory, with this year's favorite outfits being air stewardesses and French maids—and that was just the men."—Agence France-Presse (AFP) story

Relevant Websites:

www.hksevens.com
www.discoverhongkong.com
www.tseworld.com
www.pcevents.com
www.sportstravel.com
www.gotickets.com
www.premieresports.com

35

MONACO GRAND PRIX

Where?

Circuit de Monaco, the streets of Monte Carlo and La Condamine.

When?

One weekend every May.

Significance:

Since 1929, car racers have navigated the roads of Monte Carlo and La Condamine in the Monaco Grand Prix (Grand Prix de Monaco), a Formula One race held annually on the Circuit de Monaco. The prestige of the race is akin to the Indianapolis 500 and 24 Hours of LeMans. All three of those races make up the Triple Crown of Motorsport with the Monte Carlo Grand Prix serving as the jewel of that crown.

Drivers race on a narrow course that goes through the streets of Monte Carlo, complete with tight turns and changes in elevation. Grand Prix de Monaco is considered the most demanding track in Formula One Racing. On average, the speeds are lower, but that does not lessen the element of danger. Racers have compared it to riding a bike or helicopter in a living room. Careful navigation is required. The smallest of errors can be deadly.

Racing fans and local residents look forward to the Monaco Grand Prix. Six weeks of preparation goes into readying the track. A large part of Monte Carlo's annual income comes from the tourists who visit the country to see the race. Those tourists are usually welcomed with open arms, a friendly smile, and a pat on the back.

Who attends?

Racing fans meet the rich and famous in a beautiful setting.

How to get there?

Driving is not a good idea since parking is limited at best, and Monte Carlo is perched on a cliff with many hills to negotiate for even the most experienced driver. A Monaco-Monte Carlo train for day-to-day travel is highly recommended. Most people take the train via the Nice station. Five permanent bus routes are available, including Monte-Carlo to Saint Roman, Monte-Carlo to Exotic Garden, Monte-Carlo to Larvotto beaches, Railway station to Fontvieille Hospital, and Larvotto beaches to Fontvieille.

Tickets:

For primary ticket access information, consider:

Automobile Club de Monaco

23 Boulevard Albert 1er
Monaco, 98000
Phone: +377 9315 2600
www.acm.mc

For secondary ticket access, consider:

GoTickets, Inc.

2345 Waukegan Road, Suite 140
Bannockburn, IL 60015-1552
Toll-Free: 1-800-775-1617
Fax: (919) 481-9101
E-mail: sales@gotickets.com
www.gotickets.com

Accommodations:

Hotel de France

6 rue de la Turbie
Monaco, 98000
Phone: +377 9330 2464
Fax: +377 9216 1334
www.monte-carlo.mc/france
Note: In the shopping district of La Condamine, and close to the Prince's Palace and Casino de Monte-Carlo.

Hotel Metropole Monaco

4 Avenue de la Madone
Monaco, 98007
Phone: +377 9315 1515
www.metropole.com
Note: At the center of Monte Carlo. In fact, the race runs right in front of it. Also close to restaurants, bars, and shops, but make sure to look both ways before crossing the street.

Fairmont Monte Carlo

12 Avenue des Spélugues
Monaco, 98000
Phone: +377 9350 6500
Fax: +377 9330 0157
Toll-Free: 1-800-257-7544
www.fairmont.com/montecarlo
Note: Just thirty-five minutes from the airport, this resort and convention complex juts over the Mediterranean with a beautiful view of the Grand Prix Racecourse.

Hotel Miramar

1 Avenue JF Kennedy
Monaco, 98000
Phone: +377 9205 6300
www.miramar.monaco-hotel.com
Note: In the heart of Monte Carlo and close to the Casino, Grimaldi Forum, the train station, and beaches.

On-Site Hospitality:

Being onsite means anywhere along the race course in Monte Carlo and La Condamine. Plenty of local establishments are close by to grab a bite or have a drink. Some places even include a terrace view of the race with the price of food and drink. Take in the culture and still enjoy the race.

Travel Packages:

If you are going to travel to this event, I would recommend using a reliable company to work with you on making the necessary arrangements. The suppliers listed in this book have solid references and are by far the most trusted in the business. Below are some of the organizations to try for this Top 100 Must See Sporting Event.

Premiere Corporate Events

14 Penn Plaza, Suite 925
New York, NY 10122
Phone: (212) 695-9480
Fax: (212) 564-8098
Toll-Free: 1-877-621-5243
E-mail: requests@tseworld.com
www.tseworld.com
www.pcevents.com

Premiere Sports Travel

201 Shannon Oaks Circle, Suite 205
Cary, NC 27511
Phone: (919) 481-9511
Fax: (919) 481-1337
Toll-Free: 1-800-924-9993
E-mail: sales@sportstravel.com
www.sportstravel.com

Dining:

Café de Paris

Place du Casino
Monaco, 98000
Phone: 377 9806 2525
Fax: +377 9216 3862
www.casino-monte-carlo.com

Note: Advertises itself to be the premier "see and be seen" spot. An international menu with food and drink served inside and outside. Those under eighteen are not admitted.

Le Venezia Monaco

27 Boulevard Albert Ier
Monaco, 98000
Phone: +377 9315 9727
www.venezia-monaco.com

Note: A popular destination, located 220 meters from both the start and finish lines of the race, so be sure to make a reservation.

Rampoldi

3 Avenue des Spélugues
Monaco, 98000
Phone: +377 9330 7065
Fax: +377 9350 4384
www.rampoldi.restaurants-montecarlo.com

Note: More Italian fare than French cuisine. Choose from tortellini, ravioli, sea bass, veal kidneys, and, of course, crêpes suzette.

Airport:

Aéroport Nice Côte d'Azur

CCINCA, BP 3331
Cedex 3, Nice, 06206, France
Phone: +33 (4) 8988 9828
www.nice.aeroport.fr

Sports Travel Insider's Edge:

Best way to watch the action:

You will find many people selling tickets on the streets close to the authorized ticket booths. Try the ticket booths first and make sure you have a map of the circuit so you know the exact location of your seat. The best sections are A1, A4, V, Z1, Z2, and O.

Best place to get up close:

Many local residents are more than happy to rent their terraces for you to watch the event. Look for their ads in the *International Herald Tribune* and the *Nice Monaco Matin* newspapers. Also, area restaurants and hotels offer special lunch menus with prices, which include watching the race from their terraces.

Best travel tip:

After the race activities end for the day, walk where the drivers just raced. In fact, everyone walks in Monte Carlo. It is a friendly atmosphere that gets a little friendlier around race time.

Notable Quotes:

"The Monaco circuit is very challenging for the drivers and cars. . . . Historically Monaco is a great circuit, but as it is unique to any other in F1, every moment you are on the track you need precision."—TAKUMA SATO, Japanese auto racer

"Racing a Formula One car around Monaco is like flying a helicopter in your bedroom. You could not describe the race in a better way."—RALF SCHUMACHER, former BMW Williams F1 Team driver

"Winning Monaco was always special because it had more glamour, more color, more excitement: The Mediterranean on one side, the Martine Alps on the other side, the restaurants, the hotels, the beautiful people. It was at the time of the Cannes Film Festival every year, so you had the stars coming along. For me, I knew it was the last time I was ever going to drive a racing car around Monaco. Therefore, to win at Monaco under those circumstances was very important."—JACKIE STEWART, ESPN.com

Relevant Websites:
www.yourmonaco.com/grand_prix
www.visitmonaco.com
www.tseworld.com
www.pcevents.com
www.sportstravel.com
www.gotickets.com
www.premieresports.com

36

RUNNING OF THE BULLS

Where?
The streets of central Pamplona, located in the northern Spanish province of Navarra.

When?
The first or second week of July.

Significance:
The Encierro, a.k.a. the "Running of the Bulls," started in 1910 during a festival where drovers ran bulls used in bullfights for the evening from their enclosure, through sectioned-off streets in Pamplona,

and into the pens of the bullring, Plaza de Toros. Locals began the tradition of jumping in and running alongside the bulls. As time went on, they became more daring by running in front of the bulls.

Ceremonial rockets are fired from the upper balcony of Town Hall building to start the Encierro as thousands of people pop corks off bottles of Cava (champagne). The first is for the bulls. The second is for the runners. Dressed in white with red bandanas, the crowds sing songs and cheer San Fermín as the nine-day festival commences.

Today, six bulls and six steers weighing between 500 and 700 kg do anything but lumber through the streets. They move fast, covering the entire 830 meters in about three minutes. Running uphill along Santo Domingo takes about thirty seconds. With so little time, runners can ill afford to make any mistakes. Injuries from goring and trampling are all too common for both runners and bulls.

Who attends?
There are few psychological profiles of those who would impede the progress of a charging, snorting animal with sharp horns. Since 1852, men and women have donned white jeans, shirts, red bandanas, sashes, and, of course, running shoes to run the route of Santo Domingo Street, Plaza Consistorial, Estafeta Street, and the dangerously winding Mercaderes Street.

Tickets:
No tickets. Just show up donning your red cape and, again, good running shoes.

Accommodations:

Hotel AC Ciudad de Pamplona
Calle Iturrama, 21
Pamplona/Iruña, Navarra, 31007, Spain
Phone: +34 948 266 011
Fax: +34 948 173 626
www.ac-hotels.com

Note: Completely renovated, 117-room hotel conveniently located near the university areas of the city.

Zenit Pamplona
Calle, No.1
Parque Comercial Galaria
Pamplona, Navarra, 31191, Spain
Phone: +34 948 292 600
Fax: +34 948 292 601
www.zenithoteles.com
Note: Located in the middle of a shopping area. Five-minute drive from the town center and three minutes from the international airport.

El Hotel NH Iruña Park
Arcadio Mª Larraona, 1
Pamplona, Navarra, 31008, Spain
Phone: +34 948 197 119
Note: Located in the suburbs, but not far from the city's historic center.

Gran Hotel La Perla
Plaza Del Castillo 1
Pamplona/Iruña, Navarra, 31001, Spain
Phone: +34 948 223 000
Fax: +34 948 222 324
www.granhotellaperla.com
Note: Known as Ernest Hemingway's favorite hotel during his visits.

On-Site Hospitality and Events:
The Chupinazo: A recent but one of the most recognized images of the Fiesta of San Fermín, the launching of the rocket signifies the start of the festivities as Bull Run enthusiasts gather in the Plaza Consistorial. Entry to the event held every July 6th is free.

The Procession: The 7th of July is the Day of San Fermín and the main day of the fiesta. Locals have great affection for this celebration and longstanding tradition when San Fermín leaves his refuge at the Church of San Lorenzo to Pamplona. Thousands of people in white accompany the image of the saint while touring the Historical Quarter.

Local civil and religious leaders can be seen as well.

The Giants and Bigheads: From July 7th to July 14th, a company of Kings and Queens are preceded by an escort of Bigheads, Kilikis, and Zaldikos (horses) from Pamplona's Company of Giants and Bigheads. Along with the saint, these twenty-five papier mâché characters are the most beloved fixtures of the fiesta. Every morning, a procession travels through the center of the city as the giants, carried by mozos, dance to the music of pipers.

The Bullfights and the Peñas: The arena stages bullfights every afternoon at 6:30 P.M., while Peñas (San Fermín clubs), 5,000 strong, fill the stands. Each adorned in loose-hanging shirts with a shield, anthem, brass band, and banner, they are the feature and very noisy attraction of this event.

Travel Packages:
If you are going to travel to this event, I would recommend using a reliable company to work with you on making the necessary arrangements. The suppliers listed in this book have solid references and are by far the most trusted in the business. Below are some of the organizations to try for this Top 100 Must See Sporting Event.

Premiere Corporate Events
14 Penn Plaza, Suite 925
New York, NY 10122
Phone: (212) 695-9480
Fax: (212) 564-8098
Toll-Free: 1-877-621-5243
E-mail: requests@tseworld.com
www.tseworld.com
www.pcevents.com

Premiere Sports Travel
201 Shannon Oaks Circle, Suite 205
Cary, NC 27511
Phone: (919) 481-9511
Fax: (919) 481-1337

Toll-Free: 1-800-924-9993
E-mail: sales@sportstravel.com
www.sportstravel.com

Dining:

Food and drinks are pricey during the festival and are based on whether you are sitting at a table or standing at the bar. Meals of bull stew or Navarra trout can be found in the area, along with liters and liters of sangria.

Café Roch

Calle Comedias 6
Pamplona/Iruña, Navarra, 31001, Spain
Phone: +34 948 222 390

Note: Famous for the tosta (large piece of bread, side up) with Roquefort and tosta with green peppers.

Café Bar Gaucho

Calle Espoz Y Mina, 4
Pamplona, Navarra, 31001, Spain
Phone: +34 948 225 073
www.cafebargaucho.com

Note: Famous for the fried pepper and other fried foods.

Casa Otano

Calle San Nicolás 5
Pamplona/Iruña, Navarra, 31001, Spain
Phone: +34 948 227 036
Fax: +34 948 212 012
www.casaotano.com

Note: Famous for "montados," which are small pieces of bread with a little piece of chorizo, tortilla, ham, cheese, etc. They're very popular in Spanish restaurants.

La Navarra

Calle Santa Engracia 13
Pamplona/Iruña, Navarra, 31014, Spain
Phone: +34 948 130 411
www.grupolanavarra.com

Note: Famous for their tortilla de patatas . . . this is the Spanish egg and potato omelette.

La Olla

Avenida Roncesvalles 2
Pamplona/Iruña, Navarra, 31002, Spain
Phone: +34 948 229 558
www.laolla.com

Note: Famous for their montados/montaditos with Spanish cured ham.

El Burgalés

Calle Comedias 5
Pamplona/Iruña, Navarra, Spain 31001
Phone: +34 948 225 158

Note: Pinchos are small bites of something . . . a lot of pinchos make a tapa, and tapas are famous in Spain.

El Burladero

Calle Emilio Arrieta 9
Pamplona/Iruña, Navarra, 31002, Spain
Phone: +34 948 228 034

Note: Famous for their pinchos . . . of many different things.

Monasterio

Calle Espoz Y Mina 11
Pamplona/Iruña, Navarra, 31002, Spain
Phone: +34 948 212 859

Note: Known for their fried eggs and their pincho of bacalao, a type of white fish very famous in northern dishes.

Restaurante Europa

Calle Espoz Y Mina 11
Pamplona, Navarra, 31002, Spain
Phone: +34 948 221 800
Fax: +34 948 229 235
www.hreuropa.com

Note: Navarra is the region Pamplona is in. This place is famous for their innovative Navarrian style food. More expensive option.

Hartza

Calle Juan De Labrit 19
Pamplona/Iruña, Navarra, 31001, Spain
Phone: +34 948 224 568

Note: Traditional food from the Navarra region. More expensive option.

San Ignacio
Avenida San Ignacio 10
Pamplona, Navarra, 31002, Spain
Phone: +34 948 227 033

Note: Mediterranean cuisine and regional food from Navarra—good and relatively cheap.

Don Pablo
Calle Navas De Tolosa 19
Pamplona, Navarra, 31002, Spain
Phone: +34 948 225 299
www.restaurantedonpablo.com

Note: Their specialty is fish and seafood, as the northern part of Spain is famous for good quality seafood because the water up north is very cold and shellfish are better in cold waters.

Café con Sal
Calle Juan De Labrit 29
Pamplona/Iruña, Navarra, 31001, Spain
Phone: +34 948 227 927

Note: Designer food at reasonable prices.

Airports:
The airport in Noáin is 6 kilometers from Pamplona with daily flights to and from Barcelona or Madrid.

Bilbao airport is 150 kilometers from Pamplona with international flights coming in with passengers taking buses to attend the Encierro.

Sports Travel Insider's Edge:

Best way to watch the action:
A boat load of euros will get you a rented balcony from a local resident. Those looking for renters will usually hang a notice from their balcony. Free seating is available in the bullring at the end of the run.

Best way to partake in the action and get up close:
Recognize the risks and dangers of running with the bulls. Appropriate clothing, particularly running shoes, is highly recommended. You must be over eighteen and it

is recommended that you be sober and well rested. Have someone hold a purse or backpack for you. Keep running and be aware of your surroundings. Do not try to make contact with or distract a bull, as a lone bull is more dangerous than the overall herd. Finally, if you fall, lie still with your head covered. My advice if you definitely don't want to deal with a horn in your leg is to watch instead of run. It's certainly a little safer that way but then again it's an experience. . . .

Best travel tip:
Arrive between 5:30 and 6:30 A.M. to avoid the crowds and dress warm for the cooler Pamplona mornings.

Notable Quotes:

"We will definitely be back again. My brother will never run [in the festival] again, but he would like to come back to celebrate."—LAWRENCE LENAHAN, after he and his brother Michael were gored at the Running of the Bulls

"You can either sit on the couch and watch life go by, or you can go out and try to do these things around the world. If that means getting a horn in the leg, I guess that's the chance I took."—MICHAEL LENAHAN, Running of the Bulls participant, on being gored by a bull

Relevant Websites:
www.sanfermin.com
www.tseworld.com
www.pcevents.com
www.sportstravel.com
www.premieresports.com

37

RUGBY WORLD CUP

When?
October, every four years.

Future Locations:
2011–New Zealand
2015–TBD

Significance:
Rugby players aspire to one day compete in the Rugby World Cup, one of the largest international sporting events in the world, and the premier international rugby union tournament. Sanctioned by the International Rugby Board (IRB), the sport's governing body, rugby players have met every four years since 1987 to determine who is truly the best of the best among IRB nations.

IRB member nations vote on the tournament hosts and announce the tournament's location six years before it is held. That gives the host country or countries time to build or upgrade facilities to house the World Cup, a common practice due to the honor of being selected and the international fan following of the sport itself. Nations where rugby is a popular sport take precedence.

Currently, twenty nations compete for over a month in a qualifying tournament. Teams are seeded based on standings from the previous year's tournament, and divided into four pools. The winner and runner-up of each pool qualify to play in the quarterfinals until a champion is given the William Webb Ellis Cup, named for the Rugby School student credited with inventing the game.

Who attends?
Rugby fans from all walks of life throughout the world, young and old alike.

History
Even though the Rugby World Cup started in 1987, the idea goes as far back as the 1950s. IRB union opposition quelled those discussions in resistance to the tournament concept. Detractors were not as strong when the discussions resumed in the 1980s. Even with strong opposition and an initial tie vote of 8-8, the IRB approved the inaugural cup that was co-hosted by Australia and New Zealand.

Sixteen nations competed in the initial invitation-only tournament with the All Blacks of New Zealand taking home the championship by decimating France 29-9. In 1991, the tournament was changed to a format where thirty-five teams had to qualify for sixteen slots. An upset for the ages and a moment of pure emotion when the South African team shocked the All Blacks with a win in 1995 during the Rugby World Cup in South Africa. In 1999, the IRB adopted the twenty-team format that continues to this day.

Notable Athletes:
Jonny Wilkinson, England
Gavin Hastings, Scotland
Michael Lynagh, Australia
Grant Fox, New Zealand
Andrew Mehrtens, New Zealand

Records:
Most overall points accumulated in the final stages: Jonny Wilkinson, England, 243, 1999, 2003, and 2007

Most points in one competition: Grant Fox, New Zealand, 126, 1987

Most appearances: Jason Leonard, England, 22, 1991–2003

Most points in a match: Simon Culhane, New Zealand, 45, 1995, vs. Japan

Most conversions in a match: Simon Culhane, New Zealand, 20, 1995, vs. Japan

Most tries in a match: Marc Ellis, New Zealand, 6, 1995, vs. Japan

Most overall tries in the final stages: Jonah Lomu, New Zealand, 15, 1995–1999

Most tries in one competition (Tie): Jonah

Lomu, New Zealand, 8, 1999, and
Bryan Habana, South Africa, 8, 2007

Most points scored in a game: New Zealand, 145 (1995)

Widest point margin: Australia vs. Namibia, 142 (2003)

Things to know before you go:

Any player may score, carry, kick, or pass the ball. Passes must be made to the back or to the side, never forward. Only the ball carrier may be tackled and, once down on the ground, must immediately release the ball.

Three ways to score: Try (5 points), Conversion (2 points), and Goal (3 points).

Forwards: Loose Head Prop, Hooker, Tight Head Prop, Second Rows, or Locks (2), Wing Forwards or Flankers (2), and Number 8.

Backs: Scrumhalf, Flyhalf, Inside Center, Outside Center, Wings (2), and Fullback.

Pitch: A rugby field of 69 meters (75 yards) wide and not more than 144 meters (157 yards) long.

In-Goal Area: Rugby equivalent of an end zone.

Side: Team of fifteen players.

Try: Touching down the ball in the opponent's in-goal area.

Conversion: Place-kicking the ball over the crossbar of the goal post attempted from the point where the ball was touched down.

Goal (Penalty or Dropped): Dropping the ball and, on its first bounce, kicking it over the opponent's crossbar.

Scrum: A ball put back into play after an infraction with each team's forwards locked together to position the scrum so the team's hooker can kick the ball to the number 8 to gain possession.

Ruck: After a ball carrier is tackled and the ball is loose.

Maul: The ball carrier is tackled, but still on his feet and the opposing team members are trying to take the ball.

Tickets:

For primary ticket access information, consider: www.rugbyworldcup.com.

For secondary ticket access, consider:

GoTickets, Inc.
2345 Waukegan Road, Suite 140
Bannockburn, IL 60015-1552
Toll-Free: 1-800-775-1617
Fax: (919) 481-9101
E-mail: sales@gotickets.com
www.gotickets.com

Travel Packages:

If you are going to travel to this event, I would recommend using a reliable company to work with you on making the necessary arrangements. The suppliers listed in this book have solid references and are by far the most trusted in the business. Below are some of the organizations to try for this Top 100 Must See Sporting Event.

Premiere Corporate Events
14 Penn Plaza, Suite 925
New York, NY 10122
Phone: (212) 695-9480
Fax: (212) 564-8098
Toll-Free: 1-877-621-5243
E-mail: requests@tseworld.com
www.tseworld.com
www.pcevents.com

Premiere Sports Travel
201 Shannon Oaks Circle, Suite 205
Cary, NC 27511
Phone: (919) 481-9511
Fax: (919) 481-1337
Toll-Free: 1-800-924-9993
E-mail: sales@sportstravel.com
www.sportstravel.com

Notable Quotes:

"You can feel the anticipation and the tension growing because the serious stuff starts this week. Whether you're a rugby player in South Africa or England we're in World Cup countdown and suddenly it feels very real. And that's just the way it should be—because we're close now. We're very close."— SCHALK BURGER, Springbok flanker

"Everyone had a crack last when we got together afterwards once we got to the hotel so, every single guy has had a sip out of the cup. It is hard not to take your eyes off it; we've worked so hard for it."—JOHN SMIT, Springbok hooker

Relevant Websites:

www.rugbyworldcup.com
www.tseworld.com
www.pcevents.com
www.sportstravel.com
www.gotickets.com
www.premieresports.com

38

RED RIVER SHOOTOUT

Where?

Cotton Bowl Stadium
3750 Midway Plaza
Dallas, TX 75210
The game, as of right now, will be held here through 2015. From there, both schools will come to an agreement on a new contract and the stadium/venue may change.

When?

First weekend in October every year.

Significance:

The Red River Rivalry, the official name for the Red River Shootout since 2005, pits the University of Texas Longhorns against the University of Oklahoma Sooners. The origins of the annual game go back to 1900, predating Oklahoma's (then Oklahoma territory) entry as a state. Considered one of the greatest and most intense rivalries in American sports, the name comes from the Red River that carves a portion of the boundary between the two states. The cultural differences boil over and often lean toward bitter disputes and negative stereotyping going back and forth. Okies are country yokels, according to Texans. Texans are phony cowboys, according to the Sooner faithful.

Since the mid-forties, the Rivalry has been about more than just a moral victory over a hated rival. For over sixty years, Texas and/or Oklahoma have ranked in the top twenty-five nationally, giving their matchup significance both nationally and within their conference. Games that are more recent featured one of the eventual participants in or winners of the Bowl Championship Series National Championship game.

Three Red River Rivalry/Shootout trophies are at stake as well. The most prominent is the Golden Hat, kept by the winning school's athletic department until the next clash. Since 2003, the respective student governments have exchanged the Red River Rivalry trophy. The Governors' trophy has been traded back and forth between the governors of Texas and Oklahoma. Many times, a side bet of a side of beef is placed between the chief executives; that "trophy" goes to charity.

Who attends?

Longhorn and Sooner fans, but keep them separated. Also in attendance, a lot of good ol' college football fanatics.

How to get there?

Easily accessible from the north off US 75, east and west off I-30, and from the south off I-35E. Note that you may be directed to take a route back to a freeway system different from the one you used to get to the Cotton Bowl.

Tickets:
For primary ticket access information, consider:

AT&T Cotton Bowl Ticket Office
P.O. Box 569420
Dallas, TX 75356
Phone: 1-888-792-BOWL

UT Athletics Ticket Office
Bellmont Hall, First Floor Lobby
P.O. Box 7399
Austin, TX 78713-7399
Phone: (512) 471-3333
Toll-Free: 1-800-982-BEVO
www.TexasBoxOffice.com

Oklahoma Ticket Office
Phone: (405) 325-2424
Toll-Free: 1-800-456-GoOU
www.soonersports.com

For secondary ticket access, consider:

GoTickets, Inc.
2345 Waukegan Road, Suite 140
Bannockburn, IL 60015-1552
Toll-Free: 1-800-775-1617
Fax: (919) 481-9101
E-mail: sales@gotickets.com
www.gotickets.com

Accommodations:

Omni Mandalay
221 East Las Colinas Boulevard
Irving, TX 75039
Phone: (972) 869-5520
www.omnihotels.com

Note: Fifteen short minutes to the stadium and close to business and cultural attractions in Dallas. Luxury hotel with unique Burmese city-style design.

Hyatt Regency
300 Reunion Boulevard
Dallas, TX 75207
Phone: (214) 651-1234
Fax: (214) 742-8126
Toll-Free: 1-800-233-1234
www.dallasregency.hyatt.com

Note: Four miles from the stadium and close to shopping and other sports. Boasts the longest-running AAA four-diamond distinction among other convention hotels in Dallas.

Hilton Anatole
2201 Stemmons Freeway
Dallas, TX 75207
Phone: (214) 748-1200
Fax: (214) 761-7520
www.hilton.com

Note: Five miles from the stadium. Well-known Dallas hotel known for warm hospitality and Western lore.

On-Site Hospitality:
At the Cotton Bowl Stadium, you will have over seventy-five concession areas with specialty items located just outside of Gates 1 through 10. Chicken fajitas sizzle next to game-day staples such as hot dogs and charbroiled burgers. On each ramp, you will find express beverage services for quick thirst-quenching.

Travel Packages:
If you are going to travel to this event, I would recommend using a reliable company to work with you on making the necessary arrangements. The suppliers listed in this book have solid references and are by far the most trusted in the business. Below are some of the organizations to try for this Top 100 Must See Sporting Event.

Premiere Corporate Events
14 Penn Plaza, Suite 925
New York, NY 10122
Phone: (212) 695-9480
Fax: (212) 564-8098

Toll-Free: 1-877-621-5243
E-mail: requests@tseworld.com
www.tseworld.com
www.pcevents.com

Premiere Sports Travel
201 Shannon Oaks Circle, Suite 205
Cary, NC 27511
Phone: (919) 481-9511
Fax: (919) 481-1337
Toll-Free: 1-800-924-9993
E-mail: sales@sportstravel.com
www.sportstravel.com

Premiere College Sports
(Powered by Dodd's Athletic Tours)
308 South Neil
Champaign, IL 61820
Phone: (217) 373-5067
Fax: (217) 398-1313
Toll-Free: 1-800-553-5527
www.doddsathletictours.com
www.collegesportstravel.com

Dining:

Bread Winners Bakery and Café
3301 McKinney Avenue at Hall Street
Dallas, TX 75204
Phone: (214) 754-4940
www.breadwinnerscafe.com
Note: Known for not only crowds, but also great breakfasts that are worth the wait.

La Calle Doce
1925 Skillman Street
Dallas, TX 75206
Phone: (214) 824-9900
www.lacalledoce-dallas.com
Note: What else would you eat while in Texas? Great Mexican food and margaritas that will not disappoint.

For those fair food aficionados, the Texas State Fair can also satisfy those cravings for cotton candy and other delectables.

Airports:

Dallas/Fort Worth International Airport
3200 East Airfield Drive
DFW Airport, TX 75261
Phone: (972) 973-8888
www.dfwairport.com

Dallas Love Field
8008 Cedar Springs Road, LB 16
Dallas, TX 75235
Phone: (214) 670-6073
www.dallas-lovefield.com

Sports Travel Insider's Edge:

Best way to watch the action:
Like the fans' loyalties, the stadium is split in half when tickets are sold for the event. Wearing the team colors of red or burnt orange shows your spirit and allegiance. Just make sure you are sitting on the proper side; this is Texas versus Oklahoma, after all.

Best place to get up close:
The State Fair on game day is where plenty of Texas and Oklahoma devotees will be wandering around before the game. Team colors surround you, giving you a chance at a friendly wave to a fellow fan and a scowl at a loyalist for the opposition. Make sure to be aware of the time so you do not miss the game introductions.

Best travel tip:
The Texas State Fair is a must see while you are in Dallas for the big game. This is a Texas-sized gathering that is considered one of the best in the country. Grab a corn dog and play a game in a location that is convenient and a mere skeeball throw away from the Cotton Bowl.

Notable Quotes:

"I have been attending since 1970 and have commuted from my homes in either Atlanta or Connecticut to Dallas for games.

I once postponed colon surgery to attend the game. It wasn't minor surgery I was delaying either. It resulted in 13 inches of my large intestines and a benign tumor being removed, but I did not miss the game. And I don't regret the decision."—Jim Ross, WWE television announcer and die-hard Sooner fan

"Back in the day, I have gone to the Dallas city jail to buy tickets from fans who had been arrested for being drunk and disorderly the night before the game where downtown Dallas was turned into the biggest tailgate party/pep rally."—JIM ROSS

Relevant Websites:

www.soonersports.com
www.mackbrown-texasfootball.com
www.texassports.com
www.bigtex.com
www.dallascvb.com
www.tseworld.com
www.pcevents.com
www.sportstravel.com
www.gotickets.com
www.premieresports.com

39
NOTRE DAME FOOTBALL GAME

Where?
Notre Dame Stadium
University of Notre Dame
South Bend, IN 46556

When?
Home games are scheduled from early September to mid-November and sell out quickly.

Significance:
Notre Dame's Fighting Irish can stake claim to more modern-era consensus national championships and All-American football players than any other Division I-A school. They have had seven Heisman Trophy winners compete at the "House that Rockne Built." Notre Dame Stadium also provides a throwback experience in that there is not a JumboTron to be seen anywhere. A college football game at Notre Dame is a must experience.

Who attends?
Fanatical followers of the Fighting Irish fill the stadium to its capacity of 80,795. Even though the Fighting Irish enjoy a great deal of television time, it does not compare to the experience of being in the famed stadium.

How to get there?
Some fly to South Bend Regional Airport and take the fifteen-minute drive down Lincoln Way (west) to Indiana 933. Others choose to land at Chicago's O'Hare or Midway airports and head out by way of Route 190 to South Bend.

Tickets:
For primary market ticket access, please know that tickets are not sold via the Internet and can only be acquired beginning the Monday prior to each home game. Move fast because the tickets move faster. Your best bet for tickets is the secondary ticket market. Whether you are on a budget or willing to pay top prices, the best ticket for any Fighting Irish fan is anywhere within the confines of college football's second-ranked "cathedral," according to The Sporting News.

For secondary ticket access, consider:

GoTickets, Inc.
2345 Waukegan Road, Suite 140
Bannockburn, IL 60015-1552
Toll-Free: 1-800-775-1617
Fax: (919) 481-9101
E-mail: sales@gotickets.com
www.gotickets.com

Accommodations:

The Oliver Inn Bed and Breakfast

630 West Washington Street
South Bend, IN 46601
Phone: (574) 232-4545
Toll-Free: 1-888-697-4466
www.oliverinn.com

Note: A great choice if you're interested in a Victorian style place offering comfort and relaxation.

The Morris Inn

Notre Dame Avenue (right on campus)
Notre Dame, IN 46556
Phone: (574) 631-2000
Fax: (574) 631-2017
Toll-Free: 1-800-280-7256
www.morrisinn.nd.edu

Note: Located on the campus and within walking distance of the football stadium. Try Leahy's, a great cocktail lounge located in the Inn.

The Ivy Court Inn and Suites

1404 Ivy Court
South Bend, IN 46637
Phone: (574) 277-6500
Fax: (574) 271-0586
www.ivycourt.com

Note: Even though it is off campus, it is the closest hotel in South Bend to the campus athletic facilities.

The Inn at St. Mary's Hotel and Suites

53993 Indiana State Route 933
South Bend, IN 46637
Phone: (574) 217-4641
Fax: (574) 289-0986
www.innatsaintmarys.com

Note: Luxurious accommodations with a complimentary hot buffet breakfast every morning.

Inn on West Washington

322 West Washington Street
South Bend, IN 46601
Phone: (574) 232-5901
Toll-Free: 1-877-232-5902
www.innonwestwashington.com

Note: This bed and breakfast, located in a Victorian mansion, is considered "turn-of-the-century." This B&B is only a few years old.

Hampton Inn & Suites

52709 US 31 North
South Bend, IN 46637
Phone: (574) 277-9373
Fax: (574) 243-0128
Toll-Free: 1-800-HAMPTON
www.hamptoninn.com

Note: Fighting Irish fan favorite. Only a mile and a half from the Notre Dame campus.

On-Site Hospitality and Events:

At the stadium, make sure to buy a steak sandwich from the Knights of Columbus food stand. Blackened brats can be purchased from the student grillers as well. And it would not be a football game if the beer wasn't flowing freely, for those twenty-one and over, of course.

The Notre Dame Football Hospitality Village: Considered an ideal environment to entertain business clients, the Village is located on campus and nearby the stadium. In the heart of Fighting Irish fanaticism, one can hear the Oldest Marching Band in the Land and smell the food cooked by the tailgaters. Gold, Blue, and Green Packages can be purchased for an admittedly premium price and they include tickets, parking passes, ID credentials, and game programs. Check with featured travel package companies for details.

Football Fridays Tent Party: Every Friday before a Notre Dame home game, Downtown South Bend Inc. and the College Football Hall of Fame throw a party with food, drinks, and music. A small cover charge will get you in the door with groups of twenty or more receiving a discount for advance requests.

Friday Pep Rally: Every Saturday at around 6 P.M., the adrenaline begins to flow as the football players, cheerleaders, band members, and, yes, the Leprechaun, pump up Fighting Irish Fans. Location and tickets vary with each home game.

College Football Hall of Fame: Fans of the Fighting Irish and college football consider the Hall of Fame to be a Mecca of the sport they love. Established in 1951, the hall and the museum have given fans young and old a peek into the rich history of college football. Adult tickets can be had for a little more than ten dollars. Tickets for seniors, students, and children over twelve are a few dollars less. Children from five to twelve can get in for about half price while those younger can see the Hall for free.

For access to any of these events or parties contact the companies listed in the Travel Packages section.

Travel Packages:

If you are going to travel to this event, I would recommend using a reliable company to work with you on making the necessary arrangements. The suppliers listed in this book have solid references and are by far the most trusted in the business. Below are some of the organizations to try for this Top 100 Must See Sporting Event.

Premiere Corporate Events

14 Penn Plaza, Suite 925
New York, NY 10122
Phone: (212) 695-9480
Fax: (212) 564-8098
Toll-Free: 1-877-621-5243
E-mail: requests@tseworld.com
www.tseworld.com
www.pcevents.com

Premiere Sports Travel

201 Shannon Oaks Circle, Suite 205
Cary, NC 27511

Phone: (919) 481-9511
Fax: (919) 481-1337
Toll-Free: 1-800-924-9993
E-mail: sales@sportstravel.com
www.sportstravel.com

Premiere College Sports (Powered by Dodd's Athletic Tours)

308 South Neil
Champaign, IL 61820
Phone: (217) 373-5067
Fax: (217) 398-1313
Toll-Free: 1-800-553-5527
www.doddsathletictours.com
www.collegesportstravel.com

Dining:

Legends of Notre Dame Restaurant & Alehouse Pub

100 Legends
Notre Dame, IN 46556
Phone: (574) 631-2582
Fax: (574) 631-8099
www.legendsofnotredame.org

Note: Located in the parking lot of the football stadium. Try Mike's Buffalo Chicken Wrap, it's the most popular item on the menu. Also the toasted Beer, Bread, and Cheese selection is a must.

Fiddler's Hearth

127 North Main Street
South Bend, IN 46601
Phone: (574) 232-2853
Fax: (574) 232-2863
www.fiddlershearth.com

Note: Enjoy the food and drinks in this family-friendly place, which reflect the traditions of the Seven Celtic Nations. Only a ten-minute drive to the stadium.

Original Pancake House

1430 North Ironwood Drive
South Bend, IN 46635
Phone: (574) 232-3220
www.originalpancakehouse.com

Note: The place to eat breakfast before the game. This place has been around since 1962, and all of the batters are always homemade. You definitely have to try their signature dish, apple pancakes.

Wing Nut
1835 Lincoln Way East
South Bend, IN 46613
Phone: (574) 232-0457
Fax: (574) 232-0469
www.wingnutfamilypub.com
Note: You want wings, this is your place!

Airports:

South Bend Regional Airport
St. Joseph County Airport Authority
4477 Progress Drive
South Bend, IN 46628
Phone: (574) 233-2185
www.sbnair.com

O'Hare International Airport
10000 West O'Hare
Chicago, Illinois 60666
Phone: (773) 686-3700
www.ohare.com

Midway International Airport
5600 South Cicero Avenue
Chicago, IL 60638
Phone: (773) 838-0756
www.chicago-mdw.com

Sports Travel Insider's Edge:

Best way to watch the action:
Yes, you can see it on television, but nothing can come close to matching the Fighting Irish experience in Notre Dame Stadium. Get there early because it's about being there and watching the Irish run onto the field for the start of the game. Even the movie *Rudy* can't do it justice.

Best place to get up close:
The Friday night pep rally is a must to complete this experience and feel the magic of a Notre Dame football game. No other college football program carries the glorified tradition of Notre Dame. The night before the game at the pep rally is where you can feel it the most.

Best travel tip:
Make sure you bone up on your "Bob Wave" and get your picture taken with "Touchdown Jesus." Remember that everyone walks, so leave the car at home.

Notable Quotes:

"For a sports fan, visiting Notre Dame for a football weekend is like a pilgrimage, like going to Lourdes, or Jerusalem, or Mecca and Medina. You go there to be part of something bigger. To be a part of tradition. To be a part of history. But there's something more, something higher, involved. I can't quite explain it, even after being there. But when you're there, whether you're religious or not, I think you can feel it. Somehow, it all makes sense. You come away feeling good, no matter what happens in the game."—KIERAN DARCY, General Editor, ESPN.com's Page 2

"It's a beautiful thing."—KIERAN DARCY

Relevant Websites:
www.nd.edu
www.exploresouthbend.org
www.tseworld.com
www.pcevents.com
www.sportstravel.com
www.gotickets.com
www.doddsathletictours.com
www.collegesportstravel.com
www.premieresports.com

40

MLB ALL-STAR GAME

Where?

Held in different Major League ballparks around the country. The venue changes every year.

When?

Annually during the middle of July, marking the midway point of the season. Almost always falls on a Tuesday night.

Significance:

The "Midsummer Classic" is the second most anticipated event—next to the World Series—for fans of Major League Baseball. The Major League Baseball All-Star Game is baseball's pure interactive experience. Fans vote for the starting position players and the previous year's World Series managers select pitchers and reserve players. The best in the American League battle the best in the National League at the ceremonial (not mathematical) halfway point of the season. Pride is at stake, not to mention home field advantage in the upcoming World Series for the league who wins.

The Origin

While many pro baseball players have strained relationships with the media, it is important to note that a member of the fourth estate created the classic game. Arch Ward, sports editor for *The Chicago Tribune*, devised this brainchild. It was originally intended as a one-time only, major attraction at the 1933 World's Fair in Chicago. In honor of the sports scribe, Major League Baseball created the Arch Ward Trophy in 1962 for the MVP of the All-Star Game.

The Players

As of 2007, the rules require a team to have thirty-two players each. They are selected through fan voting via ballots distributed at the parks and the Internet. Many times, this causes larger teams with expansive fan bases—the Yankees and Red Sox come to mind—to dominate the voting. That has caused instances of alleged "ballot stuffing" where an All-Star roster includes a majority of members from the same team.

Players vote on the pitchers and one backup player for each position. Managers and the Commissioner's Office get the teams' rosters to thirty-one and also provide a list of five names for the fans to vote on for number thirty-two. They also have the authority to replace a player who is injured or declines the honor. This process, while cumbersome, is a far cry from the managers originally selecting the entire team in a very non-democratic fashion. Over time, that process caused fan interest to die down significantly.

The Managers

The managers of the respective teams are the same managers who faced off during the previous season's World Series and they select their coach staff. This allows for the possibility that a manager could coach, even though he may not be with his championship team. In 2003, Dusty Baker jumped from the National League champs San Francisco Giants to the Chicago Cubs. Retired or fired managers have come back to serve their rightful place as coach. Former Yankees skipper Bob Lemon, fired by George Steinbrenner, managed the 1979 American League team. There have been other exceptions due to death and the 1994 baseball strike.

The Uniforms

Players wore uniforms that designated their National League or American League allegiance during the inaugural event. When they switched to their team colors, they primarily competed in their alternate jerseys with a few variations. Today, players can be seen on the field in their standard team jerseys.

The Stadiums

Outside of a few exceptions, the games alternate between American and National League stadiums. Historic stadiums have hosted the All-Star Game and the newfangled ballparks will start getting their chance as well.

Who attends?

Fans of baseball rabid to see all the stars play on the same field. A true "Field of Dreams."

Tickets:

For primary ticket access information, consider: www.allstargame.com, www.mlb.com, or the website of the ballpark hosting the game.

For secondary ticket access, consider:

GoTickets, Inc.

2345 Waukegan Road, Suite 140
Bannockburn, IL 60015-1552
Toll-Free: 1-800-775-1617
Fax: (919) 481-9101
E-mail: sales@gotickets.com
www.gotickets.com

On-Site Hospitality and Events:

Next to the game itself, the All-Star FanFest is a popular and truly interactive destination for baseball fans. It is a haven that has featured the following:

FanFest Challenge: Test your baseball trivia knowledge against fellow fans.

FanFest Fielding Practice: Play on the field where the All-Stars compete and don't forget your glove.

Home Run Derby: Your opportunity to hit one out of the park and "touch 'em all."

Steal Home Challenge: Think you can outrun your fellow fans? Run the ninety-foot span from third base to home plate.

Batting Practice: State-of-the art batting cages put your hitting ability to the test.

Rookie League: For the younger fans to practice at the batting tees and baseball targets. Or you can play a video game, drive a radio-controlled car, or participate in other "old school" activities.

The Diamond: Baseball seminars and hands-on clinics will give you the edge in hitting, pitching, fielding, and base running. The pros will lend their expertise.

Cyber Ballpark: Modern times call for modern recreational activities, including MLB video and computer games.

Bullpen: See how your pitching holds up against a life-sized image of your favorite slugger.

You Call the Play: For the budding play-by-play announcer or color commentator.

Video Batting Cages: Life-sized video images of your favorite pitcher hurling his best at you.

Photo Opportunities: Pose by the World's Largest Baseball or have your picture taken getting that winning catch. You can also be the cover story for *Sports Weekly* or appear on your own baseball card.

Souvenirs: Autograph opportunities are everywhere with baseball legends and Hall of Famers. The Collector's Showcase is your chance to buy, sell, or trade collectibles and memorabilia of America's Greatest Pastime. The Major League Baseball Clubhouse has a variety of items. In addition, there is a silent auction for more premium items.

All-Star Bazaar: For the fan of the "free stuff," sponsors provide complimentary gifts for the attendees.

Women on the Diamond: Fan of the "Girls of Summer"? Meet and get autographs from the All-American Girls Professional Baseball League legends and current National Pro Fastpitch players.

National Baseball Hall of Fame Museum: History comes to you when Cooperstown's major attraction puts on a display like no other.

Ballpark Foods: It wouldn't be a baseball event without a hot dog or pretzel.

Volunteer Opportunities: For fans who really want to get up close, there are opportunities to be a FanFest Ambassador or Volunteer. You must be eighteen years of age or older, sign a release and eligibility form, and undergo a background check.

If you want to get in with a ticket for the FanFest, there are packages for individuals and families. For more information, e-mail fanfestsponsors@mlb.com.

Travel Packages:

If you are going to travel to this event, I would recommend using a reliable company to work with you on making the necessary arrangements. The suppliers listed in this book have solid references and are by far the most trusted in the business. Below are some of the organizations to try for this Top 100 Must See Sporting Event.

Premiere Corporate Events

14 Penn Plaza, Suite 925
New York, NY 10122
Phone: (212) 695-9480
Fax: (212) 564-8098
Toll-Free: 1-877-621-5243
E-mail: requests@tseworld.com
www.tseworld.com
www.pcevents.com

Premiere Sports Travel

201 Shannon Oaks Circle, Suite 205
Cary, NC 27511
Phone: (919) 481-9511
Fax: (919) 481-1337
Toll-Free: 1-800-924-9993
E-mail: sales@sportstravel.com
www.sportstravel.com

Sports Travel Insider's Edge:

Best way to watch the action:

Lower-level seats between the bases are your best bet in most stadiums. And look out for the taters flying into the bleachers and outfield seating areas. Is there a bad seat at any All-Star Game?

Best place to get up close:

The Home Run Derby puts the eight best sluggers (not necessarily on the All-Star team) against each other with the American and National Leagues dividing the roster. A playoff system gives each player ten "outs" per round until a winner is declared. A lot of times this event can be more fun than the game. It usually takes place on Monday night before Tuesday's All-Star game. The best seats or most interesting for this event tend to be in the outfield or bleachers, prime space for home run balls.

Best travel tip:

It's legends versus celebrities at the All-Star Legends and Celebrity Softball Game. The annual, five-inning exhibition is played for fun with some unusual rules to determine the winners.

In addition, you can see the stars of tomorrow in the All-Star Futures Game, an annual exhibition featuring the top minor-league prospects. Each organization is represented and the roster is selected by *Baseball America* magazine.

These events usually take place on Sunday or Monday ahead of Tuesday's All-Star game.

Notable Quote:

"It's great for the game, especially the fans. The fans don't think it's another exhibition game, a showcase."—OZZIE GUILLEN, White Sox manager on getting home field advantage for the World Series by winning the All-Star Game

Relevant Websites:

www.mlb.com
www.allstargame.com
www.tseworld.com
www.pcevents.com
www.sportstravel.com
www.gotickets.com
www.premieresports.com

41

IRON BOWL AT ALABAMA

Where?

Bryant-Denny Stadium
100 Bryant Drive
Tuscaloosa, AL 35487

When?

Annually, during the week of Thanksgiving.
Every other year it takes place at Alabama.

Significance:

The Iron Bowl is the annual intercollegiate
football game between Auburn University
and the University of Alabama. The first
game was played on February 22, 1893.
The tradition almost came to an end after
the 1907 game over a dispute about expenses.
In 1948, the Iron Bowl returned when
Auburn president Dr. Ralph B. Draughon
and Alabama president Dr. John Gallalee
decided to end the dispute. With Alabama's
Legion Field being its original home, the
Iron Bowl's name comes from Birmingham's
origin of being built around large iron ore
deposits in Alabama's hill country. Now, the
rivalry takes place in both stadiums on an
alternating basis. Tickets are split evenly
between those who bleed Crimson and
those who are Tiger loyalists. Considered to
be one of the greater rivalries in sports, the
battle goes beyond the stadiums and into
the societal and political realms of those
respective areas. Friends become enemies.

Allies become adversaries. Bragging rights
are at stake with a win. A loss can affect the
overall tone of the season.

Who attends?

Now that the Iron Bowl takes place in both
Jordan-Hare and Bryant-Denny stadiums,
the crowd is evenly split between students,
alumni, and die-hard fans of both Auburn
University and the University of Alabama.
Alabama is the place to see this game.

Tickets:

University of Alabama season ticket holders
are the only ones who can get their hands
on half the tickets if the Iron Bowl is a home
game. Auburn's Tide PRIDE donor program,
faculty, staff, students, and lettermen then
receive their share. The roles are reversed
for a game in Jordan-Hare. For this event
your best bet is the secondary market.

For secondary market access, consider:

GoTickets, Inc.
2345 Waukegan Road, Suite 140
Bannockburn, IL 60015-1552
Toll-Free: 1-800-775-1617
Fax: (919) 481-9101
E-mail: sales@gotickets.com
www.gotickets.com

Accommodations:

Hotel Capstone
320 Paul W. Bryant Drive
Tuscaloosa, AL 35401
Phone: (205) 752-3200
Toll-Free: 1-800-368-7764
www.hotelcapstone.com
Note: The Alabama team stays at this on-campus
hotel the night before the game. They board the
bus on game day that takes them to the stadium in
what is known as the Parade of Champions.

Holiday Inn Express
1120 Veterans Memorial Parkway
Tuscaloosa, AL 35404

Phone: (205) 464-4000
Toll-Free: 1-800-HOLIDAY
www.hiexpress.com
Note: Three miles from the stadium, featuring an exercise room, valet laundry service, and free parking.

Hampton Inn
600 Harper Lee Drive
Tuscaloosa, AL 35404
Phone: (205) 553-9800
www.hamptoninn.com
Note: A mile away from campus and located along the banks of the Black Warrior River, providing your choice of eighty clean and comfortable rooms.

Hilton Garden Inn Tuscaloosa
800 Hollywood Boulevard
Tuscaloosa, AL 35405
Phone: (205) 722-0360
Toll-Free: 1-877-STAY-HGI
www.hgi.com
Note: Promising the latest in technology and convenience to "make the most of your stay."

Courtyard Tuscaloosa
4115 Courtney Drive
Tuscaloosa, AL 35405
Phone: (205) 750-8384
Toll-Free: 1-800-321-2211
www.marriott.com
Note: Great for business and leisure. Modern rooms with free high-speed Internet and a made-to-order breakfast buffet.

On-Site Hospitality and Events:
The stadium concession stand fare is common, but locals encourage anyone from out of town to save their money for the local restaurants that can handle large crowds.

Tailgate before the game on the Quad where there are many parties taking place. Tents are set up, so you can buy in on game day. There is also an elephant walk to the stadium led by the cheerleaders that starts at Denny Chimes, a well-known gathering place/monument on the Quad.

Travel Packages:
If you are going to travel to this event, I would recommend using a reliable company to work with you on making the necessary arrangements. The suppliers listed in this book have solid references and are by far the most trusted in the business. Below are some of the organizations to try for this Top 100 Must See Sporting Event.

Premiere Corporate Events
14 Penn Plaza, Suite 925
New York, NY 10122
Phone: (212) 695-9480
Fax: (212) 564-8098
Toll-Free: 1-877-621-5243
E-mail: requests@tseworld.com
www.tseworld.com
www.pcevents.com

Premiere Sports Travel
201 Shannon Oaks Circle, Suite 205
Cary, NC 27511
Phone: (919) 481-9511
Fax: (919) 481-1337
Toll-Free: 1-800-924-9993
E-mail: sales@sportstravel.com
www.sportstravel.com

Premiere College Sports (Powered by Dodd's Athletic Tours)
308 South Neil
Champaign, IL 61820
Phone: (217) 373-5067
Fax: (217) 398-1313
Toll-Free: 1-800-553-5527
www.doddsathletictours.com
www.collegesportstravel.com

Dining for University of Alabama:

The "Original" Dreamland BBQ
Jerusalem Heights Location
5535 15th Avenue East

Tuscaloosa, AL 35405
Phone: (205) 758-8135
Fax: (205) 758-5158
www.dreamlandbbq.com

Note: Primarily ribs and bread, but the best ribs in town, according to many Tuscaloosa residents.

Los Tarascos
1759 Skyland Boulevard East
Tuscaloosa, AL 35405
Phone: (205) 553-8896

Note: Well-known for its delicious Mexican cuisine.

Nick's in the Sticks
4018 Culver Road
Tuscaloosa, Alabama 35401
Phone: (205) 758-9316

Note: Popular hangout for Alabama students and famous for the filet (food) and the Nicodemus (drink).

Cypress Inn
501 Rice Mine Road North
Tuscaloosa, AL 35406
Phone: (205) 345-6963
Fax: (205) 345-6997
www.cypressinnrestaurant.com

Note: Located on the river across from campus. Food is in the medium price range. Try the sweet rolls. The catfish and smoked chicken in barbecue sauce are guest favorites!

Kozy's Tavern
3510 Loop Road
Tuscaloosa, AL 35404
Phone: (205) 556-0665

Note: More of a high-end dining option for Tuscaloosa.

Bob Baumhower's Wings Restaurant
500 Harper Lee Drive
Tuscaloosa, AL 35404
Telephone: (205) 556-5658
Fax: (205) 556-5639
www.baumhowers.com

Note: Founded by a former Alabama football player. The sports memorabilia on the walls will put you in the mood for the game. Try the potato skins and wings.

Airport:

Birmingham-Shuttlesworth International Airport
5900 Messer Airport Highway
Birmingham, AL 35203
Telephone: (205) 458-8002

Sports Travel Insider's Edge:

Best way to watch the action:
Being an in-state rivalry, it is the one game that is more of a mixed rooting crowd than any other home game. Alabama fans are wise to stay on the home team side.

Best place to get up close:
The game day "Parade of Champions" starts as the players get on team buses at the Hotel Capstone, taking them to the stadium about two hours prior to kickoff. Fans line up on the sides of the entrance of the north end zone to greet and root them on as they enter the stadium.

Best travel tip:
Make sure to party beforehand in the Quad. The atmosphere is already carnival like, but during the Iron Bowl, that partying is taken to another level.

Notable Quotes:

"I have never felt anything more intense than the hatred between Alabama and Auburn. Period."—Scott Brown, Alabama alumnus and co-author of *The Uncivil War*

"It's a big game and down here in the South, it's definitely Auburn and Alabama. And you have to pick a team when you move down here. And I chose Auburn because they're the winning team."—Lynsey Lyons, Auburn fan, WKRG.com

Relevant Websites:

42

EPSOM DERBY

Where?

Epsom Downs Racecourse
Epsom, Surrey, KT18 5LQ, U.K.

When?

Annually, during the first weekend in June.

Significance:

Locally they call it the Derby Stakes. Around the world, it is known as the Epsom Derby, pronounced "dar-bee" in jolly old England, one of the most prestigious flat thoroughbred horse races internationally. The Epsom Downs Racecourse in Epsom, Surrey, England, hosts the annual event.

While the first race at the Downs took place in 1661, the events in the summer of 1879 would lead to its current moniker. Edward Smith-Stanley, the 12th Earl of Derby, coordinated a race for himself and his friends to race their three-year-old fillies over 1.5 miles. Originally named the Oaks, the race took on a different identity when Earl and Sir Charles Bunbury flipped a coin to decide whose name would be attached to the competition. While Sir Charles lost the flip, Diomed, his horse, won the first race held in 1780. The namesake earl would finally secure his first victory in 1787 with a horse named Sir Peter Teazle.

Today, the famed one-mile, four-furlong race serves as a significant stepping stone for the jockeys and their horses to compete in large international races. Those include France's Prix de l'Arc de Triomphe and the Breeder's Cup in the United States. The Epsom Derby also serves as the all-important second leg of England's Triple Crown with 2,000 Guineas being the first and St. Leger filling out the trio.

Who attends?

Horse-racing enthusiasts in the United Kingdom and around the world.

How to get there?

The racecourse is located a few minutes from Epsom Town Centre at B290 Epsom Downs Road. Alternatively, you can find it off Junction 9 of the M25. During the racing season, AA signs will mark all major routes to get to the track.

Tickets:

For primary ticket access information consider: www.epsomderby.co.uk.

Tickets for the Grandstand Enclosure and Tattenham Straight Enclosure go quickly. Online ticket sales are restricted for some areas. To purchase tickets not available online, contact the Ticket Office at +44 (0)1372 470 047.

For secondary ticket access, consider:

GoTickets, Inc.

2345 Waukegan Road, Suite 140
Bannockburn, IL 60015-1552
Toll-Free: 1-800-775-1617
Fax: (919) 481-9101
E-mail: sales@gotickets.com
www.gotickets.com

Accommodations:

Holiday Inn Express at Epsom Downs
Epsom Downs
Surrey, KT18 5LQ, U.K.
Phone: +44 (0)844 801 0323
www.hiexpress.com

Note: A contemporary budget hotel located at the Downs. You cannot get any closer to the race.

The Chalk Lane Hotel
Epsom
Surrey, KT18 7BB, U.K.
Phone: +44 (0)1372 721 179
Fax: +44 (0)1372 726 311
www.chalklanehotel.com

Note: You just may hear the hooves against the tarmac from your room. Nestled between the racecourse and the town center.

Nonsuch Park Hotel
355-357 London Road
Ewell, Epsom
Surrey, KT17 2DE, U.K.
Phone: +44 (0)208 393 0771
Fax: +44 (0)208 393 1415
www.nonsuchparkhotel.com

Note: Close to the racecourse and directly opposite the historic Nonsuch Park on London Road.

On-Site Hospitality:
Epsom Downs Racecourse hospitality will satisfy your friends and clients with great food and wine. The facilities are impressive and only enhance the thrilling action and party atmosphere of race day. They provide various options based on your needs.

Phone: +44 (0)1372 477 747
E-mail: london.hospitality@
jockeyclubracecourses.com

Travel Packages:
If you are going to travel to this event, I would recommend using a reliable company to work with you on making the necessary arrangements. The suppliers listed in this book have solid references and are by far the most trusted in the business. Below are some of the organizations to try for this Top 100 Must See Sporting Event.

Premiere Corporate Events
14 Penn Plaza, Suite 925
New York, NY 10122
Phone: (212) 695-9480
Fax: (212) 564-8098
Toll-Free: 1-877-621-5243
E-mail: requests@tseworld.com
www.tseworld.com
www.pcevents.com

Premiere Sports Travel
201 Shannon Oaks Circle, Suite 205
Cary, NC 27511
Phone: (919) 481-9511
Fax: (919) 481-1337
Toll-Free: 1-800-924-9993
E-mail: sales@sportstravel.com
www.sportstravel.com

Dining:

Rubbing House
34 Langley Vale Road
Epsom Downs
Surrey, KT18 5LJ, U.K.
Phone: +44 (0)1372 745 050
www.rubbinghouse.com

Note: Nothing gets you closer to the race than this restaurant. Enjoy traditional dishes with fine wines and champagne.

A Roma Restaurant
67-69 High Street
Epsom
Surrey, KT17 1RX, U.K.
Phone: +44 (0)208 393 8810

Note: Proving that it is possible to get great, authentic Italian food in the United Kingdom.

C'est La Vie
17 High Street
Epsom
Surrey, KT17 1SB, U.K.
Phone: +44 (0)208 394 2933

Note: This family-run restaurant is known for great food and friendly service.

Airports:

Gatwick Airport (thirty-two minutes from Surrey, England)
West Sussex, RH6 0NP, U.K.
Phone: +44 (0)870 000 2468
www.gatwickairport.com

Heathrow Airport (LHR) (fifty-two minutes from Surrey, England)
234 Bath Road
Hayes, Middlesex, UB3 5AP, U.K.
www.heathrowairport.com

Sports Travel Insider's Edge:

Best way to watch the action:
Enjoy a picnic while you watch the Derby. The Tattenham Picnic Area offers race go-ers a delicious picnic located next to the Grandstand Enclosure. Picnic tables are placed on a spacious lawn with access to bars and bookmakers.

Best place to get up close:
Get your hands on the Derby Festival Two Day Badge. You gain access to the Queen's Stand on Ladies Day and Derby Day, the most exclusive area at Epsom. It provides the best view opposite the winning post. Only bearers of the badge are allowed to enter.

Best travel tip:
The dress code for the Queen's Stand mandates that gentlemen wear either black or grey morn-ing dress (formal wear) with a top hat, or what they call Service Dress. Ladies are requested to wear formal day dress or a pants suit with a hat. The Grandstand is a more smart casual style, but jeans are discouraged. Your best bet is to dress up no matter where you sit.

Notable Quotes:

"Our essential site services are paving the way for a new Grandstand and conference facilities that will help to generate the nec-essary year-round income to allow Epsom to continue to host The Derby Festival, one of the world's most famous sporting events."—GARY TURNER, Chief Executive of General Demolition

"My heart seemed to stop beating at the furlong pole and I had to pinch myself passing the post. It had all been so easy. I had expected a dog fight but it was as smooth as an oil painting. I don't know whether to laugh or cry. I will never forget this day as long as I live."—FRANKIE DETTORI, on winning the Epsom Derby

"When I find myself in the tribune of Epsom on the first Wednesday of June, a few sec-onds before the start of the two minutes and a half, the longest and most tense of the year, I know with certainty that I would not like to be in that moment in any other part of the world; this is something that one may assure in very few occasions and it is worthwhile to live three hundred and sixty five days to enjoy again such plenitude."—FERNANDO SAVATER, author of *The Play of the Horses*

Relevant Websites:
www.epsomderby.co.uk
www.surreycc.gov.uk
www.tseworld.com
www.pcevents.com
www.sportstravel.com
www.gotickets.com
www.premieresports.com

43
CALGARY STAMPEDE

Where?
Stampede Grounds
1410 Olympic Way Southeast
Calgary, AB T2G 2W1, Canada

When?
Beginning the second week of July, the an-nual event takes place for 10 days.

Significance:

The "World's Largest Rodeo" is also Canada's largest annual event. Established in 1912, the Calgary Stampede attracts approximately one million people throughout the ten-day rodeo extravaganza, including 350,000 showing up for the inaugural parade. The event itself currently costs over $6 million to run. It started more modestly as a showcase for the best cowboys throughout North America. Today, those modern-day cowboys have the opportunity to show their skills and take home a few dollars out of the millions in cash prizes. Specific competitions include Bareback, Bull Riding, Ladies Barrel Racing, Saddle Bronc, Steer Wrestling, and Tie-Down Roping.

Who attends?

While a highly anticipated event for Canadians, rodeo fans from throughout the world, and of all ages, get to see their sport on a grand scale. Cowboy hats and boots are optional, but encouraged.

Tickets:

For primary ticket access information, consider: www.cs.calgarystampede.com.

Tickets via Telephone:

Calgary Stampede Box Office
Phone: (403) 269-9822
Toll-Free: 1-800-661-1767

For secondary ticket access, consider:

GoTickets, Inc.

2345 Waukegan Road, Suite 140
Bannockburn, IL 60015-1552
Toll-Free: 1-800-775-1617
Fax: (919) 481-9101
E-mail: sales@gotickets.com
www.gotickets.com

Accommodations:

The Fairmont Palliser

133 9th Avenue Southwest

Calgary, AB T2P 2M3, Canada
Phone: (403) 262-1234
www.fairmont.com
Note: A five-star, castle-like hotel

The Westin Calgary

320 4th Avenue Southwest
Calgary, AB T2P 2S6, Canada
Phone: (403) 266-1611
www.starwoodhotels.com
Note: Located in the heart of Calgary, it boasts 525 smoke-free guest rooms and suites. Onsite WestinWorkout Gym and the Essence restaurant offer cuisine with a local flair.

Sheraton Suites Eau Claire

255 Barclay Parade Southwest
Calgary, AB T2P 5C2, Canada
Phone: (403) 266-7200
Toll-Free: 1-800-661-9378
www.sheratonsuites.com
Note: This award-winning, four-diamond hotel is suites-only and close to shopping, recreation, and other neighborhood attractions.

Hotel Arts (formerly Holiday Inn Calgary)

119 12th Avenue Southwest
Calgary, AB T2R 0G8, Canada
Phone: (403) 266-4611
Toll-Free: 1-800-661-9378
www.hotelarts.ca
Note: Close to great shopping, theater, and dining. This hotel features twelve floors of luxury rooms that include studios and suites.

Best Western Calgary Center Inn

3630 MacLeod Trail South
Calgary, AB T2G 2P9, Canada
Phone: (403) 287-3900
Toll-Free: 1-877-287-3900
www.bwcalgarycentre.com
Note: Minutes from downtown businesses, shopping, and the Calgary Stampede. Featuring oversized rooms, a continental breakfast, and an onsite exercise room.

Days Inn Calgary South
3828 MacLeod Trail Southeast
Calgary, AB T2G 2R2, Canada
Phone: **(403)** 243-5531
Toll-Free: 1-800-DAYS-INN
www.daysinn.ca

Note: Prime location near Calgary Stampede Park, the Pengrowth Saddledome, and the Chinook Centre, Calgary's largest shopping mall.

Inn on Macleod Trails
4206 Macleod Trail
Calgary, AB T2G 2R7, Canada
Phone: (403) 287-2700
Toll- Free: 1-866-554-0162
www.macleodtrailhotel.com

Note: Five minutes from Calgary and situated on the Light Rail Transit (LRT) with plenty of free parking.

On-Site Hospitality and Events:

Mavericks Dining Room & Lounge: Western-style cuisine in a casual atmosphere. Big screen and plasma televisions are available.

The Saddle & Sulky: At the north end of level two, you will find a full bar and great concession food that features hamburgers, jumbo hot dogs, sausages, and made-to-order sandwiches.

The Clubhouse: The south end of level four is a great place to see live racing within a climate-controlled venue with buffet and a la carte dining selections. Located in the Clubhouse is the Winner's Circle with a full-service bar.

Stampede Casino WildCards Café & Saloon: Reasonably priced meal options are available at WildCards, including breakfast.

Chuckwagon Racing: $1 million in prize money is at stake in the Raceland Derby.

Concerts: Featuring all types of A-list bands playing rock or country.

Vintage Tractor Pulls: Speaks for itself. Miniature donkeys and blacksmiths can be found milling about the Agricultural grounds.

Stampede Breakfasts: Along Eighth Avenue, a free pancake breakfast is provided by city officials and local residents. The Chinook Center breakfast has been running for twenty-five years. A listing of the breakfasts can be found at www.tourismcalgary.com or by calling Toll-Free at 1-800-661-1678.

Travel Packages:

If you are going to travel to this event, I would recommend using a reliable company to work with you on making the necessary arrangements. The suppliers listed in this book have solid references and are by far the most trusted in the business. Below are some of the organizations to try for this Top 100 Must See Sporting Event.

Premiere Corporate Events
14 Penn Plaza, Suite 925
New York, NY 10122
Phone: (212) 695-9480
Fax: (212) 564-8098
Toll-Free: 1-877-621-5243
E-mail: requests@tseworld.com
www.tseworld.com
www.pcevents.com

Premiere Sports Travel
201 Shannon Oaks Circle, Suite 205
Cary, NC 27511
Phone: (919) 481-9511
Fax: (919) 481-1337
Toll-Free: 1-800-924-9993
E-mail: sales@sportstravel.com
www.sportstravel.com

Dining:

Ranchman's Restaurant
9615 Macleod Trail South
Calgary, AB T2J 0P6, Canada
Phone: (403) 253-1100
Fax: (403) 259-5447
www.ranchmans.com

Note: Dining and dancing in an old-time cowboy saloon atmosphere.

Caesar's Steak House

512 4th Avenue Southwest
Calgary, AB T2P 0J6, Canada
Phone: (403) 264-1222

Note: Recognized as one of Calgary's oldest and finest steakhouses.

Buzzards

140 10th Avenue Southwest
Calgary, AB T2R 0A3, Canada
Phone: (403) 264-6959
Fax: (403) 266-6630
www.cowboycuisine.com

Note: An authentic cowboy experience. For twenty-five years in the same location, serving the best steaks and burgers in the city.

Palomino Steak House

109 7th Avenue Southwest
Calgary, AB T2P 0W5, Canada
Phone: (403) 532-1911
www.thepalomino.ca

Note: The upstairs serves great barbecue with meat smoked over applewood and cherrywood. Enjoy live music downstairs every Friday and Saturday.

Airport:

Calgary International Airport

2000 Airport Road Northeast
Calgary, AB T2E 6W5, Canada
Phone: (403) 735-1200
Fax: (403) 735-1281
Toll-Free: 1-877-254-7427
www.calgaryairport.com

Sports Travel Insider's Edge:

Best way to watch the action:
The two-hour opening day parade kicks off the Stampede. Floats from various organizations fill the streets. Best seating is on the sidewalk area. This is a must see part of the Stampede.

Best place to get up close:
Check out Olympic Plaza every day at noon. There is always something going on, lots of free entertainment, and many must see Western acts.

Best travel tip:
Even if Western wear isn't your style, donning a cowboy hat and a pair of matching boots will help you blend into the crowd.

Notable Quotes:

"This is the show."—SAL HOWELL, Cowgirl and non-pro working cow horse competitor

"We're hearing it everywhere and from everyone, patrons on the park, Calgarians across the city, and visitors from around the world, this year's Calgary Stampede was absolutely amazing. We had beautiful weather, outstanding attendance at the park, and an abundance of community activities—something for everyone. That's what makes us 'The Greatest Outdoor Show on Earth.'"—GEORGE BROOKMAN, Calgary Stampede president and chairman of the board

"Ten days every July...the city goes into a rodeo frenzy. Punks, housewives, businessmen, and kids alike all sport jeans, western shirts, cowboy hats, and cowboy boots, whether they listen to country and western music or not."—TODD KIPP, ohmynews.com

"It's one of those 'good times' everyone needs to experience for themselves at least once in their lives. So throw on your cowboy hat, slip into your sh**kickers and come see what cowtown hospitality is all about."—TODD KIPP

Relevant Websites:

www.calgarystampede.com
www.tourismcalgary.com
www.tseworld.com
www.pcevents.com
www.sportstravel.com
www.gotickets.com
www.premieresports.com

44

KOSHIEN BASEBALL TOURNAMENT

Where?
Kōshien Stadium
Kōshien-machi 1-82
Nishinomiya, Hyogo Prefecture
663-8152, Japan

When?
Beginning of June.

Significance:
Hanshin Kōshien Stadium officially opened on April 1, 1924, and boasted a capacity of 55,000. It also holds the designation as the largest stadium in Asia. The stadium was built to host the annual National High School Baseball Invitational Tournament and continues to do so to this day. High school baseball is so popular with Japanese fans that the tournament games take priority over the professional matchups. That forces the Kōshien Tigers to embark on a three-week road trip every year.

Thousands of Japanese high school baseball teams vie for a coveted spot in the tournament, but only a select few make it. Young baseball players from around the country dream of the day when they can play on the "sacred" dirt of Kōshien. Today, playing at Kōshien can make a baseball player down the street into a superstar. Winning the Kōshien Baseball Tournament gives a championship team not only a title, but also celebrity status. Many go on to play in the major leagues of Japan and the United States.

Millions of baseball fans attend the tournament and millions more watch on television. Kōshien has been compared to being the Super Bowl and the World Series all rolled up into one big event.

Who attends?
The popularity of high school baseball in Japan is akin to the following Major League Baseball enjoys in the United States. Fans count on seeing future MLB players put their talents on display. Busloads of high school students show up to support their team.

How to get there?
Take the Hanshin Dentetsu Line that starts at Osaka-Umeda Station and goes to Kobe. Get off at Kōshien Station and take a one-minute walk under the overpass and to the ballpark.

Tickets:
For primary ticket access information, consider: www.hanshin.co.jp/koshien.

For secondary ticket access, consider:

GoTickets, Inc.
2345 Waukegan Road, Suite 140
Bannockburn, IL 60015-1552
Toll-Free: 1-800-775-1617
Fax: (919) 481-9101
E-mail: sales@gotickets.com
www.gotickets.com

Accommodations:

Hilton Osaka
8-8, Umeda 1-chome, Kita-ku
Osaka, 530-001, Japan
Phone: +81 6 6347 7111
Fax: +81 6 6347 7001
www.hilton.com
Note: Linked to one of Osaka's largest shopping malls. Seven restaurants are onsite, including the Windows on the World.

Novotel Kōshien Osaka West
3-30 Kōshien Takashio-Cho
Nishinomiya
Osaka, 663-8136, Japan
Phone: +81 7984 81111
www.novotel.com

Note: Four-star hotel with 200 rooms for leisure and business travelers. Five restaurants are onsite serving Japanese and European cuisine.

Hyatt Regency Osaka
1-13-11 Nanko-Kita, Suminoe-Ku
Osaka, 559-0034, Japan
Phone: +81 6 6612 1234
Fax: +81 6 6614 7800
www.hyatt.com

Note: Located in Cosmo Square, Osaka's new business district, and just forty-five minutes from Osaka and Kansai International Airport.

RIHGA Royal Hotel
5-3-68 Nakanoshima, Kita-ku
Osaka, 530-0005, Japan
Phone: +81 (0)6 6448 1121
Fax: +81 (0)6 6448 4414
www.rihga.com

Note: In the heart of Osaka and close to traditional architectures such as Central Public Hall, Osaka City Hall, and the Museum of Oriental Ceramics.

On-Site Hospitality:
The baseball sure looks American but vendors do not serve anything resembling American ballpark fare. Hot dogs, peanuts, and Cracker Jacks are nowhere to be found. Instead, you can choose from sushi, okonomiyaki, yakitori (chicken on a stick), or dried squid.

Travel Packages:
If you are going to travel to this event, I would recommend using a reliable company to work with you on making the necessary arrangements. The suppliers listed in this book have solid references and are by far the most trusted in the business. Below are some of the organizations to try for this Top 100 Must See Sporting Event.

Premiere Corporate Events
14 Penn Plaza, Suite 925
New York, NY 10122

Phone: (212) 695-9480
Fax: (212) 564-8098
Toll-Free: 1-877-621-5243
E-mail: requests@tseworld.com
www.tseworld.com
www.pcevents.com

Premiere Sports Travel
201 Shannon Oaks Circle, Suite 205
Cary, NC 27511
Phone: (919) 481-9511
Fax: (919) 481-1337
Toll-Free: 1-800-924-9993
E-mail: sales@sportstravel.com
www.sportstravel.com

Dining:

Banjara
1-12-14 Shinbata, Kita-ku
Watanebe Bldg. No 5, 6F
Osaka, 530-0012, Japan
Phone: +81 (0)6 4802 0326
Fax: +81 (0)6 4802 0326
www.restaurant-bar-banjara.com

Note: Popular Indian restaurant serving appetizers, salads, and a selection of breads. Local draft, imported beers, and wines are available.

Kanidoraku Honten
1-6-18 Dotonbori
Osaka, 27 542-0071, Japan
Phone: +81 (0)6 6211 8975

Note: Seasonal crab is prepared in a multitude of delicious ways. Japanese cuisine is served on authentic ceramic dishes.

Bombay Kitchen Shinsaibashi
Shinsaibashi Cosumi Bldg. 1F
Osaka, 27 542-0083, Japan
Phone: +81 (0)6 6245 9495

Note: Gorge yourself on spicy, sub-continental food served in an all-you-can-eat restaurant.

Surya
Hep Navio 6F
Osaka, 27, Japan

Phone: +81 (0)6 6311 3113

Note: A smaller and very popular Indian restaurant in the Hep Navio shopping center. Seating is limited, but the wait is worth it.

Pinakana

Kappayoko-cho Square
Osaka, 27 530-0012, Japan
Phone: +81 6 6375 5828

Note: Northern Indian curry dishes baked in charcoal ovens by experienced Indian chefs.

Airports:

Kansai International Airport

Phone: +81 (0)7245 52500
www.kansai-airport.or.jp

Itami International Airport

Terminal Building, 3-555
Nishimachi, Hotarugaike, Toyonaka
Osaka, 560, Japan
Phone: +81 6 6843 1121
www.osaka-airport.co.jp/ (in Japanese)
www.osaka-itm.airports-guides.com (English)

Sports Travel Insider's Edge:

Best way to watch the action:

The tradition in Japanese stadiums is for the home team fans to sit in right field and the away team boosters to sit in left field. However, due to the fanatical local following at Kōshien, the visiting fans will likely take up a small portion of that left field area.

Best place to get up close:

While it will set you back a few thousand yen, the best place to watch the game up close is a green seat directly behind home plate.

Best travel tip:

If you still want to experience Kōshien baseball, you do not have to shell out a lot of money for a premium seat. Instead, sit in an outfield seat. It is an affordable option, but make sure you are sitting on the side of the team you are supporting.

Notable Quotes:

"Our Kanō team traditions were actually just like those of the Japanese teams. If you have ever seen Kōshien [championship] games on television, you will see that after every game the losing team will cry, some even sobbing loudly with their noses running. But we Kanō players would never cry after losing; we would only cry after winning."—Su Zhengsheng, "Tianxia zhi Jianong"

"If the baseball gods really wanted the Red Sox to play in Japan, they would have steered them to the 84-year-old Hanshin Kōshien Stadium. Not that a stadium is needed to enhance enjoyment of a baseball game, but as any Fenway Park visitor understands, a special ballpark always does. Kōshien Stadium is that kind of a special ballpark."—Michael Silverman, *Boston Herald*

Relevant Websites:

www.hanshin.co.jp/koshien
www.tseworld.com
www.pcevents.com
www.sportstravel.com
www.gotickets.com
www.premieresports.com

45

SPECIAL OLYMPICS

Where?

2010–Lincoln and Omaha, NE
2014–Sochi, Russia

For the most up-to-date information on the upcoming locations, visit www.special-olympics.org.

When?

Every four years in July.

Significance:

In 1968, Eunice Kennedy Shriver founded the Special Olympics at the first Olympic-style competition in Chicago Park supported by the Kennedy Foundation. Her sister, the late Rosemary Kennedy, had an intellectual disability and served as an inspiration to her sibling and many others. Prior to that announcement, in 1962 Shriver started Camp Shriver, a day camp at her home in Potomac, Maryland, for children with intellectual disabilities. With a focus on physical activity and competition, the seeds were planted for what would become the Special Olympics six years later.

The Special Olympics have grown in participation and prominence. In 1988, the event was recognized by the International Olympic Committee as the only sports organization allowed to use the name Olympics in its title. The Special Olympics offers year-round training and competition in thirty Olympic-style summer and winter sports every four years. It ensures that events are accommodating to a variety of ability levels so these athletes can compete on a level playing field.

The Special Olympics Oath sums it up best: "Let me win. But if I cannot win, let me be brave in the attempt."

Who attends?

The Special Olympics is attended by fans who like to watch exceptional people do extraordinary things.

Tickets:

For all ticket access information, consider: www.specialolympics.org for the latest information.

Accommodations:

Omaha:

Doubletree Hotel
1616 Dodge Street
Omaha, NE 68102
Phone: (402) 346-7600
Fax: (402) 346-5722
www.doubletree.com

Note: Nine miles from the stadium and in the heart of downtown Omaha.

Embassy Suites Hotel-Downtown Omaha
555 South 10th Street
Omaha, NE 68102
Phone: (402) 346-9000
Fax: (402) 346-4236
Toll-Free: 1-800-EMBASSY
www.embassysuites.com

Note: For the guest who prefers a more upscale, full-service environment, not to mention a full suite.

Courtyard Omaha Downtown
101 South 10th Street
Omaha, NE 68102
Phone: (402) 346-2200
Fax: (402) 346-7720
Toll-Free: 1-866-204-9388
www.marriott.com

Note: A view of the Mississippi River and the restored brick buildings of the Old Market. Walking distance from Rosenblatt Stadium.

Lincoln:

Embassy Suites Lincoln
1040 P Street
Lincoln, NE 68508
Phone: (402) 474-1111
Fax: (402) 474-1144
www.embassysuites.com

Note: This full-service hotel boasts all suites. Located in downtown Lincoln.

The Cornhusker-Marriott

333 South 13th Street
Lincoln, NE 68508
Phone: (402) 474-7474
Fax: (402) 474-1847
www.marriott.com

Note: Distinguished ten-story downtown hotel combines antique tapestries with modern décor.

Hampton Inn Lincoln-Heritage Park

5922 Vandervoort Drive
Lincoln, NE 68516
Phone: (402) 420-7800
Toll-Free: 1-800-733-5916
www.hamptoninn.com

Note: Close to the Nebraska State Capitol, Lincoln Children's Museum, and the Sheldon Memorial Sculpture Garden.

Sochi, Russia:

Radisson SAS Lazurnaya Hotel, Sochi

103 Kurortny Prospect
Sochi, 354024, Russia
www.radissonsas.ru

Note: Located on the southeast coast beach of the Black Sea. Many recreational activities and a casino onsite.

Radisson SAS Lazurnaya Peak Hotel, Sochi

77 Zaschitnikov Kavkaza
Krasnaya Polyana
Sochi, 354594, Russia
www.peakhotel.ru

Note: South of the Russian Black Sea coast in the mountains. Onsite swimming pool, fitness center, and spa.

Travel Packages:

If you are going to travel to this event, I would recommend using a reliable company to work with you on making the necessary arrangements. The suppliers listed in this book have solid references and are by far the most trusted in the business. Below are some of the organizations to try for this Top 100 Must See Sporting Event.

Premiere Corporate Events

14 Penn Plaza, Suite 925
New York, NY 10122
Phone: (212) 695-9480
Fax: (212) 564-8098
Toll-Free: 1-877-621-5243
E-mail: requests@tseworld.com
www.tseworld.com
www.pcevents.com

Premiere Sports Travel

201 Shannon Oaks Circle, Suite 205
Cary, NC 27511
Phone: (919) 481-9511
Fax: (919) 481-1337
Toll-Free: 1-800-924-9993
E-mail: sales@sportstravel.com
www.sportstravel.com

Dining:

Omaha:

Bohemian Café

1406 South 13th Street
Omaha, NE 68108
Phone: (402) 342-9838
www.bohemiancafe.net

Note: A local favorite since 1964. Czech and European cuisine are on the menu with everything from roast duck to homemade apple strudel.

Lo Sole Mio Ristorante

3001 South 32nd Avenue
Omaha, NE 68105
Phone: (402) 345-5656
Fax: (402) 345-5859
www.losolemio.com

Note: Authentic Italian dishes from freshly made pastas and sauces in a casual, informal setting. Prides itself on having "The best Italian food in town."

Greek Island

3821 Center Street
Omaha, NE 68105
Phone: (402) 346-1528
Fax: (402) 345-7248

Note: Best known for gyros, Athenian salads, and other Greek delectables. Fully stocked bar includes imported Greek wines and beers.

Flatiron Café

1722 Saint Mary's Avenue
Omaha, NE 68102
Phone: (402) 344-3040
www.theflatironcafe.com

Note: Upscale restaurant located in the historic Flatiron Building. The seasonal menu is ever changing with Miso Marinated Sea Bass and Grilled Breast of Duck.

Spaghetti Works Restaurant

502 South 11th Street
Omaha, NE 68108
Phone: (402) 422-0770
Fax: (402) 341-9833
www.spagworks.com

Note: Casual Italian dining with big plates of pasta and your choice of sauces. Sandwiches and ribs are available as well. No reservations.

Lincoln:

The Oven

201 North 8th Street, Suite 117
Lincoln, NE 68508
Phone: (402) 475-6118
Fax: (402) 475-1281
www.theoven-lincoln.com

Note: Great Indian food. Considered by many to be the best restaurant in Lincoln.

JTK Cuisine & Cocktails

201 North 7th Street
Lincoln, NE 68508
Phone: (402) 435-0161

Note: Their cuisine stands out in an area filled with Italian restaurants and burger joints.

La Paz Mexican Fare & Cuisine

321 North Cotner Boulevard
Lincoln, NE 68505
Phone: (402) 466-9111
Fax: (402) 466-9244
www.lapazmexican.biz

Note: Good food and drinks at reasonable prices with great service from an attentive staff.

Skeeter Barnes

5800 South 58th Street
Lincoln, NE 68506
Phone: (402) 421-3340
Fax: (402) 421-3468
www.skeeterbarnes.com

Note: Serving Nebraska Corn-fed Beef, including steaks, prime rib, and burgers.

Sochi, Russia:

American Diner

3 Chernomorskaya ulitsa
Sochi, Russia
Phone: +7 8622 66 1881

Note: A very American restaurant reminiscent of Elvis Presley's heyday. It is located inside the Zamchuzhina Hotel on the second floor.

Filibuster

3 Chernomorskaya ulitsa
Sochi, 354002, Russia

Note: Located on the beach and features live Gypsy dancing and music.

Limpopo

3 Chernomorskaya ulitsa
Sochi, Russia

Note: Good food and located near two swimming pools.

Lubava

3 Chernomorskaya ulitsa
Sochi, 354002, Russia

Note: Serving Russian and European cuisine and magnificent fish dishes in a cozy setting. Not for children due to the erotic shows.

Airports:

Omaha:

Eppley Airfield
4501 Abbott Drive, Suite 2300
Omaha, NE 68110
Phone: (402) 661-8000
Fax: (402) 661-8025
www.eppleyairfield.com

Lincoln:

Lincoln Airport
2400 West Adams Street
Lincoln, NE 68524
Phone: (402) 458-2480
Fax: (402) 458-2490
www.lincolnairport.com

Sochi, Russia:

Sochi International Airport
Sochi, 354355, Russia
www.sochi-airport.com

Notable Quotes:

"If we give a chance to our special athletes, they can do beautiful things and we feel greatness inside us. If we believe the children can make it, we can see it become true."—JOANNA DESPOTOPOULOU, Special Olympics Hellas president

"My understanding of Olympic spirits is that one day we can realize what is beautiful, the great and the true. We try to inspire others to give people of disabilities an equal chance to be included in the societies no matter how different they are."— JOANNA DESPOTOPOULOU

Relevant Websites:

www.specialolympics.org
www.tseworld.com
www.pcevents.com
www.sportstravel.com
www.premieresports.com

46

SOCCER GAME AT MARACANÃ STADIUM IN RIO

Where?
Maracanã Stadium
Rua Professor Eurico Rabelo
Rio de Janeiro, Brazil

When?
During football, a.k.a. soccer, season.

Significance:
Maracanã Stadium (the Estádio Jornalista Mário Filho, commonly known as Estádio do Maracanã) is one of the largest and most famous football/soccer stadiums in the world. Soccer is Brazil's national pastime bordering on obsession with Brazilians filling the Maracanã beyond its official capacity of 90,000. The finals of the 1950 championship saw 199,500 people pack into the stadium. In 1969, 183,341 fans crammed in to see Pelé make his 1,000th goal. This is a facility not just for soccer fans, but also for those who live and breathe the sport, coming to the Maracanã to worship at what has been called the "World's Temple to Soccer."

Brazil's selection to host the 1950 FIFA World Cup necessitated the government to build the type of facility that would handle such an event. While construction was not complete (no bathrooms and no press stands), soccer fans filled the stadium to see Didi score the very first goal in the opening match which featured The Rio de Janeiro All-Stars defeating the São Paulo All-Stars 3-1. Today, the Maracanã hosts key games involving both local teams as well as competition between international soccer clubs.

Who attends?
Brazilian soccer fanatics that number well into the hundreds of thousands. Fans sing

---

songs, wave flags, do cartwheels, play samba drums, and shed a tear or two.

How to get there?
The stadium is easily accessible by the metro at Maracanã Station on Line 2, or by Bus 462 or 463 from Copacabana, 461 from Ipanema, or 460 from Leblon. Taxi services are available and highly recommended following a game.

Tickets:
For primary ticket access information, consider: www.cbf.com.br

For secondary ticket access, consider:

GoTickets, Inc.
2345 Waukegan Road, Suite 140
Bannockburn, IL 60015-1552
Toll-Free: 1-800-775-1617
Fax: (919) 481-9101
E-mail: sales@gotickets.com
www.gotickets.com

Accommodations:

Windsor Asturias Hotel
Rua Senador Dantas 14
Rio de Janeiro, 20031-203, Brazil
Phone : +55 21 2195 1500
Fax: +55 21 2195 1515
www.windsorhoteis.com
Note: Near the Municipal Theater and the Museum of Modern Art. The hotel features an international restaurant and bar, outdoor pool, sauna, and a gym.

Ipanema Plaza Hotel
Rua Farme de Amoedo 34
Ipanema
Rio De Janeiro, 22420-020, Brazil
Phone: +55 21 3687 2000
www.ipanemaplazahotel.com.br/pt-br
Note: Located eight miles from the stadium, fifty meters to Ipanema Beach, and a five-minute drive to the Copacabana. Close to shops and other cultural activities.

Windsor Excelsior Hotel
Avenida Atlantica 1800
Rio De Janeiro, 22021-001, Brazil
Phone: +55 21 2195 5800
Fax: +55 21 2257 1850
www.windsorhoteis.com
Note: Six miles to soccer mayhem and close to cultural options, including theaters and museums.

Sheraton Rio Hotel
Av Niemeyer 121 Leblon
Rio de Janeiro, Brazil
Phone: +55 21 2274 1122
Fax +55 21 2239 5643
www.sheraton.com
Note: One of two hotels that is not separated from the beach by a multilane boulevard. The ocean's waves are close, but tend to be unruly and unpredictable.

On-Site Hospitality:
Official tours through the Maracanã are offered for roughly fifty dollars or you can just show up early during a home game. The stadium and its museum can be visited most days of the week from 9 A.M. to 5 P.M. with an admission cost of just a few dollars. Ask a Portuguese speaker to call ahead to check. Burgers and beers are sold in the parking lot on game day outside the Maracanã.

Travel Packages:
If you are going to travel to this event, I would recommend using a reliable company to work with you on making the necessary arrangements. The suppliers listed in this book have solid references and are by far the most trusted in the business. Below are some of the organizations to try for this Top 100 Must See Sporting Event.

Premiere Corporate Events
14 Penn Plaza, Suite 925
New York, NY 10122
Phone: (212) 695-9480
Fax: (212) 564-8098

Toll-Free: 1-877-621-5243
E-mail: requests@tseworld.com
www.tseworld.com
www.pcevents.com

Premiere Sports Travel

201 Shannon Oaks Circle, Suite 205
Cary, NC 27511
Phone: (919) 481-9511
Fax: (919) 481-1337
Toll-Free: 1-800-924-9993
E-mail: sales@sportstravel.com
www.sportstravel.com

Dining:

Confeitaria Colombo

Rua Gonçalves Dias 32
Rio de Janeiro, Brazil
Phone: +55 21 2505 1500
www.confeitariacolombo.com.br
Note: Authentic South American cuisine.

Doce Delicia

Rua Dias Ferreira 48
Rio de Janeiro, Brazil
Phone: +55 21 2249 2970
www.docedelicia.com.br
Note: The food is great, but Doce Delicia is better known for their pies.

Porcao Rio's

Rua Barão da Torre, 218 (Ipanema)
Rio de Janeiro, Brazil
Phone: +55 21 3389 8989
www.porcao.com.br
Note: Get a glimpse of Brazil's celebrity lot, including actors and soccer players. Servers make the rounds with sizzling spits of juicy beef, chicken, and pork.

Celeiro

Rua Dias Ferreira 199
Rio de Janeiro, Brazil
Phone: +55 21 2274 7843
www.celeiroculinaria.com.br
Note: A salad bar with a variety of vegetables.

The adjoining café serves snacks, sandwiches, and coffee.

Antiquarius

Rua Aristides Espinola 19
Rio de Janeiro, Brazil
Phone: +55 21 2294 1049
www.antiquarius.com.br
Note: Considered one of the best restaurants in Brazil. The chef combines traditional Portuguese dishes with exotic Brazilian spices and ingredients. Boasts an impressive wine cellar.

Airport:

Rio de Janeiro Airport

Avenida 20 de Janeiro
Ilha do Governador
Rio de Janeiro, 21942-900, Brazil
Phone: +55 21 3398 5050
www.infraero.gov.br

Sports Travel Insider's Edge:

Best way to watch the action:

You have a choice to make. The white section has the best view from above, but some of the other sections have the most extreme, animated fans straining to see the action. The action in some of the sections is almost better than that on the field.

Best place to get up close:

In the stands is where the excitement never fails. Screaming and sometimes weeping fans are all around. A view of the field might be a challenge from some of the seats in this large stadium seating close to 100,000. What makes it even tougher on the view is that most people will stand and wave their hands for the entire game. You might feel like you are at a carnival and not at a soccer game with all the drumming and people partying. It makes for an incredible experience.

Best travel tip:

Try and stay away from the stadium unless it's a game day and there are crowds of people around. The pedestrian bridge that connects the subway station with the stadium is a common place for robberies. Take the Avenue below. When you are there, dress down and make sure you know which team's rooting area you are sitting in. That way you can buy the appropriate souvenirs before the game.

Notable Quotes:

"Today Brazil has the biggest and most perfect stadium in the world, dignifying the competence of its people and its evolution in all branches of human activity. Now we have a stage of fantastic proportions in which the whole world can admire our prestige and sporting greatness."—*A Noite* newspaper

"If you ask a Brazilian what his dream is, the answer will probably be to score a goal in a World Cup Final at a packed Maracanã."—ALEX BELLOS, author of *Futebol: The Brazilian Way of Life*

Relevant Websites:

www.fifa.com
www.riodejaneiro-turismo.com.br/en/
    home.php
www.tseworld.com
www.pcevents.com
www.sportstravel.com
www.gotickets.com
www.premieresports.com

Where?

Ratliff Stadium
Yukon and Grandview
Odessa, TX 79765

or

Permian High School
1800 East 42nd Street
Odessa, TX 79762

When?

Friday nights during the high school football season.

Significance:

With the big money associated with professional football and the prestige of the big-time college gridiron, high school football tends to be forgotten. Not in Odessa, Texas. Before *Friday Night Lights* became a successful major motion picture and subsequent television show, Odessa residents had turned out to Ratliff Stadium to cheer on the Permian Panthers, not to mention chanting, "Mojo." A football tradition for over forty years, Permian is the third high school for Odessa and is located in the northern part of town. Five years after its inception, a state football championship came home to the school. Their story and overall history inspired a bestselling book, critically acclaimed movie, and TV series. Throughout the country, high school football is one of the most popular interscholastic sports. In Texas, it is a way of life with chants of "Mojo" ringing out from a certain town called Odessa.

Who attends?

Everyone in the town, along with many college scouts and recruiters looking for talent.

How to get there?

Take I-20 and go north on the East Loop 388. Take a left on Yukon Road. The bright lights will lead you there.

Tickets:

For primary ticket access information, call (432) 332-9151.

Tickets can be purchased prior to the game at the Permian High School Administration Building. Be warned that fans camp out days before the big game to get their tickets, which usually go on sale Tuesday morning of that week. Call the school for information.

Accommodations:

MCM Eleganté Hotel

5200 East University Boulevard
Odessa, TX 79762
Phone: (432) 368-5885
Fax: (432) 362-8958
Toll-Free: 1-866-368-5885
www.mcmelegante.com

Note: Considered the nicest hotel in Odessa and located less than five minutes from the stadium.

Fairfield Inn Odessa

3933 John Ben Shepperd Parkway
Odessa, TX 79762
Phone: (432) 363-1900
Fax: (432) 363-0094
www.fairfieldinn.com

Note: Comfortable, clean, and well-lit rooms. Just a quick three-minute trip to the high school.

Hampton Inn Odessa

3923 John Ben Shepperd Parkway
Odessa, TX 79762
Phone: (432) 363-2900
Fax: (432) 363-2950
www.hamptoninn.com

Note: The rooms are excellent, service is great, and the location is very convenient.

On-Site Hospitality:

Tailgating is an important part of Permian high school football. RVs are parked everywhere. In addition, the local booster club will usually coordinate a tailgate prior to the game. Check out www.odessapermian.com for information on weekly tailgates and events.

Travel Packages:

If you are going to travel to this event, I would recommend using a reliable company to work with you on making the necessary arrangements. The suppliers listed in this book have solid references and are by far the most trusted in the business. Below are some of the organizations to try for this Top 100 Must See Sporting Event.

Premiere Corporate Events

14 Penn Plaza, Suite 925
New York, NY 10122
Phone: (212) 695-9480
Fax: (212) 564-8098
Toll-Free: 1-877-621-5243
E-mail: requests@tseworld.com
www.tseworld.com
www.pcevents.com

Premiere Sports Travel

201 Shannon Oaks Circle, Suite 205
Cary, NC 27511
Phone: (919) 481-9511
Fax: (919) 481-1337
Toll-Free: 1-800-924-9993
E-mail: sales@sportstravel.com
www.sportstravel.com

Dining:

Shrimp Boat

5200 East University Boulevard
Odessa, TX 79762
Phone: (432) 363-6237

Note: Award-winning chef serving up great shrimp in the MCM Elegante Hotel.

Harrigans
2701 John Ben Shepperd Parkway
Odessa, TX 79762
Phone: (432) 617-8300
Fax: (432) 617-8302
www.harrigansdining.com
Note: All-American menu featuring chicken-fried steak.

La Bodega
1024 East 7th Street
Odessa, TX 79761
Phone: (432) 333-4469
Fax: (432) 333-9831
Note: Nachos and the Rueda (Mexican pizza) come highly recommended.

Airport:

Midland International Airport
9506 Laforce Boulevard
Midland, TX 79706
Phone: (432) 560-2200
www.midlandinternational.com

Sports Travel Insider's Edge:

Best way to watch the action:
Where else should you sit but on the home team side? The adrenaline felt from the Permian fans is exciting and infectious. You can have your Dallas Cowboys and Houston Texans. This is what football should be. Not about money. Not about television ratings. Here it is only about the players, their loyal fans, and the towns they play in.

Best place to get up close:
Following the game, Permian fans line up against the fence on the north end of the field. Whether their team wins or loses, they cheer them on as they board the bus near the locker room. Don't forget that Odessa is a small town with residents who love their team.

Best travel tip:
If you are looking to relive those high school memories, take in a game-day pep rally at

Permian's field house as the school day is starting. Halloween-time is especially fun with costumed fans everywhere.

Notable Quote:

"Stop reading the news clippings. You're small and you're going to be smaller every week. There ain't going to be no growth spurt between now and the first game. You're going to use your minds! You're going to play with your heart! And that is what you're going to use to win the State Championship."—BILLY BOB THORNTON as Coach Gary Gaines, *Friday Night Lights*

Relevant Websites:
www.odessapermian.com
www.mojoland.net
www.odessacvb.com
www.tseworld.com
www.pcevents.com
www.sportstravel.com
www.premieresports.com

48

U.S. OPEN
TENNIS TOURNAMENT

Where?
The USTA Billie Jean King National Tennis Center
Flushing Meadows Corona Park
Meridian Road at Grand Central Parkway
Queens, NY 11368

When?
Two weeks every year in August and September, around Labor Day.

Significance:
The United States Open tennis tournament serves as the fourth and final event of the Grand Slam tennis tournaments. Five championships are on the line, including men's

and women's singles, men's and women's doubles, and mixed doubles. There are also tournaments for senior, junior, and wheelchair players. With a history going back to 1881 at the Newport (Rhode Island) Casino, the U.S. Open started as a men's singles and doubles tournament. Today, 650,000 fans crowd the USTA Billie Jean King National Tennis Center to get a glimpse of their favorite tennis player, if not a little history. Stars are born, as are future millionaires. U.S. Open prize money is over $20 million dollars—a far cry from the $100,000 purse in 1968.

Who attends?

Many hardcore New York tennis fans and the country club set come together to see the best in professional tennis. The casually dressed join the more formally attired and cheer on their favorite player. Fans can even get a glimpse of tennis legends of the past, including the namesake of the USTA Billie Jean King National Tennis Center.

How to get there?

Driving is not a wise option due in part to the proximity of the Tennis Center to Citi Field where the Mets play. Better options are public transportation and shuttle buses that usually run from parking lots at Orchard Beach in the Bronx. New Yorkers will tell you that the best option is the #7 MTA Subway train, which runs all the way from Times Square and Grand Central Station in Manhattan. It operates on an expanded schedule during the U.S. Open, so waiting to catch a ride back to Manhattan should not be an issue. Another great option from Manhattan is to catch the Long Island Rail Road out to the Tennis Center in Flushing.

Tickets:

For primary ticket access information, consider: www.usopen.org, www.ticketmaster.com, or www.usta.com.

Ticketmaster locations and the USTA Billie Jean King National Tennis Center box office make tickets available as well. The best seats go to Full Series Ticket Subscription holders who have the opportunity to upgrade their seats through a series of annual renewals. For quality seating you should look at the secondary market as your best option.

For secondary ticket access, consider:

GoTickets, Inc.
2345 Waukegan Road, Suite 140
Bannockburn, IL 60015-1552
Toll-Free: 1-800-775-1617
Fax: (919) 481-9101
E-mail: sales@gotickets.com
www.gotickets.com

Arthur Ashe Stadium is one of the largest tennis stadiums around. I definitely recommend sitting only in the courtside, loge, and low rows of the upper promenade.

Accommodations:

The first three hotel selections are to be considered if you're interested in staying close to the center in Queens. New York City hotel options are also listed.

The Crowne Plaza at LaGuardia
104-04 Ditmars Boulevard
East Elmhurst, NY 11369
Phone: (718) 457-6300
Fax: (718) 899-9768
www.cplaguardia.com
Note: The Crowne Plaza is located two blocks from LaGuardia Airport and is mere minutes from the U.S. National Tennis Center. A nice option if you want to get to the event and then get home.

The LaGuardia Marriott
102-05 Ditmars Boulevard
East Elmhurst, NY 11369
Phone: (718) 565-8900
Fax: (718) 898-4955

Toll-Free: 1-800-228-9210
www.marriott.com

Note: No other hotel in Queens, NY, compares to the New York LaGuardia Marriott. This is a good bet if you're planning on staying close to the tennis center.

Sheraton LaGuardia

135-20 39th Avenue
Flushing, NY 11354
Phone: (718) 460-6666
Fax: (718) 445-2615
www.sheraton.com

Note: Enjoy a warm welcome and a distinctly Asian flair at the beautiful Sheraton LaGuardia East Hotel. Located in Chinatown, Queens. The hotel is just three miles away from the LaGuardia airport, accessible by an airport shuttle. A quick stroll over to the U.S. Open.

The Waldorf Astoria

301 Park Avenue
New York, NY 10022-6897
Reservations: 1-800-925-3673
Telephone: (212) 355-3000
Guest Fax: (212) 872-7272
www.waldorf.com

Note: Since 1893, this hotel has epitomized the quintessential luxury hotel experience. The hotel tends to get a large tennis crowd during the Open.

Grand Hyatt on 42nd Street

109 East 42nd Street at Grand Central Terminal
New York, NY 10017
Phone: (212) 883-1234
Fax: (212) 697-3772
www.hyatt.com

Note: Right next to Grand Central Station for easy access to the #7 subway line out to Flushing Meadows.

On-Site Hospitality:

Note that Aces and a few other restaurants require a courtside ticket or luxury suite ticket to enter. Check the official U.S. Open website for up-to-date information.

Aces: Famed chef Ed Brown of The Sea Grill at Rockefeller Center provides flavorful dishes in a beautiful facility with an elegant wine bar. It is considered the ultimate in stadium dining experiences. Specialty items include Plateau Royale, the Ultimate Seafood Platter, and Black Angus Filet Mignon. Private dining events include samples of wine and menu items.

Champions Bar & Grill: A traditional clubhouse atmosphere with a contemporary setting. Steaks, chops, seafood, and salads are offered throughout the day and evening. Specialty items include a Gourmet Appetizer Platter, hand-selected Angus beef, and Coldwater Hardshell Lobster. Visit them for happy hour and watch the U.S. Open events unfold on one of the many televisions.

U.S. Open Club: Subscription Series ticket (for a nominal entrance fee) and Silver Loge Box seat holders (part of their package) can enjoy a grand buffet of American cuisine throughout the day and evening. Specialty items include Prime Rib, Rotisserie Chicken, BBQ Brisket, and Summer Berries with Whipped Cream.

Patio Café: All ticket holders can enjoy the outdoor café offering seasonal sandwiches and salads. Specialty items include Spicy Thai Chicken Wings with Pineapple, Steakhouse Cheeseburger, and Bittersweet Chocolate Layer Cake.

Mojito Restaurant & Bar: A 1950's Havana-style tropical oasis awaits those who visit the Mojito. Specialty items include Chicken Picadillo, BBQ Pork Bocaditos, Coconut Caramel Flan, and, of course Mojitos, Sangrias, Margaritas, and Daiquiris.

Heineken Red Star Café: A more traditional sports bar offering snacks, specialty beers, and frozen cocktails.

U.S. Open Food Village: Regional cuisine and specialty items are provided by Bakery Café, Barilla's Pasta, Pizza & Salad Kitchen, Ben & Jerry's Ice Cream Shop, Drop Shot Cocktails, Franks and Fries, Fresca Mexicana, Fulton Seafood Exchange, Glatt Kosher Stand, Java Court, NY Deli, Savory & Sweet Crepes, and Sushi Court.

Travel Packages:

If you are going to travel to this event, I would recommend using a reliable company to work with you on making the necessary arrangements. The suppliers listed in this book have solid references and are by far the most trusted in the business. Below are some of the organizations to try for this Top 100 Must See Sporting Event.

Premiere Corporate Events

14 Penn Plaza, Suite 925
New York, NY 10122
Phone: (212) 695-9480
Fax: (212) 564-8098
Toll-Free: 1-877-621-5243
E-mail: requests@tseworld.com
www.tseworld.com
www.pcevents.com

Premiere Sports Travel

201 Shannon Oaks Circle, Suite 205
Cary, NC 27511
Phone: (919) 481-9511
Fax: (919) 481-1337
Toll-Free: 1-800-924-9993
E-mail: sales@sportstravel.com
www.sportstravel.com

Dining:

Il Toscano

42-05 235th Street
Flushing, NY 11363-1526

Phone: (718) 631-0300
Fax: (718) 225-5223
www.iltoscanony.com

Note: Great Northern Italian cuisine in Queens. Il Toscano opened its doors in 1985 and their consistency of great food has kept them as one of Queens's favorite Italian Restaurants. They offer 180 wines from around the world.

La Baraka Restaurant

25509 Northern Boulevard
Little Neck, NY 11362
Phone: (718) 428-1461
www.labarakarest.com

Note: La Baraka restaurant gathered foodies' interest by being one of the first in the '70s to introduce couscous, the grainy semolina essential to North Africa.

Buccaneer Diner

9301 Astoria Boulevard
Flushing, NY 11369
Phone: (718) 429-5188

Note: The Buccaneer Diner is a great place to grab a quick meal at any time, as they are open twenty-four hours a day, seven days a week.

The Parkside Restaurant

107-01 Corona Avenue
Flushing, NY 11368
Phone: (718) 271-9871
Fax: (718) 271-2454
www.parksiderestaurantny.com

Note: This place is perennially booked, with wait times for walk-ins often topping an hour, as befits a destination Italian landmark in the heart of Corona. Check out the wicker-filled greenhouse dining area, complete with name plaques citing fans like Jackie Collins and former Met and Yankee Lee Mazzilli.

Michael Jordan's The Steak House

Located inside Grand Central Terminal
23 Vanderbilt Avenue

New York, NY 10017
Phone: (212) 655-2300
Fax: (21) 655-4915
www.theglaziergroup.com
Note: A better slab of New York strip sirloin would be hard to find. A perfect meal inside Grand Central before heading out to the matches.

Airports:

John F. Kennedy International Airport (JFK)
JFK Airport
Jamaica, NY 11430
Phone: (718) 244-4444
www.panynj.gov

LaGuardia Airport (LGA)
Ditmars Boulevard and 94th Street
Flushing, NY 11371
Phone: (718) 533-3400
www.panynj.gov

Sports Travel Insider's Edge:

Best way to watch the action:
While you will pay a premium price, the Arthur Ashe Stadium reserved tickets are the only tickets that allow access to the main stadium court and all other side courts, except for Louis Armstrong Stadium. These seats are especially beneficial if you want to see a certain match being played at center court. A grounds pass will not suffice. Make sure you stay away from the top tier Promenade seats in Arthur Ashe unless you can purchase lower rows in this section. The seats at the top of the Promenade are not very good for viewing tennis. Courtside and Loge seats are the way to go inside the stadium.

Best place to get up close:
The early sessions are your best bet to see some great tennis up close. Score yourself a grounds pass for the first few sessions and walk the Disneyland-like grounds. Open seating is available on the outer courts and you can literally sit several feet away from the court and take in the best tennis in the world. If you love tennis, this is the best way to go.

Best travel tip:
While there is not a formal dress code, old traditions live on with country club attire preferred. However, leave your fancy purse at home if you want to avoid long security lines. And don't forget to warm up your voice. Unlike other tennis tournaments, this one is in New York and the local fans loudly encourage or heckle the players. South Gate entry is best as morning lines fill the East Gate. While you're in town, check out a Yankees, Mets, Giants, Jets, or Brooklyn Cyclones game. New York is immersed in sports at this time of year. And of course, it would not be a true trip to New York if you did not attend a Broadway show.

Notable Quotes:

"You know, you can just feed off the energy. It's a show. You know, you're just pushing each other. It's a competitive environment. When you feel like both people are playing up to their abilities. Obviously the crowd. You walk out there, you're part of a very small percentage of people who can go out there and hear someone cheer for them, compete on that stage with that amount of hype. So I think, like I said, I'd have to be totally out of touch not to realize that and appreciate it."—ANDY RODDICK, professional tennis player

"I realize actually what kind of a big-time event this is, you know, with 24,000 people in the stadium, the city. Just the difficulty to win here. I wasn't aware of it in the very beginning when I came on tour really. For me, the U.S. Open is the second biggest one we have on tour. To have won those two the most times, it's just incredible for me."—ROGER FEDERER, four-time U.S. Open champion

Relevant Websites:
www.usta.com
www.nycvisit.com
www.tseworld.com
www.pcevents.com
www.sportstravel.com
www.gotickets.com
www.premieresports.com

49

USC VS. UCLA
BASKETBALL GAME
AT PAULEY PAVILION

Where?
Edwin W. Pauley Pavilion
UCLA
650 Westwood Plaza
Los Angeles, CA 90095

When?
During NCAA basketball season from the end of December until March.

Significance:
Once again, proximity is the culprit in an NCAA basketball feud. The University of California, Los Angeles (UCLA) is not just down the road from the University of Southern California (USC); they reside in the same city with campuses a mere ten miles apart. Is there a word stronger than "intense" to describe a rivalry where opposing students and alumni can bump into each other just walking down the street?

As far as success on the court, the UCLA Bruins have thirty conference championships to the USC Trojan's seven to date. UCLA can claim eleven NCAA Men's Division I Basketball championships. Compared to USC, UCLA's domination of its conference has resulted in a 2:1 ratio of games won. Yet, for the seemingly disproportionate level of success, this feud rages on with notable and competitive games. When USC shows up at the Edwin W. Pauley Pavilion, they are David ready to do battle with their cross-town rival, Goliath.

Who attends?
Since the schools are so close, fans from both teams can easily get to the Pauley Pavilion to see the latest chapter in the Trojan versus Bruin rivalry.

How to get there?
From Los Angeles International Airport (LAX), take the 405 Freeway North to the Wilshire Boulevard East exit. Continue east on Wilshire for several blocks and move into the left lane. Take a left on Westwood Boulevard and follow it into campus.

Tickets:
For primary ticket access information, consider: www.tickets.ucla.edu.

For secondary ticket access, consider:

GoTickets, Inc.
2345 Waukegan Road, Suite 140
Bannockburn, IL 60015-1552
Toll-Free: 1-800-775-1617
Fax: (919) 481-9101
E-mail: sales@gotickets.com
www.gotickets.com

Accommodations:

Holiday Inn Express West Los Angeles
11250 Santa Monica Boulevard
Los Angeles, CA 90025
Phone: (310) 478-1400
Fax: (310) 478-1401
Toll-Free: 1-800-308-5432
www.hiewestla.com
Note: A boutique hotel in Century City and close to Beverly Hills, Westwood, and UCLA.

Luxe Hotel on Sunset Boulevard
11461 Sunset Boulevard
Los Angeles, CA 90049
Phone: (310) 476-6571

Fax: (310) 471-6310
www.luxehotels.com

Note: Stylish and comfortable hotel on seven secluded acres in one of Southern California's most accessible and exceptional locations.

Beverly Hills Plaza Hotel
10300 Wilshire Boulevard
Los Angeles, CA 90024
Phone: (310) 275-5575
Fax: (310) 278-3325
www.beverlyhillsplazahotel.com

Note: Close to Rodeo Drive, Century City, and Westwood Village, this intimate sized hotel offers personalized service of the highest quality.

Hilgard House Westwood Village
927 Hilgard Avenue
Los Angeles, CA 90024
Phone: (310) 208-3945
Fax: (310) 208-1972
www.hilgardhouse.com

Note: Modern European-style hotel located at the southern edge of the UCLA campus. Walking distance to museums and minutes from shopping, entertainment, and the beach.

Royal Palace Westwood Hotel
1052 Tiverton Avenue
Los Angeles, CA 90024
Phone: (310) 208-6677
www.royalpalacewestwood.com

Note: Perfect for an overnight business trip or weeklong vacation.

On-Site Hospitality:
Current concession stands are considered meager at best, but planned renovations should improve the hospitality of Pauley.

Travel Packages:
If you are going to travel to this event, I would recommend using a reliable company to work with you on making the necessary arrangements. The suppliers listed in this book have solid references and are by far the most trusted in the business. Below are some of the organizations to try for this Top 100 Must See Sporting Event.

Premiere Corporate Events
14 Penn Plaza, Suite 925
New York, NY 10122
Phone: (212) 695-9480
Fax: (212) 564-8098
Toll-Free: 1-877-621-5243
E-mail: requests@tseworld.com
www.tseworld.com
www.pcevents.com

Premiere Sports Travel
201 Shannon Oaks Circle, Suite 205
Cary, NC 27511
Phone: (919) 481-9511
Fax: (919) 481-1337
Toll-Free: 1-800-924-9993
E-mail: sales@sportstravel.com
www.sportstravel.com

Dining:

Tengu
10853 Lindbrook Drive
Los Angeles, CA 90024
Phone: (310) 209-0071
www.tengu.com

Note: Named after the Japanese god of mischief, this restaurant serves American classics and pan-Asian dishes.

Clementine
1751 Ensley Avenue
Los Angeles, CA 90024
Phone: (310) 552-1080
Fax: (310) 552-4774
www.clementineonline.com

Note: A sidewalk café for those with a sweet tooth. Homemade soup and sandwiches are available, but it's the cookies, cupcakes, and mini-key lime pies that will keep you coming back.

The Blvd. (at the Wilshire hotel)
9500 Wilshire Boulevard
Los Angeles, CA 90212

Phone: (310) 275-5200
www.fourseasons.com

Note: Great wine selection in a restaurant located at one of the most well-known intersections in Beverly Hills.

Airports:

Burbank/Bob Hope Airport
2627 North Hollywood Way
Burbank, CA 91505
Phone: (818) 840-8840
www.burbankairport.com

LAX
1 World Way
Los Angeles, CA 90045
Phone: (310) 646-5252
www.lawa.org/lax

Sports Travel Insider's Edge:

Best way to watch the action:
Grab one of the 1,750 seats in the student section and enjoy the game as it was meant to be. That is, unless you are a USC fan.

Best place to get up close:
Make a large donation to UCLA or buddy up to a major donor who already shelled out a lot of money. North and south side court seats are reserved for those generous individuals with deep pockets or their designated substitute.

Best travel tip:
What is there not to see in Los Angeles? Culture abounds with various museums. Star-gazing for celebrities in the area. A tour through a major Hollywood Studio. You've gotten your sports fix, now get your tourist on.

Notable Quotes:

"A visit to Pauley Pavilion takes you to a place the scholarly Wooden still haunts and gives you the ultimate lesson in college hoops history. On occasion, you can catch the 97-year-old signing his books here.

But he already has left his name all over UCLA."—Doug Ward, ESPN.com

"Beating USC is not a matter of life and death. It's more important than that."—Red Sanders, legendary Bruins football coach

Relevant Websites:
www.uclabruins.com
www.usctrojans.com
www.discoverlosangeles.com
www.tseworld.com
www.pcevents.com
www.sportstravel.com
www.gotickets.com
www.premieresports.com

50
LE MANS 24

Where?
Automobile Club de l'Ouest
Circuit des 24 Heures
72019 Le Mans Cedex 2
Sarthe, France

When?
A weekend in mid-June every year.

Significance:
The 24 Hours of Le Mans, a.k.a. 24 Heures du Mans, is a test of endurance, ability, and reflexes. Held annually since May 26, 1923, despite three interruptions due to the Great Depression and World War II, race enthusiasts have descended upon Le Mans, Sarthe, a small town in France, to watch the race.

The "Grand Prix of Endurance" is organized by the Automobile Club de l'Ouest (ACO). The course is composed of public roads meant to put drivers to the test over a 24-hour period. Le Mans provides a unique type of challenge for the driver and the vehicle they are operating. This race is not about the quickness of the car; reliability, aerodynamics, and fuel efficiency at high speeds are the key features in making a car that will stand the test of Le Mans. That plays a vital role for an automobile that must travel continuously over a long span of time with pit visits kept to a minimum.

After qualifying races and test runs, 24 Heures du Mans begins in earnest on Saturday afternoon. Originally, drivers had their cars lined up along the pit wall in the order in which they qualified. When the French flag dropped to start the race, they would dash to their cars and, without help from a pit crew, start it and commence the grueling race. A risky practice, to say the least. After various complaints and protests, the procedure was done away with in 1970 with drivers already in their cars. In 1971, an Indianapolis-style "rolling start" would begin the race, a tradition that continues today.

Who attends?

Weather conditions be damned. Come rain or shine, hundreds of thousands of Le Mans fans camp out around the track to watch one of the most unique and thrilling car races in the world.

How to get there?

During Le Mans, the city establishes special bus lines to pick up passengers from various locations in the city center and the train station. That is considered the best way to get to Le Mans, so leave your car at the parking lot and avoid the difficulties of traffic and finding a parking space. Buses leave every fifteen minutes and drop you off right at the main entrance. From there, free shuttles will take you to observation points in Arnage and Mulsanne's Corner.

Information about the public transit system can be found at www.setram.fr. The ability to read French is helpful, to say the least.

Tickets:

For primary ticket access information, consider: www.lemans.org.

For secondary ticket access, consider:

GoTickets, Inc.
2345 Waukegan Road, Suite 140
Bannockburn, IL 60015-1552
Toll-Free: 1-800-775-1617
Fax: (919) 481-9101
E-mail: sales@gotickets.com
www.gotickets.com

Accommodations:

Citotel Levasseur
5, Boulevard René Levasseur
Le Mans, 72100, France
Phone: +33 2 43 39 61 61
Note: Twelve minutes to the race track, but a great value.

Campanile Le Mans
23, Boulevard Pablo Néruda
Zac de Gazonfier
Le Mans, 72000, France
Phone: +33 2 4372 1872
Fax: +33 2 4372 9139
www.campanile-le-mans-centre.fr
Note: Conveniently located close to the racetrack, town center, and the train station.

Ibis Le Mans Est Pontlieue
rue Clement Marot
Le Mans, 72100, France
Phone: +33 2 4386 1414
Fax : +33 2 4384 1021
www.ibishotel.com
Note: Staying here will put you closest to Le Mans at only nine minutes away.

On-Site Hospitality:

If camping out is not your style, you can watch Le Mans from a terrace overlooking the Ford Curve and the entrance to the pit lane. Waiting inside is the Hospitality Marquee with a large bar, reception area, and, most important, a reserved seat in a great restaurant. TV screens will allow you to keep up with the latest Le Mans happenings. The price also includes parking in Garage Blue and a general admission ticket.

Travel Packages:

If you are going to travel to this event, I would recommend using a reliable company to work with you on making the necessary arrangements. The suppliers listed in this book have solid references and are by far the most trusted in the business. Below are some of the organizations to try for this Top 100 Must See Sporting Event.

Premiere Corporate Events
14 Penn Plaza, Suite 925
New York, NY 10122
Phone: (212) 695-9480
Fax: (212) 564-8098
Toll-Free: 1-877-621-5243
E-mail: requests@tseworld.com
www.tseworld.com
www.pcevents.com

Premiere Sports Travel
201 Shannon Oaks Circle, Suite 205
Cary, NC 27511
Phone: (919) 481-9511
Fax: (919) 481-1337
Toll-Free: 1-800-924-9993
E-mail: sales@sportstravel.com
www.sportstravel.com

Dining:

La Chamade
9 rue Dorée
Le Mans, France
Phone: +33 (0)2 4328 2296
Note: A traditional French restaurant with outstanding food and service coupled with a great selection of French wines.

La Rose d'Ispahan
11 rue Trois Sonnettes

Le Mans, France
Phone: +33 (0)2 4377 1228
Note: Classic Persian restaurant with high quality menu items and a range of French and Oriental wines.

L'Andalouse
23 pl Eperon
Les Mans, France
Phone: +33 (0)2 4323 9308
Note: Enjoy sangria, paella, and tapas in this fine Spanish restaurant.

La Ciboulette
14 rue Vieille Porte
Le Mans, France
Phone: +33 (0)2 4324 6567
Note: A smaller restaurant with only six to eight tables. Quality makes up for the quantity with excellent food, wine, and service.

Le Baobab
4 rue Vieille Porte
Le Mans, France
Phone: +33 (0)2 4324 8485
Note: Enjoy authentic cuisine from various regions in Africa. They also serve unique cocktails that include ginger-based drinks as well as South African red wines.

La Cantina
18 rue des Trois Sonnettes
Le Mans, France
Phone: +33 (0)2 4323 3959
Note: A very enjoyable dining experience if you are in the mood for Mexican cuisine.

Airport:

Le Mans Airport
Route Angers
Le Mans, 72100, France
Phone: +33 (0)2 4384 3485

Sports Travel Insider's Edge:

Best way to watch the action:
While you may be fighting a little traffic,

renting a car gives you a more complete Le Mans experience. You can drive to different cities and places along the track, providing a unique perspective on the race and the chance to sightsee throughout the country. If traveling around the countryside is not for you, Les 24 Heures will offer twelve giant television screens for spectators to follow the race.

Best place to get up close:

Get a close look at the drivers in a parade that takes place the Friday night before the event. Don't worry about not getting a good look. For that one night, the drivers will be moving much slower.

Best travel tip:

A traditional Le Mans experience involves camping out at various parts of the track to see the race. The weather may not cooperate, but it is an excellent way to experience all things Le Mans and bond with your fellow car racing fans from around the world.

Notable Quotes:

"Anything can happen at Le Mans."— ANDREA PICCINI, Italian motor racer

"Le Mans feels like home to me. I have raced here many times and it is one of the best tracks in my opinion. It's really particular, also thanks to the weather conditions which are really bizarre. The weather can change at any time, making each race simply unique."—SYLVAIN GUINTOLI, French motorcycle racer

Relevant Websites:

www.lemans-sensations.com
www.lemans.org
www.tseworld.com
www.pcevents.com
www.sportstravel.com
www.gotickets.com
www.premieresports.com

51

IRONMAN WORLD CHAMPIONSHIP

Where?
The Big Island of Hawaii.

When?
Every year during the second week of October.

Significance:
If you get winded walking up the stairs, the Ironman World Championship is not for you. However, it is a true spectacle for a sports fan to see. The top athletes of the world compete in a triathlon that includes 2.4 miles of swimming and 112 miles of biking. If that isn't enough, you can add a 26.2 mile marathon to put the "tri" in triathlon. Twelve Navy Seals started the competition in 1978. The limit today is 1,700 and the competition is not limited to Navy Seals. Luc Van Lierde of Belgium set the current course record in 1996 with a winning time of 8 hours, 4 minutes, and 8 seconds.

Who attends?
Competitors and fans. In fact, it is the high point of any triathlete's career. If you can qualify through any one of the twenty plus formal competitions worldwide or register for a lottery to participate, this race is the ultimate for any Ironman racer. Some focus on personal records or what triathletes like to call PR's, but for most the satisfaction is in the achievement of just finishing. If anything, you can shout, "I am an Ironman," and it would be true. Wannabe triathletes and followers of the sport populate the starting and finish lines to experience the most dramatic parts of the Ironman World Championship.

Tickets:

No tickets necessary. A flight to Hawaii and an early arrival at the start or finish line will get you a good vantage point.

Accommodations:

Four Seasons Hualalai

72-100 Ka`upulehu Drive
Kailua-Kona, HI 96740
Phone: (808) 325-8000
Fax: (808) 325-8200
Toll-Free: 1-888-340-5662
www.fourseasons.com

Note: Secluded, not isolated, with a taste of Hawaii's "golden age." Grab a round of golf on the private Jack Nicklaus signature course.

Sheraton Keauhou Bay Resort

78-128 Ehukai Street
Kailua-Kona, HI 96740
Phone: (808) 930-4900
Fax: (808) 930-4800
Toll-Free: 1-866-837-4256
www.sheratonkeauhou.com

Note: Ideal for the family or a great destination for honeymooners. Enjoy an authentic luau or take a day's drive to Hawaii Volcanoes National Park.

Keauhou Beach Resort

78-6740 Alii Drive
Kailua-Kona, HI 96740
Phone: (808) 322-3441
Fax: (808) 322-3117
Toll-Free: 1-800-688-7444
www.outrigger.com

Note: Spacious condo units on eighteen acres of oceanfront lava rock overlooking Keauhou Bay. Relax with swimming, tennis, or snorkeling.

On-Site Hospitality:

As official Ironman World Championship sponsors, beverage companies and nutrition bar/gel sponsors make their respective drink and energy products available to those racing. That is the only hospitality this course will offer triathletes. As is the case with any Ironman race there is always a much better food selection for those just watching. Displays featuring other sponsors' products and local fare provide many meal options for spectators. In fact it's likely that if you are there to watch a friend, you can probably get three meals in before he/she finishes the race!

Travel Packages:

If you are going to travel to this event, I would recommend using a reliable company to work with you on making the necessary arrangements. The suppliers listed in this book have solid references and are by far the most trusted in the business. Below are some of the organizations to try for this Top 100 Must See Sporting Event.

Premiere Corporate Events

14 Penn Plaza, Suite 925
New York, NY 10122
Phone: (212) 695-9480
Fax: (212) 564-8098
Toll-Free: 1-877-621-5243
E-mail: requests@tseworld.com
www.tseworld.com
www.pcevents.com

Premiere Sports Travel

201 Shannon Oaks Circle, Suite 205
Cary, NC 27511
Phone: (919) 481-9511
Fax: (919) 481-1337
Toll-Free: 1-800-924-9993
E-mail: sales@sportstravel.com
www.sportstravel.com

Do you want to actually compete in this race? Try Trilife.org, an Ironman training group located in New York City.

Dining:

Four Season Hualalai: Pahu i`a *and* **The Hualalai Grille**

72-100 Ka`upulehu Drive
Kailua-Kona, HI 96740
Phone: (808) 325-8000
Fax: (808) 325-8200
www.fourseasons.com
Note: Depending on the availability of certain meats, fish, and produce, the menu changes regularly. Extensive and well-chosen wine list. Enjoy your meal inside or outside.

Roy's in the Waikoloa Kings Shops
250 Waikoloa Beach Drive
Kohala Coast, HI 96738
Phone: (808) 886-4321
www.roysrestaurant.com
Note: Featuring Euro-Asian food prepared by world-renowned chef Roy Yamaguchi. Top-ranking and award-winning restaurant in several dining publications.

Merriman's up in Waimea
Opelo Plaza
Highway 19 and Opelo Road
Waimea, HI 96743
Phone: (808) 885-6822
Fax: (808) 886-8756
www.merrimanshawaii.com
Note: Fresh from the farm ingredients in a restaurant located in the heart of the Big Island farm country. Try the Wok Charred Ahi or Peter's Organic Caesar salad.

Kailua Kona-Huggo's (oceanside, great sunsets)
75-5828 Kahakai Road
Kailua Kona, HI 96740
Phone: (808) 329-1493
www.huggos.com
Note: Oceanside location providing great sunsets.

Airports:

Kona International Airport of Keahole
Phone: (808) 836-6413
www.state.hi.us

One transfer is likely along the west coast of the United States or at Honolulu/Oahu International Airport.

Sports Travel Insider's Edge:

Best way to watch the action:
Stay until the very end. While the pros finish in eight to nine hours, there are still a few straggling in. Midnight marks the seventeen-hour cutoff. Witnessing and cheering the "walking dead" cross the finish line is considered by many to be a magical experience.

Best place to get up close:
The prior day's swim course warm-ups are entertaining to watch. Being that it takes place in a very public ocean, you can try to swim alongside your favorite Ironman athlete.

Best travel tip:
Dress for the elements. Those elements are usually heat and wind. In addition, eight to fifteen hours of being a spectator is grueling in and of itself. Eat and drink to maintain your own endurance.

Also, make time to play golf in some of the best courses in the world and visit the lava flows on the south of the island.

Notable Quotes:

"I started thinking about why I was here. God gave me a door, and I'm going to run through it.... Not finishing was not an option. Even if I had to crawl."—Scott Rigsby, a double-amputee who completed the 2007 Ironman.

"'Whoever finishes first, we'll call the Ironman,' said Cdr. Collins.... The pre-race rules and course description included a handwritten note on the last page: 'Swim 2.4 miles! Bike 112 miles! Run 26.2 miles! Brag for the rest of your life!'"
—Article from Active.com

"It does not have to be fun to be fun."
—Ross Galitsky, head coach TriLife

Relevant Websites:

www.ironman.com
www.visitkailuakona.com
www.tseworld.com
www.pcevents.com
www.sportstravel.com
www.trilife.org
www.premieresports.com

52

IOWA VS. IOWA STATE WRESTLING MEET AT IOWA

Where?

Carver-Hawkeye Arena
Iowa City, IA 52242-1020

When?

During college wrestling season, between November and February.

Significance:

Between Iowa City, home of the University of Iowa, and Ames-based Iowa State University lies 137 miles. Yet, 137 miles is not a safe enough distance for the warring factions that compose the two schools' wrestling programs. With crowds surpassing 15,000 in 1983, 1986, and 1992, Iowa college wrestling remains immensely popular, particularly when Iowa faces Iowa State. The rivalry seems to intensify with every passing year, even though Iowa has dominated the series with its in-state rival. In 2006, interest in the annual meeting peaked when Tom Brands became coach of Iowa and Cael Sanderson was announced as the head of Iowa State's wrestling program. It only added fuel to an already blazing fire. The jawing continues. The accusations of various wrongdoings and unsportsmanlike conduct fly to and fro. While the drama may resemble pro wrestling, watching Iowa battle Iowa State is not just a casual pas-

time. The event where these two schools meet can become very personal.

Who attends?

Iowa college wrestling is truly a way of life and the annual Iowa vs. Iowa State tête-à-tête attracts students and alumni of both colleges and college wrestling fans from throughout the state.

Tickets:

For primary ticket access information, consider:

University of Iowa
Athletic Department Ticket Office
Phone: 1-800-IA-HAWKS
www.hawkeyesports.com

For secondary ticket access, consider:

GoTickets, Inc.
2345 Waukegan Road, Suite 140
Bannockburn, IL 60015-1552
Toll-Free: 1-800-775-1617
Fax: (919) 481-9101
E-mail: sales@gotickets.com
www.gotickets.com

Accommodations:

Heartland Inn
87 2nd Street
Coralville, Iowa 52241
Phone: (319) 351-8132
Fax: (319) 351-2916
Toll-Free: 1-800-334-3277
www.heartlandinns.com
Note: Best value for your money. Smoke-free rooms with "heartland" hospitality.

Holiday Inn Conference Center, Iowa City
1220 1st Avenue
Coralville, IA 52241
Phone: (319) 351-5049
Fax: (319) 354-4214
Toll-Free: 1-800-315-2605
www.ichotelsgroup.com

Note: Located just about two miles away from all the action, this hotel is considered home of the University of Iowa's Hawkeyes.

Coralville Marriott Hotel and Conference Center
300 East 9th Street
Coralville, IA 52241
Phone: (319) 688-4000
Toll-Free: 1-800-228-9210
www.marriott.com

Note: Luxury accommodations located along the Iowa River.

Sheraton Iowa City
210 South Dubuque Street
Iowa City, IA 52240
Phone: (319) 337-4058
Fax: (319) 337-9045
Toll-Free: 1-800-325-3535
www.starwoodhotels.com

Note: Near city attractions and sidewalk cafés. 234 guest rooms are 100 percent smoke free.

On-Site Hospitality:
While there is currently no onsite hospitality, new renovations to the arena are under discussion to enhance the experience for anyone visiting. For updates, visit www.hawkeyesports.com.

Travel Packages:
If you are going to travel to this event, I would recommend using a reliable company to work with you on making the necessary arrangements. The suppliers listed in this book have solid references and are by far the most trusted in the business. Below are some of the organizations to try for this Top 100 Must See Sporting Event.

Premiere Corporate Events
14 Penn Plaza, Suite 925
New York, NY 10122
Phone: (212) 695-9480
Fax: (212) 564-8098
Toll-Free: 1-877-621-5243

E-mail: requests@tseworld.com
www.tseworld.com
www.pcevents.com

Premiere Sports Travel
201 Shannon Oaks Circle, Suite 205
Cary, NC 27511
Phone: (919) 481-9511
Fax: (919) 481-1337
Toll-Free: 1-800-924-9993
E-mail: sales@sportstravel.com
www.sportstravel.com

Dining:

The Vine Tavern
529 South Gilbert Street
Iowa City, IA
Phone: (319) 354-8767
www.azeats.com/vinetavern

Note: A common haunt for college wrestling fans before and after the meet.

The Wig and Pen Pub
1220 Highway 6 West
Iowa City, IA 52246
Phone: (319) 354-2767
www.wigandpeneast.com

Note: They serve what is considered to be the best pizza in town.

Josephs Steak House
212 South Clinton Street
Iowa City, IA 52240
Phone: (319) 358-0776
Fax: (319) 358-0810
www.josephssteak.com

Note: Highest quality steaks and seafood. They only serve vegetarian organically fed Angus beef and free-range natural chickens.

Airport:

Iowa City Municipal Airport
1801 South Riverside Drive # D
Iowa City, IA 52246
Phone: (319) 356-5045
www.icgov.org

Sports Travel Insider's Edge:

Best way to watch the action:
Since the arena was built with the idea that wrestling meets would be held there, it does not contain a bad seat for this event. Sellouts are likely due to Iowa's dominance in the NCAA in both competition and attendance. The opposite side of the announcer table at center court between rows 6 and 30 is best.

Best place to get up close:
After the meet, the party starts. The Hawk Club party serves as a pep rally of sorts. The location (on private property) is announced at the meet. Everyone is invited to attend, however Hawk Club members receive discounted prices. This is truly a party atmosphere where the wrestlers and hardcore Hawk fans get fired up.

Best travel tip:
During the event, there are many things going on in the area. Traditionally, Iowa plays Iowa State in other sports within a week or so of the match. Check the athletic calendar to find other clashes between the rival schools.

Notable Quote:

"When I was growing up in Oklahoma I thought the enthusiasm for wrestling was outstanding but when I got to the University of Iowa it took me to an entirely different level. These people are something else when it comes to wrestling."—MARK PERRY, JR., Iowa wrestler and two-time National Champion

Relevant Websites:

www.cyclones.com
hawkeyesports.cstv.com
www.iowacitycoralville.org
www.tseworld.com
www.pcevents.com
www.sportstravel.com
www.gotickets.com
www.premieresports.com

53

GOLDEN GLOVES AT MADISON SQUARE GARDEN

Where?
The Theater at Madison Square Garden
Madison Square Garden
4 Pennsylvania Place
New York, NY 10001

When?
The preliminaries take place from January to March, leading up to the finals in April at MSG.

Significance:
The chance to catch a legend in the making has made this event a must see.

What started as a way to settle intercity, and more specifically New York–Chicago rivalries in 1927 is now a high-profile tournament for amateur boxers. Sponsored by the *New York Daily News*, up-and-coming fighters duke it out for a coveted Golden Glove title. Past winners and champions include boxing legends such as Mike Tyson, Oscar De La Hoya, George Foreman, and "The Champ" Muhammad Ali.

Who attends?
Boxing fans weary of the controversy of the sport and price tag of tickets and pay-per-views can get a glimpse of future title-holders. Managers and promoters come to the event to find the next "Ali" or "Tyson." Boxing followers and aficionados look forward to the annual tourney to see the latest and greatest pugilist that the "Sport of Kings" has to offer.

How to get there?
MSG is located on Seventh Avenue between 31st and 33rd Streets. All forms of public transit, from subways to taxis to trains, will get you there.

Tickets:

For primary ticket access information, consider: www.thegarden.com or www.ticketmaster.com.

For secondary ticket access, consider:

GoTickets, Inc.
2345 Waukegan Road, Suite 140
Bannockburn, IL 60015-1552
Toll-Free: 1-800-775-1617
Fax: (919) 481-9101
E-mail: sales@gotickets.com
www.gotickets.com

Accommodations:

Hotel New Yorker
481 Eighth Avenue
New York, NY 10001
Phone: (212) 244-0719
Fax: (212) 629-6536
Toll-Free: 1-800-272-6232
www.nyhotel.com

Note: A value hotel in the process of renovation to restore it to its original prominence. Two blocks from MSG.

W Times Square
1567 Broadway
New York, NY 10036
Phone: (212) 930-7400
Toll-Free: 1-877-W-HOTELS
www.whotels.com

Note: Less than a ten-block walk to MSG down 7th Avenue. A small lounge popular with the "hip crowd" can be found on the check-in floor for a quick drink.

Hilton Times Square
234 West 42nd Street
New York, NY 10036
Phone: (212) 840-8222
Toll-Free: 1-877-326-5200
www.hilton.com

Note: The place to stay in New York. Located near Central Park, but still close enough for a walk to MSG on a nice day in the city.

On-Site Hospitality:
All Star Bar: Located at Gate 60
End Court Bar: Between Gates 63 and 64
Food Courts: Located at Gates 61 and 65. Between Gates 71 and 72 and Gates 76 and 77.
Note: This may vary for events at the Theater.

Travel Packages:
If you are going to travel to this event, I would recommend using a reliable company to work with you on making the necessary arrangements. The suppliers listed in this book have solid references and are by far the most trusted in the business. Below are some of the organizations to try for this Top 100 Must See Sporting Event.

Premiere Corporate Events
14 Penn Plaza, Suite 925
New York, NY 10122
Phone: (212) 695-9480
Fax: (212) 564-8098
Toll-Free: 1-877-621-5243
E-mail: requests@tseworld.com
www.tseworld.com
www.pcevents.com

Premiere Sports Travel
201 Shannon Oaks Circle, Suite 205
Cary, NC 27511
Phone: (919) 481-9511
Fax: (919) 481-1337
Toll-Free: 1-800-924-9993
E-mail: sales@sportstravel.com
www.sportstravel.com

Dining:

Lazzaras Pizza
221 West 38th Street (between 7th and 8th Avenues)
Manhattan, NY 10018
Phone: (212) 944-7792
www.lazzaraspizza.com

Note: Considered by many to be the best pizza

in New York. Look closely because it's hard to find in the townhouse-type setting.

Ben's Deli
209 West 38th Street (between 7th and 8th Avenues)
Manhattan, NY 10018
Phone: (212) 398-2367
Fax: (212) 398-3354
www.bensdeli.net
Note: Solid New York style deli food. Popular with the Garment Center and MSG neighborhood crowd.

Lugo Café
1 Penn Plaza (33rd Street between 7th and 8th)
New York, NY 10001 Phone: (212) 760-2700
Fax: (212) 629-6618
www.lugocafe.com
Note: One of the only fine dining options in the neighborhood. Popular get-together place prior to the fights.

Airports:

John F. Kennedy International Airport (JFK)
JFK Airport
Jamaica, NY 11430
Phone: (718) 244-4444
www.panynj.gov

LaGuardia Airport (LGA)
Ditmars Boulevard and 94th Street
Flushing, NY 11371
Phone: (718) 533-3400
www.panynj.gov

Newark Liberty International Airport (EWR)
North Avenue & Spring Street
Elizabeth, NJ 07201
Phone: (973) 961-6000
www.panynj.gov

Sports Travel Insider's Edge:

Best way to watch the action:
If you live close to NYC or are in town a few weeks prior to the finals, some of the best boxing takes place during the weekly tournament rounds. These matches take place in smaller gyms and arenas across the five boroughs. *The Daily News*, a longtime supporter of the Gloves, will usually list a schedule on their website of all early round matchups, times, and locations.

Best place to get up close:
While in town, be sure to visit Gleason's Gym. Brooklyn's legendary boxing gym is home to many current and former Gloves champions. It is also where Hilary Swank trained for her Academy Award winning role in *Million Dollar Baby.*

Best travel tip:
If you plan to be in town for the final rounds in April, you can also coordinate a day at Yankee Stadium or Citi Field depending upon the home team's early season schedules.

Notable Quotes:

"To me, it meant a lot just to be in the Gloves. I would always think about Sugar Ray Robinson and all the great fighters who had fought in the Gloves. Everyone knew about the *Daily News* Golden Gloves, to be in the paper. Even in the Kid Gloves and Junior Olympics, all anyone would talk about was getting to the Gloves. It was the big thing. To this day, people come up to me on the street and talk to me about how they remember me from the Golden Gloves. They don't talk about the Olympics, they want to talk about the Golden Gloves."—MARK BRELAND, Five-time *Daily News* Golden Gloves champion, Olympic gold medalist, and world welterweight champion

"Joe Louis, Ali, Frazier, everyone left their footprints…to know you're putting your feet where these great, great fighters once fought."—Teddy Atlas, boxing trainer and fight commentator

Relevant Websites:

www.nydailynews.com/features/golden-gloves
www.nycvisit.com
www.tseworld.com
www.pcevents.com
www.sportstravel.com
www.gotickets.com
www.premieresports.com

54

FRENCH OPEN

Where?
Stade de Roland Garros
2 Avenue Gordon Bennett
Paris, Ile de France, 75016
France

When?
Annually from mid-May to early June.

Significance:
Tournoi de Roland-Garros (Tennis French Internationals of Roland Garros) is the premier clay court tennis tournament in the world. Many know it by its other name, the French Open. The annual event calls Roland Garros Stadium (named after a famous World War I pilot) home.

The French Open started as a national tournament in 1891 for tennis players licensed in France, a tradition that ended in 1924. Originally a men's-only tournament, a women's tournament was added six years later. By 1912, the surface was changed to red clay made from crushed red brick. That surface makes for slow play and balls that bounce high, earning it a reputation as the most physically demanding tennis tournament in the world. That standing is a result of not only the surface, but also the five-set men's single matches without a tiebreak in the final set.

The challenging play does not diminish the importance of the French Open. The second of the Grand Slam tournaments is broadcast to a worldwide television audience. Today the French Open features professionals and amateurs from all over the world. They play for not only the French Open championship, but also individual prizes that include the Prix Orange for sportsmanship and press-friendliness, Prix Bourgeon for being the tennis player revelation of the year, and the McEnroe-like Prix Citron for strongest character and personality.

Who attends?
Tennis players and their fans, including high-profile celebrities such as Sean Connery, Antonio Banderas, Jennifer Aniston, and Vince Vaughn.

How to get there?

Metro:
Line 9: Mairie de Montreuil - Pont de Sèvres (use stations Michel-Ange Auteuil, Michel-Ange Molitor, or Porte de Saint-Cloud)
Line 10: Gare d'Austerlitz-Boulogne (Porte d'Auteuil station) BUS Line 22: Opéra - Porte de Saint Cloud (get off at last stop)

Buses:
Line 22: Opéra - Porte de Saint-Cloud (get off at Michel-Ange-Auteuil)
Line 32: Gare de l'Est - Porte d'Auteuil (get off at last stop)
Line 52: Opéra - Pont de Saint-Cloud (get off at Porte d'Auteuil or la Tourelle)
Line 62: Cours de Vincennes - Porte de Saint Cloud (get off at last stop)
Line 72: Hôtel de Ville - Pont de Saint-Cloud (get off at la Tourelle)

Line 123: Porte d'Auteuil - Mairie d'Issy (get off at Roland-Garros)
Line 241: Suresnes - Porte d'Auteuil (get off at Suzanne-Lenglen)
PC1: Petite Ceinture (get off at Porte d'Auteuil, Porte Molitor, or Porte de Saint-Cloud)

Taxis:

During the tournament, two temporary taxi ranks are set up for the public on the corner at the bottom of Rue Gordon-Bennett and Boulevard d'Auteuil, and on the corner at the top of Rue Gordon-Bennett and Boulevard d'Auteuil.

Tickets:

For primary ticket access information, consider: www.fft.fr.

For secondary ticket access, consider:

GoTickets, Inc.

2345 Waukegan Road, Suite 140
Bannockburn, IL 60015-1552
Toll-Free: 1-800-775-1617
Fax: (919) 481-9101
E-mail: sales@gotickets.com
www.gotickets.com

Accommodations:

Marriott Paris, Champs-Elysées Hotel

70 Avenue des Champs-Elysées
Paris, 75008, France
Phone: +33 1 5393 5500
Fax: +33 1 5393 5501
Toll-Free: 1-800-90-8333
www.marriott.com
Note: The beautiful atrium lobby greets you during your stay at this seven-story hotel on the Champs-Elysées and is conveniently located near the Arc de Triomphe, Eiffel Tower, and Louvre.

Hotel Raphael

17 Avenue Kléber
Paris, 75116, France
Phone: +33 (0)1 5364 3200
Fax: +33 (0)1 5364 3201
www.raphael-hotel.com
Note: Located close to the famed Arc de Triomphe and the Champs-Elysées, this is a hotel with a classic French atmosphere.

Hotel Elysées Union

44 rue de l'Amiral Hamelin
Paris, 75116, France
Phone: +33 (0)1 4553 1495
Fax: +33 (0)1 4755 9479
www.elysees-paris-hotel.com
Note: Smaller and more intimate hotel in the downtown area between the Champs-Elysées and the Eiffel Tower.

Hotel Elysées Régencia Paris

41, Avenue Marceau
Paris, 75116, France
Phone: +33 1 4720 4265
Fax: +33 1 4952 0342
www.hotelelyseesregencia.com
Note: Recently renovated, this four-star design boutique hotel is just a short walk from the Champs-Elysées.

Lancaster Hotel

7 rue de Berri - Champs Elysées
Paris, 75008, France
Phone: +33 (0)1 4076 4076
Fax: +33 (0)1 4076 4000
www.hotel-lancaster.fr
Note: A remodeled nineteenth-century mansion located off of the Champs-Elysées, featuring eight stories of spacious rooms.

On-Site Hospitality:

The Roland-Garros Restaurant: In the heart of the clay court, this restaurant offers traditional and new French culinary creations. You will be surrounded by glass panels and brick walls that house the rotisserie and fireplace. The garden side features a terrace filled with flowers that faces Centre Court.

Stade de Roland Garros Tours: Learn about the stadium's history, the Musketeers, and "The Divine" Suzanne Leglen and other French Open champions. You will get a close-up view of the player's private area, changing rooms, media center, and, of course, Philippe-Chatrier Court. Guides are provided that can speak either French or English for this one-hour tour. For booking, call +33 (0)1 4743 4848.

Travel Packages:

If you are going to travel to this event, I would recommend using a reliable company to work with you on making the necessary arrangements. The suppliers listed in this book have solid references and are by far the most trusted in the business. Below are some of the organizations to try for this Top 100 Must See Sporting Event.

Premiere Corporate Events

14 Penn Plaza, Suite 925
New York, NY 10122
Phone: (212) 695-9480
Fax: (212) 564-8098
Toll-Free: 1-877-621-5243
E-mail: requests@tseworld.com
www.tseworld.com
www.pcevents.com

Premiere Sports Travel

201 Shannon Oaks Circle, Suite 205
Cary, NC 27511
Phone: (919) 481-9511
Fax: (919) 481-1337
Toll-Free: 1-800-924-9993
E-mail: sales@sportstravel.com
www.sportstravel.com

Dining:

Ratatouille

168 rue Montmartre
Paris, France, 75002
Phone: +33 (0)1 4013 0880
www.paris-restaurant-ratatouille.com

Note: A traditional French restaurant offering classic cuisine and fine wines. Close to the Grands Boulevards subway.

Le Vin dans les Voiles

8 rue Chapu
Paris, 75016, France
Phone: +33 (0)1 4647 8398
www.vindanslesvoiles.com

Note: The English translation of this wine restaurant is "Wine in the Sails." Close to Exelmans and Chardon Lagache subways.

La Grille Montorgueil

50, rue Montorgueil
Paris, 75002, France
Phone: +33 (0)1 4233 2121
www.paris-restaurant-grillemontorgueil.com

Note: Great atmosphere and reasonably priced food in this classic French bistro.

Apicius

20, Rue d'Artois
Paris, 75008, France
Phone: +33 (0)1 4380 1966
www.restaurant-apicius.fr

Note: Located near the Champs-Elysées.

Café de Flore

172, Boulevard St Germain
Paris, 75006, France
Phone: +33 (0)1 4548 5526
www.cafe-de-flore.com

Note: Famed French café perfect for people watching.

Lancaster Hotel

7 rue de Berri – Champs-Elysées
Paris, 75008, France
Phone : +33 (0)1 4076 4076
Fax: +33 (0)1 4076 4000
www.hotel-lancaster.fr

Note: Smaller menu, but the meals are carefully selected by the head chef.

Dinner can also be picked up at any market. Fresh and warm bread, famed French cheese, and fruit make for a great meal.

Airport:

Paris Charles de Gaulle Airport (fifteen miles from Paris's city center)
Phone: +33 (0)1 4862 2280
Fax: +33 (0)1 4862 6389
www.paris-cdg.com

Sports Travel Insider's Edge:

Best way to watch the action:
It doesn't get any better than watching the French Open on a terrace while surrounded by beautiful flowers. The Roland-Garros Restaurant offers food, drink, and a perfect view of Centre Court.

Best place to get up close:
Take a tour of Stade de Roland Garros, the home of the French Open. See where the players change, relax, and compete. Even if you do not speak French, English tour guides are provided upon request.

Best travel tip:
While the French Open provides its own history, make sure to check out the famed landmarks of Paris, including the Champs-Elysées, Arc de Triomphe, Eiffel Tower, and Louvre.

Notable Quotes:

"I have a lot of respect for this tournament. I want to play it. Like I've said from the beginning of the year when people asked me, you know, what was gonna be my next goal, I said the French is probably going to be the most challenging event that I'm going to play in my career. And I play tennis because I love challenges. I love going out here and I love competing.... I know it's going to be the toughest thing in my career to win this tournament, but I'm willing to do it."—MARIA SHARAPOVA, professional tennis player

"It's just a great feeling, playing at the French Open—the surface, the fact that it's a long love story between the French and me. It's like my garden. It's very emotional. As soon as I'm there I feel magic is happening. It's unique."—JUSTINE HENIN, former professional tennis player

Relevant Websites:

www.fft.fr
www.visit-paris.com
www.tseworld.com
www.pcevents.com
www.sportstravel.com
www.gotickets.com
www.premieresports.com

55

BASEBALL GAME AT FENWAY PARK

Where?
Fenway Park
4 Yawkey Way
Boston, MA 02215

When?
During the Major League Baseball season (late March–October).

Significance:
Fenway Park, named for its location in the Fenway district of Boston, is the oldest Major League Baseball stadium and current home to the Boston Red Sox and a certain Green Monster residing in left field. Opening on April 20, 1912, Fenway is one of two remaining classic parks in Major League Baseball, a distinction it shares with Chicago's Wrigley Field. While not a distinction, Fenway and Wrigley both have a significant number of obstructed-view seats, particularly the pillars that hold up the upper deck.

Although improvements have been made, Fenway has not changed much over its near 100-year existence. Manual scoreboards are still used with green and red lights signaling balls, strikes, and outs. The park's odd geometric shape has wreaked havoc on left-handed pitchers. In fact, Fenway is a place that southpaws dread. That is, unless you're Babe Ruth, who as a pitcher posted a career record of 94 wins and 46 losses. On top of that, a home run over the right roof continues to remain elusive to the most powerful of hitters.

Fans have trouble seeing. Lefties can't pitch well. Throws have injured pigeons. Hits have killed them. Yet, for all its supposed shortcomings, Fenway remains a rare blast from the past, a stadium without the bells and whistles. For Boston Red Sox fans, they have one word to describe Fenway: home.

Who attends?
Thousands of Red Sox fanatics of all ages.

How to get there?
Take US-1 S/Fenway. Keep right at the fork and follow signs for Boylston Street Outbound/Riverway. A slight right at Boylston Street and then turn right at Yawkey Way.

Note: The Boston Red Sox organization encourages all of those coming to Fenway to take public transportation. Locals will tell you that you're crazy not to. Backups on local streets begin about an hour before the game.

Tickets:
For primary ticket access information, consider: boston.redsox.mlb.com.

For secondary ticket access, consider:

GoTickets, Inc.
2345 Waukegan Road, Suite 140
Bannockburn, IL 60015-1552
Toll-Free: 1-800-775-1617
Fax: (919) 481-9101

E-mail: sales@gotickets.com
www.gotickets.com

Accommodations:

Hotel Commonwealth
500 Commonwealth Avenue
Boston, MA 02215
Phone: (617) 933-5000
Fax: (617) 266-6888
www.hotelcommonwealth.com

Note: With its many modern accoutrements this Kenmore Square hotel satisfies visiting college parents and stylish tourists.

The Lenox Hotel
61 Exeter Street at Boylston
Boston, MA 02116
Phone: (617) 536-5300
Fax: (617) 424-0703
www.lenoxhotel.com

Note: A Boston landmark in the historic Back Bay. Old world charm meets modern technology in this 214-room luxury boutique hotel.

Boston Marriott Copley Place
110 Huntington Avenue
Boston, MA 02116
Phone: (617) 236-5800
Fax: (617) 236-5885
Toll-Free: 1-800-228-9290
www.marriott.com

Note: This award-winning hotel is centrally located in the historic Back Bay district of Boston. It's located minutes from various attractions, including Fenway Park.

Courtyard Boston Copley Square
88 Exeter Street
Boston, MA 02116
Phone: (617) 437-9300
Fax: (617) 437-9330
www.courtyardboston.com

Note: A building well over 100 years old houses this hotel with modern amenities and vibrant designs.

The Charlesmark Hotel
655 Boylston Street
Boston, MA 02116
Phone: (617) 247-1212
Fax: (617) 247-1224
www.thecharlesmark.com
Note: Great location and cozy touches distinguish this Boylston boutique hotel.

On-Site Hospitality:
The Ultimate Deck Package: Allows you and nineteen friends, family members, or clients to sit atop the Budweiser Right Field Roof Deck. Package includes private tables, VIP tour of Fenway, access to the Green Monster area during batting practice, authentic Red Sox player jerseys for everyone, dedicated servers, unlimited in-game food and beverages, and a customized in-game message on the centerfield scoreboard.

The Ultimate Monster Package: Provides a private section for you and twenty-seven of your friends, family members, or clients atop Fenway's most popular attraction, the Green Monster. The package includes on-field access during pre-game player batting practice, VIP tour of Fenway, authentic Red Sox player jersey for all guests, dedicated servers, unlimited in-game food and beverages (beer and wine included), and a customized in-game message on the centerfield scoreboard.

Travel Packages:
If you are going to travel to this event, I would recommend using a reliable company to work with you on making the necessary arrangements. The suppliers listed in this book have solid references and are by far the most trusted in the business. Below are some of the organizations to try for this Top 100 Must See Sporting Event.

Premiere Corporate Events
14 Penn Plaza, Suite 925
New York, NY 10122
Phone: (212) 695-9480
Fax: (212) 564-8098
Toll-Free: 1-877-621-5243
E-mail: requests@tseworld.com
www.tseworld.com
www.pcevents.com

Premiere Sports Travel
201 Shannon Oaks Circle, Suite 205
Cary, NC 27511
Phone: (919) 481-9511
Fax: (919) 481-1337
Toll-Free: 1-800-924-9993
E-mail: sales@sportstravel.com
www.sportstravel.com

Dining:

Cactus Club
939 Boylston Street
Boston, MA 02115
Phone: (617) 236-0200
Fax: (617) 236-0419
www.bestmargaritas.com
Note: The website address says it all. Great margaritas combined with Mexican cuisine heat up the Back Bay's answer to Southwestern chic.

Boston Beer Works
61 Brookline Avenue
Boston, MA 02114
Phone: (617) 536-BEER
Fax: (617) 536-3325
www.beerworks.net
Note: Acclaimed beers, generous bar-food portions, and a relaxed environment attract young, sports-enthused masses to Boston's oldest brewpub.

Vinny T's of Boston
867 Boylston Street
Boston, MA 02116
Phone: (617) 262-6699
Fax: (617) 437-7310
www.vinnytsofboston.com
Note: A favorite spot of area families and hungry tourists, delivering gargantuan portions of straightforward Italian fare in kitschy environs.

Al Dente

109 Salem Street
Boston, MA 02113
Phone: (617) 523-0990
Fax: (617)227-4002
www.aldenteboston.com

Note: Simply put, the best pasta in Boston. Make sure to call ahead for a reservation.

The Bova Bakery

134 Salem Street
Boston, MA 02113
Phone: (617) 523-5601
www.northendboston.com/bovabakery

Note: This place never closes. There is nothing more quintessentially Boston than this bakery.

Airport:

Boston Logan International Airport

1 Harborside Drive
Massport, East Boston, MA 02128
Phone: (617) 561-1800
www.massport.com

Sports Travel Insider's Edge:

Best way to watch the action:

Unlike other ballparks doubling as cathedrals, Fenway maintains a small and intimate environment where there are no bad seats. Well, unless you are behind a pole that may obstruct your enjoyment of the Sox. Those tickets should be marked obstructed view.

Best place to get up close:

Walk down Lansdowne Street or Yawkey Way before a game. Those streets border the park and represent the best way to take in the smells and flavors of Fenway. The aromas of sausage and beer are part of the overall experience. Get there early for a leisurely stroll around this historic stadium.

Best travel tip:

Springtime in Boston means graduation for many of the area colleges and universities. Be aware of that when you pick your weekend to visit Fenway. Any game in May will find you scrambling for a hotel room or parking. June is a better option, provided that the Bruins or the Celtics are not playing for a championship in their respective sports.

Notable Quotes:

"As a player at Fenway, the fans are right on top of the field and there's so much history you can feel it. Everything surrounding Fenway makes it such a fun place to play, especially the neighborhood it's in. It's one of the best parks in baseball for the players on the field."—BRIAN McRAE, former Kansas City Royals center fielder

"Fenway Park...allows us to imagine what baseball was like when Ted Williams galloped around in left field, when Lou Gehrig sent towering fly balls into the right-field bleachers, when Carlton Fisk hit the most-replayed home run in baseball history."—ROB NEYER, ESPN.com

Relevant Websites:

boston.redsox.mlb.com
www.bostonusa.com
www.tseworld.com
www.pcevents.com
www.sportstravel.com
www.gotickets.com
www.premieresports.com

56

BELMONT STAKES

Where?

Belmont Park
2150 Hempstead Turnpike
Elmont, NY 11003

When?

Annually on the first Saturday in June.

Significance:

You cannot win horse racing's Triple Crown without a final victory at the Belmont Stakes. When a horse wins the Kentucky Derby and the Preakness Stakes, their next and only step is the famed 1.5 mile race at Belmont Park. The "Run for the Carnations," named for the blanket of carnations draped around the winner's neck, began in 1866 (with an interruption in 1911 and 1912 by short-lived anti-betting legislation) by Leonard Jerome, a stock market speculator. The name "Belmont" comes from August Belmont, who financed the inaugural event. With initial races held at Jerome Park and Morris Park, the race finally found a permanent home in 1905—Belmont Park in Elmont, New York.

Carnations are not the only prize for winning the Belmont Stakes. A silver bowl made by Louis Comfort Tiffany and donated by the Belmont family is given to the winner, a tradition that started in 1926. However, the biggest prize may be winning the elusive Triple Crown. As the final leg, Belmont has come to be known as the "Test of the Champion." That test comes not only from the pressure of winning the coveted crown, but also the entire lap around the large Belmont main track. Three-year-olds lack the experience and ability to maintain a winning speed, making positioning and timing vital for victory.

Traditions at Belmont include elegant attire worn by the ladies and gentlemen attending the race, although it is not a requirement. In addition, "New York, New York" is sung by the audience following the call to the post. In 1997, that song replaced the longtime "Sidewalks of New York," but continued a ritual that is also followed by the Kentucky Derby, "My Old Kentucky Home," and the Preakness, "Maryland, My Maryland."

Who attends?

New Yorkers and racing fans from all walks of life.

How to get there?

From Manhattan and Brooklyn, take the Long Island Expressway. From Queens, take Grand Central Parkway. From Staten Island, take the Verrazano Bridge to Belt Parkway. All points from there lead east to Cross Island Parkway and to Exit 26-D.

Parking gates open early around 8:15 A.M. on Belmont Stakes day. Admission gates open at 8:30 A.M. Courtesy Shuttle Bus service is available from some of the lots located further away. No valet parking available.

Mass Transit is definitely recommended because of the large crowds on Stakes day.

Trains:

For up to date information call the Long Island Rail Road at (718) 217-LIRR.

Subway:

Take the F train to 169th Street or 179th Street, then take the N6 or the Q2 bus to Belmont, or take the E train to Jamaica Center (Parsons Boulevard) and then take the Q110 bus (MTA Bus Company) to Belmont.

Bus:

N6 (MSBA Line) operates along Hempstead Turnpike between Hempstead, West Hempstead, Franklin Square, Elmont, Hollis, and Jamaica. Q110 and Q2 are available.

Tickets:

For primary ticket access information, consider: www.nyra.com, (516) 488-6000 or (718) 641-4700.

You can also e-mail admpark@nyrainc.com for a Belmont Stakes Lottery application. Please be sure to provide your complete mailing address.

For secondary ticket access, consider:

GoTickets, Inc.
2345 Waukegan Road, Suite 140
Bannockburn, IL 60015-1552
Toll-Free: 1-800-775-1617
Fax: (919) 481-9101
E-mail: sales@gotickets.com
www.gotickets.com
Note: Admission is included with all reserved seats and dining tickets.

Accommodations:

Garden City Hotel
45 Seventh Street
Garden City, NY 11530
Phone: (516) 747-3000
Fax: (516) 747-1414
Toll-Free: 1-800-547-0400
www.gardencityhotel.com
Note: A nightclub is onsite, along with a pool, spa, salon, restaurants, and a lounge. 24-hour room service is available.

Floral Park Motor Lodge
30 Jericho Turnpike
Floral Park, NY 11011
Phone: (516) 775-7777
Fax: (516) 775-0451
www.floralparkmotorlodge.com
Note: Free parking. Free newspaper every morning. Free continental breakfast.

Inn at Great Neck
30 Cutter Mill Road
Great Neck, NY 11021
Phone: (516) 773-2000
Fax: (516) 773-2020
www.innatgreatneck.com
Note: All rooms contain mini-bars with 24-hour room service available. Located two blocks from the Long Island Rail Road train to Manhattan.

Long Island Marriott
101 James Doolittle Boulevard
Uniondale, NY 11553
Phone: (516) 794-3800
Fax: (516) 794-5936
Toll-Free: 1-800-228-9210
www.marriott.com
Note: Great hotel with a pool, spa, restaurant, and lounge.

Roslyn Claremont Hotel
1221 Old Northern Boulevard
Roslyn, NY 11576
Phone: (516) 625-2700
Fax: (516) 625-2731
Toll-Free: 1-800-626-9005
www.roslynclaremonthotel.com
Note: European-style luxury accommodations, fitness club, restaurant, and lounge.

La Quinta Inn & Suites Garden City
821 Stewart Avenue
Garden City, NY 11530
Phone: (516) 705-9000
Fax: (516) 705-9100
www.lq.com
Note: 24-hour business center, fitness center with a whirlpool, and complimentary continental breakfast.

Holiday Inn of Westbury
369 Old Country Road
Carle Place, NY 11514
Phone: (516) 997-5000
Fax: (516) 997-3623
Toll-Free: 1-866-259-5740
www.hiwestbury.com
Note: Business and fitness centers, complimentary continental breakfast, and a free newspaper. Walking distance to the train station.

On-Site Hospitality:

The Garden Terrace Dining Room located on the fourth floor of the Clubhouse provides great a la carte selections and a buffet menu on race day. Elegant attire is preferred and appreciated.

Kids can enjoy the state-of-the-art playground and duck pond in the Backyard. Coolers may be brought to this area, but not in the park itself.

Concession stands at Belmont provide food and drink for all attendees.

Also remember in accordance with the New York State Clean Indoor Air Act smoking is not permitted in the building or in any seating or dining areas. Smoking is permitted in the backyard and apron areas.

Travel Packages:

If you are going to travel to this event, I would recommend using a reliable company to work with you on making the necessary arrangements. The suppliers listed in this book have solid references and are by far the most trusted in the business. Below are some of the organizations to try for this Top 100 Must See Sporting Event.

Premiere Corporate Events

14 Penn Plaza, Suite 925
New York, NY 10122
Phone: (212) 695-9480
Fax: (212) 564-8098
Toll-Free: 1-877-621-5243
E-mail: requests@tseworld.com
www.tseworld.com
www.pcevents.com

Premiere Sports Travel

201 Shannon Oaks Circle, Suite 205
Cary, NC 27511
Phone: (919) 481-9511
Fax: (919) 481-1337
Toll-Free: 1-800-924-9993
E-mail: sales@sportstravel.com
www.sportstravel.com

Dining:

Note: All restaurants listed are located on the same road as the racetrack and will be easy to find before or after the race.

El Cantinero

491 Hempstead Turnpike
Elmont, NY 11003
Phone: (516) 488-6798

Note: Ideal for the connoisseur of good Mexican cuisine.

Stop 20 Diner

1336 Hempstead Turnpike
Elmont, NY 11003
Phone: (516) 358-7142

Note: Longtime diner known for plentiful plates of food at reasonable prices.

Villa Mar Restaurant

481 Hempstead Turnpike
Elmont, NY 11003
Phone: (516) 326-7643

Note: Affordable American and Italian dishes are served piping hot, from burgers to chicken marsala.

Airports:

Long Island MacArthur (Islip) Airport

100 Arrivals Avenue
Ronkonkoma, NY 11779
Phone: (631) 467-3210
www.macarthurairport.com

John F. Kennedy International Airport (JFK)

Jamaica, NY 11430
Phone: (718) 244-4444
www.panynj.gov

LaGuardia Airport (LGA)

Ditmars Boulevard and 94th Street
Flushing, NY 11369
Phone: (718) 533-3400
www.panynj.gov

Newark Liberty International Airport (EWR)

North Avenue and Spring Street
Elizabeth, NJ 07201
Phone: (973) 961-6000
www.panynj.gov

Sports Travel Insider's Edge:

Best way to watch the action:

If you plan on camping out in the grandstand picnic area, make sure you arrive early. Bring blankets to ensure that your spot is held. Crowds arrive quickly, so you want to be sure you have your area set. Prepare for a long day as the Belmont Stakes post time is approximately 6:40 P.M. Try and get as close to the main grandstand and clubhouse structure for easy access in and out. Coolers are restricted to the grandstand backyard area only. Patrons carrying coolers must enter the track at either the paddock or the west end grandstand admission gates. Coolers are not allowed through the clubhouse gate.

Best place to get up close:
Try and pick out some of those famous sketches on the wall that line some of the clubhouse corridors. There is so much history that has been made at this track and so many people who have been a part of it. See whom you know.

Best travel tip:
With 100,000 people rushing to beat the traffic, getting out of the parking lot is nothing short of a New York nightmare. Parking farther away and walking is your best bet for a quick exit. The time it takes to walk will be nowhere near the wait to get out of the main parking lots. The wait for trains on the LIRR can be excruciatingly long heading out of Belmont. There are many people heading back toward New York City.

Notable Quotes:

"Just like winning the world."—PRINCE AHMED BIN SALMAN, owner of Point Given, the winner of the 133rd Belmont Stakes

"The Belmont Stakes is our biggest event. With the recent success of the Belmont, fueled by the run of Triple Crown hopefuls, we've been able to bring the Belmont Stakes and Belmont Park to a new audience. When people come out here for the

first time, especially on a big day, they realize what a beautiful, magnificent venue it is and what a great day Belmont Stakes day is. The fact that it's the best value in big-time sports, with a $5 admission price, really helps us."—BILL NADER, New York Racing Association senior vice-president

Relevant Websites:
www.nyra.com
www.tseworld.com
www.pcevents.com
www.sportstravel.com
www.gotickets.com
www.premieresports.com

57
KANGAROOS AUSTRALIAN FOOTBALL GAME

Where?
Telstra Dome
740 Bourke Street
Docklands, VIC 3008, Australia

When?
April to November

Significance:
Take your pick for a moniker. They are officially nicknamed the Kangaroos. Unofficially, they are known as the "Shinboners," a name derived from their butcher shop origins. No matter what you call them, the North Melbourne Football Club is rich with history and influence in Australian rules football and enjoys a loyal following from local fans.

The Kangaroos are part of the Australian Football League (AFL). The AFL ranks at the top of professional sporting leagues in both attendance and television ratings. Six million fans have gone through the gates of various arenas during a regular season with an average attendance of 36,000. This is the second highest of any professional sports league in the world.

Clad in the famed blue and white, the Kangaroos embrace their club's motto of *Victoria Amat Curan*, Latin for "Victory Means Dedication." They have had their share of victories and setbacks, but their dedication is never in question. Their origin dates back to 1869 when local cricketers were clamoring for a competitive sport to keep them occupied during the winter months. While not its founder, James Henry Gardiner had a hand in those important early years—around fifty to be exact—of Australian rules football.

Today, the Kangaroos claim two home stadiums, the Telstra Dome and the Melbourne Cricket Ground. However, Telstra is the more common place to see a Kangaroo game. The arena has since been immortalized in the movie *Ghost Rider*, although a logo for SoBe Dome was digitized over Telstra.

Who attends?

North Melbourne Australian rules football fans who know every word to "Join in the Chorus" and can sing it or shout it proudly.

How to get there?

For all train, tram, and bus information, including timetables, visit www.victrip.com.au.

Train: Spencer Street Station is the closest train station to Melbourne Docklands The Bourke Street Pedestrian Bridge winds around to the southern side of Telstra Dome.

Tram: The free City Circle Tram runs through Docklands and along the waterfront on Harbour Esplanade in both directions. Hours are from 10:00 A.M. to 6:00 P.M. seven days a week, except for Christmas Day and Good Friday. Daylight savings extends the hours from 10 A.M. to 9 P.M. every Thursday, Friday, and Saturday.

Bus: The Fishermans Bend bus 236 travels along Lorimer Street, Docklands.

Taxis: Taxi ranks are located on Harbour Esplanade, Bourke Street, NewQuay, and at the coach terminus at Spencer Street Station. During a North Melbourne game, taxi ranks are provided on LaTrobe Street near the Gate 6 entrance, and Bourke Street near the Spencer Street intersection.

Driving: The main road running along the Melbourne Docklands is Harbour Esplanade that connects to Wurundjeri Way (via Dudley Street and Bourke Street extension) and LaTrobe Street. The Westgate Freeway connects to Docklands via the off ramp to Lorimer Street. CityLink's western section connects to Docklands via Footscray Road.

Tickets:

For primary ticket access information, consider: www.ticketmaster.com.au.

For secondary ticket access, consider:

GoTickets, Inc.
2345 Waukegan Road, Suite 140
Bannockburn, IL 60015-1552
Toll-Free: 1-800-775-1617
Fax: (919) 481-9101
E-mail: sales@gotickets.com
www.gotickets.com

Accommodations:

Crowne Plaza Melbourne
1-5 Spencer Street
Melbourne, VIC 3000, Australia
Phone: +61 3 9648 2777
Fax: +61 3 9629 5631
Reservations: 1-877-227-6963
www.ichotelsgroup.com
Note: A short walk to enjoy Australian rules football at the Telstra Dome.

Vibe Savoy Hotel Melbourne
630 Little Collins Street
Melbourne, VIC 3000, Australia

Phone: +61 3 9622 8888
Fax: +61 3 9622 8888
www.vibehotels.com.au

Note: At the corner of Spencer and Little Collins streets, this modern hotel has an art deco style. The service is friendly and the hotel rooms are considered very stylish.

Clarion Suites Gateway
1 William Street
Melbourne, VIC 3000, Australia
Phone: +61 3 9296 8888
Fax: +61 3 9296 8880
www.clarionsuitesgateway.com.au

Note: Luxury and hospitality await guests at the corner of William and Flinders Street. Perfect for both leisure and business travelers.

Radisson on Flagstaff Gardens
380 William Street
Melbourne, VIC 3000, Australia
Phone: +61 3 9322 8000
Fax: +61 3 9322 8888
www.radisson.com

Note: Near many major landmarks, including the Flagstaff Gardens, Queen Victoria Market, and, of course, the Telstra Dome.

On-Site Hospitality:
The Telstra Dome boasts sixty-six superbly appointed suites. Whether you are entertaining friends or clients, the electric atmosphere of an Australian rules football game will impress them. Each suite has twelve to sixteen seats.

Travel Packages:
If you are going to travel to this event, I would recommend using a reliable company to work with you on making the necessary arrangements. The suppliers listed in this book have solid references and are by far the most trusted in the business. Below are some of the organizations to try for this Top 100 Must See Sporting Event.

Premiere Corporate Events
14 Penn Plaza, Suite 925
New York, NY 10122
Phone: (212) 695-9480
Fax: (212) 564-8098
Toll-Free: 1-877-621-5243
E-mail: requests@tseworld.com
www.tseworld.com
www.pcevents.com

Premiere Sports Travel
201 Shannon Oaks Circle, Suite 205
Cary, NC 27511
Phone: (919) 481-9511
Fax: (919) 481-1337
Toll-Free: 1-800-924-9993
E-mail: sales@sportstravel.com
www.sportstravel.com

Dining:

Bellissimo Cucina & Trattoria
427 Docklands Drive
Waterfront City, Docklands, VIC 3008, Australia
Phone: +61 3 9326 6636
Fax: +61 3 9326 6186
www.bellissimo.net.au

Note: Traditional Italian cuisine includes many pasta, meat, and seafood options. Bellissimo also has a wide range of wine, spirits, and beer.

Steakhouse
Pier 35 Marina, 263-329 Lorimer Street
Port Melbourne, VIC 3207, Australia
Phone: +61 3 9646 0606
www.steakhouse.net.au

Note: Featuring prime quality Certified Australian Beef, including Angus and Wagyu steaks cooked over a flame right before your eyes. A large seafood and vegetarian menu is available as well.

The Lounge Room
28 NewQuay Promenade
Docklands, VIC 3008, Australia
Phone: 03 9600 0565

Note: The lounge-bar restaurant provides a great view of the city and waterfront access. Stop in to sample modern Australian cuisine or just get together with friends for drinks.

Mecca Bah

55A NewQuay Promenade
Docklands, VIC 3008, Australia
Phone: +613 9642 1300
Fax: +613 9642 1299
www.meccabah.com

Note: Moroccan and Middle Eastern style await you with a menu that features minced lamb and Lebanese sausages.

Airport:

Melbourne Airport

Airport Drive
Melbourne, VIC 3045, Australia
Phone: +61 3 9297 1600
Fax: +61 3 9297 1886
www.melbourneairport.com.au

Sports Travel Insider's Edge:

Best way to watch the action:

The Medallion Club is the place to go to get the best seats in the Telstra Dome. Membership will get you into the finest restaurants and bars, which allow you to enjoy Australian rules football in a unique and exclusive way.

Best place to get up close:

If you truly want to get up close and personal and ensconce yourself in Australian rules football, learn "Join in the Chorus," the official anthem of the Kangaroos. You can sing it or shout along with the crowd. Mind you, it is no "Tie Me Kangaroo Down."

Best travel tip:

Parking underground seems like a good idea when you get there. However, trying to leave is another story altogether after the game is over. You'll have to kill time with several rounds of "Join in the Chorus."

Notable Quotes:

"...Australian football still has a charm, a depth of feeling, that is lost when sport simply becomes a function of the entertainment industry, when players become performers employed by a franchise known to their fans through staged media events, when supporters become customers who go to a game as they might otherwise go to the cinema, except they barrack for one side."—Martin Flanagan, www.theage.com.au

"Our game will never lose its lustre as a spectacle for the simple reason that it is spectacular. Over the past century, a variety of visitors to Australia, including Sir Arthur Conan Doyle, the creator of Sherlock Holmes, and C. B. Fry, the gifted amateur who represented England at three sports, have attested to its wonder as sport."—Martin Flanagan

Relevant Websites:

www.kangaroos.com.au
www.melbourne.vic.gov.au
www.tseworld.com
www.pcevents.com
www.sportstravel.com
www.ticketmaster.com.au
www.premieresports.com

58

HEAVYWEIGHT TITLE FIGHT AT MADISON SQUARE GARDEN

Where?

Madison Square Garden
4 Pennsylvania Plaza
New York, NY 10001

When?

You never know when a fight for the World Heavyweight Championship belt or nowadays "belts" will take place. It could be any time during the year, but it is usually announced months prior to the big day.

Significance:

Madison Square Garden is a place of history. Many athletes have competed in the famed structure. However, many frequent attendees of MSG would say a lot of its heritage comes from those heavyweights who compete in the squared circle. After all, The Garden is considered "the Mecca."

Aspiring boxers dream of the day when they can compete where legends once fought. The deafening crowd noise from the "Fight of the Century" on March 8, 1971, featuring Muhammad Ali and the world champion Joe Frazier, still echoes throughout the building.

Fans and athletes agree that there is something truly special about Madison Square Garden. Boxing world titles have changed hands many times in this building. Legends have done battle in the center of the arena. Chances are that if a fight happens in MSG, the fans in attendance are likely to see history right before their eyes. No other arena can create the energy and excitement of The Garden.

Who attends?

Boxing fans of all ages mixed in with many celebrities.

How to get there?

Any train into Pennsylvania Station will put you right there.

Tickets:

For primary ticket access information, consider: www.thegarden.com.

For secondary ticket access, consider:

GoTickets, Inc.
2345 Waukegan Road, Suite 140
Bannockburn, IL 60015-1552
Toll-Free: 1-800-775-1617

Fax: (919) 481-9101
E-mail: sales@gotickets.com
www.gotickets.com

Accommodations:

Hotel New Yorker

481 8th Avenue (between 34th and 35th Street)
New York, NY 10001
Phone: (212) 244-0719
Fax: (212) 629-6536
www.nyhotel.com

Note: Value hotel in the process of a major renovation to restore it to its original prominence. Two blocks from MSG.

W Times Square

1567 Broadway (at the corner of 47th Street)
New York, NY 10036
Phone: (212) 930-7400
Fax: (212) 930-7500
Toll-Free: 1-877-W-HOTELS
www.whotels.com

Note: Less than a ten-block walk to MSG down 7th Avenue. A small lounge popular with the "hip crowd" can be found on the check-in floor for a quick drink.

The Hilton New York

1335 6th Avenue and 53rd Street
New York, NY 10019
Phone: (212) 586-7000
Fax: (212) 315-1374
www.hilton.com

Note: A favorite hotel for many when in New York. Located near Central Park, but still close enough for a walk to MSG on a nice day.

On-Site Hospitality:

The Club Bar and Grill: Located on the Club Terrace. An exclusive restaurant offers a great pre-game dinner option before the event. You must have a club seat or be a suite ticket holder to enter.

Play by Play Sports Bar and Restaurant: Located inside The Garden. A great option for pre- and post-event fun. You must have a club seat or be a suite holder to enter.

All Star Bar: Located at Gate 60.

End Court Bar: Between Gates 63 and 64.

Full Service Food Courts: Located at Gates 61, 65, 71, and 76.

Travel Packages:

If you are going to travel to the match, I would recommend using a reliable company to work with you on making the necessary arrangements. The suppliers listed in this book have solid references and are by far the most trusted in the business. Below are some of the organizations to try for this 100 Must See Sporting Event.

Premiere Corporate Events
14 Penn Plaza, Suite 925
New York, NY 10122
Phone: (212) 695-9480
Fax: (212) 564-8098
Toll-Free: 1-877-621-5243
E-mail: requests@tseworld.com
www.tseworld.com
www.pcevents.com

Premiere Sports Travel
201 Shannon Oaks Circle, Suite 205
Cary, NC 27511
Phone: (919) 481-9511
Fax: (919) 481-1337
Toll-Free: 1-800-924-9993
E-mail: sales@sportstravel.com
www.sportstravel.com

Dining:

Lazzaras Pizza Café and Restaurant
221 West 38th Street (between 7th and 8th Avenues)
Manhattan, NY 10018
Phone: (212) 944-7792
www.lazzaraspizza.com

Note: Considered by many New Yorkers to be the best pizza in Manhattan. Look closely because it's hard to find since it is located in a townhouse.

Ben's Deli
209 West 38th Street (between 7th and 8th Avenue)
Manhattan, NY 10018
Phone: (212) 398-2367
Fax: (212) 398-3354
www.bensdeli.net

Note: Solid New York style deli food that is popular with the Garment Center crowd.

Lugo Café
1 Penn Plaza
New York, NY 10001 (33rd Street between 7th and 8th Avenue)
Phone: (212) 760-2700
www.lugocafe.com

Note: One of the only fine dining options in the neighborhood. Offers outdoor seating when the weather is right.

Nick & Stef's Steakhouse (located in MSG)
9 Penn Plaza (33rd Street between 7th and 8th Avenue)
New York, NY 10001
Phone: (212) 563-4444
Fax: (212) 563-9184
www.patinagroup.com

Note: If they like you, they will show you the special door that leads from the restaurant into The Garden.

Tir Na Nog
5 Penn Plaza (8th Avenue between 33rd and 34th Street)
New York, NY 10001
Phone: (212) 630-0249
Fax: (212) 630-0247
www.tirnanognyc.com

Note: A great place for dinner and a solid post-event location for drinks.

Local West

1 Penn Plaza (corner of 8th Avenue and
33rd Street)
New York, NY 10119
Phone: (212) 629-7070
www.localcafenyc.com

*Note: If the weather is nice, the outdoor bar
upstairs overlooking MSG is the perfect location to pre-party before the event.*

Airports:

John F. Kennedy International Airport (JFK)

JFK Airport, Jamaica, NY 11430
Phone: (718) 244-4444
www.kennedyairport.com

LaGuardia Airport (LGA)

Ditmars Boulevard and 94th Street
Flushing, NY 11369
Phone: (718) 533-3400
www.panynj.gov

Newark Liberty International Airport (EWR)

North Avenue and Spring Street
Elizabeth, NJ 07201
Phone: (973) 961-6000
www.panynj.gov

Sports Travel Insider's Edge:

Best way to watch the action:
MSG makes available a wide variety of different level seating options for its major
boxing matches. Their premium level ring-
side seating option, although a considerable
amount, is well worth it for a heavyweight
title fight.

Best place to get up close:
Enjoy the pre-fight weigh in and interviews, which usually takes place at The
Garden the day before the fight. This event
is open to the public and depending upon
the characters involved it is usually very
entertaining.

Best travel tip:
This is New York and depending upon
when you are going there is a lot to do be-
fore or after the heavyweight bout. Make
sure to score tickets to a Broadway show,
Yankees game, or ballet at Lincoln Center.
A heavyweight fight at The Garden is just as
New York as these other events so make it a
New York weekend.

Notable Quotes:

"I figured that watching the heavyweight
championship of the world at Madison
Square Garden must be like touching the
face of God—well beyond my reach."—
MICHAEL J. FOX, actor

"You're damn right I do. I'm in Madison
Square Garden getting the sh** knocked
out of me."—BOXER WILLIE PASTRANO, when
asked by the ring doctor if he knew where
he was

Relevant Websites:

www.thegarden.com
www.nycvisit.com
www.tseworld.com
www.pcevents.com
www.sportstravel.com
www.gotickets.com
www.premieresports.com

59

ALL BLACKS RUGBY GAME

Where?

While there is no "official" stadium for the
All Blacks, they play in various arenas in
New Zealand and throughout the world.

When?

The All Blacks can be seen in the Iveco
Series and Tri Nations tournament, which
take place annually in June and July. They

also participate in the Rugby World Cup in September and October of every year.

Significance:

The New Zealand National Rugby team, also known as the All Blacks, is recognized worldwide for its dominance and it ranks at the top of international rugby teams. Established in 1884, the All Blacks boast a winning record against all opposing teams throughout the world. They have held the Rugby World Cup while holding multiple World Cup records. The All Blacks compete every year against the Wallabies, the Australian Rugby Team, and South Africa's Springboks in the Tri Nations Series. They also face Australia annually for the Bledisloe Cup. They are the 2006 International Rugby Board (IRB) Team of the Year and many team members hold membership in the IRB Hall of Fame.

Wellington provides an exciting and unique atmosphere for an All Blacks game. Games against the Wallabies or Springboks show the competitive nature between New Zealand and those countries. Simply put, the games are guaranteed excitement with All Black fans at their most fanatical. Australia is just across "the ditch." South Africa provides strong opposition, making the competitive match one of the better to attend.

Who attends?

All Black fans and those who want the "All Black experience."

Tickets:

For primary ticket access information, consider: www.ticketmaster.co.nz, or

Wellington Office

Williment Travel Group
43–47 Hanson Street
Mt. Cook
Wellington 6021
P.O. Box 589 / DX SP20034
Wellington, 6140, New Zealand
Phone: +64 4 380 2500

E-mail: wlgsales@williment.co.nz
www.williment.co.nz

Auckland Office

Williment Sports Travel Ltd
Unit D3, 27 William Pickering Drive
P O Box 101032 NSMC/
DX: BP 63518
Albany, Auckland, 0632, New Zealand
Phone: +64 9 448 0299
E-mail: aklsales@williment.co.nz

For secondary ticket access, consider:

GoTickets, Inc.

2345 Waukegan Road, Suite 140
Bannockburn, IL 60015-1552
Toll-Free: 1-800-775-1617
Fax: (919) 481-9101
E-mail: sales@gotickets.com
www.gotickets.com

Accommodations:

Wellington Hotels:

Note that while there are many hotels in Wellington to choose from, there will be limited availability when the All Blacks are playing. Make your reservations early.

Holiday Inn

75 Featherston Street
Wellington, 6000, New Zealand
Hotel Front Desk: +64 4 499 8686
Fax: +64 4 498 3763
Toll-Free: 1-877-863-4780
www.ichotelsgroup.com

Note: Located close to the railway station and the stadium (ten-minute walk). Many restaurants and hotels nearby.

Corpthorne Hotel

100 Oriental Parade
Wellington, 6011, New Zealand
Phone: +64 4 473 3750
www.millenniumhotels.co.nz

Note: Located on Wellington's beautiful harbor front, providing for an excellent view of rooms

facing the harbor, the restaurant, and the bar. Twenty-minute walk or ten-minute taxi ride to the stadium.

Auckland Hotels:

SkyCity Hotel
90 Federal Street
Auckland, 1010, New Zealand
Phone: +64 9 363 6000
Fax: +64 9 363 6383
www.skycityauckland.co.nz
Note: Four-star hotel with 344 rooms. Considered ideal for visitors; has several restaurants, bars, and two casinos.

SkyCity Grand
90 Federal Street
Auckland, 1010, New Zealand
Phone: +64 9 363 7000
Fax: +64 9 363 6383
www.skycityauckland.co.nz
Note: Luxurious five-star hotel with 316 rooms, allowing visitors to enjoy luxury and sophistication in the heart of bustling city life.

On-Site Hospitality:
Hot dog and burger stands that serve food and alcoholic and non-alcoholic beverages can be found throughout the Westpac Trust Stadium, a.k.a. "The Cake Tin."

Travel Packages:

Williment Travel Group
43-47 Hanson Street
Mt. Cook
Wellington, 6140, New Zealand
Phone: +64 4 380 2500
Fax: +64 4 380 2501
www.williment.co.nz

Auckland Office
Premier Events Hospitality Ltd
11 York Street, Level 2
Parnell, Auckland, New Zealand
E-mail: sales@premierhospitality.co.nz
Phone: +64 9 307 0770

Christchurch Office
Premier Events Hospitality Ltd.
22 Birmingham Drive
Addington, Christchurch, New Zealand
Phone: +64 3 338 0053
E-mail: krist@premierhospitality.co.nz

If you are going to travel to this event, I would recommend using a reliable company to work with you on making the necessary arrangements. The suppliers listed in this book have solid references and are by far the most trusted in the business. Below are some of the organizations to try for this Top 100 Must See Sporting Event.

Premiere Corporate Events
14 Penn Plaza, Suite 925
New York, NY 10122
Phone: (212) 695-9480
Fax: (212) 564-8098
Toll-Free: 1-877-621-5243
E-mail: requests@tseworld.com
www.tseworld.com
www.pcevents.com

Premiere Sports Travel
201 Shannon Oaks Circle, Suite 205
Cary, NC 27511
Phone: (919) 481-9511
Fax: (919) 481-1337
Toll-Free: 1-800-924-9993
E-mail: sales@sportstravel.com
www.sportstravel.com

Dining:

Wellington Dining:

The Tasting Room
2 Courtenay Place
Wellington, New Zealand
Phone: +64 4 384 1159
www.thetastingroom.co.nz
Note: Casual dining located in a cozy and inviting restaurant at the top end of Courtenay Place.

Capitol

Embassy Theatre
Kent Terrace
P.O. Box 19 174
Wellington, New Zealand
Phone: +64 4 384 2855
www.capitolrestaurant.co.nz

Note: Small and friendly restaurant located on Kent Terrace. Head down early, as they do not take reservations.

Boulcott Street Bistro

99 Boulcott Street
Wellington, New Zealand
Phone: +64 4 499 4199
Fax: +64 4 499 3879
www.boulcottstreetbistro.co.nz

Note: A bistro set in a Victorian house. Reservations are only necessary for lunch.

St. Johns Bar

5 Cable Street
Central City
Wellington, New Zealand
Phone: +64 4 801 8017
www.stjohnsbar.co.nz

Note: Waterfront location close to hotels and the national museum, Te Papa. Perfect for a quick bite and a beer.

Arbitrageur

125 Featherstone Street
Wellington Central
Wellington, 6011, New Zealand
Phone: +64 4 499 5530
Fax: +64 4 499 5535
www.arbitrageur.co.nz

Note: Upper-class fine dining boasts excellent food and wine.

Logan Brown

192 Cuba Street
Wellington, New Zealand
Phone: +64 4 801 5114
www.loganbrown.co.nz

Note: Fine dining in the heart of the city, offering a la carte or bistro-style menus.

Auckland Dining:

Euro Restaurant & Bar

Shed 22 Princes Wharf Quay Street
Auckland City, New Zealand
Phone: +64 9 309 9866
Fax: +64 9 308 9189
www.eurobar.co.nz

Note: Located on Auckland's Viaduct Harbour. Well-made cocktails and fine wines complement meals perfectly.

Orbit

Sky Tower
17 Federal Street
Auckland, 1010, New Zealand
Phone: +64 9 363 6000
www.skycityauckland.co.nz

Note: Revolving restaurant located in the Sky Tower. Classy in its look, but casual in its dining.

Airports:

Auckland International Airport

P.O. Box 73020
Auckland Airport
Manukau, 2150, New Zealand
Telephone: +64 9 275 0789
Fax: +64 9 275 5835
www.auckland-airport.co.nz

Wellington International Airport Ltd.

P.O. Box 14175
Wellington, New Zealand
Phone: +64 4 385 5100
Fax: +64 4 385 5139
www.wellington-airport.co.nz

Sports Travel Insider's Edge:

Best way to watch the action:

Check the schedule to see when the All Blacks play their neighborly rivals, Australia. No matter how entertaining the game may be, the fans will be that much more entertaining with their cheers and jeers. This is All Blacks at its best!

Best place to get up close:

With the famed shape of the Westpac Trust Stadium, there is not a bad view in the "Cake Tin." Wearing the opposing team's colors is not recommended and could be hazardous to your health. In other words, wear all black. Get there early for the traditional haka (Maori posture dance) before each match.

Best travel tip:

Make sure you extend your stay and afford yourself ample time to explore the beautiful country of New Zealand. Many who have never been there are amazed by New Zealand's pure beauty.

Notable Quote:

"When you're an All Black and you lose, whatever the game at whatever the time, there's big fall-out. New Zealand is a small country and it's front-page stuff...People call for heads to roll."—TAINE RANDELL, former All Blacks captain

Relevant Websites:

www.allblacks.com
www.tseworld.com
www.pcevents.com
www.sportstravel.com
www.gotickets.com
www.ticketmaster.com.nz
www.premieresports.com

60

ACC BASKETBALL TOURNAMENT

When?

Beginning of March every year.

Future Locations:

2009–March 12-15, Georgia Dome, Atlanta, GA

2010–March 11-14, Greensboro Coliseum, Greensboro, NC

2011–March 10-13, Greensboro Coliseum, Greensboro, NC

2012–Georgia Dome, Atlanta, GA

2013-2015–Greensboro Coliseum, Greensboro, NC

Significance:

The ACC Men's Basketball Tournament is considered "the Granddaddy of College Hoops Tourneys." The ACC is composed of twelve teams along the Atlantic coast, including Boston College, Clemson University, Duke University, Florida State University, Georgia Tech, University of Maryland, University of Miami, University of North Carolina, North Carolina State University, University of Virginia, Virginia Tech, and Wake Forest University.

The ACC conference itself is geographically compact, resulting in various rivalries. The four "Tobacco Road" schools in North Carolina are natural adversaries due to pure proximity. The two Florida and two Virginia schools have no love lost for each other as well.

At the conclusion of the regular season, all twelve teams in the ACC compete in the season-ending conference championship tournament. The tournament format is single elimination with the top four seeds receiving a first-round bye. On Thursday, the fifth through twelfth ranked teams compete in the first round with two games occurring in the afternoon and two games in the evening. The winners advance to play the top four seeds on Friday. Again, two games are played in the afternoon and two in the evening. On Saturday both semifinals are played in the evening. An automatic birth to the NCAA National Tournament is on the line on Sunday when the final teams compete for the Conference Championship and, more than likely, a top four seed in the "Big Dance."

Who attends?

You could put this tournament on the moon and loyal fans and students from all the ACC schools would make the pilgrimage.

History

On May 8, 1953, the University of South Carolina, University of North Carolina, North Carolina State University, Wake Forest University, Duke University, Clemson University, and University of Maryland broke off from the large and unwieldy Southern Conference to form the Atlantic Coast Conference. By December, the University of Virginia bolted and joined the group, making the ACC an eight-school conference.

While the motivation to break away was based on problems with the football programs, it would be basketball that put the ACC on the map. The tournament was a hit from the very beginning. It quickly became one of the most successful conferences in men's basketball, thanks to North Carolina State coach Everett Case and North Carolina coach Frank McGuire.

Case, considered the "Father of ACC Basketball," was a great coach, but an even better promoter of the conference. McGuire was his "bitter rival" and the two soon recognized that the friction and verbal jabs made money and put people in the seats. Behind the scenes, they maintained a highly secretive working relationship.

After North Carolina took the 1957 national championship, Castleman D. Chesley, a Greensboro entrepreneur, formed a five-station television network that would broadcast regular season ACC games the following season. The ACC had arrived as a basketball powerhouse that continues to this day.

Notable Athletes:

The road from the ACC to the NBA has been taken by many, including:

Mitch Kupchak, UNC
Michael Jordan, UNC
Horace Grant, Clemson
Tim Duncan, Wake Forest
Antawn Jamison, UNC
James Worthy, UNC
Elton Brand, Duke

Records:

Overall ACC tournament championships (to date):

Duke: 16
UNC: 15
NC State: 10
Wake Forest: 4
Maryland: 3
Georgia Tech: 3
South Carolina: 1
University of Virginia: 1

Traditions:

ACC Fan Fest: What would a sports tournament be without a fan fest? The ACC has its share of fans, and that number grows every year. The ACC Fan Fest is an interactive event with something for everyone of all ages. Interactive games and daily giveaways await the true ACC basketball fan. Food and beverages are available. Don't forget to pick up your favorite team t-shirt or other merchandise at the Official Tournament Merchandise Store.

ACC Legends: A group of former standout players from each ACC school is honored at both the tournament and the ACC Legend's Brunch each year.

Things to know before you go:

Even if you are not a student of an ACC school, you can still act like one. Find out who the "favorite" teams are to be in the final game and learn their school fight songs. You will fit right in by singing along and cheering with the rest of the fans.

Tickets:

There has not been a public sale of ACC Tournament tickets since 1966. All tickets are divided equally among the twelve schools.

Be aware of the matchups and what day you want to go. Saturday is the high-priced day. A Sunday game ticket is easier to find with dejected fans of a school that lost on Saturday ready to bolt out of town and looking to sell their tickets. This is a great way to get a "cheaper" ticket.

For secondary ticket access, consider:

GoTickets, Inc.
2345 Waukegan Road, Suite 140
Bannockburn, IL 60015-1552
Toll-Free: 1-800-775-1617
Fax: (919) 481-9101
E-mail: sales@gotickets.com
www.gotickets.com

Travel Packages:

If you are going to travel to this event, I would recommend using a reliable company to work with you on making the necessary arrangements. The suppliers listed in this book have solid references and are by far the most trusted in the business. Below are some of the organizations to try for this Top 100 Must See Sporting Event.

Premiere Corporate Events
14 Penn Plaza, Suite 925
New York, NY 10122
Phone: (212) 695-9480
Fax: (212) 564-8098
Toll-Free: 1-877-621-5243
E-mail: requests@tseworld.com
www.tseworld.com
www.pcevents.com

Premiere Sports Travel
201 Shannon Oaks Circle, Suite 205
Cary, NC 27511
Phone: (919) 481-9511
Fax: (919) 481-1337

Toll-Free: 1-800-924-9993
E-mail: sales@sportstravel.com
www.sportstravel.com

Notable Quotes:

"The atmosphere will be electric. Because to those who know the history of the ACC, something very important is at stake. Best on the block. Ask anyone who has ever played or coached in, or cared about, the ACC."—JOHN FEINSTEIN, author and sports commentator

"When you're competing for the ACC regular season (title), you have sixteen games to win a championship and it's over two months. The ACC Tournament is more intense because for us it'll be three games in three days—four games in four days for other teams—and it's real intense and everyone's going after it."—DEMARCUS NELSON, Duke, on his favorite part of ACC Tournament

Relevant Websites:

www.theacc.com
www.accrooms.com
www.gadome.com
www.greensborocoliseum.com
www.tseworld.com
www.pcevents.com
www.sportstravel.com
www.gotickets.com
www.premieresports.com

61
CARIBBEAN WORLD SERIES

When?
Annually in February.

Future Locations:
2009–Mexicali, Mexico
2010–Venezuela

Significance:

The Caribbean World Series was the brainchild of Venezuelans Oscar "El Negro" Prieto and Pablo Morales. The annual event is sanctioned by the Confederación de Béisbol del Caribe (CBC) or Baseball Confederation of the Caribbean (in English) since 1949. The top teams from CBC member countries Panama, Puerto Rico, Venezuela, and Mexico (replacing Cuba in 1970 after a ten-year absence of the series) meet in a six-day series of doubleheader games to crown their very own World Series champion.

Each country is represented by the winning team of its respective league. However, there is no rule stopping those teams from reinforcing their roster with additional players from losing organizations. The Caribbean World Series sees each team compete in up to six games, depending on the schedule. The team with the most wins captures the championship.

Who attends?

Aside from baseball fans from all over Mexico and the Caribbean you will find fans from the United States who can't wait until spring training to start enjoying baseball, and/or those hanging on to the previous season not wanting baseball to end.

History

Seeing the success of the Serie Interamericana (Inter-American Series), Oscar "El Negro" Prieto and Pablo Morales came up with the idea for the Caribbean World Series in 1946. The two Venezuelan natives took that idea and presented it to the CBC conference in Miami in late 1948. The CBC liked the idea of their own World Series and decided to move forward with Cuba hosting the first Caribbean World Series in 1949. Teams from Panama, Puerto Rico, and Venezuela joined and were subsequently defeated by their Cuban counterparts. That victory was

the first in a string of consecutive championships for Cuba until 1960.

But Fidel Castro, holding power in Cuba, replaced all professional baseball teams with an amateur system run by the state. In response to this move, the CBC cancelled the Caribbean World Series. By 1970, the Series was revived with Mexico replacing Cuba. The union of those nations continue to compete every year in a different host country as the Caribbean World Series gains prominence in the world and is a common haunt for Major League Baseball scouts. If anything, baseball fans in the United States get a little closer to a year-round "fix."

Notable Athletes:

Many current and former Major League Baseball players competed in the Caribbean World Series, including:

Roberto Clemente
Reggie Jackson
David Ortiz
Juan Marichal
Willie Mays
Minnie Miñoso
Sammy Sosa
Bobby Abreu
Miguel Tejada
Manny Ramirez

Traditions:

The Caribbean World Series is a chance for players from Mexico, Panama, Puerto Rico, and Venezuela to shine under the bright spotlight of a championship tournament. However, it is also an opportunity to show their skills in front of Major League Baseball scouts. Those scouts want to see how the players perform in a high-pressure environment that Caribbean World Series fans provide. Fans cheer and boo and sportswriters do hold back on an embarrassing question or two from a player. A true litmus test for these players who aspire to go to the show.

Things to know before you go:

Insults fly between fans of differing countries, but they are mostly good-natured. After some verbal jousting, don't be surprised to see those fans of various allegiances dancing the merengue or the rumba together between innings. And just think, all America has is a seventh-inning stretch.

We have all seen a pitcher pulled, forced to make that long walk back to the dugout. At the Caribbean World Series, young fans have been known to jump onto the field to seek autographs during the replacement pitcher's warm-up routine. Security stays put as the players gladly sign their name and shake a few hands.

Tickets:

For primary ticket access information, consider: www.mlb.com

For secondary ticket access, consider:

GoTickets, Inc.
2345 Waukegan Road, Suite 140
Bannockburn, IL 60015-1552
Toll-Free: 1-800-775-1617
Fax: (919) 481-9101
E-mail: sales@gotickets.com
www.gotickets.com

Travel Packages:

If you are going to travel to this event, I would recommend using a reliable company to work with you on making the necessary arrangements. The suppliers listed in this book have solid references and are by far the most trusted in the business. Below are some of the organizations to try for this Top 100 Must See Sporting Event.

Premiere Corporate Events
14 Penn Plaza, Suite 925
New York, NY 10122
Phone: (212) 695-9480
Fax: (212) 564-8098
Toll-Free: 1-877-621-5243

E-mail: requests@tseworld.com
www.tseworld.com
www.pcevents.com

Premiere Sports Travel
201 Shannon Oaks Circle, Suite 205
Cary, NC 27511
Phone: (919) 481-9511
Fax: (919) 481-1337
Toll-Free: 1-800-924-9993
E-mail: sales@sportstravel.com
www.sportstravel.com

Notable Quotes:

"I've been in a lot of World Series, and enjoyed them, but I have to tell you, the Caribbean Series is more fun."—MIKE BRITO, Latin America scout for the Los Angeles Dodgers

"The entertainment value is what is important to the Caribbean Series. Fans don't go to the stadium just for the game itself. There's an attraction."—JUAN FRANCISCO PUELLO HERRERA, Caribbean Baseball Confederation president

Relevant Websites:
www.mlb.com
www.tseworld.com
www.pcevents.com
www.sportstravel.com
www.gotickets.com
www.latinobaseball.com
www.premieresports.com

62

FA CUP

When?
May

Where?
Throughout England. All matches leading up to the final are played at the home team's

stadium, which is predetermined before each match. The final is held at the new Wembley Stadium.

Significance:

The Football Association Challenge Cup, more commonly called the FA Cup, is the oldest football/soccer competition in the world. It is also an event that can provide the most excitement because it attracts clubs at all levels from the English football league system. Non-league groups can also participate if they competed in the previous year's FA Cup, FA Trophy, or FA Vase competition. Their play must be deemed acceptable by the league and they must have a suitable stadium. In the 2007–2008 season, 731 clubs entered.

The competitions start in August and continue until a champ is crowned in May. The "knockout tournament" pairings are drawn at random and there is no seeding. Qualifying rounds are regionalized to reduce travel costs for non-league teams. Still, the possibility or probability for upsets by an upstart team makes this a tournament of drama. While clubs that are more prominent may want a more inexperienced team, they also fear the possibility of an ambitious and talented football/soccer squad. Yes, a lowly underdog of little renown has the opportunity to go all the way to win the FA Cup and qualify for a first-round game in the UEFA Cup.

The FA Cup originally was much smaller than the current trophy. It was made by Messrs Martin, Hall & Co. and cost £20. Aston Villa won the cup in 1895, but the cup was stolen while on display in the window of a soccer shop in Birmingham. It was never seen again. Today's trophy, made in 1992, serves as the fourth FA Cup.

Who attends?

Dedicated and die-hard football/soccer fans of all ages from around the United Kingdom.

History

It all started with a proposal by FA Honorary Secretary Charles Alcock, which was submitted at a meeting held at the offices of The Sportsman in London on July 20, 1871. It said, in part:

> "That it is desirable that a Challenge Cup should be established in connection with the Association, for which all clubs belonging to the Association should be invited to compete."

Members of the FA approved the proposal three months later with the first competition taking place in the 1871–1872 season. Back then, only fifteen teams entered. However, it did not take long for the first of many upsets to occur. The Wanderers, a team composed of former public school and university players, defeated the Royal Engineers at Kennington Oval in front of a crowd of 2,000 for the Cup.

Not including war years, the FA Cup called Wembley Stadium home from the time of its 1923 opening until 2000. The new Wembley played host again in 2007, but the FA Cup no longer has a permanent base of operations. The tournament is not just a sports event; it's a longtime sporting tradition with strong roots, a sense of history and pageantry, and a great deal of drama thrown in for good measure.

Notable Athletes:

Luis Garcia, Liverpool
Steven Gerrard, Liverpool
Jamie Carragher, Liverpool
Ricardo Gardner, Bolton Wanderers
Gez Murphy, Nuneaton Borough
Dave Mulligan, Doncaster Rovers
Stuart Tuck, Eastbourne Borough
Alex Rodman, Leamington
Paul Brayson, Northwich Victoria
Jamie Laidlaw, Gosport Borough

Records:

Most wins by a team: Manchester United, 11

Most FA Cup final goals: Ian Rush, Liverpool, 5 (2 in 1986; 2 in 1989; 1 in 1992)

Most FA Cup appearances: Ian Callaghan, 88

Things to know before you go:

Hat Trick: Three goals scored in one game by one player.

Give and Go: A player controlling the ball passes to a teammate and runs through a open field to get a possible return pass.

Juggling: Keeping the ball off the ground by a player using their feet, thighs, chest, head, and the top of their shoulders.

Red Card: Shown by a referee to signify that a player has been sent off. The player who has been sent off must leave the field immediately and cannot be replaced during the game; their team must continue the game with one player fewer.

Yellow Card: A cautionary warning issued by the referee to a player for unsportsmanlike behavior or a variety of infractions.

Tickets:

For primary ticket access information, consider: www.thefa.com.

For secondary ticket access, consider:

GoTickets, Inc.
2345 Waukegan Road, Suite 140
Bannockburn, IL 60015-1552
Toll-Free: 1-800-775-1617
Fax: (919) 481-9101
E-mail: sales@gotickets.com
www.gotickets.com

Travel Packages:

If you are going to travel to this event, I would recommend using a reliable company to work with you on making the neces-

sary arrangements. The suppliers listed in this book have solid references and are by far the most trusted in the business. Below are some of the organizations to try for this Top 100 Must See Sporting Event.

Premiere Corporate Events
14 Penn Plaza, Suite 925
New York, NY 10122
Phone: (212) 695-9480
Fax: (212) 564-8098
Toll-Free: 1-877-621-5243
E-mail: requests@tseworld.com
www.tseworld.com
www.pcevents.com

Premiere Sports Travel
201 Shannon Oaks Circle, Suite 205
Cary, NC 27511
Phone: (919) 481-9511
Fax: (919) 481-1337
Toll-Free: 1-800-924-9993
E-mail: sales@sportstravel.com
www.sportstravel.com

Notable Quotes:

"The FA Cup Final is the greatest single match outside the World Cup Final—and it's ours."—Sir Bobby Robson, Ispwich Town's manager and Cup winner

"When I was fourteen there is no doubt that the FA Cup was the greatest competition in the world. It was 1975. West Ham played Fulham in the final and I was so excited because West Ham had Watford old boy Billy Jennings on their team. It was unbelievable. A player I had watched and cheered so many times at Vicarage Road was actually playing at Wembley in the FA Cup final. How good could things get?"—Graham Fisher, *Soccer News*

"It's the biggest game of my career. One of the biggest club competitions in the world. It's so well-known throughout the world.

To have a chance to play in it is great and I'm looking forward to it. I've not won any honours yet in my career and I'd love a winners' medal. That's what we're going out to do."—GAVIN RAE, AFC Defender, Cardiff City

Relevant Websites:
www.thefa.com
www.tseworld.com
www.pcevents.com
www.sportstravel.com
www.gotickets.com
www.premieresports.com

63

INDIANA HIGH SCHOOL BASKETBALL TOURNAMENT FINALS

Where?
Conseco Field House
125 South Pennsylvania Street
Indianapolis, IN 46204

When?
Annually at the end of March.

Significance:
Change is not necessarily a bad thing. Sure, the Indiana High School Basketball Tournament went from one big competition to a four-class system in the 1997–1998 season. Objections and debates ensued, but little has been done to lessen Hoosier Hysteria in any way. The pool is hardly diluted with multiple championships as the class system allows teams of all sizes to hold a coveted high school basketball championship. There are plenty of Davids to defeat those almighty Goliaths. Indianans' passion for basketball is well-known, filling high school gymnasiums around the state. Nine out of the ten largest high school gyms in

the nation are located in Indiana. The movie *Hoosiers* has dramatized the fanaticism. Legendary basketball players have appeared in tournaments throughout the years, including Larry Bird, Shawn Kemp, Calbert Cheaney, and Steve Alford.

Who attends?
Indiana basketball aficionados and fanatical followers.

How to get there?
The main event of the Indiana High School Basketball Tournament is the state finals, played at Conseco Fieldhouse in downtown Indianapolis. The arena is easy to access from Highways 65 or 70.

Tickets:
For primary ticket access information, contact www.consecofieldhouse.com, or the participating schools for ticket distribution hours and to be placed on the waiting list.

Accommodations:

Hilton Indianapolis
120 West Market Street
Indianapolis, IN 6204
Phone: (317) 972-0600
Fax: (317) 822-5839
Toll-Free: 1-800-HILTONS
www.hilton.com

Note: AAA 3-star property is pet friendly, just in case you want to bring your dog. With 332 rooms, it is conveniently located near major attractions throughout Indianapolis. Onsite eateries include McCormick & Schmick's and 120 West Market Restaurant.

Conrad Indianapolis
50 West Washington Street
Indianapolis, IN 46204
Phone: (317) 713-5000
Fax: (317) 638-3687
Toll-Free: 1-800-HHonors
www.conradhotels.com

Note: At one of the city's prominent intersec-

tions, *Conrad Indianapolis provides access to Artsgarden and Circle Centre Mall. Twenty-three stories house 241 guest rooms.*

Canterbury Hotel

123 South Illinois Street
Indianapolis, IN 46225
Phone: (317) 634-3000
Fax: (317) 685-2519
Toll-Free: 1-800-538-8186
www.canterburyhotel.com

Note: European, boutique-style hotel located in downtown Indianapolis. The ninety-nine guest suites include five bi-level penthouse suites and one Presidential Suite. Look out for the chocolate truffle left on your pillow.

On-Site Hospitality:

Fifty-four concession stands fill Conseco Fieldhouse featuring traditional arena fare.

Travel Packages:

If you are going to travel to this event, I would recommend using a reliable company to work with you on making the necessary arrangements. The suppliers listed in this book have solid references and are by far the most trusted in the business. Below are some of the organizations to try for this Top 100 Must See Sporting Event.

Premiere Corporate Events

14 Penn Plaza, Suite 925
New York, NY 10122
Phone: (212) 695-9480
Fax: (212) 564-8098
Toll-Free: 1-877-621-5243
E-mail: requests@tseworld.com
www.tseworld.com
www.pcevents.com

Premiere Sports Travel

201 Shannon Oaks Circle, Suite 205
Cary, NC 27511
Phone: (919) 481-9511
Fax: (919) 481-1337
Toll-Free: 1-800-924-9993

E-mail: sales@sportstravel.com
www.sportstravel.com

Dining:

St. Elmo's Steak House

127 South Illinois Street
Indianapolis, IN 46225
Phone: (317) 635-0636
Fax: (317) 687-9162
www.stelmos.com

Note: As a downtown landmark since 1902, this steakhouse has earned a national reputation for its steaks, seafood, chops, and high level of service.

Harry and Izzy's

153 South Illinois Street
Indianapolis, IN 46225
Phone: (317) 635-9594
Fax: (317) 635-9599
www.harryandizzys.com

Note: The founders of St. Elmo's established a more casual environment for their customers while maintaining the quality of the food and service.

Oceanaire

30 South Meridian Street
Indianapolis, IN 46204
Phone: (317) 955-2277
Fax: (317) 955-2278
www.theoceanaire.com

Note: Fresh seafood is flown in daily from around the world. New menus are printed every day to accommodate those new choices.

Six Lounge & Restaurant

247 South Meridian Street
Indianapolis, IN 46204
Phone: (317) 638-6660
www.6indy.com

Note: Perfect for a private party with Chef Tyler Herald serving his latest creation. A resident DJ keeps the party going.

Airport:

Indianapolis International Airport
2500 Street High School Road
Indianapolis, IN 46241
Phone: (317) 487-7243
www.indianapolisairport.com

Sports Travel Insider's Edge:

Best way to watch the action:
Nothing beats a view between the baskets.
Center court lower level seats can be found in
sections 5 and 16. Take in a full day with two
morning competitions and the evening game.

Best place to get up close:
For those who truly want to get up close and
personal with Indiana high school basketball,
travel to the tiny town of Milan, made famous
in *Hoosiers*. The Milan '54 Museum pays
homage to the 161-student school that upset Muncie Central at the 1954 Indiana State
High School Basketball Championships.

Best travel tip:
Be sure to visit 6416 Cornell Avenue, where
you can find Plumps Last Shot. Decorated
with tons of memorabilia, it is named after
the player who actually hit that famed last
shot in the 1954 State Finals.

Notable Quotes:

"This reminded me what Indiana basketball is about—passion. Passion did not
let either team give up and that's what
made it so exciting.... That is true March
Madness."—BEN CORN, Indiana Statesman

"The players also know it is special. For
the majority of players, this is as far as
their 'career' will go, the highest level of
basketball in which they'll ever participate,
and they're lucky enough to be doing it in
the one state where people are most interested in watching them."—DALE LAWRENCE,
author of *Hoosier Hysteria Road Book*

Relevant Websites:
www.indy.org
www.ihsaa.org
www.tseworld.com
www.pcevents.com
www.sportstravel.com
www.premieresports.com

64

U.S. OPEN
GOLF TOURNAMENT

When?
Mid-June

Future Locations:

Bethpage State Park (Black Course)
Farmingdale, NY
June 15–21, 2009

Pebble Beach Golf Links
Pebble Beach, CA
June 14–20, 2010

**Congressional Country Club
(Blue Course)**
Bethesda, MD
June 13–19, 2011

The Olympic Club (Lake Course)
San Francisco, CA
June 11–16, 2012

Merion Golf Club (East Course)
Ardmore, PA
June 10–16, 2013

Pinehurst Resort (Course #2)
Pinehurst, NC
2014

Chambers Bay
University Place, WA
2015

Significance:

Golfers and fans alike look forward to Father's Day, and not because they are expecting cards, gifts, and the opportunity to take it easy on a lazy Sunday. In fact, golfers look forward to working and working hard on that day by playing the final round of the U.S. Open.

The United States Open Championship is played on longer than standard golf courses with a high cut of open rough, hilly greens, and pinched fairways. Playing well is a challenge, to say the least, and a competitor must be accurate in his drive. Golfers may complain about the conditions, but the opportunity to win one of the four major championships in the PGA is worth the supposed aggravation.

Any professional or amateur with a current USGA Handicap Index not exceeding 1.4 is welcome to play. Players earn their slot by being fully exempt or successfully qualifying. Qualifying can occur at over 100 courses around the country. Sectional qualifying involves thirty-six holes played in one day at multiple U.S. courses and one course each in Europe and Japan. Winning the U.S. Open on that third Sunday in June earns a golfer not only prize money and notoriety, but also an automatic invitation to the Masters, British Open, and the PGA Championship.

A happy Father's Day, indeed.

Who attends?

Golfers and golf fans who enjoy watching the best golfers take on some of the most difficult, challenging, and frustrating U.S. golf courses.

History

With ten professionals and one amateur playing, the U.S. Open officially began on October 4, 1895, at Newport Golf and Country Club's nine-hole course in Rhode Island. After four rounds of the 36-hole Open, a twenty-one-year-old Englishman and club assistant named Horace Rawlins was the victor. He would be the first of many British players to take the championship in the United States. It wasn't until Americans such as Bob Jones began winning (1923, 1926, 1929, and 1930) that the Open started to get some attention from naysayers who considered it a mere sideshow.

The challenge that the courses present have defined a golfer's career; as it wasn't so much about winning the U.S. Open as it is about surviving the difficulties presented. Ben Hogan, Arnold Palmer, and Jack Nicklaus became household names because of the skills they displayed under those conditions. In fact, Nicklaus nabbed his first U.S. Open during his rookie season as a professional.

Notable Athletes:

Tiger Woods
Jack Nicklaus
Willie Anderson
Arnold Palmer
Hale Irwin
Sam Snead

Records:

Oldest player to qualify: Sam Snead, 61, 1973

Youngest competitor: Tyrell Garth, 14, 1941

Most consecutive victories: Willie Anderson, 3

Oldest champion: Hale Irwin, 45 years and 15 days, 1990

Youngest champion: John McDermott, 19 years and 315 days, 1911

Things to know before you go:

Ace: A hole-in-one.

Front nine: The first half of a round of golf.

Back nine: The second half of a round of golf.

Fore: A warning cry to other players that your ball is headed in their direction.

Par: A certain number of shots needed to

hole your ball depending on the hole's distance and difficulty.

Birdie: One under par.

Eagle: Two under par.

Albatross: Three under par.

Bogey: One over par. Double and triple bogeys are self-explanatory.

Tickets:

For primary ticket access information, consider: www.www.usopen.com.

For secondary ticket access, consider:

GoTickets, Inc.
2345 Waukegan Road, Suite 140
Bannockburn, IL 60015-1552
Toll-Free: 1-800-775-1617
Fax: (919) 481-9101
E-mail: sales@gotickets.com
www.gotickets.com

Travel Packages:

If you are going to travel to this event, I would recommend using a reliable company to work with you on making the necessary arrangements. The suppliers listed in this book have solid references and are by far the most trusted in the business. Below are some of the organizations to try for this Top 100 Must See Sporting Event.

Premiere Corporate Events
14 Penn Plaza, Suite 925
New York, NY 10122
Phone: (212) 695-9480
Fax: (212) 564-8098
Toll-Free: 1-877-621-5243
E-mail: requests@tseworld.com
www.tseworld.com
www.pcevents.com

Premiere Sports Travel
201 Shannon Oaks Circle, Suite 205
Cary, NC 27511
Phone: (919) 481-9511
Fax: (919) 481-1337
Toll-Free: 1-800-924-9993

E-mail: sales@sportstravel.com
www.sportstravel.com

Sports Travel Insider's Edge:

Best way to watch the action:
Sitting at the 18th hole grandstand will always give you a bird's-eye view of the action as the Open comes to an end. You can not only see the dramatic and not-so-dramatic finishes and the winning putt, but also have the rare opportunity to sit.

Best place to get up close:
Some golf holes are more crowded than others. Seeking out an area without a crowd or watching the tee off is a way to see your favorite golfer up close and in action. Practice rounds which take place at the beginning of the week are also a cheaper option that provide an up-close feel in a much looser environment.

Best travel tip:
A week of watching the pros can make any golfer excited to play. Make sure to split your viewing of the tournament with actual playing. A good idea might be to substitute one day of spectating with a day of golfing. Since the event takes place in June the weather usually provides for a nice day on the course.

Notable Quotes:

"The U.S. Open is my favorite tournament to play. I love the fun. Americans are noisier than us, and I like that. I love the atmosphere, the way the tournament is run, I love how tough the course is."— NICK DOUGHERTY, golfer

"This is a tournament that I dreamt of winning as a kid, that I spent hours practicing I mean, countless hours practicing, dreaming of winning this tournament, came out here weeks and months in advance to get ready."—PHIL MICKELSON, golfer

Relevant Websites:

www.usopen.com
www.tseworld.com
www.pcevents.com
www.sportstravel.com
www.gotickets.com
www.premieresports.com

65

MIDNIGHT MADNESS AT UNIVERSITY OF KENTUCKY

Where?

Rupp Arena
430 West Vine Street
Lexington, KY 40507

When?

Annually on the first Saturday in October.

Significance:

Madness over college basketball extends beyond midnight at the University of Kentucky. The front yard of Rupp Arena is usually filled with tents. In Kentucky, they call it "Big Blue Madness" and those happy campers want one of the coveted 23,000 free tickets for the practice that starts when the clock strikes time. They come from all walks of life, from college students to captains of industry. Kentucky fans clearly take their basketball seriously, in spite of the perceived madness. They camp out and shoot hoops, making it an all-night sleepover and a celebration of everything college basketball. Traditions have sprouted up around the event, including slam-dunk contests and the famous "Tuition Shot" where a student making a half-court shot can win tuition, room, and board at UK for the year.

Former University of Maryland head basketball coach Lefty Driesell clearly preferred to get a jump on the competition. In 1970, he came up with a brainchild. Discovering that the NCAA allowed practice to start on October 15th, he literally took advantage of every minute of that day and started at 12:01. Actually, he just had his players run a mile for bragging rights before commencing the actual practice at 3 P.M. Nonetheless, the academia at Maryland was less than thrilled. "Midnight Madness" was born.

The edge Driesell was seeking has become an annual tradition that has spread far beyond the University of Maryland campus. Coaches from around the country embraced the practice, but fans, including the Kentucky faithful, have made it true "Midnight Madness."

Who attends?

This event is for the college students who attend UK and the literal fanatics who follow college hoops.

How to get there?

From the Bluegrass Airport, turn left onto Man o' War Boulevard. Turn right on Versailles Road (US 60). As you come into downtown, the road will split into a one-way street called Maxwell Street. Follow it for two blocks and the High Street Lot is on the left. To get to the Cox Street Lot, follow Maxwell Street and take a left on South Broadway. Left on Main Street and then another left into the lot at the end of Heritage Hall.

Tickets:

For primary ticket access information, consider: www.ukathletics.com.

For secondary ticket access, consider:

GoTickets, Inc.
2345 Waukegan Road, Suite 140
Bannockburn, IL 60015-1552
Toll-Free: 1-800-775-1617
Fax: (919) 481-9101
E-mail: sales@gotickets.com
www.gotickets.com

Accommodations:

If a tent is not enough luxury or you're not the outdoorsy type, try these options:

Hyatt Regency Lexington
401 West High Street
Lexington, KY 40507
Phone: (859) 253-1234
Fax: (859) 233-7974
www.hyatt.com
Note: The hotel is attached to the arena. Rest in warmth and comfort while others sleep under the Kentucky sky.

SpringHill Suites
863 South Broadway
Lexington, KY 40504
Phone: (859) 225-1500
Fax: (859) 225-1534
Toll-Free: 1-800-MARRIOTT
www.marriott.com
Note: Conveniently located about a mile from Rupp Arena.

Embassy Suites Hotel
1801 Newtown Pike
Lexington, KY 40511
Phone: (859) 455-5000
Fax: (859) 455-5001
www.embassysuites.com
Note: Located less than two miles from Rupp Arena, each suite has a private bedroom and spacious living rooms.

Griffin Gate Marriott Resort and Spa
1800 Newtown Pike
Lexington, KY 40511
Phone: (859) 231-5100
Fax: (859) 255-9944
www.marriott.com
Note: Smoke-free hotel located 1.7 miles from Rupp Arena. Offers many dining options and the chance to get in a round of golf.

Holiday Inn Express
1000 Export Street
Lexington, KY 40504
Phone: (859) 389-6800
Fax: (859) 389-6801
www.hiexpress.com
Note: Reasonably priced and at the heart of campus just 1.4 miles from Rupp Arena.

Gratz Park Inn
120 West 2nd Street
Lexington, KY 40507
Phone: (859) 231-1777
Fax: (859) 233-7593
Toll-Free: 1-800-752-4166
www.gratzparkinn.com
Note: Boutique Inn located in the beautiful Gratz Park Historic District.

On-Site Hospitality:

Bringing your own tent means bringing your own food and beverages leading up to the event. Once you get in, concession stands can be found throughout the building.

Travel Packages:

If you are going to travel to this event, I would recommend using a reliable company to work with you on making the necessary arrangements. The suppliers listed in this book have solid references and are by far the most trusted in the business. Below are some of the organizations to try for this Top 100 Must See Sporting Event.

Premiere Corporate Events
14 Penn Plaza, Suite 925
New York, NY 10122
Phone: (212) 695-9480
Fax: (212) 564-8098
Toll-Free: 1-877-621-5243
E-mail: requests@tseworld.com
www.tseworld.com
www.pcevents.com

Premiere Sports Travel
201 Shannon Oaks Circle, Suite 205
Cary, NC 27511
Phone: (919) 481-9511
Fax: (919) 481-1337

Toll-Free: 1-800-924-9993
E-mail: sales@sportstravel.com
www.sportstravel.com

Dining:

Jimmy D's East Coast Café
1395 West Main Street
Lexington, KY 40508
Phone: (859) 246-1708
www.jimmydcafe.com
Note: Known for their Reubens and authentic Philly Cheese Steak.

Joe Bologna's
120 West Maxwell Street
Lexington, KY 40508
Phone: (859) 252-4933
www.joebolognas.com
Note: Great Italian food to enjoy as the clock ticks to midnight.

daSha's
101 North Broadway
Lexington, KY 40507
Phone: (859) 259-3771
Fax: (859) 254-1602
www.deshas.com
Note: Considered one of the best meals in downtown Lexington.

Big Blue Martini
369 West Vine Street
Lexington, KY 40507
Phone: (859) 231-9000
Note: Grab a martini or another cocktail of your choice prior to the game. Located in the Radisson Plaza Hotel.

Pazzo's Pizza Pub
385 South Limestone
Lexington, KY 40508
Phone: (859) 255-5125
www.pazzospizzapub.com
Note: Popular hangout for Wildcats fans. Great pizza and pub food.

Airports:

Blue Grass Airport (twelve miles to UK)
4000 Terminal Drive, Suite 206
Lexington, KY 40510
Phone: (859) 425-3114
Fax: (859) 233-1822
www.bluegrassairport.com

Cincinnati/Northern KY Airport (one hour and thirty-one minutes to UK)
Donaldson Road & Lincoln Road
Florence, KY 41022
Phone: (859) 767-3151
www.cvgairport.com

Sports Travel Insider's Edge:

Best way to watch the action:
Due to NCAA rule changes, the event starts closer to 9 P.M. nowadays. Lower-level center court seats provide the best view of all events, starting with the men's and women's player introductions and the women's scrimmage. Following the men's player introduction, you can see the dunk contest and the three-point competition. Keep an eye out for former players known to make cameo appearances toward the end of the scrimmage.

Best place to get up close:
The only way to get a great view of this game is to camp out for your tickets on Wednesday morning. The tickets are sold on a first-come, first-serve basis and the good seats go quickly. Traditionally, all tickets are sold in less than forty-eight hours.

Best travel tip:
Midnight Madness usually takes place on Friday during football season. There is a possibility that the football team will be in town, making for an all-Wildcat weekend.

Notable Quotes:

"It feels right; it feels like home. I loved the kindness of the coaches, just the atmosphere of the school. Kentucky is Kentucky basketball. That's all there is. They treat the men's basketball team like kings. I want to be King Curtis. They really care about their players."—CURTIS BROWN, after witnessing his first Midnight Madness

"It really is madness. This is the standard everyone measures their opening practice by."—MICKIE DEMOSS, former University of Kentucky women's head basketball coach

Relevant Websites:
www.ukathletics.com
www.visitlex.com
www.rupparena.com
www.tseworld.com
www.pcevents.com
www.sportstravel.com
www.gotickets.com
www.premieresports.com

66
PREAKNESS STAKES

Where?
Pimlico Race Course
5201 Park Heights Avenue
Baltimore, MD 21215

When?
Third weekend in May.

Significance:
While the first race in horse racing's Triple Crown has intrigue and the third leg has drama, the Preakness Stakes is a rare opportunity to see both rematches from the Kentucky Derby and previews of the Belmont Stakes. The Preakness, the shortest of the three races, is an American Grade 1 stakes thoroughbred horse race lasting 1 3/16 miles. Every year, race fans crowd the Pimlico Race Course in Baltimore, Maryland, to see the best colts, fillies, and geldings. Fans expect to see the winner of the Kentucky Derby attempt to

make it two races in a row toward the three needed for the Triple Crown.

Predating the Kentucky Derby by two years, the Preakness launched a stakes race for three-year-olds in 1873. Then-Maryland Governor Oden Bowie officially named the race after a colt from the Preakness Stables in Preakness, Wayne Township, New Jersey. The famed race is also known as "The Run for the Black-Eyed Susans," a moniker derived from the official state flower of Maryland formed into a horseshoe. The winner proudly wears the odd-shaped bouquet of black-eyed Susans.

Who attends?
Racing fans and those that can't miss a good party.

How to get there?
From the South of Baltimore, take 95 North to 695 West (a.k.a. Baltimore Beltway). Take Exit 18 East, Lochearn (Liberty Road). Left at Northern Parkway. Right on Park Heights Avenue. Left on Hayward Avenue and proceed straight into the track.

From the North of Baltimore, take 95 South to 695 West (Baltimore Beltway). Take exit 83 South and follow to Northern Parkway West. Turn left on Park Heights Avenue. Left on Hayward Avenue. Follow signs to parking.

Tickets:
For primary ticket access information, consider: www.preakness-tickets.com.

For secondary ticket access, consider:

GoTickets, Inc.
2345 Waukegan Road, Suite 140
Bannockburn, IL 60015-1552
Toll-Free: 1-800-775-1617
Fax: (919) 481-9101
E-mail: sales@gotickets.com
www.gotickets.com

Accommodations:

Henderson's Wharf Hotel
1000 Fell Street
Baltimore, MD 21231
Phone: (410) 522-7777
Fax: (410) 522-7087
Toll-Free: 1-800-522-2088
www.hendersonswharf.com

Note: A unique and charming place to stay. This converted nineteenth-century brick to-bacco warehouse is just a twenty-minute drive to Pimlico.

Hampton Inn Baltimore – Camden Yards
550 Washington Boulevard
Baltimore, MD 21230
Phone: (410) 685-5000
Fax: (410) 685-5002
Toll-Free:1-800-HAMPTON
www.hamptoninn.com

Note: Excellent view of Camden Yards and a quick walk to the Inner Harbor area.

Baltimore Marriott Waterfront
700 Aliceanna Street
Baltimore, MD 21202
Phone: (410) 385-3000
Fax: (410) 895-1900
Toll-Free: 1-800-228-9290
www.marriott.com

Note: Located on the edge of Baltimore's historic Inner Harbor. Close to downtown.

Radisson Hotel at Cross Keys
5100 Falls Road
Baltimore, MD 21210
Phone: (410) 532-6900
Fax: (410) 532-2403
Toll-Free: 1-800-333-3333
www.radisson.com

Note: A little over two miles from the track.

On-Site Hospitality:

Enjoy the Preakness in comfort and luxury. You can choose from various packages, including the Chalet Package, Corporate Tent Package, Turf Club Tent Package, Turfside Terrace, and Clubhouse Turn Reserved.

Terrace Dining: Overlooking the racetrack, you can enjoy four-star dining.

Hall of Fame Room: Attached to the Terrace Dining Room. This is a place with comfortable seating and a delicious buffet. Make your Black-Eyed Susan Day and/or Preakness Day a day (or days) to remember.

Sports Palace: Fifty-five televisions, including two 42-inch screens, show the Black-Eyed Susan and Preakness Day live racing and simulcast racing.

Travel Packages:

If you are going to travel to this event, I would recommend using a reliable company to work with you on making the necessary arrangements. The suppliers listed in this book have solid references and are by far the most trusted in the business. Below are some of the organizations to try for this Top 100 Must See Sporting Event.

Premiere Corporate Events
14 Penn Plaza, Suite 925
New York, NY 10122
Phone: (212) 695-9480
Fax: (212) 564-8098
Toll-Free: 1-877-621-5243
E-mail: requests@tseworld.com
www.tseworld.com
www.pcevents.com

Premiere Sports Travel
201 Shannon Oaks Circle, Suite 205
Cary, NC 27511
Phone: (919) 481-9511
Fax: (919) 481-1337
Toll-Free: 1-800-924-9993
E-mail: sales@sportstravel.com
www.sportstravel.com

Dining:

Ambassador Dining Restaurant
3811 Canterbury Road
Baltimore, MD 21218
Phone: (410) 366-1484
Fax: (410) 366-1484
www.ambassadordiningroom.com
Note: Known for great breakfasts and plentiful brunches.

The Prime Rib
1101 North Calvert Street
Baltimore, MD 21202
Phone: (410) 539-1804
Fax: (410) 837-0244
www.theprimerib.com
Note: Romantic setting for the racing couple. Take your time and enjoy your prime rib in leisure.

Bop Brick Oven Pizza
800 South Broadway
Baltimore, MD 21231
Phone: (410) 563-1600
www.boppizza.com
Note: Child-friendly restaurant offering fun for the entire family.

Airport:

Baltimore/Washington International Thurgood Marshall Airport
Aviation Boulevard and Elm Road
Baltimore, MD 21240
www.bwiairport.com

Sports Travel Insider's Edge:

Best way to watch the action:
A Turf Club Tent is the most affordable of the premium packages. Luxury on a smaller scale includes seating at Pimlico, views of the course, a private mutuel window, and an official souvenir program to commemorate the day.

Best place to get up close:
A premium price will get you a VIP view along the Preakness Village rail. Find seventy-nine of your closest friends to enjoy the day in a climate-controlled setting with a buffet and open bar. Bet at the private mutuel window and enjoy the entertainment.

Best travel tip:
Do not stray far from the Inner Harbor. Yes, it's twenty minutes from the track, but it is the ultimate in Baltimore nightlife after a long day watching and perhaps wagering on the ponies.

Notable Quote:

"It's a vital thing to have as far as the racing industry is concerned. Someone said having the Preakness is like having the Super Bowl in town every year. It's like the Super Bowl every third weekend in May."—MIKE HOPKINS, Executive Director of the Maryland Racing Commission

Relevant Websites:
www.preakness.com
www.baltimore.org
www.preaknesscelebration.com
www.preakness-tickets.com
www.tseworld.com
www.pcevents.com
www.sportstravel.com
www.gotickets.com
www.premieresports.com

67
NFL DRAFT

Where?
Radio City Music Hall
1260 Avenue of the Americas
New York, NY 10020

When?
April of every year.

Significance:

The National Football League draft has been held in New York City since 1965. As it has grown in prominence and popularity, bigger venues were located to house the fans. The draft has called Madison Square Garden and the Javits Convention Center home. Currently, the annual event is held in Radio City Music Hall. Draftees are put under a bright spotlight on a big stage, literally and figuratively. The best and brightest of college football are selected for their new NFL homes. It is a football fan's first glimpse at future starters, Hall of Famers, and legends—a true opportunity to say, "I was there when." Fantasy football players lay the groundwork for the coming season, not to mention their own drafts. A true sporting event has drama, intrigue, and a bit of mystery over the outcome. While the only sweat comes from worry and stress, the NFL draft is a major event in the sports world.

Who attends?

Die-hard football fans can be seen throughout Radio City Music Hall getting a glimpse of the latest and greatest draft selection. Plus, they are not afraid to jeer when they feel a team has picked incorrectly in their eyes. Look out for all the New York Jets fans.

How to get there?

Bus:
Take M5, M6, M7, or M27/M50 buses to Rockefeller Center/50th Street.
www.mta.nyc.ny.us

Train:
Take the B, D, or F subway to Rockefeller Center/50th Street.

NY City Transit
Phone: (718) 330-1234
www.mta.nyc.ny.us/nyct

Metro North Commuter Railroad
Phone: (212) 532-4900
www.mta.nyc.ny.us/mnr

Long Island Rail Road
Phone: (718) 217-5477
www.mta.nyc.ny.us/lirr

MTA Customer Service
Phone: (718) 330-3322
www.mta.nyc.ny.us

NJ Transit
Phone: (973) 762-5100
www.njtransit.com

Tickets:

Tickets are free and first-come, first-serve. Available at Radio City's box office on the morning of the draft. Beware, long lines form as they impose a one ticket per person policy. Arrive early and be prepared to wait.

Accommodations:

Flatotel
135 West 52nd Street (between 6th and
    7th Avenue)
New York, NY 10019
Phone: (212) 887-9400
Fax: (212) 887-9795
Toll-Free: 1-800-352-8683
www.flatotel.com

Note: Touted on their website as a "contemporary, intimate, and cosmopolitan hotel in midtown Manhattan."

The Barclay
111 East 48th Street (between Park and
    Lexington Avenue)
New York, NY 10017
Phone: (212) 755-5900
Fax: (212) 644-0079
Toll-Free: 1-800-980-6429
www.InterContinental.com

Note: Recently restored to its original 1926 neo-Federal style that still provides luxury for its guests.

Hilton New York

1335 Avenue of the Americas (6th Avenue
and 53rd Street)
New York, NY 10019
Phone: (212) 586-7000
Fax: (212) 315-1374
Toll-Free: 1-800-445-8667
www.hiltonfamilynewyork.com
*Note: Conveniently located close to Radio City
Music Hall, Broadway theaters, Times Square,
and Central Park.*

Sheraton New York Hotel and Towers

811 7th Avenue (7th Avenue and 53rd
Street)
New York, NY 10019
Phone: (212) 581-1000
Fax: (212) 262-4410
Toll-Free: 1-800-325-3535
www.starwoodhotels.com
*Note: Centralized location in Manhattan's
Midtown business and entertainment district.*

On-Site Hospitality:

Concession stands are located in Radio City.
Bringing in outside food and drink is prohibited.

Travel Packages:

If you are going to travel to this event, I
would recommend using a reliable company to work with you on making the necessary arrangements. The suppliers listed in
this book have solid references and are by
far the most trusted in the business. Below
are some of the organizations to try for this
Top 100 Must See Sporting Event.

Premiere Corporate Events

14 Penn Plaza, Suite 925
New York, NY 10122
Phone: (212) 695-9480
Fax: (212) 564-8098
Toll-Free: 1-877-621-5243
E-mail: requests@tseworld.com

www.tseworld.com
www.pcevents.com

Premiere Sports Travel

201 Shannon Oaks Circle, Suite 205
Cary, NC 27511
Phone: (919) 481-9511
Fax: (919) 481-1337
Toll-Free: 1-800-924-9993
E-mail: sales@sportstravel.com
www.sportstravel.com

Dining:

Burger Heaven

20 East 49th Street at 5th Avenue
New York, NY 10017
Phone: (212) 755-2166
www.burgerheaven.com
*Note: The name says it all. Reasonably priced
burgers served quickly for over fifty years.*

Del Frisco's Double Eagle Steak House

1221 6th Avenue (6th Avenue and 49th
Street)
New York, NY 10020
Phone: (212) 575-5129
www.delfriscos.com
*Note: High-end steakhouse described as so-
phisticated, elegant, romantic, legendary, and
award-winning.*

The Rainbow Room

30 Rockefeller Plaza (between 5th and 6th
Avenue)
New York, NY 10112
Phone: (212) 632-5100
www.rainbowroom.com
*Note: Famed restaurant providing a night of
dinner and dancing. A live big band orchestra
plays selected Fridays and Saturdays.*

Sea Grill Rockefeller Center

19 West 49th Street (between 5th and 6th
Avenue)
New York, NY 10020
Phone: (212) 332-7610

www.rapatina.com/seagrill

Note: Classic and contemporary with an ocean-inspired menu from an Ivy Award-winning restaurant.

Airports:

John F. Kennedy International Airport (JFK)
Jamaica, NY 11430
Phone: (718) 244-4444
www.panynj.gov

LaGuardia Airport (LGA)
Ditmars Boulevard and 94th Street
Flushing, NY 11371
Phone: (718) 533-3400
www.panynj.gov

Newark Liberty International Airport (EWR)
North Avenue & Spring Street
Elizabeth, NJ 07201
Phone: (973) 961-6000
www.panynj.gov

Sports Travel Insider's Edge:

Best way to watch the action:
Line up early to get a good seat as they are distributed on a first-come, first-serve basis. The closer to the action, the better the experience. Once you are inside, note that the wait between draft selections has been reduced significantly by NFL mandate. Make sure you get there early because the NFL will cut off fans in line once all the seats are filled up.

Best place to get up close:
Rub shoulders with various football luminaries and draft picks at any number of parties taking place throughout the city. The New York Jets sponsor several draft-day parties and the higher draft picks get in on the action too with their own get-togethers which usually take place Saturday night after the first day of the draft.

Best travel tip:
While it is an important date on any NFL fan's calendar, remember that the event takes place in April and New York is a baseball town. After the draft, take in a Yankees or Mets game if they are home.

Notable Quotes:

"It just takes one team to like you for you to get up there. That's where you get a big pot and boil the crawfish and you put corn and potatoes in the boil. It will only be about 10 people total, I imagine. We'll sit around and watch. Actually, I don't know if I can sit through the whole thing and wait, and wait...."—BRAD COTTAM, former University of Tennessee and Kansas City Chiefs tight end

"I want to go as high as I can. I'd have to be fooling myself if I said I didn't want to be a first round pick. That's what I always dreamt of as a kid...Just because you go in the first round doesn't mean you're going to be a great football player. It doesn't mean that you're going to have a career in the NFL and it doesn't mean you're going to be what they thought you'd be. It just means that you have a little bit more money than somebody else. I am more excited about the opportunity to play than worried about what round I get drafted in."—LAWRENCE JACKSON, Seattle Seahawks and former USC defensive lineman

Relevant Websites:
www.radiocity.com
www.nycvisit.com
www.tseworld.com
www.pcevents.com
www.sportstravel.com
www.premieresports.com

68

NATIONAL FINALS RODEO

Where?
Thomas & Mack Center
UNLV
4505 South Maryland Parkway
Las Vegas, NV 89119

When?
Annually for ten days in December.

Significance:
Saddle up, partner. For ten days, Las Vegas takes on a Western flair as rodeo cowboys mosey their way on into Sin City. It is man (and woman) versus livestock in a battle for the ages that is one of the more popular athletic competitions in the city. The National Finals Rodeo (NFR) is the jewel in the crown (or oversized belt buckle) of the Professional Rodeo Cowboys Association. Referred to as the "Super Bowl of Rodeo," the event takes place during the first full week of December at the Thomas & Mack Center.

Since 1959, the NFR, now known as the Wrangler National Finals Rodeo, has showcased the crowning of world champions in calf roping, steer wrestling, bull riding, saddle bronc riding, bareback bronc riding, and team roping. After stays in Dallas and Oklahoma City, the NFR found its permanent and longtime Las Vegas home in 1984. With 170,000 fans packing Thomas & Mack throughout the ten days, the city has been more than accommodating. Major hotels and casinos air the event in their sports books, host special parties for fans, and book country and western acts during the event.

To qualify, a rodeo athlete has to rank in the Top 15 of money winners. World championships are awarded to the winning cowboy or cowgirl. In addition, the highest-earning athlete who has competed in more than one event during the year is recognized as the "World All-Around Rodeo Champion."

Who attends?
Rodeo fans of all ages and from all walks of life, including celebrities.

How to get there?
On the corner of Tropicana and Swenson. Not far from the Strip and easily accessible from I-15 South, I-95 South, and Las Vegas Boulevard.

Rodeo fans in need of transportation to and from the NFR can use complimentary shuttle bus service with routes from the Las Vegas Convention Center and NFR official host hotels on the Las Vegas Strip and Downtown to the Thomas & Mack Center. Shuttle buses will pick them up in front of the NFR Cowboy Christmas Gift Show located at the Las Vegas Convention Center. This "One Way Only" route will serve as the Rodeo Express Shuttle running from the North Hall of the Las Vegas Convention Center directly to Thomas & Mack.

Tickets:
For primary ticket access information, consider: www.unlvtickets.com.

For secondary ticket access, consider:

GoTickets, Inc.
2345 Waukegan Road, Suite 140
Bannockburn, IL 60015-1552
Toll-Free: 1-800-775-1617
Fax: (919) 481-9101
E-mail: sales@gotickets.com
www.gotickets.com

Accommodations:
Note that athletes in different divisions stay in specific hotels, including:

Bareback Riders:

Gold Coast Casino
4000 West Flamingo Road
Las Vegas, NV 89103

Phone: (702) 367-7111
Fax: (702) 367-8575
Toll-Free: 1-888-402-6278
www.goldcoastcasino.com
Note: Spanish-style hotel just one mile west of
The Strip and a half mile to Chinatown.

Steer Wrestlers:

Hooters Casino and Hotel
115 East Tropicana Avenue
Las Vegas, NV 89109
Phone: (702) 739-9000
Toll-Free: 1-866-584-6687
www.hooterscasinohotel.com
Note: The name says it all. 696 Floridian-style
rooms with a great atmosphere.

Team Roping:

Golden Nugget
129 East Fremont Street
Las Vegas, NV 89101
Phone: (702) 385-7111
Toll-Free: 1-800-846-5336
www.goldennugget.com
Note: A great place to stay for the Fremont
Street Experience. Eight miles from McCarran
International Airport.

Saddle Bronc Riders:

Luxor
3900 Las Vegas Boulevard South
Las Vegas, NV 89119
Phone: (702) 262-4444
Toll-Free: 1-800-288-1000
www.luxor.com
Note: A unique, pyramid-shape design with
a Sphinx replica goes well with the overall
Egyptian theme.

Tie-Down Ropers:

The Mirage
3400 Las Vegas Boulevard South
Las Vegas, NV 89109
Phone: (702) 791-7111

Fax: (702) 791-7446
Toll-Free: 1-800-374-9000
www.themirage.com
Note: They boast a South Seas vibe combined
with Strip excitement. A popular hotel and
casino at the heart of Las Vegas.

Barrel Racers:

Excalibur Hotel and Casino
3850 Las Vegas Boulevard South
Las Vegas, NV 89109
Phone: (702) 597-7777
Fax: (702) 597-7009
Toll-Free: 1-877-750-5464
www.excalibur.com
Note: Medieval themes inspired by Camelot with four
towers, castle gates, and spires of varying colors.

Bull Riders:

Las Vegas Hilton
3000 Paradise Road
Las Vegas, NV 89109
Phone: (702) 732-5111
Toll-Free: 1-888-732-7117
www.lvhilton.com
Note: Luxurious hotel with world-class entertainment options and a 40,000 square-foot
casino. For the younger lot or the kid in all of
us, they boast the city's best video arcade.

Other:

MGM Grand
3799 Las Vegas Boulevard South
Las Vegas, NV 89109
Phone: (702) 891-1111
Toll-Free: 1-877-880-0880
www.mgmgrand.com
Note: One of the best-known Las Vegas hotels
and casinos. Iconic part of Sin City history.

The Venetian Resort Hotel Casino
3355 Las Vegas Boulevard South
Las Vegas, NV 89109
Phone: (702) 414-1000
Fax: (702) 414-1100

Toll-Free: 1-877-883-6423
www.venetian.com

Note: An all-suite hotel providing luxury and comfort after a long day of rodeo action.

Treasure Island
3300 Las Vegas Boulevard South
Las Vegas, NV 89109
Phone: (702) 894-7111
Fax: (702) 894-7414
Toll-Free: 1-800-288-7206
www.treasureisland.com

Note: More affordable with a little something for everyone.

On-Site Hospitality:
With 9.7 million square feet of meeting space and over 136,000 hotel rooms in Las Vegas alone, the Las Vegas Convention Center is the perfect spot for leisure or business.

Travel Packages:
If you are going to travel to this event, I would recommend using a reliable company to work with you on making the necessary arrangements. The suppliers listed in this book have solid references and are by far the most trusted in the business. Below are some of the organizations to try for this Top 100 Must See Sporting Event.

Premiere Corporate Events
14 Penn Plaza, Suite 925
New York, NY 10122
Phone: (212) 695-9480
Fax: (212) 564-8098
Toll-Free: 1-877-621-5243
E-mail: requests@tseworld.com
www.tseworld.com
www.pcevents.com

Premiere Sports Travel
201 Shannon Oaks Circle, Suite 205
Cary, NC 27511
Phone: (919) 481-9511
Fax: (919) 481-1337

Toll-Free: 1-800-924-9993
E-mail: sales@sportstravel.com
www.sportstravel.com

Dining:

Aqua Knox
3355 South Las Vegas Boulevard
Las Vegas, NV 89109
Phone: (702) 414-3772
Fax: (702) 414-3872
www.aquaknox.net

Note: Great place to get seafood if you don't mind paying a bit more.

Joe's
3500 South Las Vegas Boulevard
Las Vegas, NV 89109
Phone: (702) 792-9222
Fax: (702) 369-8384
www.icon.com/joes

Note: Seasonal seafood offerings from around the world with carry-out and children's menus.

Red Square
3950 Las Vegas Boulevard South
Las Vegas, NV 89119
Phone: (702) 632-7777
Fax: (702) 632-7234
Toll-Free: 1-877-632-7000
www.mandalaybay.com

Note: Pricey, but great food and a selection of over 100 different kinds of vodka.

Baja Beach Café
2400 North Rancho Drive
Las Vegas, NV 89130
Phone: (702) 631-7000
Toll-Free: 1-800-731-7333

Note: Great food with even greater values, including the Fiesta Burger and fries for only $2.99!

Blondie's Sports Bar & Grill at Miracle Mile Shops
Planet Hollywood Resort and Casino
3663 Las Vegas Boulevard

Las Vegas, NV 89109
Phone: (702) 737-0444
Note: Traditional bar menu with great appetizers and entrées.

Airport:

McCarran International Airport - Las Vegas
5757 Wayne Newton Boulevard
Las Vegas, NV 89119
Phone: (702) 261-5211
www.mccarran.com

Sports Travel Insider's Edge:

Best way to watch the action:
For over twenty years, the rodeo has been a consistent sellout. A bull seems to be easier to rope than a ticket. The event lasts ten days with a winner announced each night. If you can only get a ticket for one night, try for the finale. The last night of the rodeo determines the individual champions and the overall title-holder for the year.

Best place to get up close:
The announcer's side is the best place to sit and gives you a great view of the rough stock stomping out of the chutes. The building adjacent to the Thomas & Mack Center serves as a hospitality venue. There you can see a Walk of Fame with pictures and biographies of past stars and all-around champions. The "walk" also includes autograph sessions with your favorite cowboys onsite.

Best travel tip:
You're at the NFR. You might as well dress appropriately. The Cowboy Christmas Gift Show at the Las Vegas Convention Center North Hall is promoted as "the longest running and only original gift show" of the NFR. 400 vendors fill 300,000 square feet with booths selling customized jewelry, western wear, boots, and spurs. If you want to take something home, there is furniture, original art, handmade crafts, and pottery

for sale as well. You can also pick up official Wrangler NFR and PRCA merchandise.

Notable Quotes:

"The Finals is 'the greatest show on earth.' It kind of ruins watching other rodeos for you. The best cowboys and cowgirls in the world riding the best bucking horses, best bulls, and the best timed-event horses in the world. It's good watching on TV; but when you are there it is electric."—A diehard and unnamed NFR fan

"The camaraderie in rodeo is different than any other sport. I helped a bunch of people all week long, too. It's all about making money, but you want to see your friends win as much as you."—JASON MILLER, Steer Wrestling world champion

Relevant Websites:
www.nfrexperience.com
www.prorodeo.com
www.unlvtickets.com
www.lasvegas24hours.com
www.tseworld.com
www.pcevents.com
www.sportstravel.com
www.gotickets.com
www.premieresports.com

69
BASKETBALL GAME AT PHOG ALLEN FIELDHOUSE

Where?
Phog Allen Fieldhouse
University of Kansas
Naismith Drive
Lawrence, KS 66044

When?
Every year during NCAA basketball season.

Significance:

When the University of Kansas hired their first head basketball coach, they truly picked the most qualified. "I invented the game of basketball" is an impressive item on a resumé. Dr. James Naismith did just that and coached Kansas basketball. Ironically, he has another distinction as the only coach in Kansas basketball history—boasting the winningest program in all of college basketball—to have a losing record. However, he did leave the team in good hands when he mentored and groomed his successor, Dr. Forrest C. "Phog" Allen, recognized as the "Father of Basketball Coaching" and the Jayhawks' head coach for thirty-nine years.

Phog Allen Fieldhouse is a place of tradition. Before a home game starts, the National Anthem is sung, followed by the school alma mater, "Crimson and Blue," and the Rock Chalk Jayhawk chant. After the introduction of the home team, the Jayhawk faithful in the 4,000-seat student section close to the playing floor pick up copies of the college newspaper as if to act disinterested in the visiting team's introductions. Those papers serve a greater purpose as the students use it for confetti.

"The Phog" was dedicated on March 1, 1955, and the Jayhawks went on to defeat Kansas State, 77-76. The official attendance was 17,228, exceeding the capacity of 17,000. The Fieldhouse has also hosted thirty-seven NCAA tournament games and championship matchups. Phog Allen has been good to the Jayhawks as they won sixty-two consecutive games between January 30, 1994, and November 21, 1998. The previous record was an equally impressive fifty-five-game streak between February 22, 1984, and January 30, 1988. Perhaps opposing teams should follow the advice on a banner hung high in the rafters: "Pay heed all who enter: Beware of The Phog!"

Who attends?

Jayhawk fans, college students, alumni, and family.

How to get there?

From Kansas City Airport, take 435 to Interstate 70. Take the 2nd Lawrence Exit (Iowa Street) taking you to Kansas campus. A left onto 19th Street and a left onto Naismith will take you to the Fieldhouse.

Tickets:

For primary ticket access information, consider: www.kuathletics.com.

For secondary ticket access, consider:

GoTickets, Inc.
2345 Waukegan Road, Suite 140
Bannockburn, IL 60015-1552
Toll-Free: 1-800-775-1617
Fax: (919) 481-9101
E-mail: sales@gotickets.com
www.gotickets.com

Accommodations:

The Eldridge
701 Massachusetts
Lawrence, KS 66044
Phone: (785) 749-5011
Toll-Free: 1-800-527-0909
www.eldridgehotel.com

Note: A hotel promising that history and hospitality will come together in the heart of downtown.

Holiday Inn Express, Lawrence
3411 South West Iowa Street
Lawrence, KS 66046
Phone: (785) 749-7555
Fax: (785) 749-0232
Toll-Free: 1-866-695-0459
www.hiexpress.com

Note: Reasonably priced and conveniently located two miles from the KU campus.

SpringHill Suites

1 Riverfront Plaza
Lawrence, KS 66044
Phone: (785) 841-2700
Fax: (785) 749-1477
Toll-Free: 1-800-MARRIOTT
www.marriott.com

Note: Located on the Kansas River in downtown Lawrence.

The Halcyon House

Bed and Breakfast
1000 Ohio Street
Lawrence, KS 66044
Phone: (785) 841-0314
Toll-Free: 1-888-441-0314
www.thehalcyonhouse.com

Note: Nine distinctly styled bedrooms, not to mention warm, homemade breakfasts.

On-Site Hospitality:

Concession stands are located throughout "The Phog."

Travel Packages:

If you are going to travel to this event, I would recommend using a reliable company to work with you on making the necessary arrangements. The suppliers listed in this book have solid references and are by far the most trusted in the business. Below are some of the organizations to try for this Top 100 Must See Sporting Event.

Premiere Corporate Events

14 Penn Plaza, Suite 925
New York, NY 10122
Phone: (212) 695-9480
Fax: (212) 564-8098
Toll-Free: 1-877-621-5243
E-mail: requests@tseworld.com
www.tseworld.com
www.pcevents.com

Premiere Sports Travel

201 Shannon Oaks Circle, Suite 205
Cary, NC 27511

Phone: (919) 481-9511
Fax: (919) 481-1337
Toll-Free: 1-800-924-9993
E-mail: sales@sportstravel.com
www.sportstravel.com

Dining:

Milton's

920 Massachusetts Street
Lawrence, KS 66044
Phone: (785) 832-2330

Note: Great breakfast, including their famous French Toast. Expect to be greeted by lines to enter, but hang in there because it's worth the wait.

Ingredient

947 Massachusetts Street
Lawrence, KS 66044
Phone: (785) 832-0100
www.ingredientrestaurant.com

Note: Healthier fare and fast service.

Free State Brewing Company

636 Massachusetts Street
Lawrence, KS 66044-2236
Phone: (785) 843-4555
www.freestatebrewing.com

Note: Sample various beers from the first legal brewery in Kansas.

The Wheel

14th and Ohio Street
Lawrence, KS 66044
Phone: (785) 841-0488

Note: Considered by Jayhawk fans and all to be the best bar in town.

Quinton's

615 Massachusetts Street
Lawrence, KS 66044
Phone: (785) 842-6560

Note: Well-known for great soups and sandwiches.

Teller's

746 Massachusetts Street
Lawrence, KS 66044

Phone: (785) 843-4111

www.tellerslawrence.com

Note: An old bank converted into a restaurant. Teller's. Get it?

First Watch
2540 Iowa Street, Suite D

Lawrence, KS 66046

Phone: (785) 842-7999

www.firstwatch.com

Note: Join Jayhawk fans for Sunday breakfast.

Airports:

Kansas City International Airport, MO
(about fifty minutes to KU)

601 Brasilia Avenue

Kansas City, MO 64153

Phone: (816) 243-5237

www.flykci.com

Sports Travel Insider's Edge:

Best way to watch the action:
The student section is the place to sit, but not just because of its proximity to the playing floor. It is a true Jayhawk experience that will likely keep you on your feet, cheering KU on to victory. And don't forget that student newspaper for shunning the opposition and making confetti.

Best place to get up close:
Join pre-game traditions where students and alumni lock arms and sway to the alma mater. It would be a good idea to know the "Rock Chalk" chant because that comes after the singing. Get close to the locker room exit to receive a few Jayhawk high-fives. Does it get any closer?

Best travel tip:
With the layout of the campus, you want to make sure you have a car. Bring good walking shoes as well, since the walk from the parking lot to Phog Allen is about ten minutes.

Notable Quote:

"I tell everybody there's not a place around—I know Chapel Hill, Pauley Pavilion, Cameron, you name it. They are pretty special, but there's nothing like this. All the guys who scout, I always tell them, 'You'll never have an experience like [Phog] Allen Fieldhouse.' This is how a college fieldhouse is supposed to be."—LARRY BROWN, former KU coach and Hall of Famer

Relevant Websites:
www.ku.edu

www.visitlawrence.com

www.tseworld.com

www.pcevents.com

www.sportstravel.com

www.gotickets.com

www.premieresports.com

70
BASKETBALL GAME AT MADISON SQUARE GARDEN

Where?
Madison Square Garden

4 Pennsylvania Plaza

New York, NY 10001

When?
Throughout the year, this Mecca hosts NBA and WNBA games, college hoops, charity hoops, and a few boys and girls high school basketball tournaments.

Significance:
Anyone who has ever laced up basketball sneakers has dreamed of playing on this court.

They don't call it the "World's Most Famous Arena" for nothing. The building located in Manhattan on 7th Avenue, between 31st and 33rd Streets, is a place where sports history happens. Athletes of all sports dream of competing under the bright lights and stage of Madison Square Garden. Basketball players from high school to professional want to be a part of that history. While the current Garden boasts commerce and business, it is still the Mecca of sports and entertainment.

The New York Knickerbockers make their home in Madison Square Garden. The Knicks are truly a team that matches the history of the building where they compete. Along with the Boston Celtics, they are the only NBA team still residing in their original city. They have held elite status in three different eras, the most recent being the early- to late-nineties, led by center Patrick Ewing.

College players know that many "firsts" have occurred in the Mecca. That includes the first college basketball doubleheader in 1934 and the inaugural National Invitational Tournament (NIT) in 1938. Nowadays St. John's University plays many of its home games at MSG and the Big East Basketball Tournament is one of many that The Garden holds.

The New York Public Schools Athletic League hosts boys and girls high school basketball championships. While those tournaments have seen their fair share of mischief and violent altercations, security has been increased and sportsmanlike conduct of the players and fans seems to be on the rise.

Who attends?

Celebrities can be seen sitting courtside in front of fanatical professional, college, or high school basketball fans. The fans are considered the most knowledgeable of all basketball fans in the world.

Tickets:

For primary ticket access information, consider: www.thegarden.com or www.ticketmaster.com.

For secondary ticket access, consider:

GoTickets, Inc.
2345 Waukegan Road, Suite 140

Bannockburn, IL 60015-1552
Toll-Free: 1-800-775-1617
Fax: (919) 481-9101
E-mail: sales@gotickets.com
www.gotickets.com

Accommodations:

Hotel New Yorker
481 Eighth Avenue
New York, NY 10001
Phone: (212) 244-0719
Fax: (212) 629-6536
Toll-Free: 1-800-272-6232
www.nyhotel.com

Note: Two blocks from MSG, this value hotel is being renovated to restore the building to its original prominence.

W Times Square
1567 Broadway
New York, NY 10036
Phone: (212) 930-7400
Toll-Free: 1-877-W-HOTELS
www.whotels.com

Note: This is less than a ten-block walk to MSG down 7th Avenue and located in Times Square. It houses a small lounge where guests can grab a quick drink prior to the game.

Hilton Times Square
234 West 42nd Street
New York, NY 10036
Phone: (212) 840-8222
Toll-Free: 1-877-326-5200
www.hilton.com

Note: The place that many tourists like to stay in New York. Located near Central Park, but still close enough for a walk to MSG on a nice day in the city.

On-Site Hospitality:

All Star Bar: Gate 60

End Court Bar: Between Gates 63 and 64

Food Courts: Gates 61, 65, 71, and 76

Club Bar and Grill Restaurant: Between Gates 60 and 67. Open only during Knicks games for Club Seat Ticket holders only. Reservations are required. Phone: (212) 465-6290

Play By Play Sports Restaurant: Between Gates 60 and 67. The premier sports bar in NYC is open during Knicks games for Club Seat Ticket holders only. Reservations not required, but get there early. Phone: (212) 465-5888

Travel Packages:

If you are going to travel to this event, I would recommend using a reliable company to work with you on making the necessary arrangements. The suppliers listed in this book have solid references and are by far the most trusted in the business. Below are some of the organizations to try for this Top 100 Must See Sporting Event.

Premiere Corporate Events

14 Penn Plaza, Suite 925
New York, NY 10122
Phone: (212) 695-9480
Fax: (212) 564-8098
Toll-Free: 1-877-621-5243
E-mail: requests@tseworld.com
www.tseworld.com
www.pcevents.com

Premiere Sports Travel

201 Shannon Oaks Circle, Suite 205
Cary, NC 27511
Phone: (919) 481-9511
Fax: (919) 481-1337
Toll-Free: 1-800-924-9993
E-mail: sales@sportstravel.com
www.sportstravel.com

Dining:

Lazzaras Pizza

221 West 38th Street (between 7th and 8th Avenues)
Manhattan, NY 10018
Phone: (212) 944-7792
www.lazzaraspizza.com

Note: Considered by many to be the best pizza in Manhattan. Look closely because it's hard to find in the townhouse-type setting.

Ben's Deli

209 West 38th Street (between 7th and 8th Avenues)
Manhattan, NY 10018
Phone: (212) 398-2367
Fax: (212) 398-3354
www.bensdeli.net

Note: Solid New York style deli food and popular with the Garment Center and MSG neighborhood crowd.

Lugo Café

1 Penn Plaza (33rd Street between 7th and 8th)
New York, NY 10001
Phone: (212) 760-2700
Fax: (212) 629-6618
www.lugocafe.com

Note: One of the only fine dining options in the neighborhood. It is located right across the street from The Garden and Penn Station. The crab cakes with house-made bread and butter pickles are delectable. Also try their house special lemonades.

Airports:

John F. Kennedy International Airport (JFK)

Jamaica, NY 11430
Phone: (718) 244-4444
www.panynj.gov

LaGuardia Airport (LGA)

Ditmars Boulevard and 94th Street
Flushing, NY 11371
Phone: (718) 533-3400
www.panynj.gov

Newark Liberty International Airport (EWR)

North Avenue & Spring Street
Elizabeth, NJ 07201
Phone: (973) 961-6000
www.panynj.gov

Sports Travel Insider's Edge:

Best way to watch the action:

The Garden will sell "VIP Courtside" tickets, better known as "Spike Lee seats," for most college and high school basketball games. The cost is a mere fraction of what a comparable Knicks game would set you back. While you are not watching the pros, you are still witnessing the future greats of the sport with a prime front-row seat. Even the younger players enjoy playing to the crowd at MSG.

Best place to get up close:

A trip downtown to Greenwich Village and the West 4th Street basketball court better known as the "Cage" is a must for all hoop lovers while in town. New Yorkers and tourists line the fence five deep to watch the physical battles that happen on this tiny court.

Best travel tip:

Timing is everything. Planning your trip to Madison Square Garden carefully can allow you to see multiple NBA, college, and high school games all within one week in March.

Check the calendar and see if you can make it to The Garden then.

Notable Quote:

"None of the other venues have the audacity to call themselves 'the world's most famous arena.' But then, none of the other arenas have made the hair on the back of my neck stand up or made my heart beat a bit faster just by walking into the building. I start to feel it when I get a couple blocks from the arena. Maybe it's the millions of commuters that pass beneath in the cavernous Penn Station. Or perhaps it's because The Garden sits in the heart of the most exciting city in the world."
—MATTHEW MODINE, actor

Relevant Websites:

www.thegarden.com
www.knicks.com
www.nba.com
www.nycvisit.com
www.tseworld.com
www.pcevents.com
www.sportstravel.com
www.gotickets.com
www.premieresports.com

71

PREFONTAINE CLASSIC

Where?

Hayward Field
University of Oregon
1580 East 15th Street
Eugene, OR 97403

When?

One day every year in early June.

Significance:

The Prefontaine Classic is recognized as the premier track and field meet in the United States and the only chance that fans have of seeing the World Athletics Tour on North American soil. Outside of Europe, this is the top-ranked annual track and field meet by the IAAF, a designation the Classic has enjoyed since 2000.

To qualify for the Prefontaine Classic, track and field athletes must be ranked in the Top 50 in the world for their respective events. This is an elite event with only the best competing. It draws the largest United States crowds for a track and field competition.

The annual event is named in honor of Steve Prefontaine, a track and field legend who was considered America's greatest distance runner at the time of his 1975 death at the age of twenty-four. You may know him from two critically acclaimed movies based on his life: *Prefontaine* in 1997 and *Without Limits* in 1998.

Hayward Field is the home of the Prefontaine Classic. The track and field–only facility is named after Bill Hayward, the first track and field coach for the University of Oregon from 1904 to 1947. "Track City USA," as it is known, not only attracts the best in track and field from thousands of miles away, but fans well-versed in the sport, not to mention enthusiastic and downright loud.

Who attends?
Dedicated and savvy track and field fans who have to wait an entire year to see the best track and field stars from around the world in what they consider to be "dream matches."

How to get there?
From the airport, take Highway 999 South to the Beltline Highway East. Take the Delta Highway Exit South. Merge left onto I-105 E/OR-126 East. Take Country Club Road (exit #2) to Coburg Road and take a right. Follow Coburg as it forks to the left and winds around downtown to the North edge of the campus. Take a right on Agate Street. Hayward Field is between 15th and 18th Avenues.

Tickets:
For primary ticket access information, consider: www.goducks.com.

For secondary ticket access, consider:

GoTickets, Inc.
2345 Waukegan Road, Suite 140
Bannockburn, IL 60015-1552
Toll-Free: 1-800-775-1617
Fax: (919) 481-9101
E-mail: sales@gotickets.com
www.gotickets.com

Accommodations:

Americas Best Value Inn
1140 West 6th Avenue
Eugene, OR 97402

Phone: (541) 343-0730
Fax: (541) 343-8443
Toll-Free: 1-877-646-2466
www.bestvalueinneugene.com
Note: A hotel that lives up to its claim of being "cheerful, comfortable, and convenient."

Campbell House Inn & Restaurant
252 Pearl Street
Eugene, OR 97401
Phone: (541) 343-1119
Fax: (541) 343-2258
Toll-Free: 1-800-264-2519
www.campbellhouse.com
Note: Restored nineteenth-century building in the style of a fine European hotel. Conveniently located in downtown Eugene.

Campus Inn & Suites
390 East Broadway
Eugene, OR 97401
Phone: (541) 343-3376
Fax: (541) 485-9392
Toll-Free: 1-800-888-6313
www.campus-inn.com
Note: Guests enjoy 24-hour desk service and Starbucks coffee served with their continental breakfast. Near downtown Eugene.

On-Site Hospitality:
There is no upscale onsite hospitality, so grab a seat and enjoy the races.

Travel Packages:
If you are going to travel to this event, I would recommend using a reliable company to work with you on making the necessary arrangements. The suppliers listed in this book have solid references and are by far the most trusted in the business. Below are some of the organizations to try for this Top 100 Must See Sporting Event.

Premiere Corporate Events
14 Penn Plaza, Suite 925
New York, NY 10122
Phone: (212) 695-9480

Fax: (212) 564-8098
Toll-Free: 1-877-621-5243
E-mail: requests@tseworld.com
www.tseworld.com
www.pcevents.com

Premiere Sports Travel
201 Shannon Oaks Circle, Suite 205
Cary, NC 27511
Phone: (919) 481-9511
Fax: (919) 481-1337
Toll-Free: 1-800-924-9993
E-mail: sales@sportstravel.com
www.sportstravel.com

Dining:

The Cooler Restaurant & Bar
20 Centennial Loop
Eugene, OR 97401
Phone: (541) 484-4355
Fax: (541) 434-6201
www.thecoolerbar.com

Note: Popular race-day haunt since 1968. Great food, cold drinks, sports on the televisions, live music, and even the chance to get up and belt out a karaoke tune.

Adam's Place
30 East Broadway
Eugene, OR 97401
Phone: (541) 344-6948
Fax: (541) 344-1266
www.adamsplacerestaurant.com

Note: Seven Wine Spectator awards can't be wrong. Plus, they serve an organic menu of local meats and seafood.

Ambrosia Restaurant
174 East Broadway
Eugene, OR 97401
Phone: (541) 342-4141
Fax: (541) 345-6965

Note: Fine Northern Italian cuisine and specialty pizzas cooked in a wood-fired oven. Enjoy drinks that include rare Italian wines and espresso coffees.

Airport:

Eugene Airport (EUG)
28855 Lockheed Drive
Eugene, OR 97402
Phone: (541) 682-5430

Sports Travel Insider's Edge:

Best way to watch the action:
As preparation for the U.S. Olympic trials for the 2008 Summer Games in Beijing, Hayward Field now boasts several new renovations, in particular a brand-new scoreboard with real-time video and replays. Seating in the West Grandstand's Section B is a great vantage point as is the Southeast side where you can sit in the grass at Powell Plaza.

Best place to get up close:
A chronological display of Oregon track and field history is located on the outside of Powell Plaza. Learn about Steve Prefontaine, Bill Bowerman, Bill Hayward, and other track and field pioneers. No tickets are necessary and you can view it at any time.

Best travel tip:
Your own film festival with a double-feature of *Prefontaine* and *Without Limits* will provide you a background of the legendary Steve Prefontaine, and more importantly, get you in the spirit of the Classic. For an outside activity, go visit the Nike Campus located about ninety minutes from the track.

Notable Quotes:

"But the loudest, the loudest I've ever heard it, was in 2001, beginning in the first turn of the last lap of the mile. World-record holder Hicham El Guerrouj of Morocco had the lead and was on his way to breaking 3:50. But the knowing crowd, Bowerman's crowd, Pre's crowd, was watching a Virginia high school kid, Alan Webb, back in eighth place, moving out and beginning to pass. Webb took NCAA champion Bryan Berryhill on the turn, then Adil Kaouch of Morocco and Raymond Yator of Kenya on the backstretch. By then the sound was of such an order that stadium announcer Scott Davis, realizing that he couldn't be heard, turned off the mike and willed the 18-year-old on."—TOM JORDAN, Steve Prefontaine Biographer and Prefontaine Classic Meet Director for over twenty years.

"Most people run a race to see who is fastest. I run a race to see who has the most guts."—STEVE PREFONTAINE

"They've named Eugene Tracktown, USA for a reason. It's always an honor to come here and race."—GAIL DEVERS, sprinter, Olympic gold medalist

Relevant Websites:
www.preclassic.com
www.visitlanecounty.org
www.goducks.com
ato.goducks.com
www.tseworld.com
www.pcevents.com
www.sportstravel.com
www.gotickets.com
www.premieresports.com

72

MLB OPENING DAY IN CINCINNATI

Where?
Great American Ballpark
100 Joe Nuxhall Way
Cincinnati, OH 45202

When?
Opening day or sometimes evening of baseball season, usually at the end of March.

Significance:
Opening Day for baseball in Cincinnati carries special meaning. After all, the city is the home of the first professional sports team. The Cincinnati Reds are the only baseball team to open the season at home every year. Needless to say, Opening Day is a big event and an unofficial city holiday. Interestingly enough, there is a rise in workers and schoolchildren "falling ill," yet ending up at the ballpark. The only people working are the owners and staff at bars and restaurants opening early in the morning. By lunchtime, good luck finding a place to sit.

For many years, the honor of that first pitch on the Monday that kicked off the major league season fell upon the Cincinnati Reds. With Sunday night games and openers outside the country kicking off baseball's season, the first pitch is now more ceremonial. However, that does not diminish its significance as it is still considered the traditional opener across the land. Opening Day in Cincinnati and throughout the country is not just about the first of 162 games. It is a sign that spring is here and the winter doldrums are over. Plus, underperforming teams from the previous season can boast their new, nonlosing record of 0-0, if only for a little while.

Who attends?
Baseball fanatics and traditionalists who have been counting the days and putting "Xs" on their calendars since the end of the previous year's World Series.

How to get there?
Located in the Downtown/Riverfront area of Cincinnati on Second Street/Joe Nuxhall Way, the Great American Ballpark is easily accessible from I-75, I-71, I-471, and Highway 50.

Tickets:
For primary ticket access information, consider: cincinnati.reds.mlb.com.

For secondary ticket access, consider:

GoTickets, Inc.
2345 Waukegan Road, Suite 140
Bannockburn, IL 60015-1552
Toll-Free: 1-800-775-1617
Fax: (919) 481-9101
E-mail: sales@gotickets.com
www.gotickets.com

Accommodations:

The Westin Cincinnati
21 East 5th Street
Cincinnati, OH 45202
Phone: (513) 621-7700
www.starwoodhotels.com
Note: A convenient and centralized downtown location with the Great American Ballpark less than a half-mile away.

Cincinnati Marriott at RiverCenter
10 West RiverCenter Boulevard
Covington, KY 41011
Phone: (859) 261-2900
Fax: (859) 261-0900
Toll-Free: 1-800-228-9290
www.marriott.com
Note: Perfect for business-types and leisure travelers. Additionally, it's close to major landmarks, including a half-mile jaunt to the Great American Ballpark.

Hyatt Regency Cincinnati
151 West 5th Street
Cincinnati, OH 45202
Phone: (513) 579-1234
Toll-Free: 1-800-233-1234
www.hyatt.com
Note: Conveniently connected to downtown via a second-level skywalk. Three blocks from Paul Brown Football Stadium and six blocks to the Great American Ball Park.

Embassy Suites RiverCenter
10 East Rivercenter Boulevard
Covington, KY 41011

Phone: (859) 261-8400
Fax: (859) 261-8486
Note: Whether on vacation or traveling for business, this all-suite hotel provides a full range of services. Located on the south bank of the Ohio River, and close to dining and other attractions.

Holiday Inn Riverfront
600 West 3rd Street
Covington, KY 41011
Phone: (859) 291-4300
Fax: (859) 491-2331
Toll-Free: 1-800-HOLIDAY
www.holidayinn.com
Note: About a mile from the Great American Ballpark and in the heart of Covington, Kentucky's business and entertainment district.

On-Site Hospitality and Events:

Diamond Seats: An all-inclusive ticket includes membership into the private Diamond Club, complimentary food and beverage, extra-wide padded seats with in-seat food service, complimentary parking, and concierge service.

Club Seats: Amenities include access to FSN Ohio Club 4192 with extended beverage service and a wide selection of food, in-seat service on more comfortable seating, preferred parking, complimentary membership to the Riverfront Club, ticket purchases without surcharges or fees, Opening Day bonus tickets, and guaranteed options for playoff tickets.

Premium Sales Department Phone: (513) 765-7210

Findlay Market Opening Day Parade: Floats, high school bands and choirs, and other Cincinnati residents help ring in Opening Day of the baseball season. The parade was established in 1920 to celebrate the Reds' 1919 World Series victory over the Chicago White Sox. Now, you cannot imagine Opening Day in Cincinnati without it.

Travel Packages:

If you are going to travel to this event, I would recommend using a reliable company to work with you on making the necessary arrangements. The suppliers listed in this book have solid references and are by far the most trusted in the business. Below are some of the organizations to try for this Top 100 Must See Sporting Event.

Premiere Corporate Events

14 Penn Plaza, Suite 925
New York, NY 10122
Phone: (212) 695-9480
Fax: (212) 564-8098
Toll-Free: 1-877-621-5243
E-mail: requests@tseworld.com
www.tseworld.com
www.pcevents.com

Premiere Sports Travel

201 Shannon Oaks Circle, Suite 205
Cary, NC 27511
Phone: (919) 481-9511
Fax: (919) 481-1337
Toll-Free: 1-800-924-9993
E-mail: sales@sportstravel.com
www.sportstravel.com

Dining:

Pre-Game:

Hathaway's

441 Vine Street
Cincinnati, OH 45202
Phone: (513) 621-1332
Note: A classic diner complete with a soda fountain and counter seating. Top off a great meal with a hand-dipped milkshake.

Arnold's Bar and Grill

210 East 8th Street
Cincinnati, OH 45202

Phone: (513) 421-6234
www.arnoldsbarandgrill.com
Note: Since 1861, three generations of the Arnold family have lived upstairs and served food and drink downstairs. Check out the historic photos of the Reds on the walls.

Pomodori's Pizzeria

7880 Remington Road
Cincinnati, OH 45219
Phone: (513) 794-0080
Note: A great pizza place, and campus staple, popular with the local college kids.

Game Day Café

537 East Pete Rose Way
Cincinnati, OH
Phone: (513) 744-9096
www.gamedaysportscafe.com
Note: Pre-game hot spot where Reds fans congregate for a few beers before their heroes take the field.

Post-Game:

Madonna's

11 East 7th Street
Cincinnati, OH 45202-2401
Phone: (513) 621-8838
Note: Enjoy an imported beer with your burger. End your meal with a cigar. Conveniently located near the Aronoff and Taft theaters.

Tina's

350 West 4th Street
Cincinnati, OH 45202-2603
Phone: (513) 621-3567
Note: Unwind at this neighborhood bar with a burger or a game of pool or darts.

In Between Tavern

307 Sycamore Street
Cincinnati, OH 45202-4107
Phone: (513) 621-7009
Note: The patio beer garden is a game-day fixture with Reds fans hungry for a burger or wings and thirsty for a brew.

Head First Sports Café

218 West 3rd Street
Cincinnati, OH 45202
Phone: (513) 721-3767
www.headfirstsportscafe.com

Note: Popular sports bar across from Paul Brown Stadium. Perfect for a beer to celebrate a victory or drown your sorrows over a loss.

Mount Adams Pavilion

949 Pavilion Street
Cincinnati, OH 45202
Phone: (513) 744-9200

Note: Two-level, upscale bar. Top level has a DJ and the more relaxed lower level has a bar and pool tables. Four levels of outdoor patios are popular during the summer months.

Montgomery Inn

925 Riverside Drive
Cincinnati, OH 45202
Phone: (513) 721-7427
www.montgomeryinn.com

Note: Cincinnati Reds legend Ken Griffey, Jr., asserts that this restaurant has "the greatest ribs in the U.S.A."

Newport on the Levee

1 Levee Way #1113
Newport, KY 41071
Phone: (859) 291-0550
www.newportonthelevee.com

Note: What are you in the mood for? Here you will find a variety of six great restaurants to choose from for a great dining experience.

Bars:

Cadillac Ranch

38 Fountain Square Plaza
Cincinnati, OH 45202
Phone: (513) 621-6200
www.cadillacranchcincinnati.com

Note: Open for lunch and dinner. Enjoy a steak, overstuffed sandwich, or burger. Then work off those calories by riding on the mechanical bull or dancing the night away.

Airport:

Cincinnati/Northern Kentucky International Airport

Donaldson Road and Lincoln Road
Florence, KY 41048
Phone: (859) 767-3144
www.cvgairport.com

Sports Travel Insider's Edge:

Best way to watch the action:

Along the left field line (sections 408-410) are nearly 400 Mezzanine seats in the all-inclusive food and ticket area. All-you-can-eat, traditional ballpark food awaits you for one low price. You can enjoy the game and not worry about going hungry.

Best place to get up close:

The Diamond Club Seats will get you the best look at the batters for the Reds and their opposition. In fact, your view of the batter is closer than the pitcher on the field!

Best travel tip:

Can't get in the spirit of opening day? While you are traveling to the ballpark, read *Why Time Begins on Opening Day* by Thomas Boswell. If that doesn't pump you up for Reds baseball, nothing will.

Notable Quote:

"It's known around the country that Opening Day in Cincinnati is different than anywhere else. Opening Day in Cincinnati has become an event that's more than just the game."—NEIL LUKEN, Findlay Market Opening Day Parade chairman

Relevant Websites:

www.mlb.com
cincinnati.reds.mlb.com
www.cincyusa.com
www.tseworld.com
www.pcevents.com

www.sportstravel.com
www.gotickets.com
www.premieresports.com

73

NATHAN'S
HOT DOG EATING CONTEST

Where?
Coney Island
1310 Surf Avenue
Brooklyn, NY 11224
Phone: (212) 352-8651

When?
July 4th of every year.

Significance:
Probably not exactly what the Founding Fathers had in mind for Independence Day. Nathan's International July Fourth Hot Dog Eating Contest is a Major League Eating sanctioned eating contest held every July 4th on the corner of Surf and Stillwell Avenues in Brooklyn's Coney Island. In 1916, legend has it that four immigrants engaged in their own gastronomical competition at the Nathan's Famous stand in Coney Island. At stake, perhaps, who was the most patriotic? James Mullen proved his allegiance to the United States by downing thirteen hot dogs in twelve minutes. Today, over 30,000 fans crowd the event with 1.5 million watching on ESPN. Names like Joey Chestnut and Takeru "Tsunami" Kobayashi, referred to as the "Babe Ruth" of competitive eating, dominate the sport. Yes, many consider it a sport. Weigh-ins start the event and the contestants arrive with pageantry in the "Bus of Champions." A bejeweled, yellow title belt, dubbed the "Coveted Mustard Yellow Belt," awaits the champion and has traveled to such places as the Imperial Palace in Saitama, Japan.

At the 2008 contest, viewers got a real treat, seeing a number of firsts. With the introduction of the new ten-minute time limit, came the first tie and eat off since 1980. In a five-dog overtime Joey "Jaws" Chestnut came up victorious against Kobayashi for the second straight year.

To be one of the twenty qualifying competitors, contestants/athletes must be adults, eighteen years of age or older who either are the reigning champion, have won a regional qualifying contest for the season, qualify as one of two "wildcards," or have received a special invitation from Major League Eating. The rules are simple. Whoever consumes the most hot dogs and buns (HDBs) in twelve minutes is declared the winner. A designated scorekeeper for each contestant—called a "Bunnette"—keeps track of the progress. The winner gets that coveted, mustard-colored belt. Gentlemen (and ladies), start your digestion!

Who attends?
Fans of competitive eating and the athletes that participate in the event. Those with a weak stomach may not want to watch the gorging and a few after-effects.

How to get there?
Subway: D, F, N, or Q train to Stilwell Avenue.

Driving: Belt Parkway to Exit 6. South on Cropsey Avenue toward Coney Island. Cropsey becomes West 17th Street. Take a left onto Surf Avenue to Coney Island's amusement area.

Tickets:
Free to the public. Just show up in Coney Island, but get there early.

Accommodations:

In Brooklyn:

New York Marriott at the Brooklyn Bridge
333 Adams Street
Brooklyn, NY 11201

Phone: (718) 246-7000
Fax: (718) 246-0563
Toll-Free: 1-800-228-9290
www.marriott.com

Note: Located across the river from Manhattan, this hotel is ideal for business types and leisure travelers.

SoHo Grand

310 West Broadway
New York, NY 10013
Phone: (212) 965-3000
Fax: (212) 965-3200
Toll-Free: 1-800-965-3000
www.sohogrand.com

Note: Make your stay in Manhattan. Hotel guests are in the midst of fashion, industry, culture, and, of course, the New York nightlife in Soho.

Ritz-Carlton, Battery Park

2 West Street
New York, NY 10004
Phone: (212) 344-0800
Fax: (212) 344-3801
Toll-Free: 1-800-704-5643
www.ritzcarlton.com

Note: Close to cultural and historical attractions with a view of the Statue of Liberty, Ellis Island, and the New York Harbor.

On-Site Hospitality:

It's Coney Island. Plenty of concessions, including the well-known Nathan's Famous.

Travel Packages:

If you are going to travel to this event, I would recommend using a reliable company to work with you on making the necessary arrangements. The suppliers listed in this book have solid references and are by far the most trusted in the business. Below are some of the organizations to try for this Top 100 Must See Sporting Event.

Premiere Corporate Events

14 Penn Plaza, Suite 925
New York, NY 10122

Phone: (212) 695-9480
Fax: (212) 564-8098
Toll-Free: 1-877-621-5243
E-mail: requests@tseworld.com
www.tseworld.com
www.pcevents.com

Premiere Sports Travel

201 Shannon Oaks Circle, Suite 205
Cary, NC 27511
Phone: (919) 481-9511
Fax: (919) 481-1337
Toll-Free: 1-800-924-9993
E-mail: sales@sportstravel.com
www.sportstravel.com

Dining:

Gargiulo's

2911 West 15th Street
Brooklyn, NY 11224
Phone: (718) 266-4891
Fax: (718) 714-5833
www.gargiulos.com

Note: Established in 1907, a longtime tradition of Neapolitan hospitality and cuisine.

Nathan's Famous

1310 Surf Avenue
Brooklyn, NY 11224
Phone: (718) 946-2202
www.nathansfamous.com

Note: You can't go to this event and not visit Nathan's Famous for a hot dog. There will be plenty left over after the contest.

Atlantic Oceana

1029 Brighton Beach Avenue
Brooklyn, NY 11235
Phone: (718) 743-1515

Note: Great place to grab reasonably priced seafood.

Café Glechik

3159 Coney Island Avenue
Brooklyn, NY 11235
Phone: (718) 616-0766

Note: Known for great food in a cozy atmosphere.

Peter Luger's
178 Broadway
Brooklyn, NY 11211
Phone: (718) 387-7400
Fax: (718) 387-3523
www.peterluger.com
Note: Voted in 2006 as one of the 1,000 places to see before you die in the United States and Canada.

Junior's Cheesecake Restaurant
386 Flatbush Avenue, Extension at Dekalb
Avenue
Brooklyn, NY 11201
Phone: (718) 852-5257
www.juniorscheesecake.com
Note: World's best cheesecake. Enough said.

River Café
1 Water Street
Brooklyn, NY 11201
Phone: (718) 522-5200
www.rivercafe.com
Note: Well-known for great service, food, and the view.

Difara Pizza
1424 Avenue J
Brooklyn, NY 11230
Phone: (718) 258-1367
Note: Grab a slice of a true New York-style pie.

L & B Spumoni Gardens Pizza
2725 86th Street
Brooklyn, NY 11223
Phone: (718) 449-1230
www.spumonigardens.com
Note: "Home of the World's Famous Pizza and Spumoni."

Airports:

John F. Kennedy International Airport (JFK)
Jamaica, NY 11430
Phone: (718) 244-4444
www.panynj.gov

LaGuardia Airport (LGA)
Ditmars Boulevard and 94th Street
Flushing, NY 11371
Phone: (718) 533-3400
www.panynj.gov

Newark Liberty International Airport (EWR)
North Avenue & Spring Street
Elizabeth, NJ 07201
Phone: (973) 961-6000
www.panynj.gov

Sports Travel Insider's Edge:

Best way to watch the action:
The lines form along Surf Avenue in the early morning for this afternoon event, so get there as soon as you can. Front row is ideal because the view is challenging the farther back you stand.

Best place to get up close:
Having a Nathan's hot dog is part of the entire experience. Yes, it is likely their busiest day with hot dogs made and sold, with that number registering in the 10,000s. Waits are twenty to thirty minutes, but well worth it for a frank, fries, and large soda.

Best travel tip:
While some would consider a hot dog eating contest a freak show, Coney Island actually has its own Freak Show, hearkening back to the carnival days of old. Or you can go around the corner and see a Brooklyn Cyclones ball game if they are in town.

Notable Quote:

"The greatest moment in American Sports history!"—ESPN, when Joey Chestnut won the "Mustard Belt"

Relevant Websites:
www.ifoce.com
www.visitbrooklyn.org
www.nathansfamous.com
www.tseworld.com

www.pcevents.com
www.sportstravel.com
www.premieresports.com

74

IDITAROD

Where?

While the ceremonial kickoff starts in Anchorage, the official start, or "restart," changed locations from year to year until finding a permanent home close to Anchorage in Willow. The route changes every other year, alternating between northern and southern routes.

When?

The first Sunday in March.

Significance:

The Iditarod Trail is not for the faint of heart. It doesn't just test a dog's will and perseverance, but the musher guiding the sled as well. Nearly 1,160 miles of Alaskan terrain greet racers every year, not to mention temperatures plummeting to -100° F (-75° C). There is little time to enjoy the picturesque scenery over the two-week race. While they do race through large metropolitan areas, mushers and their dogs must focus on more treacherous terrain that includes mountain ranges, forests, and frozen rivers. The cold, darkness, and wind-blown snow are unforgiving at best.

Teams of twelve to sixteen dogs with their mushers compete in what is known as "The Last Great Race on Earth." These mushers can be fishermen, miners, artists, doctors, or lawyers. Natives and non-natives alike, they usually spend an entire year in preparation, whether they hold down a full-time job or not. The dogs are as diverse as their owners. Each has its own ability and stamina. Dogs must be fed meals and snacks throughout the race. Some run in the day. Some run at night.

The event hearkens to the historical past of the trail serving as a route for mail, supplies, and gold, all via dogsled. Dorothy G. Page, a.k.a. the "Mother of the Iditarod," created the race in 1967 with the support of Joe Redington, a.k.a. the "Father of the Iditarod." Named the Iditarod (derived from the Athabaskan *haiditarod*, meaning "far distant place"), it originally covered twenty-five miles near Anchorage. The race was extended more than 1,000 miles in 1973, considered the year of the first true Iditarod.

Who attends?

Local residents when the race comes to their town, along with supportive friends and family of the competitors.

How to get there?

Fly into Ted Stevens Anchorage International Airport and find any one of the checkpoints along the Iditarod Trail.

Tickets:

No ticket needed, only warm clothing.

Accommodations:

Anchorage Hilton Hotel
500 West 3rd Avenue
Anchorage, AK 99501
Phone: (907) 272-7411
Fax: (907) 265-7044
Toll-Free: 1-800-245-2527
www.hilton.com
Note: In the heart of downtown Alaska and ten minutes from the airport.

Hawthorn/Clarion Suites
1110 West 8th Avenue
Anchorage, AK 99501
Phone: (907) 222-5005
Fax: (907) 222-5215
Toll-Free: 1-800-527-1133
www.hawthorn.com

Note: Three-story hotel on spacious grounds. Close to shopping and the Anchorage Museum.

Sheraton Anchorage Hotel

401 East 6th Avenue
Anchorage, AK 99501
Phone: (907) 276-8700
Fax: (907) 276-7561
www.sheraton.com

Note: Prominent Anchorage landmark close to many businesses, restaurants, and shopping.

On-Site Hospitality:

Anchorage provides various ways to add to the excitement of your Iditarod trip. Day cruises on Resurrection Bay, the Iditarod Start Banquet, or even your own dog sled and sleigh ride trips. Heartier travelers can venture off to the rougher terrain where the "onsite hospitality" varies.

Dining:

Orso's Restaurant

737 West 5th Avenue
Anchorage, AK 99501
Phone: (907) 222-3232
Fax: (907) 792-3701
www.orsoalaska.com

Note: Wonderful fresh fish dishes. Make sure to check their hours because they change depending on the season.

Glacier Brewhouse

737 West 5th Avenue, Suite 110
Anchorage, AK 99501
Phone: (907) 274-BREW
Fax: (907) 277-1033
www.glacierbrewhouse.com

Note: Award-wining, hand-crafted ales and classic cocktails. Lunch and dinner is served.

Snow Goose Restaurant

717 West 3rd Avenue
Anchorage, AK 99501
Phone: (907) 277-7727
Fax: (907) 277-0606
www.alaskabeers.com

Note: Restaurant and brewery in one. A deck with a view and a great menu with nationally recognized beers.

Sacks Café and Restaurant

328 G Street
Anchorage, AK 99501
Phone: (907) 274-4022
Fax: (907) 276-3548
www.sackscafe.com

Note: Award-winning restaurant serving Alaskan seafood, choice meats, and pasta.

Snow City Café

1034 West 4th Avenue
Anchorage, AK 99501
Phone: (907) 272-2489
Fax: (907) 272-6338
www.snowcitycafe.com

Note: Considered by many to be the best breakfast and lunch in Anchorage.

The Crows Nest

939 West 5th Avenue
Anchorage, AK 99501
Phone: (907) 276-6000
www.captaincook.com

Note: English pub and gourmet restaurant in one, no joke! Serving seafood and gourmet pizza. This restaurant is located inside The Hotel Captain Cook.

Airport:

Ted Stevens Anchorage International Airport

4600 Postmark Drive
Anchorage, AK 99502
www.dot.state.ak.us

Sports Travel Insider's Edge:

Best way to watch the action:

While not the actual start to the race, the ceremonial Iditarod kickoff in Anchorage provides spectators with a hands-on, interactive experience, along with the chance to cheer on the sleds. They help mushers prepare for the start. An online auction allows anyone to buy a seat on a sled and ride down the streets.

Best place to get up close:
It would not be a true Iditarod experience without the Musher's Banquet. Mushers and other Alaskan luminaries gather on the Thursday night before the race. Spectators are more than welcome to attend and rub shoulders with some legends.

In addition, four-time Iditarod champ Martin Buser opens up his Happy Trails Kennel for tours. Visitors can look around and even ride with the dogs. Mr. Buser welcomes his guests warmly and is known for his hospitality.

Best travel tip:
Does anyone need to be told to dress warm? Dress warm! Do not let the weather prevent you from seeing this event that is truly a part of Alaska's and America's heritage.

Notable Quotes:

"Over the years, the Iditarod Trail Sled Dog Race's origins have been closely linked with the 'great mercy race' to Nome. Most people believe the Iditarod was established to honor drivers and dogs that carried the diphtheria serum, a notion the media have perpetuated. The race was patterned after the Sweepstakes races, not the serum run."—DOROTHY PAGE, co-founder of the Iditarod, in *Iditarod*, by Bill Sherwonit

"Travel over 1,000 arctic miles in under ten days with man's best friend, little sleep, storms and glaciers, bareground, and glare ice and you know you're on the Iditarod Trail. The world's longest sled dog race is the most challenging sporting event. The driver is nurse, cook, coach, and caretaker of sixteen of the world's best athletes who take over a million steps in any weather and terrain that Mother Nature throws at

you. Drivers and dogs overcome countless physical and mental challenges together to traverse the state of Alaska, visiting with friends in the villages as well as traveling in solitude day and night. Getting to Nome is never the same and after twenty-five years of racing, it's still exciting and dynamic."— MARTIN BUSER, four-time Iditarod Sled Dog Race winner

Relevant Websites:
www.iditarod.com
www.anchorage.net
www.buserdog.com
www.tseworld.com
www.pcevents.com
www.sportstravel.com
www.premieresports.com

75

LITTLE 500

Where?
Bill Armstrong Stadium at Indiana University.

When?
Every Spring, but the dates vary year-to-year.

Significance:
The Little 500—a.k.a. the "Little Five" or the "World's Greatest College Weekend"— is the nation's premier intramural collegiate cycling event with teams of four riding 200 laps relay-style around a quarter-mile cinder track. Teams include the famed Cutters team and collections of students from dormitories, current fraternities, and exiled frat houses.

After witnessing an impromptu bicycle race in a dormitory, Howard "Howdy" Wilcox, Executive Director of the Indiana University Foundation, established the annual event in 1950. A single race known only to the local community became a nationwide sensation after the release of the Oscar-winning motion picture *Breaking Away*. Frequent attendees of Bill Armstrong Stadium include David Letterman, John Mellencamp, and Lance Armstrong. Bragging rights and a combined $1 million in scholarship money is at stake, but don't bring your own customized bike to win. Official Little 500 bikes are provided to all teams. They are single gear, coaster brake racing bicycles with new versions made every year.

Who attends?

Indiana University students and hometown celebrities look forward to attending this event each and every year. *Breaking Away* raised the profile of the event and attracts racing enthusiasts from around the world.

Tickets:

For primary ticket access information, consider: www.iusf.org.

For secondary ticket access, consider:

GoTickets, Inc.
2345 Waukegan Road, Suite 140
Bannockburn, IL 60015-1552
Toll-Free: 1-800-775-1617
Fax: (919) 481-9101
E-mail: sales@gotickets.com
www.gotickets.com

Accommodations:

Indiana Memorial Union/Biddle Hotel and Conference Center
900 East 7th Street
Bloomington, IN 47405
Phone: (812) 855-2536
Toll-Free: 1-800-209-8145
www.imu.indiana.edu/hotel
Note: Elegant hotel in the heart of the campus for families and business people. Luxurious suites and individual rooms are available. Amenities include free on-campus parking, wireless Internet, and local phone calls.

Fourwinds Resort Marina
9301 South Fairfax Road
Bloomington, IN 47401-8962
Phone: 812-824-BOAT
Fax: 812-824-9816
Toll-Free: 1-800-824-BOAT
www.fourwindsresort.com
Note: Fifteen minutes from the campus with beautiful guest rooms and suites, most overlooking Lake Monroe. Many family-oriented resort activities.

Courtyard Bloomington
310 South College Avenue
Bloomington, IN 47403
Phone: (812) 335-8000
Fax: (812) 336-9997
Toll-Free: 1-800-321-3211
www.marriott.com
Note: Newly renovated rooms have ergonomic workspaces, complimentary weekday paper, and in-room coffee. Onsite lounge, indoor pool, and exercise room.

Hilton Garden Inn
245 North College Avenue
Bloomington, IN 47404
Phone: (812) 331-1335
Fax: (812) 331-1060
Toll-Free: 1-877-STAY-HGI
www.stayhgi.com
Note: Minutes from Indiana University, Lake Monroe, and Brown County State Park. An onsite business center is open to guests twenty-four hours a day.

On-Site Hospitality and Events:

Multiple screenings of *Breaking Away* are shown around Indiana University during the week leading up to the race. Information on those screenings and Little 500 related events can be found on the college website's Little 500 page and bulletins located throughout the campus.

Travel Packages:

If you are going to travel to this event, I would recommend using a reliable company to work with you on making the necessary arrangements. The suppliers listed in this book have solid references and are by far the most trusted in the business. Below are some of the organizations to try for this Top 100 Must See Sporting Event.

Premiere Corporate Events

14 Penn Plaza, Suite 925
New York, NY 10122
Phone: (212) 695-9480
Fax: (212) 564-8098
Toll-Free: 1-877-621-5243
E-mail: requests@tseworld.com
www.tseworld.com
www.pcevents.com

Premiere Sports Travel

201 Shannon Oaks Circle, Suite 205
Cary, NC 27511
Phone: (919) 481-9511
Fax: (919) 481-1337
Toll-Free: 1-800-924-9993
E-mail: sales@sportstravel.com
www.sportstravel.com

Dining:

Nick's English Hut

423 East Kirkwood Avenue
Bloomington, IN 47408
Phone: (812) 332-4040
www.nicksenglishhut.com

Note: A Bloomington tradition for over eighty years. World-famous pizza, Stromboli, and burgers.

The Bluebird

215 North Walnut Street
Bloomington, IN 47408
Phone: (812) 336-3984
www.thebluebird.ws

Note: Touting over thirty years of rock and roll, it is the place close to campus for great live music and cocktails.

Bear's Place

1316 East 3rd Street
Bloomington, IN 47401
Phone: (812) 339-3460
www.bearsplacebar.com

Note: Home of good food, good music, and a good time.

Hinkle's Hamburgers

206 South Adams Street
Bloomington, IN 47404
Phone: (812) 339-3335

Note: A particular favorite of the alums and considered by many to have the best hamburger in America.

Village Deli

409 East Kirkwood Avenue
Bloomington, IN 47408
Phone: (812) 336-2303
www.villagedeli.biz

Note: Widely considered to have the best omelets around.

Airports:

Monroe County Airport

972 South Kirby Road
Bloomington, IN 47403
Phone: (812) 825-5406
www.co.monroe.in.us

Indianapolis International Airport
(fifty-two miles to Bloomington)

2500 South High School Road., Suite 100
Indianapolis, IN 46241–4941
Phone: (317) 487-7243
www.indianapolisairport.com

Sports Travel Insider's Edge:

Best way to watch the action:

With the oval track, surrounding grandstands, and a lawn to sit on, there is not a bad seat to watch the event. Keep an eye out for the actual Cutters team competing against the frats, dorms, and Greeks. They have remained quite competitive since

Shaun Cassidy played a Cutter on the small screen. Action abounds all week as the celebration leads up to the main event with plenty of hoopla and drinking.

Best place to get up close:
Breaking Away is the story of the actual Cutters (yes, they are real) and the Little 500. Leading up to the actual Little 500, the famed movie is shown on big screens throughout campus. Catch the movie once or multiple times at the public showings. The Indiana University website will provide more information on their Little 500 page.

Best travel tip:
Preparation in advance and patience when you get there. Hotels are full and there will be a certain amount of walking. Restaurants are crowded and the alcohol flows freely.

Notable Quotes:

"I've attended Super Bowls, World Series, and the Monaco Grand Prix, but the coolest event I ever attended was the Little 500."—LANCE ARMSTRONG, Tour de France champion

"There is no event like the Little 500. You can't find an event quite like this at any other school. It makes everyone proud to feel like we go to a really unique university."—BILL COLBERT, Delta Upsilon team

Relevant Websites:
www.visitbloomington.com
www.tseworld.com
www.pcevents.com
www.sportstravel.com
www.premieresports.com

76

BASKETBALL GAME AT RUCKER PARK, HARLEM, NY

Where?
155th Street & Frederick Douglass Boulevard
Harlem, NY 10039

When?
In 1986, the Rucker Tournament became the Entertainers Basketball Classic. The league starts in late June and runs through August. Games are usually held between 6 and 10 P.M. each night of the week.

Significance:
In the shadow of Yankee Stadium and right across the street from the Polo Grounds Houses where the famed Polo Grounds Baseball Stadium once stood, consider your search for the best "streetball" in the world over.

The Entertainers Basketball Classic, formerly the Rucker Pro Am, was started in 1946 by Holcombe Rucker and has continued at its current site since 1965. It boasts the highest level of play on the traditional green and red painted court. While the talent level is considered the best in the nation, this is not your traditional basketball game. Make no mistake about it. This is "streetball" at its finest. The coaching style is relaxed as the players focus on what they do best. Basketball stars such as Allen Iverson, Stephon Marbury, Kobe Bryant, Wilt Chamberlain, and Julius Irving have played in this annual event. Don't be surprised to see celebrities such as Denzel Washington, Bill Clinton, David Stern, Fat Joe, Jay Z, and Snoop Dogg, who fields his own team. Basket MC's provide play-by-play and a bit of trash talking to the players for all to hear. The games sometimes air on MSG Networks and ESPN.

Who attends?

Future superstars and basketball fans come together for this unique event. Celebrities to hoop lovers from around the world look forward to the annual event.

Tickets:

No tickets and the only seat you can possibly hope for is one on the B or D Train that will get you there. The bleachers are, at best, rickety. However, if you are there to play, get ready to go up against the best basketball players in the nation. If you are there to sit, get there early, as the seating capacity will only hold 2,000 people.

Accommodations:

Courtyard Marriott, Upper East Side
1st & York, 410 East 92nd Street
New York, NY 10128
Phone: (212) 410-6777
Fax: (212) 423-1236
Toll-Free: 1-800-321-2211
www.marriott.com
Note: Clean, comfortable, and close enough to Rucker.

Grand Hyatt New York
109 East 42nd Street at Grand Central Terminal
New York, NY 10017
Phone: (212) 883-1234
Fax: (212) 697-3772
Toll-Free: 1-800-233-1234
www.grandnewyork.hyatt.com
Note: Most big league teams have been staying here for years. Close to Grand Central with easy access to the subway up to Rucker.

The Roosevelt Hotel
45 East 45th Street
New York, NY 10007
Phone: (212) 661-9600
Fax: (212) 885-6161
Toll-Free: 1-888-TEDDY-NY
www.therooseveltbotel.com

Note: Named after former President Theodore Roosevelt, this hotel combines old school charm with modern amenities. Close to Grand Central with easy access to the subway up to Rucker, where the players speak loudly and carry a big stick.

On-Site Hospitality:

Only one block away, Mama's Fried Chicken serves basic fried chicken, burgers, and all types of junk food at very affordable prices.

Nas Deli provides sandwiches/subs for the hungry lot at Rucker Park.

Stop by Associated Supermarket, across the street next to the Polo Grounds Houses, to load up on Gatorade and water.

Dining:

Sylvia's
328 Lenox Avenue
New York, NY 10027
(212) 996-0660
www.sylviassoulfood.com
Note: People from around the world have been eating here for some great "soul food" since 1962.

Amy Ruth's
113th West 116th Street
New York, NY 10026
Phone: (212) 280-8779
Fax: (212) 280-3109
www.amyruthsharlem.com
Note: According to some, it's the best "soul food" north of the Mason-Dixon Line.

IHOP Restaurant
2294 Adam Clayton Powell Jr. Boulevard
New York, NY 10030
Phone: (212) 234-4747
www.ihop.com
Note: Everyone goes over to IHOP after the game for pancakes.

Airports:

John F. Kennedy International Airport (JFK)
Jamaica, NY 11430
Phone: (718) 244-4444
www.panynj.gov

LaGuardia Airport (LGA)
Ditmars Boulevard and 94th Street
Flushing, NY 11371
Phone: (718) 533-3400
www.panynj.gov

Newark Liberty International Airport (EWR)
North Avenue & Spring Street
Elizabeth, NJ 07201
Phone: (973) 961-6000
www.panynj.gov

Sports Travel Insider's Edge:

Best way to watch the action:
There is only one way to watch ball at the Rucker. Get to Rucker Park early for a seat in the bleachers.

Best way to get up close:
The only way to get any closer than the bleachers at Rucker is to get in the game. If you really can play, we're talking hang with pros and your game has style, then you might have to grab a ball and hoop. It's been done many times.

Best travel tip:
Insiders will tell you that to see the best talent, show up on Monday and Thursday nights. Recent years have also seen the establishment of kids' leagues during the day. This will give you a chance to spot the next Michael Jordan or Lloyd "Sweet Pea" Daniels. Female talent can usually be seen during the late afternoon on Wednesday, prior to the evening's festivities.

Notable Quotes:

"If your swagger isn't there, people in New York, they taste blood really quickly. I had to lie a little bit. I had to act like I had it, but I really didn't."—JOAKIM NOAH, Chicago Bulls center, on playing at Rucker Park

"Earl 'The Goat' Manigault. Herman 'Helicopter' Knowings. Joe 'The Destroyer' Hammond. Richard 'Pee Wee' Kirkland. These and dozens of other colorfully nicknamed men are the 'Asphalt Gods,' whose astounding exploits in the Rucker Tournament, often against multi-millionaire NBA superstars, have made them playground divinity."—VINCENT MALLOZZI, from his book *Asphalt Gods*

Relevant Websites:
www.nycvisit.com
www.tseworld.com
www.pcevents.com
www.sportstravel.com
www.ebcsports.com
www.premieresports.com

77

BOSTON MARATHON

Where?
The streets of Boston, Massachusetts, starting at Hopkington and ending in Copley Square.

When?
Held annually on the third Monday in April and serves as the centerpiece of "Patriots Day," a local Boston holiday. The race starts at noon and the 26.2 miles are usually completed by the last runners around 5:30 to 6 P.M.

Significance:
One of the oldest and best marathons in the world.

The Boston Marathon, one of the five events of the World Marathon Majors, is an annual racing event rich in history. Established in 1886, the race now attracts an average of 20,000 to 25,000 registered participants per year with the high point being the 100th anniversary where 38,000 registered. Yes, there are cash prizes, but runners are more motivated to participate in a race of such prestige and renown. Registering is not enough. You must qualify to gain entry. Qualifying for and completing the Boston Marathon is an achievement in and of itself. For the more elite participants, the chance to win is the pinnacle of any runner's career.

Who attends?

The Boston Marathon is recognized as New England's most widely viewed sporting event. One million spectators from the immediate area and around the world fill the streets and cheer on their favorite runner or everyone who participates. The attendees serve as one of the largest cheering sections in professional and amateur sports at any level.

Tickets:

Tickets are not necessary. However, if you want to sit in a certain location, get there early to avoid the rush. The wait is well worth it.

Accommodations:

The Charlesmark Hotel

655 Boylston Street
Boston, MA 02116
Phone: (617) 247-1212
Fax: (617) 247-1224
www.thecharlesmark.com

Note: Great location and cozy touches distinguish this Boylston boutique hotel.

Midtown Hotel

220 Huntington Avenue
Boston, MA 02119

Phone: (617) 262-1000
Fax: (617) 262-8739
Toll-Free: 1-800-343-1177
www.midtownhotel.com

Note: Tourist-class hotel offers great prices and a convenient Back Bay location.

Hotel Commonwealth

500 Commonwealth Avenue
Boston, MA 02215
Phone: (617) 933-5000
Fax: (617) 266-6888
www.hotelcommonwealth.com

Note: With its many modern accoutrements, this Kenmore Square hotel satisfies visiting college parents and stylish tourists. This one is right in the action of the marathon and some rooms offer a perfect view of the course.

The Eliot Hotel

370 Commonwealth Avenue
Boston, MA 02215
Phone: (617) 267-1607
Fax: (617) 536-9114
Toll-Free: 1-800-443-5468
www.eliothotel.com

Note: Intimate hotel with service and style befitting its posh Back Bay address. Also located right along the course.

Howard Johnson Inn

1271 Boylston Street
Boston, MA 02215
Phone: (617) 267-8300
Fax: (617) 267-2763
Toll-Free: 1-800-654-2000
www.hojo.com

Note: If you want a great view of Fenway Park and easy access to the race course, this is where you should be staying.

Hilton Back Bay

40 Dalton Street
Boston, MA 02115
Phone: (617) 236-1100

Fax: (617) 867-6104
Toll-Free: 1-800-445-8667
www.hilton.com
Note: New England–style charm and sophistication located in the historic Back Bay area of Boston.

Four Seasons Boston
200 Boylston Street
Boston, MA 02116
Phone: (617) 338-4400
Fax: (617) 423-0154
Toll-Free: 1-800-332-3442
www.fourseasons.com
Note: Overlooking the famous Public Gardens and Beacon Hill, this hotel offers elegant simplicity coupled with old-world Boston charm.

Travel Packages:
If you are going to travel to this event, I would recommend using a reliable company to work with you on making the necessary arrangements. The suppliers listed in this book have solid references and are by far the most trusted in the business. Below are some of the organizations to try for this Top 100 Must See Sporting Event.

Premiere Corporate Events
14 Penn Plaza, Suite 925
New York, NY 10122
Phone: (212) 695-9480
Fax: (212) 564-8098
Toll-Free: 1-877-621-5243
E-mail: requests@tseworld.com
www.tseworld.com
www.pcevents.com

Premiere Sports Travel
201 Shannon Oaks Circle, Suite 205
Cary, NC 27511
Phone: (919) 481-9511
Fax: (919) 481-1337
Toll-Free: 1-800-924-9993
E-mail: sales@sportstravel.com
www.sportstravel.com

Marathon Tours
261 Main Street
Boston, MA 02129
Toll-Free: 1-800-444-4097
Fax: (617) 242-7686
E-mail: info@marathontours.com
www.marathontours.com

Dining:

Cactus Club
939 Boylston Street
Boston, MA 02115
Phone: (617) 236-0200
www.bestmargaritas.com
Note: The website address says it all. Great margaritas combined with Mexican cuisine heats up the Back Bay's answer to Southwestern chic.

Boston Beer Works
61 Brookline Avenue
Boston, MA 02114
Phone: (617) 896-BEER
www.beerworks.net
Note: Acclaimed beers, generous bar-food portions, and a relaxed environment attract young, sports-enthused masses to Boston's oldest brewpub.

Vinny T's of Boston
867 Boylston Street
Boston, MA 02116
Phone: (617) 262-6699
www.vinnytsofboston.com
Note: A favorite of area families and hungry tourists, delivering gargantuan portions of straightforward Italian fare in kitschy environs.

Al Denta
109 Salem Street
Boston, MA 02113
Phone: (617) 523-0990
www.aldenteboston.com
Note: Simply put, the best pasta in Boston. Open the day before the marathon, but make

sure to call ahead for a reservation as carb-loading runners will be out in force.

The Bova Bakery
134 Salem Street
Boston, MA 02113
Phone: (617) 523-5601
www.northendboston.com/bovabakery
Note: This place never closes. There is nothing more Boston than this bakery. A great place for post-race snacks.

Airport:

Boston Logan International Airport
1 Harborside Drive
Massport, East Boston, MA 02128
Phone: (617) 561-1800
www.massport.com

Sports Travel Insider's Edge:

Best way to watch the action:
Coolidge Corner provides a great vantage point to see the excitement of the race. Heartbreak Hill provides a spectacular and up-close view, but challenges exist in the difficult climb near the Boston College campus. Warm up your vocal cords and prepare to cheer on the runners at this crucial area of the race.

Also, according to famed Chicago runner Mark Buciak, pick a spot and camp out, but tell any runners you know where you will be located and where you will meet at the finish line following the race. Also, bring some form of noisemaker to make your presence known to any and all of the racers.

Best place to get up close:
The B.A.A. Freedom Run: Held the day before the Monday marathon, this 2.8 mile race allows a runner to see various attractions throughout Boston, including part of the Freedom Trail. The event is open to marathon runners and their friends and family. Progress can be tracked and alerts

are broadcast on the official Boston Marathon website.

Best travel tip:
Try and avoid the Kenmore Square area at all costs for three specific reasons: the Marathon crowd, BU students, *and* the annual 11 A.M. Red Sox Patriots Day game at Fenway Park. As the first runners are hitting Kenmore at around 1:30 P.M., the Red Sox Nation gravitates toward Kenmore.

Notable Quotes:

"I go to races all over the country and constantly hear people talking about qualifying for Boston. It's a real point of honor for them."—BILL RODGERS, Boston Marathon legend

"No marathon crowd is as spirited as Boston's, which for nearly a century has been high on this April event."—SANDY TREDWELL, author, *The World of Marathons*

"For me it's amazing because the last part of the marathon is amazing, especially this one. It's a great distraction. I found myself trying to get over to the side of the road to get that deafening crowd noise to distract and you just keep those positive thoughts going.... That's what makes this race incredible, and that's what is so encouraging when you—that the crowd doesn't—they are not real selective. They don't care if you're having your best day or worst day. They are pumped up. I saw a lot of beer cups out there and everyone was pumped up. On the tough part of the course, that's when the crowd really brings it home."—ALAN CULPEPPER, Boston Marathon runner

Relevant Websites:
www.bostonmarathon.org
www.cityofboston.gov
www.bostonusa.com
www.tseworld.com
www.pcevents.com

www.sportstravel.com
www.premieresports.com

78

COWBOYS MONDAY NIGHT FOOTBALL GAME IN DALLAS

Where?
New Cowboys Stadium (to open in 2009)
Arlington, Texas

When?
When the Cowboys play at home on Monday night during the NFL season.

Significance:
As the most successful team in the modern football era, the Dallas Cowboys are considered "America's Team." Five Super Bowl championships (including a record three within four years) and eight Conference Championships have made them a formidable football force. From 1966 to 1985, they had the most consecutive winning seasons in the NFL. They also hold the records for most seasons with ten wins, and the most appearances in the postseason and the NFC championship game.

No one would be surprised to learn that the Cowboys are also the most valuable team finance-wise, according to Forbes. When it comes to television broadcasts, the Cowboys make money for others, particularly for the producers of *Monday Night Football*. The Cowboys fan base reaches far beyond Dallas, Texas.

Monday Night Football began airing on the ABC network in 1970 and has set the standard for how football is presented on television. After *Monday Night Football* ran 555 games over thirty-six years, they became the second longest running primetime show on an American broadcast network,

just behind *60 Minutes*. Part of their success comes from airing games featuring "America's Team," particularly when they are playing the New York Giants, San Francisco 49ers, and perhaps their greatest rival, the Washington Redskins. Viewership is high with Dallas fans who want to watch the Cowboys triumph while detractors want to see them go down in defeat. There is nothing like actually being there, though, in all the energy of a Monday night.

Who attends?
Some of the rowdiest football fans and die-hard Cowboys fans you will ever meet.

How to get there?
Whatever the name ends up being, the new Cowboys Stadium will reside in Arlington, Texas. The new stadium will have sixteen points of entry as opposed to four for the old stadium. Traffic flow and roadways should be much more efficient.

Tickets:
For primary ticket access information, consider: www.dallascowboys.com.

For secondary ticket access, consider:

GoTickets, Inc.
2345 Waukegan Road, Suite 140
Bannockburn, IL 60015-1552
Toll-Free: 1-800-775-1617
Fax: (919) 481-9101
E-mail: sales@gotickets.com
www.gotickets.com

Accommodations:

Hilton Arlington Texas
2401 East Lamar Boulevard
Arlington, TX 76006
Phone: (817) 640-3322
Fax: (817) 633-1430
www.hilton.com
Note: Centrally located between Dallas and Fort Worth, and close to many major

attractions, including Six Flags Over Texas, Hurricane Harbor, and Lone Star Park.

Courtyard Dallas/Arlington
1500 Nolan Ryan Expressway
Arlington, TX 76011
Phone: (817) 277-2774
Fax: (817) 277-3103
www.marriott.com

Note: Nearby shopping, dining, and other landmarks, including the University of Texas at Arlington, Six Flags Over Texas, and Hurricane Harbor.

Sheraton Arlington Hotel
1500 Convention Center Drive
Arlington, TX 76011
Phone: (817) 261-8200
www.starwoodhotels.com

Note: In the heart of the Arlington entertainment district and only a fifteen-minute drive to downtown Dallas or Forth Worth. A Starbucks is onsite to help start your day.

Residence Inn Arlington
1050 Brookhollow Plaza Drive
Arlington, TX 76006
Phone: (817) 649-7300
Fax: (817) 649-7600
www.residenceinnarlington.com

Note: Close to the North Texas Metroplex and located less than ten miles away from the new stadium.

Omni Mandalay
221 East Las Colinas Boulevard
Irving, TX 75039
Phone: (972) 556-0800
www.omnihotels.com

Note: Advertises the "exotic charm of a Burmese city." Located on the Mandalay Canal in the Las Colinas Urban Center.

Hyatt Regency
300 Reunion Boulevard West
Dallas, TX 75207

Phone: (214) 651-1234
www.dallasregency.hyatt.com

Note: Longest running AAA Four-Diamond distinction and about twenty-five minutes to the stadium. Located near business, sports, and shopping districts.

Hilton Anatole
2201 Stemmons Freeway
Dallas, TX 75207
Phone: (214) 748-1200
www.hilton.com

Note: About thirty minutes to the stadium, this hotel promises "warm hospitality with Western lore."

On-Site Hospitality:
To be determined, but expect hospitality at the new stadium to be "Texas-sized." For Stadium Suites information call (972) 785-4430, or log on to www.dallascowboys.com/suites.cfm.

Travel Packages:
If you are going to travel to this event, I would recommend using a reliable company to work with you on making the necessary arrangements. The suppliers listed in this book have solid references and are by far the most trusted in the business. Below are some of the organizations to try for this Top 100 Must See Sporting Event.

Premiere Corporate Events
14 Penn Plaza, Suite 925
New York, NY 10122
Phone: (212) 695-9480
Fax: (212) 564-8098
Toll-Free: 1-877-621-5243
E-mail: requests@tseworld.com
www.tseworld.com
www.pcevents.com

Premiere Sports Travel
201 Shannon Oaks Circle, Suite 205
Cary, NC 27511

Phone: (919) 481-9511
Fax: (919) 481-1337
Toll-Free: 1-800-924-9993
E-mail: sales@sportstravel.com
www.sportstravel.com

Dining:

Texas Land and Cattle

2009 East Copeland
Arlington, TX 76011
Phone: (817) 461-1500
Fax: (817) 801-6600
www.texaslandandcattle.com

Note: Since 1993, they have been serving high-quality and generous portions of mesquite-grilled steaks, smoked sirloin, chicken, ribs, fish, and shrimp.

Traildust Steak House

2300 East Lamar Boulevard
Arlington, TX 76006
Phone: (816) 640-6411
www.traildust.com

Note: Over forty years in business and 19 million steaks tell the story. Committed to quality, the naturally aged beef is as tender as you will find in the Lone Star State.

Piccolo Mondo

829 East Lamar Boulevard
Arlington, TX 76011-3504
Phone: (817) 265-9174
Fax: (817) 226 3474
www.piccolomondo.com

Note: If you are looking for a good, authentic Italian meal, this is the place to go.

My Martini Wine & Bistro

859 North East Green Oaks Boulevard
Arlington, TX 76006
Phone: (817) 461-4424
Fax: (817) 801-3472
www.mymartinibistro.com

Note: Known for great martinis, appetizers, and ambiance.

Rockfish Seafood & Grill

3785 South Cooper Street
Arlington, TX 76015-3414
Phone: (817) 419-9988
Fax: (817) 419-2699
www.rockfishseafood.com

Note: A comfortable and relaxed atmosphere awaits you with menu choices that include fish tacos and New England baked stuffed fish. Ask about the Rock-a-Rita margarita.

Bobby V's Sports Gallery and Grill

4301 South Bowen Road
Arlington, TX 76016
Phone: (817) 467-9922

Note: A popular pre- and post-game gathering place to celebrate all things Cowboys.

Airports:

Dallas/Fort Worth International Airport

DFW Airport, TX 75261
Phone: (972) 973-8888
www.dfwairport.com

Dallas Love Field

8008 Cedar Springs Road, LB 16
Dallas, TX 75235
Phone: (214) 670-6073
www.dallas-lovefield.com

Sports Travel Insider's Edge:

Best way to watch the action:

With Jerry Jones, you can count on the biggest, best, and most luxurious. Scoring a seat in one of the 300 plus luxury suites will provide you the absolute best way to watch your beloved (or for some, hated) Cowboys.

Best place to get up close:

Seats on the lower level will not only allow you to get up close to the game, but also up close and personal (well, maybe not) with the Dallas Cowboy Cheerleaders. A great view, no matter what you are focused on.

Best travel tip:

If *Monday Night Football* is broadcasting a Cowboys home game in October, sneak in a Friday night Texas high school football game during your trip for an even more memorable football experience.

Notable Quote:

"They can take football away from ABC on Monday nights, but they can't take away the memories."—JOHN MADDEN, former Oakland Raiders head coach, football commentator

Relevant Websites:

www.dallascowboys.com
www.arlington.org
www.tseworld.com
www.pcevents.com
www.sportstravel.com
www.gotickets.com
www.premieresports.com

79

HEAD OF THE CHARLES REGATTA

Where?

Head of the Charles Regatta
Cambridge, MA 02238

When?

Mid to late October every year.

Significance:

Hearkening back to his native England, Harvard University sculling instructor Ernest Arlette proposed a "head of the river" race to Cambridge Boat Club members D'Arcy MacMahon, Howard McIntyre, and Jack Vincent. It would be held on the Charles River in Cambridge and feature boats and their rowers engaged in a regatta against each other and the clock. The winner would be crowned "Head of the Charles."

Since that first race in October 16, 1965, many racers have strived to be in charge of the Charles. The annual October race has spread worldwide. Cambridge boasts the largest with fifty-six different racing events, which include 8,000 athletes from around the world. Over two days, 300,000 spectators cheer on their favorite rowers as they navigate the 3.2 mile stretch of the Charles River starting at Boston University's DeWolfe Boathouse to the finish line just after the Eliot Bridge.

While the HOCR has experienced significant growth, one thing has not changed. A group of three from the Cambridge Boat Club focuses on planning the entire event, similar to the tasks of MacMahon, McIntyre, and Vincent. With the help of 1,500 volunteers, of course.

Who attends?

300,000 casual and hardcore regatta fans filling the riverbanks and bridges of Cambridge.

How to get there?

Massachusetts's Turnpike to Exit 18 East or Exit 20 West, follow signs to Cambridge. Stay straight through several traffic lights and across the River Street Bridge. Left onto Memorial Drive. Memorial Drive forks at the 1.6 mile mark (near the Cambridge Boat Club). Staying to the left, follow signs for Watertown/Newton. As you approach Eliot Bridge, follow signs for Boston/Newton. As you are crossing Eliot bridge stay to the right and an HOCR volunteer will meet your trailer and direct you to a parking space.

Tickets:

Free to watch and first-come, first-serve for the best view. Look out for those overserved.

Accommodations:

Hotel Commonwealth
500 Commonwealth Avenue
Boston, MA 02215
Phone: (617) 933-5000
www.hotelcommonwealth.com
Note: The official host hotel of the Head of the Charles Regatta is a favorite among tourists.

The Charlesmark Hotel
655 Boylston Street
Boston, MA 02116
Phone: (617) 247-1212
Fax: (617) 247-1224
www.thecharlesmark.com
Note: This Boylston boutique hotel is ideally located close to the HOCR.

Midtown Hotel
220 Huntington Avenue
Boston, MA 02115
Phone: (617) 262-1000
Fax: (617) 262-8739
www.midtownhotel.com
Note: Reasonably priced, tourist-class hotel with a convenient Back Bay location.

The Eliot Hotel
370 Commonwealth Avenue
Boston, MA 02215
Phone: (617) 267-1607
Fax: (617) 536-9114
Toll-Free: 1-800-443-5468
www.eliothotel.com
Note: Intimacy combined with great service and style to go with the posh Back Bay address.

Howard Johnson Inn
1271 Boylston Street
Boston, MA 02215
Phone: (617) 267-8300
Fax: (617) 267-2763
Toll-Free: 1-800-654-2000
www.hojo.com
Note: For those on a budget. Plus, you might get a great view of Fenway Park.

Hilton Back Bay
40 Dalton Street
Boston, MA 02115
Phone: (617) 236-1100
Fax: (617) 867-6104
Toll-Free: 1-800-445-8667
www.hilton.com
Note: One of the finer hotels in the historic Back Bay area providing local charm and sophistication.

Four Seasons Boston
200 Boylston Street
Boston, MA 02116
Phone: (617) 338-4400
Fax: (617) 423-0154
Toll-Free: 1-800-332-3442
www.fourseasons.com
Note: Elegance and charm from a hotel boasting a view of the Public Gardens and Beacon Hill.

On-Site Hospitality:

The Reunion Village: Located at the halfway point of the HOCR. Stop for a refreshment and enjoy the fun and relaxed atmosphere with your fellow regatta enthusiasts. Minimal entry fee to get in for unlimited access, and all proceeds benefit official charities. Open all day Saturday and Sunday with hours subject to change.

Vendors are also located near the Weld Boathouse and the Expo Tent, providing healthy sandwiches, burgers, fries, clam chowder, and apple cider.

Travel Packages:

If you are going to travel to this event, I would recommend using a reliable company to work with you on making the necessary arrangements. The suppliers listed in this book have solid references and are by far the most trusted in the business. Below are some of the organizations to try for this Top 100 Must See Sporting Event.

Premiere Corporate Events
14 Penn Plaza, Suite 925
New York, NY 10122
Phone: (212) 695-9480
Fax: (212) 564-8098
Toll-Free: 1-877-621-5243
E-mail: requests@tseworld.com
www.tseworld.com
www.pcevents.com

Premiere Sports Travel
201 Shannon Oaks Circle, Suite 205
Cary, NC 27511
Phone: (919) 481-9511
Fax: (919) 481-1337
Toll-Free: 1-800-924-9993
E-mail: sales@sportstravel.com
www.sportstravel.com

Dining:

Cactus Club
939 Boylston Street
Boston, MA 02115
Phone: (617) 236-0200
Fax: (617) 236-0419
www.bestmargaritas.com

Note: Best margaritas indeed. Perfect to wash down with some great Mexican food.

Boston Beer Works
61 Brookline Avenue
Boston, MA 02114
Phone: (617) 536-BEER
Fax: (617) 536-3325
www.beerworks.net

Note: Boston's oldest brewpub serves acclaimed beers that go with generous bar-food portions in a setting that attracts the young sports enthusiast.

Vinny T's of Boston
867 Boylston Street
Boston, MA 02116
Phone: (617) 262-6699
Fax: (617) 437-7310
www.vinnytsofboston.com

Note: Great Italian food in an environment that can be best described as kitschy.

Al Dente
109 Salem Street
Boston, MA 02113
Phone: (617) 523-0990
Fax: (617)227-4002
www.aldenteboston.com

Note: Considered the best pasta in Boston. A popular place, so call ahead for a reservation.

The Bova Bakery
134 Salem Street
Boston, MA 02113
Phone: (617) 523-5601
www.northendboston.com/bovabakery

Note: This bakery never closes. It would not be a trip to Boston without a visit to the Bova.

Airport:

Boston Logan International Airport
One Harborside Drive
Massport, East Boston, MA 02128
Phone: (617) 561-1800
www.massport.com

Sports Travel Insider's Edge:

Best way to watch the action:
If you prefer an overhead vantage point, find a spot on any of the six bridges, including Boston University, River Street, Western Avenue, Weeks, Anderson, or Eliot. Overlooking the race from any of those locations provides you with the best view.

Best place to get up close:
The competitors' staging area is located one mile upstream from the Lars Anderson Bridge and is open throughout the race starting on Friday afternoon. You will find the Head of the Charles Rowing and Fitness Expo with plenty of vendors selling rowing gear. The area also holds the awards ceremonies at the end.

Best travel tip:
The chance to see the Red Sox play at Fenway in the playoffs is too much to resist. Check the calendar, not to mention the standings, to see if you can catch the Sox in action.

Notable Quotes:

"It's the greatest regatta in the world."— MAHÉ DRYSDALE, Single Sculler world champion

"Given half a chance, the Head of the Charles folks can put on a damn good regatta and regatta party...the Head of the Charles is absolutely the place to be on a weekend like this."—ED HEWITT, row2k. com

Relevant Websites:
www.hocr.org
www.cityofboston.gov
www.cambridge-usa.org
www.tseworld.com
www.pcevents.com
www.sportstravel.com
www.premieresports.com

80

FLORIDA VS. GEORGIA FOOTBALL GAME

Where?
Jacksonville Municipal Stadium
1400 East Duvall Street
Jacksonville, FL 32202

When?
Annually on the last Saturday in October.

Significance:
ESPN, *College Football News*, the *Sporting News*, Fox Sports, and America's Best Online all agree the Georgia vs. Florida Football Classic is easily one of the top ten football rivalries. While nicknamed "The World's Largest Outdoor Cocktail Party," a tag organizers and the city of Jacksonville are trying to live down, the meeting between the University of Florida Gators and the University of Georgia Bulldogs is officially called the "Florida-Georgia/Georgia-Florida Game," alternating each year. The game is played at the neutral Jacksonville Municipal Stadium in Jacksonville, seventy-three miles from the Gators' home and 342 miles from the Bulldogs' dog house. The game itself is many times overshadowed by the hype and alcohol-fueled hoopla surrounding it. While the rivalry is not as intense as other warring teams, they do differ on when the teams first played each other. Georgia says 1904. Florida asserts 1915. Steve Spurrier, former Gator head coach, does his best to fan the flames with his constant disrespect toward Georgia, even going so far as to call Georgia coach Ray Goff, "Ray Goof."

Who attends?
Gator fans, Bulldog fans, and anyone else who wants to "get their drink on."

Tickets:
For primary ticket access information, consider: www.georgiadogs.com or www.ufl.edu.

For secondary ticket access, consider:

GoTickets, Inc.
2345 Waukegan Road, Suite 140
Bannockburn, IL 60015-1552
Toll-Free: 1-800-775-1617
Fax: (919) 481-9101
E-mail: sales@gotickets.com
www.gotickets.com

Accommodations:

Omni Hotel
245 Water Street
Jacksonville, FL 32202
Phone: (904) 355-6664
Fax: (904) 791-4812

Toll-Free: 1-800-843-6664
www.omnihotels.com
Note: Four-diamond luxury hotel located in the heart of downtown provides large, luxury guest rooms and a rooftop heated swimming pool.

Hyatt Regency Jacksonville Riverfront
225 East Coast Line Drive
Jacksonville, FL 32202
Phone: (904) 588-1234
Fax: (904) 634-4554
Toll-Free: 1-800-233-1234
www.hyatt.com
Note: 966 rooms with rooftop swimming pool and various onsite restaurants, from bagels to steaks.

Crowne Plaza Jacksonville
1201 Riverplace Boulevard
Jacksonville, FL 32207
Phone: (904) 398-8800
Fax: (904) 318-9170
Toll-Free: 1-800-2-CROWNE
www.cpjacksonville.com
Note: A ferry ride across the river will get you to the stadium and will only set you back about $5.

Beach Hotels:

Ponte Vedra Inn and Club
200 Ponte Vedra Boulevard
Ponte Vedra Beach, FL 32082
Phone: (904) 285-1111
Fax: (904) 285-2111
Toll-Free: 1-800-234-7842
www.pvresorts.com
Note: Outstanding hospitality, amenities, and services, but expect to pay a higher price for it.

One Ocean Resort and Spa
1 Ocean Boulevard
Atlantic Beach, FL 32233
Phone: (904) 247-0305
Toll-Free: 1-877-247-0305
www.oneoceanresort.com

Note: Nice, moderately priced resort right on the beach and close to various entertainment venues.

Sawgrass Marriott Resort & Spa
1000 PGA Tour Boulevard
Ponte Vedra Beach, FL 32082
Phone: (904) 285-7777
Fax: (904) 285-0906
Toll-Free: 1-800-457-GOLF
www.sawgrassmarriott.com
Note: Relax with a round of golf on their world-famous course.

On-Site Hospitality:
Onsite offerings change from year to year. Tons of tailgating parties abound, but they change locations as well.

Travel Packages:
If you are going to travel to this event, I would recommend using a reliable company to work with you on making the necessary arrangements. The suppliers listed in this book have solid references and are by far the most trusted in the business. Below are some of the organizations to try for this Top 100 Must See Sporting Event.

Premiere Corporate Events
14 Penn Plaza, Suite 925
New York, NY 10122
Phone: (212) 695-9480
Fax: (212) 564-8098
Toll-Free: 1-877-621-5243
E-mail: requests@tseworld.com
www.tseworld.com
www.pcevents.com

Premiere Sports Travel
201 Shannon Oaks Circle, Suite 205
Cary, NC 27511
Phone: (919) 481-9511
Fax: (919) 481-1337
Toll-Free: 1-800-924-9993
E-mail: sales@sportstravel.com
www.sportstravel.com

Premiere College Sports (Powered by Dodd's Athletic Tours)

308 South Neil
Champaign, IL 61820
Phone: (217) 373-5067
Fax: (217) 398-1313
Toll-Free: 1-800-553-5527
www.doddsathletictours.com
www.collegesportstravel.com

Dining:

Bistro Aix

1440 San Marco Boulevard
Jacksonville, FL 32207
Phone: (904) 398-1949
Fax: (904) 398-4127
www.bistrox.com

Note: Close to hotels and provides great food, drink, and overall service.

Aqua Grill

950 Sawgrass Village
Ponte Vedra Beach, FL 32082
Phone: (904) 285-3017
Fax: (904) 285-0727
www.aquagrill.net

Note: An excellent dining experience includes outdoor patio seating for sunny Florida days.

Bonefish Grill

10950 San Jose Boulevard
Jacksonville, FL 32223
Phone: (904) 370-1070
Fax: (904) 370-1071
www.bonefishgrill.com

Note: Fresh snapper and mahi mahi are served by this chain restaurant that got its start in St. Petersburg.

Tra Vini

216 Ponte Vedra Park Drive
Ponte Vedra Beach, FL 32082
Phone: (904) 273-2442
www.travinis.com

Note: Known for great wine, but be prepared to pay.

Campeche Bay

127 First Avenue North
Jacksonville Beach, FL 32250
Phone: (904) 249-3322
Fax: (904) 249-3323
www.campechebay.net

Note: Good Mexican food at an affordable price.

The Jacksonville Landing

2 Independent Drive, Suite 250
Jacksonville, FL 32202
Phone: (904) 353-1188
Fax: (904) 353-1558
www.jacksonvillelanding.com

Note: Located less than one mile from the Jacksonville Municipal Stadium, the Jacksonville Landing provides a variety of dining options. Check their website for more information.

In addition, the Southbank Riverwalk is a 1.2 mile boardwalk on the banks of the St. John's River. Dining options include chain restaurants and microbreweries. Accessible by car or water taxi.

Airports:

Jacksonville International Airport

2400 Yankee Clipper Drive
Jacksonville, FL 32218
Phone: (904) 741-4902
www.jia.aero

Craig Municipal Airport

855-1 St. Johns Bluff Road North
Suite 500
Jacksonville, FL 32225
Phone: (904) 641-7666
Fax: (904) 645-6483
www.jaa.aero

Cecil Field Airport

13365 Aeronautical Circle
Jacksonville, FL 32215
Phone: (904) 573-1611
www.jaa.aero

Sports Travel Insider's Edge:

Best way to watch the action:

If you hold no allegiance to either school, pick one. Buy some merchandise to adorn yourself with one school's colors and join that group in cheering their heroes and razzing the opposition. Being a hardcore fan, even if just for one day, is the best way to enjoy the action in stadium.

For actual seating, the lower level end zone seats at Alltel are extremely close to the field. The seating is so good in that area that after a few drinks it can make it seem like you are actually on the field.

Best place to get up close:

If you are looking for a giant tailgate party with food, drinks, and music, go to The Landing for pre- and post-game festivities. There are a multitude of restaurants, bars, clubs, and food/drink vendors to choose from. Live bands perform, while large screens play football highlights in case you can't make it to the stadium. The party goes well into the night on both Friday and Saturday.

Best travel tip:

If you cannot make it to The Landing, but are still in the mood for tailgating, you will find various tailgaters onsite at the stadium. Go from one to the other without fear of retribution for your allegiance to Florida or Georgia. This is about a celebration of school spirit with hostility at a minimum and partying at a maximum.

Notable Quotes:

"Going to the game is an experience like no other. The atmosphere that is created by the fans and by both teams is exciting. You get really excited for your family because you know how much they are going to enjoy the atmosphere. It's going to be a fun time for both teams and all of our families that are going to be there."—CHRIS LEAK, former Florida Gators quarterback

"Florida in a stand-up five, they may or may not blitz. Belue...third down on the eight. In trouble, he got a block behind him. Going to throw on the run. Complete on the 25. To the 30, Lindsay Scott 35, 40, Lindsay Scott 45, 50, 45, 40....Run Lindsay, 25, 20, 15, 10, Lindsay Scott! Lindsay Scott! Lindsay Scott."—LARRY MUNSON'S, long-time Georgia radio announcer, legendary call in the 1980 Florida vs. Georgia game where the Bulldogs won in the final seconds.

Relevant Websites:

www.ufl.edu
www.uga.edu
www.visitjacksonville.com
www.jacksonvillelanding.com
www.tseworld.com
www.pcevents.com
www.sportstravel.com
www.gotickets.com
www.premieresports.com

81

LADY VOLS
BASKETBALL GAME

Where?

Thompson-Boling Assembly Center and Arena
1600 Phillip Fulmer Way
Knoxville, TN 37996

When?

During the NCAA college women's basketball season.

Significance:

The Tennessee Lady Volunteers basketball team, a.k.a. the Lady Vols, is a dominant force in college b-ball that does not take a backseat to any other basketball program, men's or women's. For three decades they have defeated and downright decimated opponents who dared challenge them on their home turf of the Thompson-Boling Assembly Center and Arena. It's become known as a bit of a tough neighborhood to leave with a victory. Vols victories range in the 90th percentile. In the past thirty years, the Lady Vols have been fourteen-time SEC regular season champions and thirteen-time SEC tournament champions. They have appeared at the Final Four eighteen times and captured eight NCAA National championships entering the 2009 season. They are the only team to have appeared in every NCAA tournament.

Head Coach Pat Summitt has led them to their status as a powerhouse in women's basketball. No one can accuse her of taking the easy route to glory. Nearly half of their regular season games are against ranked opponents. The SEC alone is considered one of the most dominant conferences in women's basketball, yet the Lady Vols still secured a sixty-four-game conference winning streak that ended in 2006. Fans have responded to this dominance by filling up the Thompson-Boling Assembly Center and Arena with record-setting attendance and consistent sellouts.

The records are part of basketball history and the numbers don't lie. Simply put, the Tennessee Lady Vols are one of the single most successful basketball programs of all time.

Who attends?

Lady Volunteer fans, and there are a lot of them, and young basketball hopefuls.

How to get there?

Highway 129 or I-40 (via the James White Parkway Exit) will take you to Neyland Drive. The arena is off of Lake Loudon Boulevard on Phillip Fulmer Way.

Tickets:

For primary ticket access information, consider: www.tbarena.com.

For secondary ticket access, consider:

GoTickets, Inc.
2345 Waukegan Road, Suite 140
Bannockburn, IL 60015-1552
Toll-Free: 1-800-775-1617
Fax: (919) 481-9101
E-mail: sales@gotickets.com
www.gotickets.com

Accommodations:

Hilton Knoxville Downtown
501 West Church Avenue
Knoxville, TN 37902
Phone: (865) 523-2300
Fax: (865) 525-6532
Toll-Free: 1-800-HILTONS
www.hilton.com

Note: A mere five minutes to the arena, the newly renovated hotel is in the downtown business district and close to many local attractions.

Hampton Inn & Suites
618 West Main Street
Knoxville, TN 37902
Phone: (865) 522-5400
Fax: (865) 522-4000
www.hamptoninn.com

Note: Located downtown in the Historic District and close to the Women's Basketball Hall of Fame.

Knoxville Marriott
500 Southeast Hill Avenue
Knoxville, TN 37915
Phone: (865) 637-1234
Fax: (865) 637-1193
Toll-Free: 1-800-836-8031
www.marriott.com

Note: Guests have a beautiful view of the Tennessee River and the convenience of a covered walkway that leads to the Knoxville Civic Auditorium.

On-Site Hospitality:

There is no onsite hospitality, but who would want to leave their seat and miss a minute of a Lady Vols game in the first place?

Travel Packages:

If you are going to travel to this event, I would recommend using a reliable company to work with you on making the necessary arrangements. The suppliers listed in this book have solid references and are by far the most trusted in the business. Below are some of the organizations to try for this Top 100 Must See Sporting Event.

Premiere Corporate Events
14 Penn Plaza, Suite 925
New York, NY 10122
Phone: (212) 695-9480
Fax: (212) 564-8098
Toll-Free: 1-877-621-5243
E-mail: requests@tseworld.com
www.tseworld.com
www.pcevents.com

Premiere Sports Travel
201 Shannon Oaks Circle, Suite 205
Cary, NC 27511
Phone: (919) 481-9511
Fax: (919) 481-1337
Toll-Free: 1-800-924-9993
E-mail: sales@sportstravel.com
www.sportstravel.com

Dining:

Tomato Head
12 Market Square
Knoxville, TN 37902
Phone: (865) 637-4067
Fax: (865) 637-4019
www.thetomatohead.com
Note: Known for great salads and sandwiches.

Calhoun's
400 Neyland Drive
Knoxville, TN 37902
Phone: (865) 673-3399

www.calhouns.com
Note: Close to the arena and the Women's Basketball Hall of Fame. Enjoy authentic southern barbecue.

King Tut Grill
4132 Martin Mill Pike
Knoxville, TN 37920-3031
Phone: (865) 573-6021
www.kingtutgrill.com
Note: Singing and games are part of the experience here. It's BYOB and bring cash as they do not take credit cards.

Fountain City Creamery
114 Hotel Road
Knoxville, TN 37918
Phone: (865) 688-4607
Note: Considered by locals as the place to get the best burger in Knoxville. Top off your meal with some homemade ice cream.

Litton's
2803 Essary Road
Knoxville, TN 37901
Phone: (865) 688-0429
www.littonsburgers.com
Note: Another contender for the best burger in Knoxville.

Airport:

Knoxville International Airport
2055 Alcoa Highway
Alcoa, TN 37701
Phone: (865) 342-3000
www.tys.org

Sports Travel Insider's Edge:

Best way to watch the action:
If you want a view of the Lady Vols and their coach in action, get a seat opposite the benches in Sections 119-123.

Best place to get up close:
The "Guest Coach Program" is about as interactive as you can get and a Lady Vols fan's

dream come true. One individual per game is selected by the Tennessee Athletic Department to sit behind the coach, attend the halftime locker room speech, and be a fly on the wall after the game to hear the post-game debriefing.

For the remaining 16,000 or so not selected, the player introductions are considered the best in women's college basketball. Knoxville-based Bandit Lites, one of the biggest lighting companies in the world, adds to the excitement and aura of the presentation.

Best travel tip:

After a game, you may feel like you've been sitting inside long enough. Take a trip to the Great Smoky Mountains. Visit www.nps.gov for more information on a getaway.

For the indoor crowd who has just witnessed the Lady Vols in action, and probably making their own history, revel in the entire history of women's basketball at the Woman's Basketball Hall of Fame, located two miles from the arena.

Notable Quote:

"I came to Tennessee because I was one of those people lining the court. To be a fan of women's basketball is to be a fan of Tennessee. And that's a responsibility that we have to represent our school. It's something we don't take for granted."—CANDACE PARKER, former University of Tennessee and Los Angeles Sparks forward, recalling a childhood trip to DePaul to see Coach Summitt and the Lady Vols

Relevant Websites:

www.tbarena.com
www.utladyvols.com
www.knoxville.org
www.tseworld.com
www.pcevents.com
www.sportstravel.com
www.gotickets.com
www.premieresports.com

82

NBA ALL-STAR GAME

Where?

The 2010 NBA All-Star Game will be played on Sunday, February 14, at the new Dallas Cowboys Stadium in Arlington, Texas.

When?

One weekend in February.

Significance:

And you thought red versus blue was only reserved for the political realm. The premier players in the National Basketball Association's Eastern and Western Conferences have come together every year since March 2, 1951. The NBA All-Star game is a basketball fan's ultimate fantasy with once-a-year dream matchups pitting the best that the NBA has to offer.

Picking the Players and Coaches

The starting roster is selected by fan ballot while the reserves are picked by the coaches of each conference. Selecting the players they coach is forbidden. The replacement of injured players falls upon the NBA Commissioner.

The coaches are selected based upon the team that has the most wins in its conference through the Sunday two weeks before the game. The only exception to that rule is that the same coach cannot coach a team in consecutive seasons. Thank Pat Riley for that. The Los Angeles Lakers' dominance throughout the eighties resulted in repeat All-Star coaching appearances for the legendary coach, creating the need for what is now known as the "Riley Rule." When that duplication occurs, the coach with the second-best record is offered the All-Star skipper nod.

Flash and Substance

With the All-Star Game serving as a showcase for the NBA, the glitz and glamour is ramped up to the extreme. Each All-Star is given his own introduction with lighting, music, and the always-popular pyrotechnics. A major recording artist is selected to sing "The Star-Spangled Banner" and the musical performances continue in an expanded halftime show. Special uniforms are designed (red for Western, blue for Eastern). No, it is not Wrestlemania. It is the pageantry of the NBA All-Star Game.

The pageantry continues during game play with NBA stars showing what they do best with a few slam dunks and alley oops mixed in for good measure. The competitive nature is downplayed, unless the score is close in the fourth quarter. Then, the substance outweighs the flash and these guys get to work.

Who attends?

Basketball fans of all ages.

Tickets:

For primary ticket access information, consider: www.nba.com.

For secondary ticket access, consider:

GoTickets, Inc.

2345 Waukegan Road, Suite 140
Bannockburn, IL 60015-1552
Toll-Free: 1-800-775-1617
Fax: (919) 481-9101
E-mail: sales@gotickets.com
www.gotickets.com

On-Site Events:

NBA All-Star Weekend is more than just the game played on Sunday. The days leading up to it include many major events.

NBA All-Star Jam Session: An interactive theme park of basketball greets fans for a true hands-on experience. Those eighteen years or older can join the Jam Session MVP Volunteer Team. As basketball ambassadors, the volunteers welcome and work with fans of all ages. Their job is to enhance the overall Jam Session experience and make a few dreams come true. Volunteers receive limited-edition NBA gear and the chance to win tickets to the game.

NBA All-Star Practice: Get a sneak peek at the stars with a view that is touted as better than a courtside seat. Access like this comes once in a lifetime. When you are not taking pictures of your favorite superstars, cheer them on as they prepare for the big game.

Slam Dunk Contest: Perhaps the most popular and high-profile special event. Athleticism combines with creativity as the NBA's best dunkers fly through the air with the greatest of ease. Plus, they can travel and double-dribble to their hearts content.

Three-Point Shootout: The best of the three-point shooters have five opportunities from five different places around the three-point line. A shot equals one point. The last ball from each section, nicknamed the "money ball," is worth two points. The highest score wins.

Skills Challenge: Combines timed dribbling, shooting, and passing. Showmanship takes a backseat to agility and quickness.

Shooting Stars Competition: A diverse mini-All-Star Team is composed of a retired NBA legend, a current player, and a WNBA star. They represent their respective cities in a shooting competition. This event replaced the longtime Legends Classic.

Celebrity All-Star Game: While not athletes, famous actors and performers take to the court to compete in their own East versus West competition. To make it a bit more competitive and exciting, each "all-star" team gets one WNBA player.

D-League All-Star Game: The minor league of the NBA is allowed to show their stuff, giving fans another glimpse into what could become the league's future.

Travel Packages:

If you are going to travel to this event, I would recommend using a reliable company to work with you on making the necessary arrangements. The suppliers listed in this book have solid references and are by far the most trusted in the business. Below are some of the organizations to try for this Top 100 Must See Sporting Event.

Premiere Corporate Events

14 Penn Plaza, Suite 925
New York, NY 10122
Phone: (212) 695-9480
Fax: (212) 564-8098
Toll-Free: 1-877-621-5243
E-mail: requests@tseworld.com
www.tseworld.com
www.pcevents.com

Premiere Sports Travel

201 Shannon Oaks Circle, Suite 205
Cary, NC 27511
Phone: (919) 481-9511
Fax: (919) 481-1337
Toll-Free: 1-800-924-9993
E-mail: sales@sportstravel.com
www.sportstravel.com

Sports Travel Insider's Edge:

Best way to watch the action:

The NBA All-Star Game is a matchup where individual offensive talent shines. This event is not for those that want to see a great defensive battle. No matter what arena is hosting the event, secure a seat where you can watch both sides of the court. Lower level, between the baskets is ideal. But remember, the All-Star Game is the main event of a weekend filled with other activities that allow fans to enjoy their favorite players.

Those events include:

NBA All-Star Jam Session
NBA All-Star Practice
Slam Dunk Contest
Three-Point Shootout
Skills Challenge
Shooting Stars Competition
Celebrity All-Star Game
Rookie Challenge
D-League All-Star Game

Best place to get up close:

Out of all the events, the Slam Dunk contest is the most popular and competitive. The sports media gives this competition almost as much coverage as the game itself. The "must see" event places a spotlight on the best of the best in NBA dunkers. This is your chance to see your favorite star performing solo.

Best travel tip:

See a side of the NBA that is not about million-dollar players, but a love for the game. Launched in 2007, the D-League All-Star Game is growing in popularity and prominence as a preview for what is coming to the NBA in the future. This one is for basketball fans who want to see the next surprise story in the making.

Notable Quotes:

"One of the greatest honors besides winning the (NBA) Championship, is playing at the NBA All-Star Weekend. You get to see great players and you get to play with those great players."—MAGIC JOHNSON, former Los Angeles Laker

"For the players, playing in the All-Star Game is special. When you know that everyone in the world is watching. If you're a high school player, you're watching the NBA All-Star Game. If you're a college player, you're watching the NBA All-Star

Game. If you're a pro player, no matter what you say, you're watching the game. The entire basketball world is watching."—CHARLES BARKLEY, former NBA player

Relevant Websites:

www.nba.com
www.tseworld.com
www.pcevents.com
www.sportstravel.com
www.gotickets.com
www.premieresports.com

83

PIPELINE SURFING

Where?

Pipeline Beach
59-337 Ke-Nui Road
North Oahu, HI

When?

Two weeks in December every year.

Significance:

Golfers want to play at Augusta. Mountain climbers long to scale Everest. Surfers dream about the opportunity to surf the Banzai Pipeline at the Pipeline Masters. The Pipeline Reef is where those surfers congregate for the best "break" in the world. The Banzai Pipeline serves as the biggest barrel in the world among the best waves on the north shore.

Surfing the Banzai Pipeline is not for the weak of heart. It is a tubed surfing break that calls Ehukai ("Reddish Tinged Water") Beach Park on the north shore of Oahu home. Surfers call it "cranking" when the water surrounds them, but this is not a peaceful enclosure that provides a protective water cocoon. The powerful waves come up fast and break in a furious and almost violent fashion. Surfers have come out of it with cuts and a few broken bones.

The Banzai Pipeline got its nickname from Bruce Brown in the late 1950s. Brown was a surf cinematographer. Reacting to a surfer navigating a vicious wave while narrating "Surf Safari," he shouted "banzai" with the cameras rolling. The name has stuck ever since. The Banzai Pipeline and the Pipeline Masters have been immortalized in other movies, most recently *Blue Crush*, along with documentaries and books.

The Pipeline Masters is the most prestigious surfing contest and the final leg of the annual World Championship Tour. Surfers from around the world come together to find out who is the best of the best, not to mention the "master" of the Banzai Pipeline.

Who attends?

Surfers, surfing hopefuls, and wannabes can be found at the Pipeline Masters. Locals also congregate to watch the best surfers battle their hometown waves.

Tickets:

No tickets necessary. A beach towel and binoculars will suffice. And wear sunscreen.

Accommodations:

Turtle Bay, North Shore Oahu Hawaii
57-091 Kamehameha Highway
Kahuku, HI 96731
Phone: (808) 293-6000
Fax: (808) 293-9147
Toll-Free: 1-800-203-3650
www.turtlebayresort.com
Note: 443 beach cottages and guest rooms on five miles of beachfront that face the beautiful Kawela Bay, Bay View Beach Lawn, and Turtle Bay.

JW Marriott Ihilani Resort & Spa
92-1001 Olani Street
Kapolei, HI 96707
Phone: (808) 679-0079

Fax: (808) 679-0080
Toll-Free: 1-800-626-4446
www.ihilani.com

Note: A breathtaking view of one of the finest white sand beaches in Hawaii. Luxurious amenities, elegant surroundings, and private lanais.

Waikiki Beach Area (forty-five minutes from Pipeline Beach):

Aqua Palms and Spa

1850 Ala Moana Boulevard
Waikiki Beach, HI 96815
Phone: (808) 947-7256
Fax: (808) 947-7002
Toll-Free: 1-866-406-2782
www.aquaresorts.com

Note: AAA 3-Diamond-rated hotel located one block from Waikiki Beach.

Hilton Hawaiian Village Resort & Spa

2005 Kalia Road
Honolulu, HI 96815
Phone: (808) 949-4321
Fax: (808) 951-5458
Toll-Free: 1-800-345-6565
www.hiltonhawaiianvillage.com

Note: On twenty-two oceanfront acres, this resort boasts beautiful tropical gardens, waterfalls, exotic wildlife, and priceless artwork. Over twenty restaurants and lounges onsite.

On-Site Hospitality:

Nothing formal, just the beauty and majesty of the Hawaiian surroundings.

Travel Packages:

If you are going to travel to this event, I would recommend using a reliable company to work with you on making the necessary arrangements. The suppliers listed in this book have solid references and are by far the most trusted in the business. Below are some of the organizations to try for this Top 100 Must See Sporting Event.

Premiere Corporate Events

14 Penn Plaza, Suite 925
New York, NY 10122
Phone: (212) 695-9480
Fax: (212) 564-8098
Toll-Free: 1-877-621-5243
E-mail: requests@tseworld.com
www.tseworld.com
www.pcevents.com

Premiere Sports Travel

201 Shannon Oaks Circle, Suite 205
Cary, NC 27511
Phone: (919) 481-9511
Fax: (919) 481-1337
Toll-Free: 1-800-924-9993
E-mail: sales@sportstravel.com
www.sportstravel.com

Dining:

Pizza Bob's

Haleiwa Shopping Plaza
66-145 Kamehameha Highway
Haleiwa, HI 96712
Phone: (808) 637-5095

Note: In the heart of old-town Haleiwa, this restaurant serves fresh, non-greasy pizzas with large toppings over a hand-tossed crust.

Kua Aina Sandwich Shop

66-160 Kamehameha Highway
Haleiwa, HI 96712
Phone: (808) 637-6067

Note: Locals consider this the place for the best burgers in Hawaii.

Jameson's by the Sea

62-540 Kamehameha Highway
Haleiwa, HI 96712
Phone: (808) 637-6272

Note: The menu features sashimi, fried calamari, and mahi mahi. Dine on rattan furniture while listening to the music of Hawaii.

Haleiwa Café
66-460 Kamehameha Highway
Haleiwa, HI 96712
Phone: (808) 637-5516
Note: An affordable option and great meal for the budget-conscious diner.

Haleiwa Joe's
66-011 Kamehameha Highway
Haleiwa, HI 96712
Phone: (808) 637-8005
www.haleiwajoes.com
Note: Down the road from the Pipeline and a great place to get a quick lunch before watching the best surfers in the world compete.

Airport:

Honolulu International Airport
300 Rodgers Boulevard
Honolulu, HI 96819
www.honoluluairport.com

Sports Travel Insider's Edge:

Best way to watch the action:
Avoid the water and experience the Pipeline at its best. Stand on the beach with the throng of Pipeline fanatics as the sand squishes between your toes. You will notice that, at times, the crowd speaks in hushed tones, almost in reverence for the event. But when a surfer emerges from the white, join those fans in loud cheers.

Best place to get up close:
Again, avoid the water. High tide is, in a word, treacherous. Bring binoculars for an up-close look at the waves breaking far from shore. Visually, standing on the beach is as close as you want to get.

Best travel tip:
Staying on the North Shore is not only more convenient, but also less crowded than other parts of the island. After all, you're in Hawaii to relax. And what better way to relax but to take in a swim—when the surf is not up, that is.

Notable Quotes:

"Pipe is the ultimate arena and the Pipeline Masters is the most prestigious title on tour."—Wayne "Rabbit" Bartholomew, ASP President and 1978 World Champion

"This is how it should be. Beautiful day, good waves, and the Hawaiians showing the world what they can do. There's just no other spot like Pipeline."—Gerry Lopez, legendary surfer

Relevant Websites:
www.northshoreoahu.org
www.tseworld.com
www.pcevents.com
www.sportstravel.com
www.premieresports.com

84
AUSTRALIAN OPEN TENNIS TOURNAMENT

Where?
Melbourne Park
Batman Avenue
Melbourne, Australia

When?
In January, actual dates vary each year.

Significance:
As the first and hottest, temperature-wise, of the four Grand Slam tennis tournaments the Australian Open features the best of the best sweating it out in singles, mixed doubles, juniors, and master's competitions. Formerly known as the Australian Championships, the event started in 1905 at the grass courts of Kooyong.

Today, the Australian Open enjoys prominence as the first leg of the Grand Slam, attracting tennis superstars from around the world. However, the tournament hasn't been without its struggles. Remote locations, low prize money, and scheduled dates on Christmas and New Year's Day were not attracting marquee players or fans who wanted to see them.

In 1983, Ivan Lendl, Mats Wilander, and John McEnroe competed in the Australian Open, but only because they were playing the Davis Cup at Kooyong a few days after the Open. Wilander would go on to win that year. A move to Melbourne Park, then Flinders Park, in 1988 put the tournament on a hardcourt and back into prominence. The first year saw attendance rise 90 percent to well over a quarter-million tennis fans watching top tennis stars compete.

Protection from the elements is vital in an Australian climate. The Rod Laver Arena and the Vodafone Arena, the two main courts, have retractable roofs in the event of rain or extreme heat. Nonetheless, an extreme heat policy remains in effect when the thermometer reaches dangerous levels. Today, rain or shine, so to speak, the players compete on a Plexicushion acrylic surface that helps deflect the sun's rays. In Australia, it is both the heat and the humidity.

Who attends?
Tennis fans from all over the world, including many celebrities and famous athletes.

How to get there?
A five-minute drive from Melbourne's CBD. Melbourne Park is separated from the Botanic Gardens by the Yarra River. Two tram stops, route 70, a taxi rank, a river jetty, and two pedestrian bridges link the precinct with the MCG.

Tickets:
For primary ticket access information, consider: www.australianopen.com.

For secondary ticket access, consider:

GoTickets, Inc.
2345 Waukegan Road, Suite 140
Bannockburn, IL 60015-1552
Toll-Free: 1-800-775-1617
Fax: (919) 481-9101
E-mail: sales@gotickets.com
www.gotickets.com

Accommodations:

Bayview on the Park, Melbourne
52 Queens Road
Melbourne, VIC 3004, Australia
Phone: +61 3 9243 9999
Fax: +61 3 9243 9800
www.bayviewhotels.com
Note: Award-winning, four-star hotel in the heart of Melbourne's St. Kilda Road business district. Get in a quick round at Albert Park Lake and Golf Course across the street.

Grand Hyatt, Melbourne
123 Collins Street
Melbourne, VIC 3000, Australia
Phone: +61 3 9657 1234
Fax: +61 3 9650 3491
www.melbourne.grand.hyatt.com
Note: Walking distance to many tourist attractions and a thirty-minute drive from Melbourne Airport.

Hilton on the Park, Melbourne
192 Wellington Parade
East Melbourne, VIC 3002, Australia
Phone: +61 3 9419 2000
Fax: +61 3 9419 2001
www.hilton.com
Note: Features a spa, pool, and gym onsite. Have a drink in the Executive Lounge or sample tapas and wine at the Park Lounge.

Park Hyatt, Melbourne
1 Parliament Square
Melbourne, VIC 3002, Australia
Phone: +61 3 9224 1234
Fax: +61 3 9224 1200
www.melbourne.park.hyatt.com

Note: A beautiful view of a Victorian architecture district and Fitzroy Gardens. Only thirteen minutes from the airport.

The Langham, Melbourne
1 Southgate Avenue
Southbank, VIC 3006, Australia
Phone: +61 3 8696 8888
Fax: +61 3 9690 5889
Melbourne.langhamhotels.com.au
Note: Walking distance to al fresco cafés, restaurants, and boutiques. The onsite Melba Brasseries serves world-famous cuisine.

Sofitel, Melbourne
25 Collins Street
Melbourne, VIC 3000, Australia
Phone: +61 3 9653 0000
Fax: +61 3 9653 7715
www.sofitelmelbourne.com.au
Note: Close to the city's premier shopping, dining, and theater district. Rooms have floor-to-ceiling windows that provide a beautiful view.

On-Site Hospitality:

Garnier Girls Day Breakfast: A tradition at the Australian Open where you can enjoy a champagne breakfast while being surrounded and entertained by celebrities.

Private Dining Marquees: An exclusive and private setting for friends or clients. Your marquee includes an outdoor deck for pre-dinner drinks and a plasma screen to enjoy the Open in the event of rain or extreme heat. Various packages can be purchased, including some that provide all-inclusive food and beverage options.

Travel Packages:
If you are going to travel to this event, I would recommend using a reliable company to work with you on making the necessary arrangements. The suppliers listed in this book have solid references and are by far the most trusted in the business. Below

are some of the organizations to try for this Top 100 Must See Sporting Event.

Premiere Corporate Events
14 Penn Plaza, Suite 925
New York, NY 10122
Phone: (212) 695-9480
Fax: (212) 564-8098
Toll-Free: 1-877-621-5243
E-mail: requests@tseworld.com
www.tseworld.com
www.pcevents.com

Premiere Sports Travel
201 Shannon Oaks Circle, Suite 205
Cary, NC 27511
Phone: (919) 481-9511
Fax: (919) 481-1337
Toll-Free: 1-800-924-9993
E-mail: sales@sportstravel.com
www.sportstravel.com

Dining:

Baristas 101
100 Flinders La
Melbourne, VIC 3000, Australia
Phone: +61 3 9654 4377
Note: Parisian elegance meets old-fashioned appeal. While coffee is the featured attraction, there is a wide range of menu options that includes pizzas, sandwiches, and pastries. Three minutes from the arena.

Fifteen Melbourne
Basement, 115-117 Collins Street
Melbourne, VIC 3000, Australia
Phone: +61 3 86 486 000
www.fifteenmelbourne.com.au
Note: Italian-inspired dishes made with local produce and a wine list featuring 550 selections.

Vue de Monde
Normanby Chambers
430 Little Collins Street
Melbourne, VIC 3000, Australia
Phone: +61 3 9691 3888

Fax: +61 3 9600 4600

www.vuedemonde.com.au

Note: Classic French food includes Strasbourg Foie Gras, black Perigord truffles, and caviar. Enjoy wine from the great European vineyards.

Napier Hotel

210 Napier Street

Fitzroy, VIC 3065, Australia

Phone: +61 3 9419 4240

Note: A great Aussie Pub where you can rub shoulders with the locals over a beer and Bogan Burger.

Rob Roy Hotel

51 Brunswick Street

Fitzroy, VIC 3065, Australia

Phone +61 3 9419 7180

Note: Enjoy live music while relaxing with a late-night drink.

Airport:

Melbourne Airport

Airport Drive

Victoria, VIC 3045, Australia

Phone: +61 3 9297 1600

Fax: +61 3 9297 1886

www.melbourneairport.com.au

Sports Travel Insider's Edge:

Best way to watch the action:

Why suffer through the unpredictable Australian elements if you don't have to? The Private Dining Marquees provide a climate-controlled setting to enjoy the Open. Dinner and drinks are served for you and your friends while you watch from your deck or a plasma screen television.

Best place to get up close:

Rub shoulders with celebrities and tennis stars at the Garnier Girls Day Breakfast. Toast a victory with a glass of champagne that goes down perfectly with breakfast.

Best travel tip:

While the tennis players are competing on a surface that repels heat, the area you will be sitting in may not. If the roof is retracted, be aware of the Australian elements that include extreme heat. Bring the sunscreen.

Notable Quotes:

"You know, it's a great Grand Slam, great facilities, one of the best in the world.... They've been able to maintain great crowds and a great event for us players."—ROGER FEDERER, professional tennis player

"I love, when you come here, you listen to the accent. My whole life, I was watching tennis. It's like, Oh, I want to go to Australia and play the Australian Open. When I'm playing my video game, I'm playing in Australia."—SERENA WILLIAMS, professional tennis player

Relevant Websites:

www.australianopen.com

www.metlinkmelbourne.com.au

www.visitmelbourne.com

www.tickettek.com.au

www.tseworld.com

www.pcevents.com

www.sportstravel.com

www.gotickets.com

www.premieresports.com

85

BASEBALL GAME AT RICKWOOD FIELD IN ALABAMA

Where?

Rickwood Field

1137 2nd Avenue West

Birmingham, AL 35204

When?

Over 200 events from February to October.

Significance:

"America's Oldest Baseball Park" has featured the likes of Babe Ruth, Ty Cobb, "Shoeless" Joe Jackson, Dizzy Dean, Stan "The Man" Musial, Leroy "Satchel" Paige, and Willie Mays playing on the historic ball field. And just think it all started with an Alabama industrialist still in his twenties. When Rick Woodward purchased the Coal Barons, he needed to build a home for his acquisition. Fueled by a new owner's passion for baseball and $75,000, a staggering $50,000 over budget, Rickwood Field was built in 1910. Baseball fans have responded to that passion with passion of their own, filling Rickwood Field to capacity. The structure and the entire atmosphere hearkens back to a simpler time in baseball. It is intentionally out-of-date and anything but innovative. Call it a "wayback machine" for true baseball fans. Before free agency, multi-million-dollar contracts, and scandals over performance enhancements, Rickwood Field was about one thing. Baseball. Nothing more. Nothing less. It reminds us that while other sports are around and draw their fair share of fans, baseball is and will always be the National Pastime.

Who attends?

Baseball fanatics who want to be a part of continuing baseball history.

How to get there?

Conveniently located off Interstates 59 and 65. Rickwood is west of downtown Birmingham and South of the intersection of 3rd Avenue West and 12th Street West. The field is a couple of miles from Legion Field football stadium.

Tickets:

For primary ticket access information, consider: www.rickwood.com.

For secondary ticket access, consider:

GoTickets, Inc.

2345 Waukegan Road, Suite 140
Bannockburn, IL 60015-1552
Toll-Free: 1-800-775-1617
Fax: (919) 481-9101
E-mail: sales@gotickets.com
www.gotickets.com

Accommodations:

Courtyard Birmingham Downtown

1820 5th Avenue South
Birmingham, AL 35233
Phone: (205) 254-0004
Fax: (205) 254-8001
Toll-Free: 1-800-321-2211
www.marriott.com

Note: In the heart of Birmingham's medical district and just eight minutes from the ballpark. The café serves breakfast, a la carte or buffet, and lunch and dinner.

The Hotel Highland Five Points

1023 20th Street South
Birmingham, AL 35205
Phone: (205) 933-9555
Fax: (205) 933-6918
Toll-Free: 1-800-255-7304
www.thehotelhighland.com

Note: Advertised as the "city's premier luxury boutique hotel" located in the historic Southside of Birmingham. Walking distance to the heart of the entertainment district.

Doubletree Hotel Birmingham

808 20th Street South
Birmingham, AL 35205
Phone: (205) 933-9000
Fax: (205) 933-0920
Toll-Free-1-800-222-TREE
www.doubletree.com

Note: Close to Rickwood, the Alabama Sports Hall of Fame, the Birmingham Zoo, and various museums and theaters.

On-Site Hospitality:

Being an old-school ballpark, there is not much in the way of onsite hospitality except for some typical stadium fare. Just grab a hot dog and enjoy the game.

Travel Packages:

If you are going to travel to this event, I would recommend using a reliable company to work with you on making the necessary arrangements. The suppliers listed in this book have solid references and are by far the most trusted in the business. Below are some of the organizations to try for this Top 100 Must See Sporting Event.

Premiere Corporate Events

14 Penn Plaza, Suite 925
New York, NY 10122
Phone: (212) 695-9480
Fax: (212) 564-8098
Toll-Free: 1-877-621-5243
E-mail: requests@tseworld.com
www.tseworld.com
www.pcevents.com

Premiere Sports Travel

201 Shannon Oaks Circle, Suite 205
Cary, NC 27511
Phone: (919) 481-9511
Fax: (919) 481-1337
Toll-Free: 1-800-924-9993
E-mail: sales@sportstravel.com
www.sportstravel.com

Dining:

Cobb Lane Restaurant

1 Cobb Lane South
Birmingham, AL 35205
Phone: (205) 933-0462
www.birminghammenus.com/cobblane

Note: Enjoy year-round outdoor dining in a heated tent or indoors in a European style dining room. Favorites include She-Crab Soup and Chicken Divan.

Cosmos South Side Pizza

2012 Magnolia Avenue
Birmingham, AL 35205
Phone: (205) 930-9971
www.cosmossouthside.com

Note: Boasting pizza ingredients "from the simple to the sublime." A full bar is available as well.

Five Points Grill

1035 20th Street South
Birmingham, AL 35205
Phone: (205) 933-6363
www.birminghammenus.com/5ptsgrill

Note: Restaurant and bar that serves delicious Saturday and Sunday brunches. Enjoy nighttime entertainment.

Millie's and Billy's Square One

2012 Magnolia Avenue, Suite R1
Birmingham, AL 35205
Phone: (205) 365-3958
www.milliesandbillyssquare1.net

Note: Traditional supper club for fine dining and live entertainment. Enjoy a variety of appetizers, salads, soups, and entrées.

Ocean

1218 20th Street South
Birmingham, AL 35205
Phone: (205) 933-0999
www.birminghammenus.com/ocean

Note: Fresh seafood served in a restaurant that has received a four-star rating from the Birmingham News and an AAA-Four Diamond/Four Star Award.

La Mesa Grill and Cantina

1101 20th Street South
Birmingham, AL 35205
Phone: (205) 933-1544
www.enjoylamesa.com

Note: Family-style atmosphere with traditional Spanish cuisine and unique cocktails.

Airport:

Birmingham International Airport
5900 Airport Highway
Birmingham, AL 35212
Phone: (205) 595-0533
www.bhamintlairport.com

Sports Travel Insider's Edge:

Best way to watch the action:
While the Birmingham Barons are considered the main attraction, they only play one game a year after leaving in 1987. Over 200 games and numerous tournaments are still played by high schools, Miles College, and summer and men's amateur baseball leagues. High school summer ball, in particular, is a showcase event and rivals the excitement of their minor league counterparts. Tickets are open to the public and free of charge for most events.

Best place to get up close:
Two hundred dates may be on the park's calendar, but that should not prevent you from renting Rickwood to bring your team members or fellow employees together for a game. Be a part of Rickwood history. Costs are probably less than you think but will vary depending on the date you book.

Best travel tip:
If you've already visited Rickwood, you're already in a sports mood. Visit the Alabama Sports Hall of Fame nearby. Around 5,000 sports artifacts are displayed in the 33,000 square foot building. Past inductees include baseball legends Hank Aaron and Willie Mays.

While they do not currently call Rickwood home, former tenants the Birmingham Barons play home games not too far from the stadium. Visit www.barons.com for more information and game dates.

Notable Quotes:

"I love everything about Rickwood. Just the smell of this ballpark is different than the others. You can smell the hot dogs here and you don't get that anywhere else. You can really feel the energy of the park."
—B. J. LaMura, minor league pitcher

"You can have those new fields with artificial turf and sky boxes. This is a ball park! You need the sun and the wind in your face. To me, Rickwood is a one of a kind place."—Donnie Harris, former centerfielder for the Black Barons

Relevant Websites:
www.rickwood.com
www.birminghamal.org
www.tseworld.com
www.pcevents.com
www.sportstravel.com
www.gotickets.com
www.premieresports.com

86
HARLEM GLOBETROTTERS PERFORMANCE

Where?
Anywhere in the world in over 300 arenas annually. Find out for yourself at www.harlemglobetrotters.com to find the location nearest you.

When?
Between December 26 and mid-April across North America, and internationally from May to November.

Significance:
Who can hear the strains of the song "Sweet Georgia Brown" and not think of the "Ambassadors of Goodwill," a.k.a. the Harlem Globetrotters? They are more than an Amer-

ican icon. They are American and have been immortalized into mainstream media. They have vanquished their hated foes around the world, solved mysteries with Scooby-Doo, morphed into superheroes on their own Saturday morning cartoon show, and even paid a visit to Gilligan's Island.

While some institutions come and go, the Harlem Globetrotters remain to entertain the masses worldwide with hustle, humor, and hijinks. The Globetrotters are an exhibition basketball team combining amazing athleticism with a vaudevillian comic style. Their total audience encompasses well over 125 million Globetrotter fans in 118 countries. The Trotter faithful cheer them on as they face their faux foes, the Washington Generals, a "basketball team" known for consistently losing games and their basketball shorts. They have also competed against other "teams" organized by Red Klotz. Interestingly enough, those teams boasted a similar roster as the Generals. Those included the Boston Shamrocks, New Jersey Reds, Baltimore Rockets, and the Atlantic City Seagulls.

Who attends?

While families make up the core audience at Globetrotter games, the team attracts fans of all ages. Typically, parents or grandparents who were fans of "Meadowlark," "Curly," and "Geese" bring their kids and grandchildren to the games.

History

In the 1920s, a group of Wendell Phillips High School basketball players from the South Side of Chicago formed the Savoy Big Five. They were considered one of the headline attractions when the Savoy Ballroom opened in November of 1927. By 1928, a dispute over bringing back former players resulted in certain members of the roster leaving. Led by Tommy Brookins, the newly formed "Globe Trotters" toured southern Illinois throughout the spring.

In 1929, Abe Saperstein discovered the team and renamed them "The New York Harlem Globe Trotters." Saperstein selected Harlem as their "hometown" because of the association with African-American culture and to give the Trotters a certain mystique as the "away team." Ironically, it would not be until 1968 that the Globetrotters would actually play a "home game" in Harlem.

The Globetrotters initially took their basketball seriously. Commanding leads over the opposition would bring out the entertainment and comedy, but their talent brought them success in those early days. Defeating The Minneapolis Lakers in 1948 and 1949 turned heads because those wins came prior to the NBA breaking the color line. By 1950, African-American players were allowed into the league, affecting the Globetrotters' ability to attract and keep top-tier talent. Comedy became more of a staple of a Globetrotter game, combining their coordination with amazing shots. And who can forget the famous ball spinning on a Globetrotter's fingertip?

Notable Athletes:

Albert "Runt" Pullins
Tony Peyton
George "Meadowlark" Lemon
Fred "Curly" Neal
Wilt "The Stilt" Chamberlain
Connie "The Hawk" Hawkins
Nat "Sweetwater" Clifton
Marques Haynes
Jerome James
John Chaney
Reece "Goose" Tatum
Hubert "Geese" Ausbie
Bob Gibson
Ferguson Jenkins
Lynette Woodard
Joyce Walker

Records:

The Globetrotters boast well over 22,000 victories with a winning percentage of over 98 percent. A few losses have come their way throughout their existence, including:

The Washington Generals, 1962
The New Jersey Reds, January 5, 1971
Kareem Abdul-Jabbar's All-Star Team, September 12, 1995
Michigan State University, November 13, 2000
UTEP Miners, November 15, 2003
NABC College All-Stars, March 31, 2006

Traditions/Opening Ceremony:

When the "Magic Circle" commences with "Sweet Georgia Brown" playing in the background, you know the Globetrotters are ready to play. While they work as a team in that famed circle, each player is allowed to show off their unique individual skills.

Tickets:

For primary ticket access information, consider: www.harlemglobetrotters.com.

For secondary ticket access, consider:

GoTickets, Inc.
2345 Waukegan Road, Suite 140
Bannockburn, IL 60015-1552
Toll-Free: 1-800-775-1617
Fax: (919) 481-9101
E-mail: sales@gotickets.com
www.gotickets.com

Travel Packages:

If you are going to travel to this event, I would recommend using a reliable company to work with you on making the necessary arrangements. The suppliers listed in this book have solid references and are by far the most trusted in the business. Below are some of the organizations to try for this Top 100 Must See Sporting Event.

Premiere Corporate Events

14 Penn Plaza, Suite 925
New York, NY 10122
Phone: (212) 695-9480
Fax: (212) 564-8098
Toll-Free: 1-877-621-5243
E-mail: requests@tseworld.com
www.tseworld.com
www.pcevents.com

Premiere Sports Travel
201 Shannon Oaks Circle, Suite 205
Cary, NC 27511
Phone: (919) 481-9511
Fax: (919) 481-1337
Toll-Free: 1-800-924-9993
E-mail: sales@sportstravel.com
www.sportstravel.com

Sports Travel Insider's Edge:

Best way to watch the action:
Attending a Harlem Globetrotter game courtside truly gives new meaning to "up close and personal." Fans not only become part of the game, but they can also be covered in water—or is it confetti?—before the final buzzer sounds.

Best place to get up close:
Get your tickets early and be ready for a Globetrotter to pull you out of your seat to give them a helping hand against those hated Generals.

Notable Quote:

"And let me say this, you look at the ballplayers in the NBA that are standout players. How many standout players do you have in the NBA? You hear about Michael Jordan. You know why you hear about Michael Jordan. Michael Jordan plays Harlem Globetrotters type of basketball. We are role models. When you come to a Globetrotters game, the parents know that they're going to see a lot of exceptional basketball players. They know they're going to see sportsmanship and they know their kids are going to be watching a group of guys who are gonna be out there smiling, and having a great time. That's what sports is supposed to be all about. It's entertainment. It's supposed to be joy and fun. To be honest with you, we are the only basketball team that's still upholding those values. That's why we are known as Ambassadors of Goodwill."—BILLY RAY HOBLEY, former Harlem Globetrotter

Relevant Websites:

www.harlemglobetrotters.com
www.tseworld.com
www.pcevents.com
www.sportstravel.com
www.gotickets.com
www.ticketmaster.com
www.premieresports.com

87

SPRING TRAINING GAME AT TIGERTOWN

Where?
Joker Marchant Stadium
2301 Lakeland Hills Boulevard
Lakeland, FL 33805

When?
February and March, traditional spring training time for Tigers Baseball.

Significance:
Some major league baseball teams jump to different locations, or leverage their influence to get better digs. Not the Detroit Tigers. They have made Joker Marchant Stadium their home since 1965, the longest tenure of any team. Marchant Stadium is named for the late Joker Marchant, a former Lakeland parks and recreation director. There have been modifications over the years that increased the capacity to 8,500.

Lights were added in 1972, and a food and picnic court was added in 1994. Today, Marchant boasts new seats and improved seating for disabled fans, along with six luxury suites.

Tigertown is not far from Marchant. It includes a three-story dormitory that houses 190 players and coaches. Renovations in 1993 added an administrative building, a cafeteria, and a recreation center. When the Tigers are not working out the kinks of a winter layoff, the facility is the regular season home, since 1953, of the Class A Florida State League Lakeland Tigers.

Yet no matter how many alterations and additions are made to the structure or its surroundings, this is a place of baseball history. Marchant and Tigertown are where Al Kaline, Kirk Gibson, and other Tiger legends once prepared for the upcoming season.

Who attends?
Rabid and real Tiger baseball fans who simply cannot wait until Opening Day to watch their favorites take the field.

How to get there?

From Orlando:
I-4 West to Exit 33 South Lakeland. Follow the signs to the stadium, which is located 1.5 miles on the left.

From Tampa:
Exit 18, then right onto 98 North to Griffin. The stadium is located point-five miles down on the left.

From Winter Haven:
92 to Lakeland Hills Boulevard. Turn right. The stadium is located two miles down on the right.

Tickets:
For primary ticket access information, consider: www.mlb.com/springtraining.

For secondary ticket access, consider:

GoTickets, Inc.
2345 Waukegan Road, Suite 140
Bannockburn, IL 60015-1552
Toll-Free: 1-800-775-1617
Fax: (919) 481-9101
E-mail: sales@gotickets.com
www.gotickets.com

Accommodations:

Sleeps Inn and Suite
4321 Lakeland Park Drive
Lakeland, FL 33809
Phone: (863) 577-1170
Fax: (863) 577-1180
Toll-Free: 1-800-4-CHOICE
www.sleepinn.com

Note: Located four minutes from Marchant and near other attractions, including the Florida State Fairgrounds, the Florida Strawberry Festival, and the USA International Speedway.

Crestwood Suites Lakeland
4360 Lakeland Park Drive
Lakeland, FL 33809
Phone: (863) 904-2050
Fax: (863) 904-2051
www.crestwoodsuites.com

Note: Spacious rooms with great amenities, including a large LCD wall-mounted flat-panel TV and high-speed Internet service.

Hampton Inn Lakeland
4420 North Socrum Loop Road
Lakeland, FL 33809
Phone: (863) 816-2525
Fax: (863) 816-2727
Toll-Free: 1-800-426-7866
www.hamptoninnlakeland.com

Note: A mere three minutes from Marchant. The seventy-three-room hotel features an exercise room and an outdoor pool.

Lakeland Terrace Hotel
329 East Main Street
Lakeland, FL 33801

Phone: (863) 688-0800
Fax: (863) 688-0664
Toll-Free: 1-888-644-8400
www.terracehotel.com

Note: A full-service, luxury hotel with excellent service and accommodations. Considered the centerpiece of downtown Lakeland's rebirth.

On-Site Hospitality:
Beyond and behind first base, you will not just find concession stands, but a concession courtyard. Enjoy all the staples of a ball game.

Travel Packages:
If you are going to travel to this event, I would recommend using a reliable company to work with you on making the necessary arrangements. The suppliers listed in this book have solid references and are by far the most trusted in the business. Below are some of the organizations to try for this Top 100 Must See Sporting Event.

Premiere Corporate Events
14 Penn Plaza, Suite 925
New York, NY 10122
Phone: (212) 695-9480
Fax: (212) 564-8098
Toll-Free: 1-877-621-5243
E-mail: requests@tseworld.com
www.tseworld.com
www.pcevents.com

Premiere Sports Travel
201 Shannon Oaks Circle, Suite 205
Cary, NC 27511
Phone: (919) 481-9511
Fax: (919) 481-1337
Toll-Free: 1-800-924-9993
E-mail: sales@sportstravel.com
www.sportstravel.com

Dining:

Carrabba's Italian Grill
4829 South Florida Avenue
Lakeland, FL 33813

Phone: (863) 646-2518
Fax: (863) 701-0564
www.carrabbas.com

Note: Enjoy crispy calamari, chicken marsala, tender filet, unique pasta dishes, seafood, and handmade pizzas.

Louie Mack's Steakhouse

5700 South Florida Avenue
Lakeland, FL 33813
Phone: (863) 619-6500
Fax: (863) 619-6511
www.lmsteakhouse.com

Note: Upscale restaurant serving the finest aged USDA prime cuts of steak and the freshest fish in Polk County.

Harry's Seafood Bar and Grille

101 North Kentucky Avenue
Lakeland, FL 33801
Phone: (863) 686-2228
www.hookedonharrys.com

Note: With its origins as a seafood market, you know you will get the freshest fish around. Committed to quality and customer service.

Airports:

Tampa Bay Airport (forty-one miles from Lakeland)
5503 West Spruce Street
Tampa, FL 33607
Phone: (813) 870-8700
www.tampaairport.com

Orlando International Airport (fifty miles from Lakeland)
1 Airport Boulevard
Orlando, FL 32827
Phone: (407) 825-2001
www.orlandoairports.net

Sports Travel Insider's Edge:

Best way to watch the action:
The first three rows of seating between the dugouts are now fifteen feet closer to home plate. Essentially, you will be sitting closer to the game than the actual players residing in the dugout.

Best place to get up close:
Renovations replaced the old Tigers bullpen with 265 new seats behind first base. Those seats are so close that a screen was erected to protect fans from balls thrown over the first baseman's head.

Best travel tip:
You may see some "dinosaurs" milling about at Marchant, but why not check out the real thing? Dinosaur World in nearby Plant City has over 150 life-sized dinosaurs displayed outdoors in a natural environment. You can participate in the Fossil Dig and uncover a skeleton in the Boneyard.

Notable Quote:

"You exit the ever-busy Interstate 4 and begin the short drive south along Lakeland Hills Boulevard, past the obligatory Waffle House and the hole-in-the-wall saloon with three pickups parked out front, toward the idyllic baseball field where, legend has it, late one evening in the spring of '76 Mark 'The Bird' Fidrych jumped the fence and celebrated his making the team with an amorous young lady on the pitcher's mound."—JIM HAWKINS, *Oakland Press*

Relevant Websites:

www.detroit.tigers.mlb.com
www.lakelandgov.net
www.tseworld.com
www.pcevents.com
www.sportstravel.com
www.gotickets.com
www.ticketmaster.com
www.premieresports.com

88

BACKYARD BRAWL
IN MORGANTOWN

Where?

Milan Puskar Stadium
Law Drive
Morgantown, WV 26506

When?

In Morgantown this one happens every other year in late November or early December. Some games have occurred on Thanksgiving Day.

Significance:

When the University of Pittsburgh Panthers meet the West Virginia University Mountaineers, a literal "Backyard Brawl" ensues. One of the oldest and most intense college football rivalries in the United States began in 1895. As with many other gridiron grudges, the main cause of the tension is proximity. Seventy miles separate schools that often vie for the same recruits. These recruits are worth fighting over. They are true blue-chippers as approximately 400 have gone on to the National Football League with nearly thirty of them being first-round draft picks.

Pitt can claim more victories, but the Mountaineers have had their share of wins. During the 2007 "Brawl," the Panthers upset the Mountaineers by knocking them out of the BCS National Championship Game. It was the biggest upset for the Panthers and the "Game of the Year" after the votes were tallied by ESPNU. And it did nothing to quell the tension between these two neighboring schools.

Who attends?

Thousands of screaming Mountaineer and Panther fans hoping their team wins the backyard brawl.

Tickets:

For primary ticket access information, consider: www.pittsburghpanthers.com or www.wvugame.com.

For secondary ticket access, consider:

GoTickets, Inc.

2345 Waukegan Road, Suite 140
Bannockburn, IL 60015-1552
Toll-Free: 1-800-775-1617
Fax: (919) 481-9101
E-mail: sales@gotickets.com
www.gotickets.com

Accommodations:

Euro Suites

501 Chestnut Ridge Road
Morgantown, WV 26505
Phone: (304) 598-1000
Fax: (304) 599-2736
Toll-Free: 1-800-6-SUITES
www.euro-suites.com

Note: Walking distance to the stadium with comfortable rooms, and, of course, Southern hospitality.

Hampton Inn Morgantown

1053 Van Voorhis Road
Morgantown, WV 26505
Phone: (304) 599-1200
Fax: (304) 598-7331
Toll-Free: 1-800-HAMPTON
www.hamptoninn.com

Note: A great view of the mountains of West Virginia. Minutes from outdoor activities such as fishing and rafting. Also close to unique shops, restaurants, and a theater.

Historic Clarion Hotel Morgantown

127 High Street
Morgantown, WV 26505
Phone: (304) 292-8200
Fax: 1-888-241-7944
www.clarionhotel.com

Note: Located near WVU and the Morgantown

Municipal Airport. Close to the shops at
Mountaineer Mall and Morgantown Mall.

Quality Inn Morgantown
1400 Saratoga Avenue
Morgantown, WV 26505
Phone: (304) 599-1680
Fax: (304) 598-0989
Toll-Free: 1-800-424-6423
www.qualityinn.com

*Note: Walking distance from WVU and a
short drive to Coopers Rock State Forest,
Cheat Lake, and Forks of Cheat Winery.*

On-Site Hospitality:
Who has time for onsite hospitality when
you should be enjoying the type of "brawl"
that only happens once a year? Plenty of
tailgating goes on around the stadium prior
to this one. It's extra special the closer it falls
near Thanksgiving.

Travel Packages:
If you are going to travel to this event, I
would recommend using a reliable company to work with you on making the necessary arrangements. The suppliers listed in
this book have solid references and are by
far the most trusted in the business. Below
are some of the organizations to try for this
Top 100 Must See Sporting Event.

Premiere Corporate Events
14 Penn Plaza, Suite 925
New York, NY 10122
Phone: (212) 695-9480
Fax: (212) 564-8098
Toll-Free: 1-877-621-5243
E-mail: requests@tseworld.com
www.tseworld.com
www.pcevents.com

Premiere Sports Travel
201 Shannon Oaks Circle, Suite 205
Cary, NC 27511
Phone: (919) 481-9511
Fax: (919) 481-1337

Toll-Free: 1-800-924-9993
E-mail: sales@sportstravel.com
www.sportstravel.com

Premiere College Sports (Powered by Dodd's Athletic Tours)
308 South Neil
Champaign, IL 61820
Phone: (217) 373-5067
Fax: (217) 398-1313
Toll-Free: 1-800-553-5527
www.doddsathletictours.com
www.collegesportstravel.com

Dining:

Chic 'n Bones Rhythm Café
444 Chestnut Street
Morgantown, WV 26505
Phone: (304) 291-5060

*Note: You will find other Mountaineer fans
for a drink before and after the game at this
Morgantown hangout.*

West Virginia Brewing Company
1291 University Avenue
Morgantown, WV 26505
Phone: (304) 296-BREW

*Note: This local pub brews its own and is only
1.5 miles from the stadium.*

Boston Beanery Restaurant
321 High Street
Morgantown, WV 26505
Phone: (304) 292-0165
Fax: (304) 296-1253
www.bostonbeanery.com

*Note: Grilled sandwiches, hand-battered
seafood, steaks, and chicken are on the menu.
Relaxing environment for the entire family.*

Blue Moose Café
248 Walnut Street
Morgantown, WV 26505
Phone: (304) 292-8999
www.thebluemoosecafe.com

Note: Serving rich gourmet coffee and tea to

go with a bagel, pastry, or a vegetarian meal at lunch.

Maxwell's

1 Wall Street
Morgantown, WV 26505
Phone: (304) 292-0982
www.eatatmaxwells.com

Note: A Morgantown institution for over twenty years. Try their famous and plentiful Sunday brunch after the game.

Madeleine's

140 High Street
Morgantown, WV 26505-5413
Phone: (866) 466-5950
www.madeleinesrestaurantwv.com

Note: Made-from-scratch dishes and great salads in a kid-friendly environment with eclectic artwork adorning the walls.

Airport:

Morgantown Municipal Airport-Walter L. Bill Hart Field
100 Hart Field Road
Morgantown, WV 26505
Phone: (304) 291-7461, Ext.10
www.morgantownairport.com

Sports Travel Insider's Edge:

Best way to watch the action:
Any one of the ten field suites or 648 club seats will set you back a few dollars, but the view is hard to resist. The north end zone or first level of the press box provides great locations to watch the game. Simply put, there is not a bad seat in this stadium.

Best place to get up close:
First, if you can get up close, do not wear a Pitt shirt. The fans are friendly, but they do have their limits. Thanksgiving-time themed tailgating is a main attraction and longtime tradition in Morgantown. Most of the tailgating takes place in the parking lots around the stadium.

Best travel tip:
As the "Best Small City in the Nation," according to bizjournals.com, Morgantown is a "must see." Main Street has over seventy retail stores and thirty plus restaurants, bars, and cafés. You will not find many chain restaurants, but more unique places featuring an eclectic mix along the street. In addition, the Monongahela "Mon" River is the perfect setting for walking, jogging, or biking.

Notable Quotes:

"Some rivalries might be more publicized than this one, but none has more tradition than the Backyard Brawl."—RYAN MUNDY, former West Virginia safety

"When you talk about the rivalry between Pitt and West Virginia, it is a historic game. It is almost like the Hatfields and McCoys. I don't hate Pitt, but I don't like them, either."—DARYL TALLEY, WVU consensus All-American linebacker and fourteen-year NFL veteran

"Their [West Virginia's] fans just hated us with a passion. The night before that [1979] game, out in the parking lot at the hotel, people were making noise till four in the morning. They were partying, yelling...anything they could do to try to disturb us."—ESPN's MARK MAY, former member of the Pitt Panthers and Washington Redskins

Relevant Websites:

www.morgantown.com
www.wvu.edu
www.pitt.edu
pittsburghpanthers.cstv.com
www.wvugame.com
www.tseworld.com
www.pcevents.com
www.sportstravel.com
www.gotickets.com
www.premieresports.com

89

LONDON MARATHON

Where?

London, England

When?

Every year during April.

Significance:

In 1979, hours after having run the New York Marathon, the former Olympic champion Chris Brasher wrote an article for *The Observer* which began, "To believe this story you must believe that the human race be one joyous family, working together, laughing together, achieving the impossible. Last Sunday, in one of the most trouble-stricken cities in the world, 11,532 men and women from forty countries in the world, assisted by over a million black, white, and yellow people, laughed, cheered, and suffered during the greatest folk festival the world has seen." Enchanted with the sight of people coming together for such an occasion, he concluded questioning "...whether London could stage such a festival?"

Within months the London Marathon was born, with Brasher making trips to America to study the race organization and finance of big city marathons such as New York and Boston, the oldest in the world. He secured a contract with Gillette of £50,000, established the organization's charitable status, and set down six main aims for the event, which he not only hoped would echo the scenes he had witnessed in New York, but also put Britain firmly on the map as a country capable of organizing major events.

His vision was realized on March 29, 1981, with the inaugural London Marathon proving to be an instant success. More than 20,000 people applied to run: 7,747 were accepted and 6,255 crossed the finish line on Constitution Hill as cheering crowds lined the route. Since this time the event has continued to grow in size, stature, and popularity with a capacity 46,500 accepted entrants each year. In all, a total of 676,743 have completed the race since its inception with a then record 35,674 crossing the line in 2007.

Who attends?

Anyone who loves to have a great time while watching some of the world's best runners compete!

Tickets:

The only tickets you need are the ones to get you on the trains!

Accommodations:

Note that listed hotels are along the running route:

Clarendon Hotel

8-16 Montpelier Row
London, SE3 0RW, U.K.
Phone: +44 (0)20 8318 4321
Fax: +44 (0)20 8318 4378
www.clarendonhotel.com

Note: Since the 18th century, this historic hotel is popular with locals and visitors who want a place to relax, eat, and drink.

Chamberlain Hotel

130-135 Minories
London, EC3N 1NU, U.K.
Phone: +44 (0)20 7680 1500
Fax:+44 (0)20 7702 2500
www.thechamberlainhotel.com

Note: Onsite restaurant and pub with fine dining that serves some of the best ale you will find in the city. Close to the Tower Bridge and popular tourist attractions.

Mad Hatter Hotel

3-7 Stamford Street
London, SE1 9NY, U.K.
Phone: +44 (0)20 7401 9222
Fax: +44 (0)20 7401 7111
www.fullershotels.com

Note: A twentieth-century hotel behind a nineteenth-century London façade. Not far from the Borough, a well-known place to those devotees of Shakespeare and Dickens.

Sanctuary House Hotel
33 Tothill Street
London, SW1H 9LA, U.K.
Phone: +44 (0)20 7799 4044
Fax: +44 (0)20 7799 3657
www.fullershotels.com

Note: Historic sites close by include Westminster Abbey, the Houses of Parliament, and Buckingham Palace. Relax at the onsite Fuller's Ale & Pie House on the ground floor.

On-Site Hospitality:
You cannot avoid seeing a pub along the 26.2-mile path that the runners take. There are more than eighty of them with most offering marathon-related activities for their patrons. You can easily find those pubs, as they will be displaying the banners and balloons supplied by marathon organizers. Live music from over sixty bands can be found at any point along the route. Let the runners have their water while you enjoy a pint. Though many runners enjoy a pint too.

Travel Packages:
If you are going to travel to this event, I would recommend using a reliable company to work with you on making the necessary arrangements. The suppliers listed in this book have solid references and are by far the most trusted in the business. Below are some of the organizations to try for this Top 100 Must See Sporting Event.

Premiere Corporate Events
14 Penn Plaza, Suite 925
New York, NY 10122
Phone: (212) 695-9480
Fax: (212) 564-8098
Toll-Free: 1-877-621-5243
E-mail: requests@tseworld.com

www.tseworld.com
www.pcevents.com

Premiere Sports Travel
201 Shannon Oaks Circle, Suite 205
Cary, NC 27511
Phone: (919) 481-9511
Fax: (919) 481-1337
Toll-Free: 1-800-924-9993
E-mail: sales@sportstravel.com
www.sportstravel.com

Marathon Tours
261 Main Street
Boston, MA 02129
Toll-Free: 1-800-444-4097
Fax: (617) 242-7686
E-mail: info@marathontour.com
www.marathontour.com

Dining:
Note that the restaurants and pubs listed below are along the running route:

The Pilot
68 River Way
Greenwich, London SE10 0BE, U.K.
Phone: +44 (0)20 8858 5910

Note: Friendly service and affordable drinks, not to mention a beautiful beer garden. Considered one of the best-kept secrets in Greenwich.

The Moby Dick Pub
6 Russel Place, Surrey Quays
Rotherhithe, London SE16 7PL, U.K.
Phone: +44 (0)20 7231 6719
www.mobydickpub.co.uk

Note: The dining area features a stainless-steel table that seats eight. Enjoy a pint or a cup of coffee as you surf the Internet free. Great breakfasts served daily and a beer garden to enjoy in the summer.

Blacksmith Arms
257 Rotherhithe Street
London, SE16 5EJ, U.K.

Phone: +44 (0)20 7237 1349

Note: Some of the best Thai food and ale in the area. Professional service in a place with character.

Leather Exchange

15 Leathermarket Street
London, SE1 3HN, U.K.
Phone: +44 (0)20 7407 0295
www.theleatherexchange.co.uk

Note: A contemporary and cozy atmosphere greets guests. Friendly service and great food that includes ciabattas, salads, and gourmet burgers.

Cat and Canary

1-24 Fisherman's Walk
Canary Wharf, London, U.K.
Phone: +44 (0)20 7512 9187

Note: A historic London venue that has been able to maintain its original charm while keeping up with the times.

Fine Line

10-30 Fisherman's Walk
Canary Wharf, London E14 4DH, U.K.
Phone: +44 (0)20 7513 0255

Note: Surrounded by a sophisticated development area, you can enjoy a cold one and a view of the waterfront.

The Mint

12 East Smithfield
Tower Hill, London, EC3N 4QN, U.K.
Phone: +44 (0)20 7702 0370

Note: Authentic Thai food in a restaurant that can host private functions of up to fifty people. If the weather cooperates, more can be seated in the garden.

Hung, Drawn & Quartered

27 Great Tower Street
London, EC3R 5AQ, U.K.
Phone: +44 (0)20 7626 6123

Note: Traditional English menu items to eat while enjoying the telly.

The Banker

2 Cousin Lane
London, EC4R 3TE, U.K.
Phone: +44 (0)20 7283 5206

Note: Excellent views with seating along the river. Get in a few games of pool, but be aware marathon day draws large crowds.

The Ship

68 Borough Road
London, SE1 1DX, U.K.
Phone: +44 (0)20 7403 7059

Note: Great English dishes to enjoy while watching Sky Sports or in between dart games.

Airport:

Heathrow Airport (LHR)

234 Bath Road
Hayes, Middlesex, UB3 5AP, U.K.
www.heathrowairport.com

Sports Travel Insider's Edge:

Best way to watch the action:

The marathon crowd is constantly in motion. Most fans want to see the runners at more than one point. You should too. Travel light, wear comfortable clothes, especially shoes for walking, and make sure you have a map of the marathon route. Be prepared for road closures and large crowds as you move around London.

Best place to get up close:

There are two official cheering points, one is the Millwall Park and the other is the Tower Bridge at Marsh Plaza. Help cheer on the runners at these two locations, which are set up nicely for the occasion.

Best travel tip:

While the London Marathon makes its own history, you are also in the midst of London history itself. Visit the Tower Bridge, the Borough, Westminster Abbey, the Houses of Parliament, and Buckingham Palace. You do want to make that guard smile, don't you?

Notable Quote:

"The Marathon always has, and always will be, a mystical event. I have often heard that physiologists have reason to believe that the human body is ideally capable of covering 32k. The final 10k of the Marathon therefore is really testing our energy stores and true worth."—LEE TROOP, runner

Relevant Websites:

www.london-marathon.co.uk
www.visitlondon.com
www.tseworld.com
www.pcevents.com
www.sportstravel.com
www.premieresports.com

90

PENN RELAYS

Where?

Franklin Field
235 South 33rd Street
Philadelphia, PA 19104

When?

The last full week at the end of April, wrapping up on the last Saturday of the month.

Significance:

The Penn Relays, short for the Penn Relays Carnival, hosted by the University of Pennsylvania, is the nation's oldest uninterrupted track and field meet. It brings 15,000 runners from high schools, colleges, and track clubs worldwide. Over several days at the end of April, they compete in 300 events with attendance reaching 100,000 over three days, with 50,000 on that last Saturday.

On April 21, 1895, 5,000 people attended the first Carnival and dedication of Franklin Field. Originally intended for college and high school students, the event has grown to encompass everyone from elementary school runners to those seventy-five years and older in the Masters Division. Many contend that this event popularized the running of relay races by honoring it in a carnival-type, celebratory atmosphere. While everyone has their favorite race, the Penn Relays are about the entire event.

Attendance grows in Olympic years, which is ironic since the event predates the arrival of the modern Olympics by one year. Shoe companies fall over themselves to get their top athletes to show up sporting the latest in their footwear. The advent of corporate sponsorships and television coverage came to pass in 1988, providing the Penn Relays the funding they needed to continue to grow. Yet this is still an event that celebrates amateur athletic achievement, not corporate sponsorship. Participants have gone on to win gold medals in every modern Summer Olympic event, save for the 1980 Moscow games boycotted by the United States.

Who attends?

Over 100,000 track and field enthusiasts with a few family members and friends thrown in to cheer for the competitors.

How to get there?

From the New Jersey Turnpike: Take exit 4 to Whitman Bridge. Take I-76 West to the South Street exit (346A). Turn left at South Street to 33rd Street and take a right. Franklin Field is located on I-295.

From the Pennsylvania Turnpike: Take exit 24 (Valley Forge). Follow I-76 East to the South Street exit (346A). Turn right on South Street and proceed to 33rd Street. Take a right on 33rd Street to Market Street and make a left.

From the South: Follow I-95 North to PA 291 East and follow signs to I-76 West. Take I-76 West to the South Street exit (346A). Turn left onto South Street and proceed to 33rd Street where you will make another right.

Tickets:
For primary ticket access information, consider: www.ComcastTix.com.

For secondary ticket access, consider:

GoTickets, Inc.
2345 Waukegan Road, Suite 140
Bannockburn, IL 60015-1552
Toll-Free: 1-800-775-1617
Fax: (919) 481-9101
E-mail: sales@gotickets.com
www.gotickets.com

Accommodations:

Sofitel Philadelphia
120 South 17th Street
Philadelphia, PA 19103
Phone: (215) 569-8300
Fax: (215) 564-7452
Toll-Free: 1-800-763-4835
www.accorhotels.com

Note: Close to the business district and shops. Conveniently located two blocks from Rittenhouse Square. A seven-minute drive will get you to Franklin Field.

Alexander Inn
301 South 12th Street
Philadelphia, PA 19107
Phone: (215) 923-3535
Toll-Free: 1-877-ALEX-INN
www.alexanderinn.com

Note: A historic building in city center restored into a beautiful seven-story hotel. Located eight minutes from Franklin Field by car.

Sheraton University City Hotel
36th and Chestnut Street
Philadelphia, PA 19104

Phone: (215) 387-8000
Fax: (215) 387-7920
Toll-Free: 1-877-459-1146
www.philadelphiasheraton.com

Note: Located on the University of Pennsylvania campus and within walking distance of Franklin Field.

The Inn at Penn - A Hilton Hotel
3600 Sansom Street
Philadelphia, PA 19104
Phone: (215) 222-0200
Fax: (215) 222-4600
Toll-Free: 1-800-231-4587
www.theinnatpenn.com

Note: AAA Four Diamond-rated hotel located in the heart of the University of Pennsylvania. Close to museums and the Annenberg Theatre. One mile to Franklin Field.

On-Site Hospitality:
Vendors can be found hawking all types of Philly and concession-style food along Walnut Street right outside Franklin Field. Philly cheese steaks anyone?

Travel Packages:
If you are going to travel to this event, I would recommend using a reliable company to work with you on making the necessary arrangements. The suppliers listed in this book have solid references and are by far the most trusted in the business. Below are some of the organizations to try for this Top 100 Must See Sporting Event.

Premiere Corporate Events
14 Penn Plaza, Suite 925
New York, NY 10122
Phone: (212) 695-9480
Fax: (212) 564-8098
Toll-Free: 1-877-621-5243
E-mail: requests@tseworld.com
www.tseworld.com
www.pcevents.com

Premiere Sports Travel
201 Shannon Oaks Circle, Suite 205
Cary, NC 27511
Phone: (919) 481-9511
Fax: (919) 481-1337
Toll-Free: 1-800-924-9993
E-mail: sales@sportstravel.com
www.sportstravel.com

Dining:

Alma de Cuba
1623 Walnut Street
Philadelphia, PA 19103
Phone: (215) 988-1799
Fax: (215) 988-0807
www.almadecubarestaurant.com

Note: If you're in the mood for modern Cuban cuisine, this is the place to go.

Little Fish
600 Catharine Street
Philadelphia, PA 19147
Phone: (215) 413-3464
www.littlefishphilly.com

Note: Boasting sophisticated seafood dishes in a casual atmosphere. BYOB.

The Victor Café
1303 Dickinson Street
Philadelphia, PA 19147
Phone: (215) 468-3040
www.victorcafe.com

Note: Dine while listening to great music.

Airport:

Philadelphia International Airport
International Plaza Drive and Industrial
    Highway
Philadelphia, PA 19153
Phone: (215) 937-6937
www.phl.org

Sports Travel Insider's Edge:

Best way to watch the action:
With Thursday, Friday, and Saturday being ticketed days, you want to place yourself by the finish line in Section ND. The high jump event is on the east side of the stadium, pole-vaulting on the south side by the hurdles, and the long jump on the north side. Be sure to specify which side you would like to sit on when ordering tickets.

Best place to get up close:
School day events for those traveling with high school or middle school students are not only offered a discounted price, but they are also invited to a meet and greet with the organizers. The international presence ramps up on Saturday and there is usually a Jamaican fair. Irie!

Best travel tip:
Take the train right from the airport (R1, R2, or R3) as it drops you right in front of Franklin Field where the action takes place. Prepare to wait in line for security checks. Backpacks or bags larger than 12" x 12" x 12", alcohol, bottles, cans, coolers, fireworks, or any open flames, weapons, noisemakers, and laser pointers are prohibited on Franklin Field. Bags must be smaller than 11" x 17". Food must be in clear plastic bags. Any sealed plastic water bottles or cardboard juice boxes must not be larger than 11" x 17". With all these rules it will make you feel like you're back in high school.

Notable Quotes:

"It's wild and crazy. On my leg, I'll stand in one section and hear cheers and in the next section I hear boos. One moment you're a hero, the next you're a villain. Life is like that. We did a great job and put on a great show. We ran good. It was fun. It feels good that we didn't drop the baton."—JUSTIN GATLIN, sprinter, Olympic gold medalist

"The annual Penn Relay Carnival has not only been America's largest track meet, but the world's first and most recognized relay meet. The presence and prestige of the relays is extremely significant, as the relays are a rite of spring in the Philadelphia community and in the greater track and field world at large. The relays are also the place where track fans gather to see tomorrow's Olympic stars."—jamaicaobserver. com

Relevant Websites:
www.thepennrelays.com
www.gophila.com
www.pennathletics.com
www.ComcastTix.com
www.tseworld.com
www.pcevents.com
www.sportstravel.com
www.gotickets.com
www.premieresports.com

91
PRESIDENTS CUP

When?
September, every other year.

Future Locations:
2009–San Francisco, CA
2011–Melbourne, Australia

Significance:
Every two years, the top male golfers in the United States compete against an International team composed of non-European players representing the best in the world. The Presidents Cup, created and coordinated by the PGA Tour, is not so much about competition as it is about the enjoyment of golf and all-out fun. The event boasts honorary chairmen of certain renown, including past U.S. Presidents and dignitaries from other countries. Proceeds of the event are not doled out in prize money for the participants. The net revenue is distributed to charities chosen by the players, captains, and their assistants.

Members of the U.S. team are selected based on official earnings and golfers from overseas are picked based on their official world golf ranking. Often compared to its much older counterpart, the Ryder Cup, the event shares a similar format with twelve players on each side led by a non-playing captain. The set-up deviates a bit from the Ryder Cup with an extra six matches. All twelve players compete in foursome and four-ball matches on Thursday and Friday, playing six matches per session. Two players sit out each session on Saturday with a schedule of only five matches. On Sunday, each team member competes in a one-on-one singles match. Points are assigned for each victory and half-points are given for a tie. The team that scores 17.5 points or more is declared the winner.

Who attends?
Golf fans who like to watch their country team up and take on some of the world's best golf courses.

History
Non-European golfers have a rare chance to show off their skills in the Presidents Cup. Led by David Graham, they first played the United States Team, captained by Hale Irwin, from September 16–18, 1994, at the Robert Trent Jones Golf Club. The U.S. won by a score of 20–12. Chris DiMarco provided a dramatic ending when he holed a fifteen-foot birdie putt on the 18th hole to put the U.S. up by one point. The teams have traded victories, except for 2003 (the 9/11 attacks pushed the Cup to odd-numbered years), when they tied and decided to share the Cup.

Former U.S. President and avid golfer Gerald Ford served as the Honorary Chairman for the inaugural Cup. 1996 saw

George H. W. Bush, four years out of the White House, chairing the proceedings. History was made at the 2000 event when Bill Clinton became the first sitting President to be Honorary Chairman.

In the end, the winner is not the golfers or which one brings home the largest monetary winnings. The golfers may take home a Cup championship, but the charities are the real champions as their cups runneth over with millions of dollars.

Notable Athletes:

Tiger Woods
Fred Couples
Jack Nicklaus
Ernie Els
Mike Weir
Retief Goosen
Vijay Singh

Traditions:

The only tradition that matters is that the money raised by this event is always donated to different charities worldwide.

Things to know before you go:

Ace: A hole-in-one.
Front nine: The first half of a round of golf.
Back nine: The second half of a round of golf.
Fore: A warning cry to other players that your ball is headed in their direction.
Par: A certain number of shots needed to hole your ball depending on the hole's distance and difficulty.
Birdie: One under par.
Eagle: Two under par.
Albatross: Three under par.
Bogey: One over par. Double and triple bogeys are self-explanatory.

Tickets:

For primary ticket access information, consider: www.pgatour.com.

For secondary ticket access, consider:

GoTickets, Inc.

2345 Waukegan Road, Suite 140
Bannockburn, IL 60015-1552
Toll-Free: 1-800-775-1617
Fax: (919) 481-9101
E-mail: sales@gotickets.com
www.gotickets.com

Travel Packages:

If you are going to travel to this event, I would recommend using a reliable company to work with you on making the necessary arrangements. The suppliers listed in this book have solid references and are by far the most trusted in the business. Below are some of the organizations to try for this Top 100 Must See Sporting Event.

Premiere Corporate Events

14 Penn Plaza, Suite 925
New York, NY 10122
Phone: (212) 695-9480
Fax: (212) 564-8098
Toll-Free: 1-877-621-5243
E-mail: requests@tseworld.com
www.tseworld.com
www.pcevents.com

Premiere Sports Travel

201 Shannon Oaks Circle, Suite 205
Cary, NC 27511
Phone: (919) 481-9511
Fax: (919) 481-1337
Toll-Free: 1-800-924-9993
E-mail: sales@sportstravel.com
www.sportstravel.com

Notable Quotes:

"I think maybe you had to be there to recognize what it meant to the game of golf. People were arm in arm, they were singing as they came away from the greens. Everyone was absolutely ecstatic. I think it was the most special event I have ever been involved with."—JACK NICKLAUS, golfing legend

"I think the great thing about the Presidents Cup… it's played in different parts of the world…. And it's played in different countries and it boosts the golf all over the world, which we like to see. And it's also an opportunity for us as old cooks now to still be able to compete against each other."—GARY PLAYER, golfing legend

Relevant Websites:
www.pgatour.com
www.tseworld.com
www.pcevents.com
www.sportstravel.com
www.gotickets.com
www.premieresports.com

92
WORLD JUNIOR HOCKEY CHAMPIONSHIP

When?
Annually from December to January.

Future Locations:
2009 — Ottawa, Ontario, Canada
2010 — Regina/Saskatoon, Saskatchewan, Canada
2011 — Buffalo, New York
2012 — Calgary/Edmonton, Alberta, Canada

Significance:
The World Junior Hockey Championship (WJHC), known also by its formal yet cumbersome moniker of the International Ice Hockey Federation World Under 20 Championship, is where under-20 ice hockey teams from around the world compete. From late December to early January, the main "Top Division" tournament features the Top 10-ranked hockey nations worldwide as they play for the world championship. Division I, II, and III teams play in separate

tournaments to determine who moves up in the pool and who moves down.

The fact that Canada has been a perennial host for this event is apropos. Hockey is a way of life with five million Canadians involved in the sport at all levels from volunteers to high-level administrators. 1.5 million games are played and another two million practices are held in any one of the 3,000 hockey arenas in Canada. To date, Canada's National Junior Team has won a gold (3), silver (3), or bronze (1) medal at every World Junior Championship held in Canada.

Who attends?
Hardcore hockey fans get to see the professional stars of tomorrow while they are still pups.

History
The first official World Junior Hockey Championship was held in 1977 without much fanfare. At that time, the tournament existed in relative obscurity. Today, it is the premier event on the hockey calendar. Canada, along with the former Soviet Union, have dominated the tournament with the Russians taking the first four titles followed by the Canadians winning five consecutive tournaments from 1993 to 1997 and 2004 to 2008.

The WJHC allows budding hockey players to not only shine, but also increase their value for the NHL Entry Drafts. The tournament serves as a stage with a bright spotlight, featuring the superstars of tomorrow. Names such as Wayne Gretzky and Mario Lemieux cut their teeth on the ice of the WJHC and now reside in the NHL Hall of Fame.

There are moments that the WJHC would like you to forget. One of those infamous historical occasions occurred in 1987 when Canada and the Soviet Union, the two teams that dominated the tournaments, engaged in a massive, bench-clearing brawl. It started when Pavel Kostichkin took a two-handed slash at Theoren Fleury. One player after another left his seat to engage in battle.

For twenty minutes, the fight continued. Even shutting off the arena lights could not stop the violence. When the dust (or steam from the ice) cleared, the International Ice Hockey Federation declared the game null and void and the delegates called an emergency meeting. They voted 7-1 to disqualify both teams from the tournament and the player's banquet following the competition. Canada's Dennis McDonald was the dissenter.

Notable Athletes:

Sidney Crosby, Canada, 2004 and 2005
Joe Thornton, Canada, 1997
Dominik Hasek, Czechoslovakia, 1984
Sergei Fedorov, Soviet Union, 1988 and 1989
Doug Gilmour, Canada, 1983
Steve Yzerman, Canada, 1983
Jarome Iginla, Canada, 1996
Roberto Luongo, Canada, 1999
Alexander Ovechkin, Russia, 2005

Most Decorated Countries (to date):

Canada: 24 medals, including 14 Gold, 6 Silver, and 4 Bronze
Soviet Union: 13 medals, including 8 Gold, 3 Silver, and 2 Bronze
Russia: 13 medals, including 3 Gold, 6 Silver, and 4 Bronze
Finland: 12 medals, including 2 Gold, 4 Silver, and 6 Bronze
Sweden: 12 medals, including 1 Gold, 7 Silver, and 4 Bronze
Czechoslovakia: 11 medals, including 5 Silver and 6 Bronze

Records:

Most goals scored by a team in a game: Czechoslovakia, 21, 1981

Most goals in one year – player: Markus Naslund, 13, Sweden, 1993
All-time goal scoring leader: Pavel Bure, 27, Soviet Union, 1989 to 1991
All-time assist leader: Peter Forsberg, 32, Sweden, 1992 to 1993

Things to know before you go:

Assist: Awarded to a player that set up a goal and is the last to handle the puck immediately preceding the goal.
Boarding: A violent and illegal check to an opponent into the boards from behind. Considered a penalty.
Changing on the Fly: A player from the bench substitutes for a player on the ice while the clock is running.
Icing: When a player shoots the puck from his side of the red line across the opponent's goal line. Play is stopped when an opponent other than the goalie touches the puck. An infraction unless a team is shorthanded.
Face-Off: Held at the offending team's end of the ice. A team that is shorthanded can ice the puck without being penalized.
Power Play: When one team has more players on the ice than their opponent due to one or more penalties from the opposing team.

Tickets:

Primary ticket access information differs depending upon the country hosting the event.
For secondary ticket access, consider:

GoTickets, Inc.
2345 Waukegan Road, Suite 140
Bannockburn, IL 60015-1552
Toll-Free: 1-800-775-1617
Fax: (919) 481-9101
E-mail: sales@gotickets.com
www.gotickets.com

Travel Packages:

If you are going to travel to this event, I would recommend using a reliable company to work with you on making the necessary arrangements. The suppliers listed in this book have solid references and are by far the most trusted in the business. Below are some of the organizations to try for this Top 100 Must See Sporting Event.

Premiere Corporate Events

14 Penn Plaza, Suite 925
New York, NY 10122
Phone: (212) 695-9480
Fax: (212) 564-8098
Toll-Free: 1-877-621-5243
E-mail: requests@tseworld.com
www.tseworld.com
www.pcevents.com

Premiere Sports Travel

201 Shannon Oaks Circle, Suite 205
Cary, NC 27511
Phone: (919) 481-9511
Fax: (919) 481-1337
Toll-Free: 1-800-924-9993
E-mail: sales@sportstravel.com
www.sportstravel.com

Notable Quotes:

"We worked so hard from Day 1. The scars I will have with me, and this is something I will remember the rest of my life."— JONATHAN TOEWS, Chicago Blackhawks and former Team Canada player

"I've always enjoyed my Hockey Canada experiences and it's the chance of a lifetime to coach a world junior team, especially with it in our back yard in Canada."— PETER DEBOER, Florida Panthers head coach

"People back home might not understand how hard it is to win over here. At the same time, it's been very rewarding. You'd have to win a Stanley Cup to feel like this."—CRAIG HARTSBURG, Team Canada head coach

Relevant Websites:

www.tsn.ca
www.tseworld.com
www.pcevents.com
www.sportstravel.com
www.gotickets.com
www.premieresports.com

93
WESTMINSTER DOG SHOW

Where?

Madison Square Garden
4 Pennsylvania Plaza
New York, NY 10001

When?

One weekend in early February.

Significance:

Once a year, the age-old question of "Who let the dogs out?" is answered. Canine owners from around the world come to Madison Square Garden (MSG) to "unleash" their dogs and put them on display. The Westminster Kennel Club Dog Show is the second-oldest continuous sporting event in America. The Kentucky Derby has it beat by only two years.

In 1877, the Westminster Kennel Club was established, according to their bylaws, "To increase the interest in dogs, and thus improve the breeds, and to hold an Annual Dog Show in the city of New York." Back then, a small group of hunters with an interest in Pointers, Setters, and other sporting dogs met at the Westminster Hotel in New York City. The inaugural event at Gilmore's Gardens (an old railroad depot that would become MSG) focused primarily on Pointers and Setters with the top prize being pearl-handled pistols.

Requirements for entry have changed over the years. Only AKC-registered dogs were allowed starting in 1884, eliminating less-common breeds not recognized by Westminster but acknowledged by other kennel clubs. Over a century later, in 1992, the AKC further restricted entries to dogs recognized as breed champions, qualifying them for competition at Westminster.

Today, the Westminster Kennel Club Dog Show has gained prominence as the second largest and most prestigious dog show in the world with England's Crufts International Show ranking first, as it is a tribute to dogs of all breeds. Television coverage began in 1948 and the event still generates high ratings. 2,500 dogs in over 150 breeds compete in various categories, including Sporting, Hound, Working, Terrier, Toy, Non-Sporting, and Herding. They fill multiple rings during the two-day show to win the coveted Best in Group and the more coveted Best in Show.

The breed with the most Best in Show wins is the Terrier, winning nearly half of the competitions (forty-four to date) since 1907, the first year the prize was awarded.

Who attends?
Who else but dog lovers?

How to get there?
MSG is located on Seventh Avenue between 31st and 33rd Streets. All forms of public transit, from subways to taxis to trains will get you there.

Tickets:
For primary ticket access information, consider: www.thegarden.com or www.ticketmaster.com.

For secondary ticket access, consider:

GoTickets, Inc.
2345 Waukegan Road, Suite 140
Bannockburn, IL 60015-1552
Toll-Free: 1-800-775-1617

Fax: (919) 481-9101
E-mail: sales@gotickets.com
www.gotickets.com

Accommodations:

Hotel New Yorker
481 Eighth Avenue
New York, NY 10001
Phone: (212) 244-0719
Fax: (212) 629-6536
Toll-Free: 1-800-272-6232
www.nyhotel.com
Note: Value hotel in the process of renovation to restore it to its original prominence. Two blocks from MSG.

W Times Square
1567 Broadway
New York, NY 10036
Phone: (212) 930-7400
Toll-Free: 1-877-W-HOTELS
www.whotels.com
Note: Less than a ten-block walk to MSG down 7th Avenue. A small lounge popular with the "hip crowd" can be found on the check-in floor for a quick drink.

Hilton Times Square
234 West 42nd Street
New York, NY 10036
Phone: (212) 840-8222
Toll-Free: 1-877-326-5200
www.hilton.com
Note: The place to stay in New York. Located near Central Park, but still close enough for a walk to MSG on a nice day in the city.

On-Site Hospitality:
All Star Bar: Located at Gate 60
End Court Bar: Between Gates 63 and 64
Food Courts: Located throughout MSG

Travel Packages:
If you are going to travel to this event, I would recommend using a reliable company to work with you on making the neces-

sary arrangements. The suppliers listed in this book have solid references and are by far the most trusted in the business. Below are some of the organizations to try for this Top 100 Must See Sporting Event.

Premiere Corporate Events
14 Penn Plaza, Suite 925
New York, NY 10122
Phone: (212) 695-9480
Fax: (212) 564-8098
Toll-Free: 1-877-621-5243
E-mail: requests@tseworld.com
www.tseworld.com
www.pcevents.com

Premiere Sports Travel
201 Shannon Oaks Circle, Suite 205
Cary, NC 27511
Phone: (919) 481-9511
Fax: (919) 481-1337
Toll-Free: 1-800-924-9993
E-mail: sales@sportstravel.com
www.sportstravel.com

Dining:

Lazzaras Pizza
221 West 38th Street (between 7th and 8th Avenues)
Manhattan, NY 10018
Phone: (212) 944-7792
www.lazzaraspizza.com
Note: Considered by many to be the best pizza in Manhattan. Look closely because it's hard to find in the townhouse-type setting.

Ben's Deli
209 West 38th Street (between 7th and 8th Avenues)
Manhattan, NY 10018
Phone: (212) 398-2367
Fax: (212) 398-3354
www.bensdeli.net
Note: Solid New York style deli food and popular with the Garment Center and MSG neighborhood crowd.

Lugo Café
1 Penn Plaza
New York, NY 10001 (33rd Street between 7th and 8th)
Phone: (212) 760-2700
Fax: (212) 629-6618
www.lugocafe.com
Note: One of the only fine dining options in the neighborhood.

Airports:

LaGuardia Airport (LGA)
Ditmars Boulevard and 94th Street
Flushing, NY 11371
Phone: (718) 533-3400
www.panynj.gov

John F. Kennedy International Airport (JFK)
Jamaica, NY 11430
Phone: (718) 244-4444
www.panynj.gov

Newark Liberty International Airport (EWR)
North Avenue & Spring Street
Elizabeth, NJ 07201
Phone: (973) 961-6000
www.panynj.gov

Sports Travel Insider's Edge:

Best way to watch the action:
Yes, this is Madison Square Garden, the home of raucous basketball games and over-the-top wrestling events. The Westminster Kennel Club Dog Show is a different animal, so to speak. Feel free to cheer on the dogs when they come out, but keep your enthusiasm to yourself during the judging portion.

Best place to get up close:
All tickets provide access to the benching area as seating is first-come, first-serve. Your best bet is to get there early. And while watching it on television seems more convenient, the televised version encapsulates

a two-day event into six hours. You need to be there!

Best travel tip:
With the Westminster Kennel Club Dog Show being a two-day event, surely, you want to stay in New York City longer. A Broadway show will titillate the theater enthusiast while a New York Rangers hockey game will provide for a thrilling sporting event.

Notable Quotes:

"Westminster is like no other show. It's like the Super Bowl where the crowd is revved up and cheering. The dogs also feel the excitement and some dogs will respond to the crowd and turn it on, becoming the ultimate show dog."—BURTON YAMADA, Best in Show judge

"For those 15 minutes in the ring, on that particular day, a dog has to be at its very best, and the handler has to be perfectly on, too."—KRISTIN KLEEMAN, breeder

Relevant Websites:
www.westminsterkennelclub.org
www.nycvisit.com
www.thegarden.com
www.nyc.com
www.tseworld.com
www.pcevents.com
www.sportstravel.com
www.gotickets.com
www.premieresports.com

94

NFL HALL OF FAME INDUCTION

Where?
Pro Football Hall of Fame
2121 George Halas Drive North West
Canton, OH 44708

When?
Beginning of August every year.

Significance:
Canton, Ohio, is the birthplace of the National Football League. Ralph Hay, the owner of the Canton Bulldogs, huddled together with fellow football team owners to establish a professional football league on September 17, 1920. The league, then called the American Professional Football Association, had been in existence for nearly forty years when demand began to grow for a place to honor the hard-working athletes who helped establish the league as a powerhouse. It needed a home, and where else but the place the NFL was born?

After lobbying efforts by residents and dignitaries in Canton to host the Hall of Fame and over two years of planning, a groundbreaking ceremony was held on August 11, 1962. A little over one year later, on September 7, 1963, the Pro Football Hall of Fame was officially opened.

Those enshrined NFL legends are selected by a thirty-nine-member committee, called the Board of Selectors, composed of sportswriters from around the country, six at-large delegates, and one representative from the Pro Football Writers of America. Coaches retired for any length of time and players out of the game for at least five years are eligible. The Board meets the day before the Super Bowl and selects the next class of enshrinees.

Every year since its opening, football legends flock to Canton to be inducted into the hallowed Hall. Fans crowd the area and crane their necks to get a glimpse of their favorite gridiron stars from childhood. While there are many exciting events over the ten-day celebration every August, the main event is the Enshrinement Ceremony. The stars of the past give memorable speeches and a few tears are shed. Super Bowls and

Pro Bowls aside, this is a true celebration of professional football history.

Who attends?

Major sports fans and fellow teammates who want to support the football legends being inducted into the NFL Hall of Fame.

How to get there?

The Hall is located at Exit 107A (Fulton Road) off I-77. That intersects many major highways just a few minutes from Canton.

Tickets:

For primary ticket access information, consider: www.profootballhof.com.

For secondary ticket access, consider:

GoTickets, Inc.
2345 Waukegan Road, Suite 140
Bannockburn, IL 60015-1552
Toll-Free: 1-800-775-1617
Fax: (919) 481-9101
E-mail: sales@gotickets.com
www.gotickets.com

Accommodations:

Fairfield Inn
5285 Broadmoor Circle Northwest
Canton, OH 44709
Phone: (330) 493-7373
Fax: (330) 493-7373
Toll-Free: 1-800-228-2800
www.marriott.com
Note: Conveniently located just eight minutes from the Hall of Fame.

Courtyard Canton
4375 Metro Circle Northwest
North Canton, OH 44720
Phone: (330) 494-6494
Fax: (330) 494-7129
Toll-Free: 1-877-TOP-ROOM
www.courtyardcanton.com
Note: Close to the Hall of Fame, amusement parks, cultural and entertainment centers, and the Harry London Chocolate Factory.

Glenmoor Country Club
4191 Glenmoor Road Northwest
Canton, OH 44718
Phone: (330) 966-3600
Fax: (330) 966-3611
www.glenmoorcc.com
Note: You will be farther from the Hall, but you will be treated to a more resort/retreat atmosphere.

On-Site Hospitality and Events:

The Ribs Burnoff takes place over three days to accommodate the large crowd of football fans and barbecue lovers. The event has expanded year after year, so get there early.

Travel Packages:

If you are going to travel to this event, I would recommend using a reliable company to work with you on making the necessary arrangements. The suppliers listed in this book have solid references and are by far the most trusted in the business. Below are some of the organizations to try for this Top 100 Must See Sporting Event. Always need a tailgate with football!

Premiere Corporate Events
14 Penn Plaza, Suite 925
New York, NY 10122
Phone: (212) 695-9480
Fax: (212) 564-8098
Toll-Free: 1-877-621-5243
E-mail: requests@tseworld.com
www.tseworld.com
www.pcevents.com

Premiere Sports Travel
201 Shannon Oaks Circle, Suite 205
Cary, NC 27511
Phone: (919) 481-9511
Fax: (919) 481-1337
Toll-Free: 1-800-924-9993
E-mail: sales@sportstravel.com
www.sportstravel.com

Dining:

Taggarts Ice Cream Parlor
1401 Fulton Road Northwest
Canton, OH 44703
Phone: (330) 452-6844

Note: Considered to be one of the best kept secrets in Canton. Homemade ice cream for the football fan with a sweet tooth.

Peter Shears
427 East Tuscarawas Street
Canton, OH 44702
Phone: (330) 588-8300
www.petershears.com

Note: A location in the basement of a historical business gives this local restaurant a cozy ambience.

Angello's
4905 West Tuscarawas Avenue
Canton, OH 44708
Phone: (330) 477-1486

Note: Customize your pizza any way you want it. From the type of crust to the toppings, you ask, they'll make it.

Big City Chophouse
6041 Whipple Avenue Northwest
Canton, OH 44720
Phone: (330) 494-6758
www.bigcitychophouse.com

Note: Large, hand-selected cuts of meat charbroiled to your liking. Authentic Italian dishes are served as well.

Airport:

Akron Canton Airport
5400 Lauby Road North West
North Canton, OH 44720
Phone: (330) 896-2385
Toll-Free: 1-888-434-2359
www.akroncantonairport.com

Sports Travel Insider's Edge:

Best way to watch the action:
If it's football action you crave, check out the NFL Hall of Fame Game, a pre-season matchup between two teams. Past games have included the Saints versus the Steelers, Raiders versus the Eagles, Bears versus the Dolphins, and the Broncos versus the Redskins.

Best place to get up close:
Talk to a travel provider listed in the Travel Package Section about a Pro Football Hall of Fame Enshrinement package that includes a lot of add-on options. In addition to the Enshrinement Ceremony, you can attend the Enshrinees Dinner, Enshrinees Game-Day Roundtable, the Hall of Fame Game, and Fan Tailgate Parties.

Best travel tip:
Get there during the week before the induction ceremony. Many activities are going on around Canton, including Drum Corps International competitions and Food Festivals. There is fun and festivities for the entire family.

Notable Quotes:

"I should have gone to the Hall of Fame before I stepped on a football field of any kind. It would have given me that much more appreciation for the game."—MICHAEL IRVIN, former Dallas Cowboys wide receiver

"Today, I'm here to tell my family, my coaches, my teammates, and my friends that I lived the life that I had imagined. I advanced confidently in the direction of my dreams and today, with many of you present, we have come here to Canton, Ohio, to celebrate and to share this great honor on what I consider to be football's most hallowed ground."—RON YARY, former NFL offensive tackle

Relevant Websites:
www.profootballhof.com
www.cantonstarkcvb.com
www.tseworld.com
www.pcevents.com
www.sportstravel.com
www.gotickets.com
www.premieresports.com

95

NCAA MEN'S LACROSSE CHAMPIONSHIP

When?
End of May.

Significance:
While not enjoying the prominence of NCAA Men's Basketball's Final Four, the NCAA Lacrosse Championship match has it beat in attendance and drawing power. For three days in May, the Division I, II, and III champions are decided, the only NCAA event that allows three divisions at one site. A lacrosse fanatic's dream come true. Truly the best of the best battling it out on the lacrosse field.

The weekend is more than just lacrosse matches. Fan-oriented events are scheduled, including youth lacrosse clinics, interactive fan zones, and community-oriented initiatives.

Who attends?
Lacrosse hopefuls and fans from the schools making it into the NCAA Lacrosse Championships.

Fun Facts:

The average lacrosse program has anywhere from forty-five to fifty players.

From 1996 to 2006, 152 new NCAA lacrosse programs were added.

Twenty-seven new varsity lacrosse programs were started in 2008.

The NCAA National Lacrosse championships boast an attendance of 50,000 per division championship.

As of 2007, there were nearly 17,000 male college lacrosse players.

Participation in NCAA men's lacrosse has increased by over 25 percent from 1997 to 2007.

Men's lacrosse ranks fifth out of eighty NCAA sponsored championships in merchandise sales.

New York has the greatest number of men's college lacrosse teams in the country. California is a close second.

History
As the oldest sport in North America, lacrosse, the Creator's Game to Native Americans, has a history that spans centuries and once served as a preparation for war. Its roots are in Native American religion and it was used to resolve conflicts, heal the sick, and develop strong men.

In 1881, Harvard defeated Princeton 3-0 for the championship in the first intercollegiate lacrosse tournament. By 1882, Harvard, New York University, and Princeton established a formal lacrosse association. Other universities soon joined. Initially, champions were determined by regular season records alone. However, a rival Inter-University Lacrosse League started using different standards to crown their champion. The rivalry lasted until 1905 when the two groups merged to form the U.S. Intercollegiate Lacrosse League (USILL). It took the name of the U.S. Intercollegiate Lacrosse Association (USILA) in 1929 following a reorganization.

Starting in 1936, the league competed for the coveted Wingate Memorial Trophy, named for the late W. Wilson Wingate, a sportswriter for Baltimore newspapers who played lacrosse in college and covered the sport. Many credit him for giving the nickname to lacrosse of "the fastest game on two feet."

The first NCAA national lacrosse tournament was held in 1971. The Wingate trophy was presented to the first two NCAA champions and subsequently retired.

Today, lacrosse is considered the fastest growing college team sport in the country. Over 26,000 men and about 5,500 women play at the varsity or club level. That number will continue to grow with 74,000 high school students playing lacrosse for their respective schools.

Notable Athletes:

Recent MVPs include:

Mike Leveille, Syracuse, 2008

Jesse Schwartzman, John Hopkins, 2005 and 2007

Matt Ward, UVA, 2006

Mike Powell, Syracuse, 2002 and 2004

Tillman Johnson, UVA, 2003

Records:

Most wins for a division one school: John Hopkins, 9

Most goals in a tournament: Matt Ward, 16, Virginia, 2006 (3 games)

Most goals in one game (Tie): Gary Gait, 9, Syracuse vs. Navy, 1988; Oliver Marti, 9, Brown vs. Loyola (MD), 1992

Most assists in a tournament: Tim Goldstein, 16, Cornell, 1987 (3 games)

Most assists in one game: Paul Basile, 8, Navy vs. Brown, 1987

Most points in a tournament (Tie): Eamon McEneaney, 25, Cornell, 1977 (3 games); Tim Goldstein, 25, Cornell, 1987 (3 games)

Most points in one game (Tie): Ed Mullen, 12 (7 goals, 5 assists), Maryland vs. Navy, 1976; Gary Gait, 12 (9 goals, 3 assists), Syracuse vs. Navy, 1988

Most saves in a tournament: Paul Schimoler, 85, Cornell, 1988 (4 games)

Most saves in one game: Steve Kavovit, 30, Maryland vs. Brown, 1991

Things to know before you go:

Cradling: A player turning his or her wrist and arms to cradle and maintain control of the ball in the stick pocket.

Crank Shot: A shot on goal where a player takes a backswing wind-up and fires the ball underhand or sidearm.

Man Down: A team losing a player to the penalty box, forcing the team to play with fewer members on the field.

Pick: An offensive player without the ball positions himself or herself against the body of a defender to allow a teammate to get open and receive a pass or take a shot.

Pocket: The head of the stick strung with leather or mesh netting where the ball is held and carried.

Quick Stick: An offensive player catching a ball with his or her stick on a feed pass and then shooting it toward the goal in one motion.

Scooping: A player picking up a loose ground ball by bending toward the ground, sliding his or her stick under the ball, and lifting it into the netting.

Tickets:

For primary ticket access information, consider: www.ticketmaster.com.

For secondary ticket access, consider:

GoTickets, Inc.
2345 Waukegan Road, Suite 140
Bannockburn, IL 60015-1552
Toll-Free: 1-800-775-1617
Fax: (919) 481-9101
E-mail: sales@gotickets.com
www.gotickets.com

Travel Packages:

If you are going to travel to this event, I would recommend using a reliable company to work with you on making the necessary arrangements. The suppliers listed in this book have solid references and are by far the most trusted in the business. Below are some of the organizations to try for this Top 100 Must See Sporting Event.

Premiere Corporate Events

14 Penn Plaza, Suite 925
New York, NY 10122
Phone: (212) 695-9480
Fax: (212) 564-8098
Toll-Free: 1-877-621-5243
E-mail: requests@tseworld.com
www.tseworld.com
www.pcevents.com

Premiere Sports Travel

201 Shannon Oaks Circle, Suite 205
Cary, NC 27511
Phone: (919) 481-9511
Fax: (919) 481-1337
Toll-Free: 1-800-924-9993
E-mail: sales@sportstravel.com
www.sportstravel.com

Sports Travel Insider's Edge:

Best way to watch the action:
If you are looking for a more "unplugged" experience, attend the practices that are usually held on Friday. Information related to the practice schedules should be provided by the NCAA when you purchase your ticket.

Best place to get up close:
To get the greatest possible view of the best of the best in college lacrosse and even rub shoulders with them, attend the NCAA championship banquet. The event is part of the overall weekend and fans are welcome to attend.

Best travel tip:
Pack the sticks. Plenty of lacrosse youth

clinics take place onsite during the event. If your child aspires to be an NCAA champ, this is the perfect place to start them on their lacrosse career.

Notable Quote:

"Right now I think everyone in here is thinking, 'Wow, we just lost the national championship.' In a couple of weeks, maybe we'll say, 'Look what we accomplished.' But we wanted a national championship. That's what we came here for."—DAN LOFTUS, Duke Blue Devils goaltender following their loss in the 2007 NCAA Division I Championship game

Relevant Websites:

www.ncaa.com
www.tseworld.com
www.pcevents.com
www.sportstravel.com
www.gotickets.com
www.ticketmaster.com
www.premieresports.com

96

COLLEGE BASEBALL WORLD SERIES

Where?

Rosenblatt Stadium
1202 Bert Murphy Avenue
Omaha, NE 68107

When?

Every year from mid-June until the end of the month.

Significance:

While not having the stature and following of its professional counterpart, the College World Series (CWS) has a strong and loyal following among baseball fans. Sure they borrowed a bit from Major League Base-

ball's World Series moniker, but it signifies the best of the best in NCAA Division I
Baseball. Setting attendance records of over
300,000 every year, over 6 million fans have
attended since the CWS's start at "The Blatt"
in Omaha, Nebraska. Millions more watch
at home on ESPN.

In 1988, the College World Series changed
from a pure double-elimination tournament
into two four-team, double-elimination
brackets. Starting with the 1999 championship tournament, the field increased from
forty-eight to sixty-four teams. The four-team
brackets were determined by the results of
regional and super-regional play, similar to
the NCAA basketball tournament.

Winning one NCAA Division I Baseball
championship is challenging, let alone winning two consecutively. To date, only five
colleges have that distinction. Dual champions include Oregon State in 2006 and
2007, Louisiana State University in 1996
and 1997, the University of Texas in 1949
and 1950, and Stanford University in 1987
and 1988. The University of Southern
California reigned as champs from 1970 to
1974.

Who attends?

College baseball fans and family members
of the athletes, some who will likely be the
major leaguers of tomorrow.

How to get there?

Rosenblatt Stadium is located in Omaha off
of I-80 and 13th Street.

Tickets:

For primary ticket access information, consider: www.cwsomaha.com.

For secondary ticket access, consider:

GoTickets, Inc.
2345 Waukegan Road, Suite 140
Bannockburn, IL 60015-1552
Toll-Free: 1-800-775-1617

Fax: (919) 481-9101
E-mail: sales@gotickets.com
www.gotickets.com

Accommodations:

Doubletree Hotel
1616 Dodge Street
Omaha, NE 68102
Phone: (402) 346-7600
Fax: (402) 346-5722
Toll-Free: 1-800-766-1164
www.hilton.com
*Note: Nine miles from the stadium and in the
heart of downtown Omaha.*

Embassy Suites Hotel-Downtown Omaha
555 South 10th Street
Omaha, NE 68102
Phone: (402) 346-9000
Fax: (402) 346-4236
Toll-Free: 1-800-EMBASSY
www.embassySuites.com
*Note: For the guest who prefers a more up-
scale, full-service environment, not to mention
a full suite.*

Courtyard Omaha Downtown
101 South 10th Street
Omaha, NE 68102
Phone: (402) 346-2200
Fax: (402) 346-7720
Toll-Free: 1-866-204-9388
www.marriott.com
*Note: Enjoy the views of the Mississippi River
and the restored brick buildings of the Old
Market. Walking distance from Rosenblatt
Stadium.*

On-Site Hospitality:

The stadium has two meeting rooms
available. The Stadium View Club restaurant overlooks the field and the Hall
of Fame Room can provide accommodations for large groups. Reservations are

required for both rooms. In addition, an excellent assortment of concession stands with souvenirs can be found in the concourse under the seating area. There are many places to park, and best of all the parking is free.

Travel Packages:

If you are going to travel to this event, I would recommend using a reliable company to work with you on making the necessary arrangements. The suppliers listed in this book have solid references and are by far the most trusted in the business. Below are some of the organizations to try for this Top 100 Must See Sporting Event.

Premiere Corporate Events

14 Penn Plaza, Suite 925
New York, NY 10122
Phone: (212) 695-9480
Fax: (212) 564-8098
Toll-Free: 1-877-621-5243
E-mail: requests@tseworld.com
www.tseworld.com
www.pcevents.com

Premiere Sports Travel

201 Shannon Oaks Circle, Suite 205
Cary, NC 27511
Phone: (919) 481-9511
Fax: (919) 481-1337
Toll-Free: 1-800-924-9993
E-mail: sales@sportstravel.com
www.sportstravel.com

Dining:

Bohemian Café

1406 South 13th Street
Omaha, NE 68108
Phone: (402) 342-9838
www.bohemiancafe.net
Note: A local favorite since 1964. Czech and European cuisine is on the menu with everything from roast duck to homemade apple strudel.

Lo Sole Mio Ristorante

3001 South 32nd Avenue
Omaha, NE 68105
Phone: (402) 345-5656
Fax: (402) 345-5859
www.losolemio.com
Note: Authentic Italian dishes including freshly made pastas and sauces in a casual, informal setting.

Greek Island

3821 Center Street
Omaha, NE 68105
Phone: (402) 346-1528
Note: Best known for gyros, Athenian salads, and other Greek delectables. Fully stocked bar includes imported Greek wines and beers.

Flatiron Café

1722 St. Mary's Avenue
Omaha, NE 68102
Phone: (402) 344-3040
www.theflatironcafe.com
Note: Upscale restaurant located in the historic Flatiron Building. The seasonal menu is ever changing with Miso Marinated Sea Bass and Grilled Breast of Duck on the list.

Airport:

Eppley Airfield

4501 Abbott Drive
Omaha, NE 68110
Phone: (402) 661-8000
Fax: (402) 661-8025
www.eppleyairfield.com

Sports Travel Insider's Edge:

Best way to watch the action:

With multiple expansions, it's hard to claim a bad seat in the house. The seating sections run as far as the foul poles down each line. Bleacher sections occupy the outfield area. For those who want to get out of the elements, there are plenty of seats under the cover for those who desire shade from the sun and shelter from the rain.

Best place to get up close:

The Stadium View Club provides a restaurant to dine in while watching the best that college baseball has to offer. Just find 249 of your best friends to join you as the capacity is 250. Reservations are required.

Best travel tip:

If you come early or stay late, you can return to "The Blatt" to see an Omaha Royals, a Triple A affiliate of the KC Royals, Pacific Coast League baseball game. A great environment to enjoy baseball with unique promotions and giveaways from time to time.

Notable Quote:

"From a coach's standpoint, this (Omaha) is a great spot. When coaches talk to their teams and their fans they don't talk about going to the College World Series. They talk about going to Omaha. And everybody knows what that means. Anybody that knows anything about college baseball knows what going to Omaha means. We know it's a great, great spot."—DAVE KEILITZ, Executive Director, American Baseball Coaches Association (ABCA)

Relevant Websites:

www.cwsomaha.com
www.ncaa.com
www.visitomaha.com
www.tseworld.com
www.pcevents.com
www.sportstravel.com
www.gotickets.com
www.premieresports.com

97

BEANPOT HOCKEY TOURNAMENT

Where?

TD Banknorth Garden
100 Legends Way
Boston, MA 02114

When?

The first and second Monday of February. The first round takes place the first week with the winners advancing to the championship the following Monday.

Significance:

Since 1952, the Boston Beanpot has invited the best Boston-based NCAA Men's Hockey teams to compete in the high-profile tournament. Those cross-town rivals include Boston University, Northeastern University, Boston College, and Harvard University. Teams fight for the tournament trophy and bragging rights. Individual awards include the Beanpot MVP, and the Eberly Trophy for the goaltender with the highest save percentage in both team games. The first Monday of February features the initial round, while the second week showcases the finals in a typically sold-out TD Banknorth Garden. Speaking of bragging rights, Boston University has won the lion's share of the Beanpot tournaments since its inception.

Who attends?

Hockey fanatics and college students along the east coast crowd the arena to cheer on the Terriers, Eagles, Huskies, or Crimson. Team jerseys can be found throughout the arena, particularly in the student section.

How to get there?

For the best ambiance, take the Green Line Eastbound to North Station. When you get there, you will be ensconced in the spirit of the Beanpot tournament. College students can be seen everywhere donning their team jerseys and preparing for battle.

Tickets:

For primary ticket access information, consider: www.tdbanknorthgarden.com or www.ticketmaster.com

For secondary ticket access, consider:

GoTickets, Inc.
2345 Waukegan Road, Suite 140
Bannockburn, IL 60015-1552
Toll-Free: 1-800-775-1617
Fax: (919) 481-9101
E-mail: sales@gotickets.com
www.gotickets.com

Accommodations:

Ritz-Carlton, Boston Common
10 Avery Street
Boston, MA 02111
Phone: (617) 574-7100
Fax: (617) 574-7200
Toll-Free: 1-888-709-2027
www.ritzcarlton.com
Note: Boasting a commanding presence on the Boston skyline and overlooking Boston Common, the oldest public park in the United States.

The Fairmont Copley Plaza
138 St. James Avenue
Boston, MA 02116
Phone: (617) 267-5300
Fax: (617) 267-7668
Toll-Free: 1-800-441-1414
www.fairmont.com
Note: Dedicated staff provides incomparable hospitality in this hotel offering 383 guest-rooms and suites.

Bulfinch Hotel
107 Merrimac Street
Boston, MA 02114
Phone: (617) 624-0202

Fax: (617) 624-0211
Toll-Free: 1-877-267-1776
www.bulfinchhotel.com
Note: Close to the arena, great restaurants, and the train. Onsite fitness center, restaurants, and a lounge.

Holiday Inn Boston at Beacon Hill
5 Blossom Street
Boston, MA 02114
Phone: (617) 742-7630
Fax: (617) 742-4192
Toll-Free: 1-800-HOLIDAY
www.holidayinn.com
Note: A convenient walk to the train, this hotel has fourteen floors with 303 rooms with a restaurant and lounge onsite.

Liberty Hotel
215 Charles Street
Boston, MA 02114
Phone: (617) 224-4000
Fax: (617) 224-4001
www.libertyhotel.com
Note: Member of Leading Hotels of the World with sixteen floors with 298 rooms, not to mention 24-hour room service.

Onyx Hotel
155 Portland Street
Boston, MA 02114
Phone: (617) 557-9955
Fax: (617) 557-0005
Toll-Free: 1-800-546-7866
www.onyxhotel.com
Note: Ranked 4-diamonds with AA, 112 rooms with a restaurant and fitness center onsite.

On-Site Hospitality:

Banners: Level 6 of the TD Banknorth Garden features an upscale dining restaurant. Reservations are strongly recommended and can be made by calling (617) 624-2501.

The Premium Club Restaurant: More casual dining can be found on Level 5 in a restaurant that is usually open two hours prior to all events and close when the games end. Patrons can enjoy pizza, deli food, and more at various food stations. Reservations are not accepted.

The Sports Museum: A museum devoted to the best in Boston sports history. Call (617) 624-1234 for hours.

Travel Packages:

If you are going to travel to this event, I would recommend using a reliable company to work with you on making the necessary arrangements. The suppliers listed in this book have solid references and are by far the most trusted in the business. Below are some of the organizations to try for this Top 100 Must See Sporting Event.

Premiere Corporate Events

14 Penn Plaza, Suite 925
New York, NY 10122
Phone: (212) 695-9480
Fax: (212) 564-8098
Toll-Free: 1-877-621-5243
E-mail: requests@tseworld.com
www.tseworld.com
www.pcevents.com

Premiere Sports Travel

201 Shannon Oaks Circle, Suite 205
Cary, NC 27511
Phone: (919) 481-9511
Fax: (919) 481-1337
Toll-Free: 1-800-924-9993
E-mail: sales@sportstravel.com
www.sportstravel.com

Dining:

T. Anthony's

1016 Commonwealth Avenue
Boston, MA 02215
Phone: (617) 734-7708
Note: Custom-made for BU fans and will put you in a Terrier mood. Pick up a slice before the big game.

The Harp

Sports/Irish
85 Causeway Street
Boston, MA 02114
Phone: (617) 742-1010
www.harpboston.com
Note: The Harp is usually crowded due to reasonable bar and food prices and live music Thursdays through Saturdays. Being a sports/ Irish bar located right next to the Fleet Center doesn't hurt either.

Fours

166 Canal Street
Boston, MA 02114
Phone: (617) 720-4455
www.thefours.com
Note: This classic English pub stands out above the other run-of-the-mill watering holes and sports bars around the Fleet Center.

McGann's

197 Portland Street
Boston, MA 02114
Phone: (617) 227-4059
Note: Usually packed before and after events at TD Banknorth Garden, but worth getting a few drinks to celebrate your team's victory or just drown your sorrows.

Boston Beer Works

61 Brookline Avenue
Boston, MA 02114
Phone: (617) 536-BEER
Note: Closer to Boston University and Boston College campuses, this microbrewery features a wide variety of home brews made onsite. Their menu combines standard bar fun with fairly unique specialties.

Airport:

Boston Logan International Airport

1 Harborside Drive
East Boston, MA 02128
Phone: (617) 561-1800
www.massport.com

Sports Travel Insider's Edge:

Best way to watch the action:
Sit near the student sections. What the seats lack in closeness, they make up for in excitement. Spirited chanting and jarring between the student sections cannot help but entertain. Listen for the Harvard students cheering if their team is losing, "It's all right. It's okay. You're going to work for us one day anyway."

Best place to get up close:
Most years the best place to see the players up close and personal is at the 4-man Team Burrito Eating Contest with BU, BC, Harvard, and Northeastern vying for the gastronomic crown. That event is followed by a Battle of the Bands at Paradise Lounge on Commonwealth Avenue.

Best travel tip:
In the week between tournament rounds, stick around Boston for some other NCAA college sports events or you can watch the pros at a Celtics or Bruins game.

Notable Quotes:

"I haven't felt anything like this in my life. We're drinking out of this thing tonight. It's the greatest feeling. You've got to love it."—PAUL FENTON, one-time Boston University boys hockey team captain

"The Beanpot may not be a life or death matter for most of us. But it is a big deal and has been a big deal for most of its half century of inspiring athletes and entertaining fans. It is a half century that has seen great changes in the world, in amateur athletics, and in college hockey itself. But for all the changes, the competition for the 'Pot' has remained relatively unaffected by all that has evolved around it."—JOE BERTAGNA, goalie for Harvard, 1972 and 1973 Beanpot tournaments.

Relevant Websites:
www.beanpothockey.com
www.tdbanknorthgarden.com
www.bostonusa.com
www.tseworld.com
www.pcevents.com
www.sportstravel.com
www.gotickets.com
www.ticketmaster.com
www.premieresports.com

98
BAYOU CLASSIC

Where?
The Louisiana Superdome
1500 Sugar Bowl Drive
New Orleans, LA 70112

When?
During the NCAA Football season.

Visit www.gram.edu or www.subr.edu for up-to-date game-day information.

Significance:
Fans converge on the Superdome. Friends and old classmates reunite. Football players workout. Band members warm up their instruments. Nearly 200,000 fans descend upon New Orleans, and over 76,000 pack the Louisiana Superdome every year for the famed Bayou Classic that pits the Grambling State University Tigers against the Southern University Jaguars.

New Orleans's Tulane Stadium hosted the inaugural Bayou Classic. In 1974, Grambling and Southern faced off for the first time, and 76,753 fans were on hand to witness history and the start of a storied rivalry as Grambling stopped Southern by a score of 21-0. That domination continued for many years until Southern embarked on an eight-game winning streak that ended in 2001, the longest in the history of the Bayou Classic.

This is not just a football game. It is a highly anticipated event for both schools to showcase their best and not just on the football field. The McDonald's Battle of the Bands and Greek Show has become as big a part of this extravaganza as the game itself in opening and closing the event and providing the most incredible half-time entertainment.

Who attends?
Students, alumni, and loyalists of the Grambling State University Tigers and the Southern University Jaguars. Not to mention fans of their band programs awaiting their battle as well.

How to get there?
I-10 to the Superdome Exit. For those coming from the West, do not take the Poydras Exit.

Tickets:
For primary ticket access information, consider: www.ticketmaster.com.

For primary tickets to the McDonald's Battle of the Bands and Greek Show tickets, consider: www.statefarmbayouclassic.com.

For secondary ticket access, consider:

GoTickets, Inc.
2345 Waukegan Road, Suite 140
Bannockburn, IL 60015-1552
Toll-Free: 1-800-775-1617
Fax: (919) 481-9101
E-mail: sales@gotickets.com
www.gotickets.com

Accommodations:

New Orleans Marriott
555 Canal Street
New Orleans, LA 70130
Phone: (504) 581-1000
Fax: (504) 523-6755

Toll-Free: 1-888-364-1200
www.neworleansmarriott.com
Note: Conveniently located a little over one mile from the stadium.

Hotel Le Cirque
936 St. Charles Avenue
New Orleans, LA 70130
Phone: (504) 962-0900
Fax: (504) 962-0901
Toll-Free: 1-800-684-9525
www.hotellecirqueneworleans.com
Note: Touted as "New Orleans's hottest and hippest new property." Conveniently located in the Arts District and close to the Convention Center and the French Quarter.

Holiday Inn Express
221 Carondelet Street
New Orleans, LA 70130
Phone: (504) 962-0800
Fax: (504) 962-0701
Toll-Free: 1-877-863-4780
www.hiexpress.com
Note: Located in the heart of New Orleans's French Quarter, making it an exciting place to stay and walking distance from the Superdome.

Hilton New Orleans Riverside
2 Poydras Street
New Orleans, LA 70140
Phone: (504) 561-0500
Fax: (504) 568-1721
Toll-Free: 1-800-445-8667
www.hilton.com
Note: Oversized guest rooms with French provincial styling featuring views of numerous courtyards.

Astor Crowne Plaza
739 Canal Street
New Orleans, LA 70130
Phone: (504) 962-0500
Fax: (504) 962-0501
Toll-Free: 1-800-972-2791
www.CrownePlaza.com

Note: Promises elegance and comfort in a perfect location.

Monteleone Hotel
214 Royal Street
New Orleans, LA 70130
Phone: (504) 523-3341
Fax: (504) 528-1019
Toll-Free: 1-800-535-9595
www.hotelmonteleone.com
Note: A hotel of history located on Royal Street.

Royal Sonesta
300 Bourbon Street
New Orleans, LA 70130
Phone: (504) 586-0300
Fax: (504) 586-0335
Toll-Free: 1-800-766-3782
www.sonesta.com
Note: Spacious rooms with great service from an attentive staff.

On-Site Hospitality:
The competition in the McDonald's Battle of the Bands and Greek Show is as intense as the game itself. Southern and Grambling compete on a musical performance level before the game, during halftime, and after the gridiron competition is over. Anticipation for the battle of the bands rivals the game itself.

Travel Packages:
If you are going to travel to this event, I would recommend using a reliable company to work with you on making the necessary arrangements. The suppliers listed in this book have solid references and are by far the most trusted in the business. Below are some of the organizations to try for this Top 100 Must See Sporting Event.

Premiere Corporate Events
14 Penn Plaza, Suite 925
New York, NY 10122
Phone: (212) 695-9480
Fax: (212) 564-8098

Toll-Free: 1-877-621-5243
E-mail: requests@tseworld.com
www.tseworld.com
www.pcevents.com

Premiere Sports Travel
201 Shannon Oaks Circle, Suite 205
Cary, NC 27511
Phone: (919) 481-9511
Fax: (919) 481-1337
Toll-Free: 1-800-924-9993
E-mail: sales@sportstravel.com
www.sportstravel.com

Dining:

The Rib Room
621 St. Louis Street
New Orleans, LA 70140
Phone: (504) 529-5333
www.omnihotels.com
Note: Located inside the French Quarter's Omni Royal Orleans Hotel. Serving prime rib, fowl, and seafood prepared on giant French rotisseries and mesquite grills.

Commander's Palace
1403 Washington Avenue
New Orleans, LA 70130
Phone: (504) 899-8221
www.commanderspalace.com
Note: Reservations and proper dress will get you into this famed restaurant in the Garden District. Emeril Lagasse served as head chef from 1982 to 1990.

Allegro Bistro
1100 Poydras Street
New Orleans, LA 70163
Phone: (504) 582-2350
Note: Adjacent to the Superdome, offering contemporary, Cajun, and Creole dishes.

Johnny White's Sports Bar
720 Bourbon Street
New Orleans, LA 70116
Phone: (504) 524-4909

Note: Always open with nearby street performers. What else would you expect from a bar in the French Quarter?

Acme Oyster House

724 Iberville Street
New Orleans, LA
Phone: (504) 522-5973
www.acmeoyster.com

Note: Serves raw oysters, jambalaya, and other entrées. The long wait is well worth it.

Mango Mango

201/236/333/400 Bourbon Street
New Orleans, LA
Phone: (504) 566-1113
www.mangodaiquiris.com

Note: Did you know that there are twelve different daiquiris? Only available at the four Mango Mango locations on Bourbon Street.

Dragos
Hilton New Orleans Riverside

2 Poydras Street
New Orleans, LA 70140
Phone: (504) 584-3911
www.dragosrestaurant.com

Note: Home of the first ever Charbroiled Oyster. Do not leave before trying one.

Mother's Restaurant

401 Poydras Street
New Orleans, LA 70130
Phone: (504) 523-9656
www.mothersrestaurant.net

Note: The world's best baked ham, which is also one of many ingredients on their po'boy.

Pat O'Brien's Bar

718 St. Peter Street
New Orleans, LA 70116
Phone: (504) 525-4823
www.patobriens.com

Note: A great local place to grab a drink or something to eat at any time, day or night. Be sure to taste their signature drink, the Hurricane.

Airports:

Louis Armstrong New Orleans International Airport

900 Airline Drive
Kenner, LA 70064
Phone: (504) 464-0831
www.flymsy.com

New Orleans Lakefront Airport

6001 Stars and Stripes Boulevard
New Orleans, LA 70126
Phone: (504) 243-4010
www.lakefrontairport.com

Sports Travel Insider's Edge:

Best way to watch the action:

The Superdome is immense and was able to house thousands of families displaced during Hurricane Katrina. The second-level sideline seats give you the best view of the game, particularly the first several rows, or what is known as the 200 level.

Best place to get up close:

Bands at any game will get you in the mood prior to the game, entertain you at halftime, and conclude the exciting event. Fans and loyalists know that the football field is not the only place where Southern and Grambling battle. The band room is also on the front line of this school war. While the game is the proverbial "main event," the McDonald's Battle of the Bands and Greek Show has become a vital part of the Bayou Classic. Friday nights before the game feature the legendary battle. Do not miss it.

Best travel tip:

The Bayou Classic is so much more than the game. A fan festival, coaches' luncheon, golf tournament, job fair, and college fair will keep you plenty busy. Plan ahead if you want to attend multiple events. Also, keep in mind that as with any gathering in New Orleans, be prepared to party or witness a great deal of partying. Sleep is a rare commodity at best.

Notable Quote:

"It's a rare chance to see prosperous black people from all over the country come together for no reason other than to have a good time. That makes the Classic beautiful."—BOMANI JONES, an alumnus of Clark Atlanta University

Relevant Websites:

www.superdome.com
www.statefarmbayouclassic.com
www.gram.edu
www.soulofneworleans.com
www.subr.edu
www.tseworld.com
www.pcevents.com
www.sportstravel.com
www.gotickets.com
www.ticketmaster.com
www.premieresports.com

99

LITTLE LEAGUE WORLD SERIES

Where?
Howard J. Lamade Stadium
539 U.S. Highway 15
Williamsport, PA 17702

When?
Every year in the middle of August.

Significance:
Are you tired of million-dollar athletes more concerned about paychecks than playing? Do you want to watch good baseball played for the love of it, not the financial benefits? The players in the Little League World Series may be smaller in stature then their counterparts in the major leagues, but they make up for it with heart and determination.

Since 1947, the Little League World Series has brought the best eleven- to thirteen-year-old players together in one stadium. Start-

ing as a showcase for U.S. players with four teams competing for the title, the tournament has grown in size and scope to include eight teams from the United States and eight teams from other countries. Divided into U.S. and International brackets, the teams compete in a round-robin tournament until a champion is declared. The two best rosters that emerge battle it out in Howard J. Lamade Stadium in Williamsport, Pennsylvania, for the world championship.

The Little League World Series makes its television home on ESPN after several years at ABC. Coverage includes the regional tournaments in addition to the main event.

Who attends?
Baseball fans and family members of the players, including those parents living vicariously through their children.

How to get there?
The Little League complex is easily found from Interstate 80 and Route 15 in Williamsport, Pennsylvania.

Tickets:
For primary tickets, a lottery is held for the general public to the World Championship game. You can write to the address below requesting tickets.

Attention: World Series Tickets
Little League Baseball International
539 U.S. Route 15 Highway
P.O. Box 3485
Williamsport, PA 17701

Everyone is notified, including those selected and those who were not. Tickets must be picked up at the will call window of Lamade Stadium during the week prior or during the World Series. For those who did not win, fear not. The terraced hills at the stadium provide a view of the game for free. You will have to bring lawn chairs or blankets.

For the other games, a ticket is not needed as it is first-come, first-served.

Accommodations:

All of these hotels are less than one mile from the stadium:

Holiday Inn – Downtown Williamsport
100 Pine Street
Williamsport, PA 17701
Phone: (570) 327-8231
Fax: (570) 322-2957
Toll-Free: 1-800-HOLIDAY
www.holidayinn.com
Note: Comfortable guest rooms and The James, a restaurant and bar to enjoy meals and cocktails. Kids eat free.

Old Corner Hotel
328 Court Street
Williamsport, PA 17701
Phone: (570) 326-4286
Note: Located in the heart of Williamsport. They boast a restaurant with a unique menu that includes mesquite-smoked duck, tuna steak, prosciutto, and much more.

Jefferson Square Corporate Suites
726 Washington Boulevard
Williamsport, PA 17701
Phone: (570) 322-7623
Note: More than a room, this is a temporary home away from home. Perfect for vacationers and business travelers.

On-Site Hospitality and Events:

One of the more pleasant surprises of Lamade Stadium is the reasonable prices of concession food and beverages. Fans accustomed to paying a small fortune for snacks will appreciate the low prices, not to mention the accessibility, friendly service, and short lines.

Annual Grand Slam Parade: The official kickoff of the tournament features each of the regional champions who will be competing for the World Series title. Fans cheer on their favorites as they enjoy good food and music. An impressive fireworks display ends the night. The parade will also be your first opportunity to get a glimpse of Dugout, the official Little League Mascot.

Peter J. McGovern Little League Museum: Relive Little League's past and honor the players who have gone on to bigger and better things. Interactive displays allow you to learn about the history of the league, making for a truly entertaining and educational experience.

Pin Trading: A favorite pastime where collectible pins are exchanged at the trading pavilion between Volunteer Stadium and Lamade Stadium.

Travel Packages:

If you are going to travel to this event, I would recommend using a reliable company to work with you on making the necessary arrangements. The suppliers listed in this book have solid references and are by far the most trusted in the business. Below are some of the organizations to try for this Top 100 Must See Sporting Event.

Premiere Corporate Events
14 Penn Plaza, Suite 925
New York, NY 10122
Phone: (212) 695-9480
Fax: (212) 564-8098
Toll-Free: 1-877-621-5243
E-mail: requests@tseworld.com
www.tseworld.com
www.pcevents.com

Premiere Sports Travel
201 Shannon Oaks Circle, Suite 205
Cary, NC 27511
Phone: (919) 481-9511
Fax: (919) 481-1337
Toll-Free: 1-800-924-9993

E-mail: sales@sportstravel.com
www.sportstravel.com

Dining:

Huckleberry's Family Restaurant
445 River Avenue
Williamsport, PA 17701
Phone: (570) 327-5200

Note: Family restaurant located in Faxon Bowling Lanes. Fuel up for a day of baseball with their hearty breakfasts.

Mulberry Street Café
166 Mulberry Street
Williamsport, PA 17701
Phone: (570) 322-9423

Note: A favorite for the locals in downtown Williamsport. The menu includes Italian dishes, steaks, seafood, and salads.

Airport:

Williamsport Regional Airport
700 Airport Road
Montoursville, PA 17754
Phone: (570) 368-2444
www.flyipt.com

Sports Travel Insider's Edge:

Best way to watch the action:
Those seeking shade will want to sit in the right field stands for late afternoon games. Don't let the sun keep you from seeing the best that the Little League has to offer.

Best place to get up close:
Keep your fingers crossed and hope you are selected in the LLWS lottery. Tickets for the qualifying games are first-come, first-serve, so get to Lamade Stadium early. Better yet, volunteer to be a Little League coach and take your team all the way to the world title!

Best travel tip:
For the lottery losers and the ticketless fans out of options to get into the facility, Lamade Stadium boasts a tiered bank that rises over 100 feet above the field. Bring a chair or blanket and enjoy the game from the ultimate in cheap seats.

Notable Quotes:

"It was awesome. Coming from a small town like Trail, British Columbia, and then playing in front of all those people at eleven years old was just amazing. It's something I'll never forget."—JASON BAY, MLB All-Star

"Oh yeah I've been wanting to come here since I was a kid. And lo and behold . . . I finally get to come here."—LATROY HAWKINS, relief pitcher

"In Little League you learn how you have to depend on teammates, because even on no-hitters there's someone behind you making a play."—KEVIN COSTNER, actor

"Little League has a big, positive impact in my life."—BRUCE SPRINGSTEEN, singer/song-writer

Relevant Websites:
www.littleleague.org
www.centralpacvb.org
www.tseworld.com
www.pcevents.com
www.sportstravel.com
www.premieresports.com

100
UFC TITLE FIGHT

Where?
While the venue changes, one of Las Vegas's major casinos or hotels usually host the events, including the MGM Grand and the Mandalay Bay Resort.

When?
Annually from May to July.

Significance:

Once disregarded as "human cockfighting," the Ultimate Fighting Championship (UFC) is enjoying a surge in mainstream popularity as the largest and most high-profile Mixed Martial Arts (MMA) organization in the United States. UFC started as a tournament to find the world's best fighters regardless of style and embracing the "No Holds Barred" philosophy. It caught the attention of fight fans looking for a little something more. It also got the attention of prominent politicians looking to put an end to the up-and-coming sporting event.

UFC wisely reformed itself and began to implement stricter rules. The "No Holds Barred" tag was dropped in favor of "Mixed Martial Arts." The organization also became recognized by athletic commissions in California, Florida, Nevada, New Jersey, Ohio, and Pennsylvania. Mainstream media attention has come their way, resulting in increased pay-per-view buys, and their Spike TV *Ultimate Fighter* and *UFC Fight Night* shows deliver top ratings in the all-important male 18-34 demographic for the cable network. Markets in Canada, Mexico, and Germany are being explored as the UFC is looking to go international. Today the United States, tomorrow the world.

Weight classes:

Lightweight: Over 145 lbs. to 155 lbs.
Welterweight: Over 155 lbs. to 170 lbs.
Middleweight: Over 170 lbs. to 185 lbs.
Light Heavyweight: Over 185 lbs. to 205 lbs.
Heavyweight: Over 205 lbs. to 265 lbs.

Duration of bouts:

Non-championship bouts are three rounds. Championship bouts are five rounds.
All rounds are five minutes in duration.
A one-minute rest period occurs between each round.

Who attends?

A growing legion of fans who may be getting bored with the same old boxing matches and professional wrestling bouts.

Tickets:

For primary ticket access information, consider: www.ufc.com.

For secondary ticket access, consider:

GoTickets, Inc.
2345 Waukegan Road, Suite 140
Bannockburn, IL 60015-1552
Toll-Free: 1-800-775-1617
Fax: (919) 481-9101
E-mail: sales@gotickets.com
www.gotickets.com

Accommodations:

Gold Coast Casino
4000 West Flamingo Road
Las Vegas, NV 89103
Phone: (702) 367-7111
Fax: (702) 367-8575
Toll-Free: 1-888-402-6278
www.goldcoastcasino.com
Note: Spanish-style hotel just one mile west of The Strip and a half-mile to Chinatown.

Hooters Casino and Hotel
115 East Tropicana Avenue
Las Vegas, NV 89109
Phone: (702) 739-9000
Toll-Free: 1-866-584-6687
www.hooterscasinohotel.com
Note: The name says it all. 696 Floridian style rooms with a great atmosphere.

Golden Nugget
129 East Fremont Street
Las Vegas, NV 89101
Phone: (702) 385-7111
Toll-Free: 1-800-846-5336
www.goldennugget.com
Note: A great place to stay for the Fremont

Street Experience. Eight miles from McCarran International Airport.

Luxor
3900 Las Vegas Boulevard South
Las Vegas, NV 89119
Phone: (702) 262-4444
Toll-Free: 1-800-288-1000
www.luxor.com

Note: A unique, pyramid-shape design with a Sphinx replica that goes with the overall Egyptian theme.

The Mirage
3400 Las Vegas Boulevard South
Las Vegas, NV 89109
Phone: (702) 791-7111
Fax: (702) 791-7446
Toll-Free: 1-800-374-9000
www.themirage.com

Note: They boast a South Seas vibe combined with Strip excitement. A popular hotel and casino at the heart of Las Vegas.

Excalibur Hotel and Casino
3850 Las Vegas Boulevard South
Las Vegas, NV 89109
Phone: (702) 597-7777
Fax: (702) 597-7009
Toll-Free: 1-877-750-5464
www.excalibur.com

Note: Medieval themes inspired by Camelot with four towers, castle gates, and spires of varying colors.

Las Vegas Hilton
3000 Paradise Road
Las Vegas, NV 89109
Phone: (702) 732-5111
Toll-Free: 1-888-732-7117
www.lvhilton.com

Note: Luxurious hotel with world-class entertainment options and a 40,000 square-foot casino. For the younger lot, or simply the kid in all of us, they boast the city's best video arcade.

MGM Grand
3799 Las Vegas Boulevard South
Las Vegas, NV 89109
Phone: (702) 891-1111
Toll-Free: 1-877-880-0880
www.mgmgrand.com

Note: One of the best known Las Vegas hotels and casinos. Iconic and part of Sin City history.

The Venetian Resort Hotel Casino
3355 Las Vegas Boulevard South
Las Vegas, NV 89109
Phone: (702) 414-1000
Fax: (702) 414-1100
Toll-Free: 1-877-883-6423
www.venetian.com

Note: An all-suite hotel providing luxury and comfort.

Treasure Island
3300 Las Vegas Boulevard South
Las Vegas, NV 89109
Phone: (702) 894-7111
Fax: (702) 894-7414
Toll-Free: 1-800-944-7444
www.treasureisland.com

Note: More affordable with a little something for everyone.

On-Site Hospitality:
Depends on the venue where the event is held.

Travel Packages:
If you are going to travel to this event, I would recommend using a reliable company to work with you on making the necessary arrangements. The suppliers listed in this book have solid references and are by far the most trusted in the business. Below are some of the organizations to try for this Top 100 Must See Sporting Event.

Premiere Corporate Events
14 Penn Plaza, Suite 925
New York, NY 10122

Phone: (212) 695-9480
Fax: (212) 564-8098
Toll-Free: 1-877-621-5243
E-mail: requests@tseworld.com
www.tseworld.com
www.pcevents.com

Premiere Sports Travel
201 Shannon Oaks Circle, Suite 205
Cary, NC 27511
Phone: (919) 481-9511
Fax: (919) 481-1337
Toll-Free: 1-800-924-9993
E-mail: sales@sportstravel.com
www.sportstravel.com

Dining:

Aqua Knox
3355 South Las Vegas Boulevard
Las Vegas, NV 89109
Phone: (702) 414-3772
Fax: (702) 414-3872
www.aquaknox.net
Note: Great place to get seafood if you don't mind paying a bit more.

Joe's
3500 South Las Vegas Boulevard
Las Vegas, NV 89109
Phone: (702) 792-9222
Fax: (702) 369-8384
www.icon.com/joes
Note: Seasonal seafood offerings from around the world with carry-out and children's menus.

Red Square
3950 Las Vegas Boulevard South
Las Vegas, NV 89119
Phone: (702) 632-7777
Fax: (702) 632-7234
Toll-Free: 1-877-632-7000
www.mandalaybay.com
Note: Pricey, but great food and a selection of over 100 different kinds of vodka.

Baja Beach Café
2400 North Rancho Drive
Las Vegas, NV 89130
Phone: (702) 631-7000
Toll-Free: 1-800-731-7333
Note: Great food with even greater values, including the Fiesta Burger and fries for only $2.99!

Blondie's Sports Bar & Grill at Miracle Mile Shops
Planet Hollywood Resort and Casino
3663 Las Vegas Boulevard
Las Vegas, NV 89109
Phone: (702) 737-0444
Note: Traditional bar menu with great appetizers and entrées.

Airport:

McCarran International Airport-Las Vegas
5757 Wayne Newton Boulevard
Las Vegas, NV 89119
Phone: (702) 261-5211
www.mccarran.com

Sports Travel Insider's Edge:

Best way to watch the action:
While some choose cable and pay-per-view, the live experience is unmatched in its excitement and energy, particularly in Las Vegas. The cage may impede the view, so the closer you can get, the better. Cheaper seats will give you a more aerial view. Plus, you're liable to rub shoulders with the hardcore and more "bloodlusty" UFC fans.

Best way to get up close:
The battles take place in the confines of a steel cage, so you can only get so close to the fighting. Picking up a season of Spike TV's *Ultimate Fighter* on DVD will show you how a UFC contender is born and works his way through the ranks. It will give you a behind-the-scenes look at the struggles and strife of a potential UFC champion.

Best travel tip:
You're in Vegas already! When you're not watching the bloody battles or a new UFC champion being crowned, check out any one of many casinos, live shows, or other sporting events.

Notable Quotes:

"If I had my choice between being a Super Bowl Champion, a World Series Champion, an NBA titlist, or a UFC Champion, my personal choice would be UFC Champion. To me, that's the pinnacle of everything in the greatest sport there is."—MARK COLEMAN, UFC Hall of Famer

"I think one of the things that makes us more of a sport than a fighting league is—like I said earlier—the sportsmanship. When two teams play each other, yeah, you might have some teams that are rivals and they really don't like each other that much. That happens in fighting, too. But most of the time, these guys that go out to fight each other are like two teams playing. . . . They go out before the fight, they can hang out at the press conference and the weigh-in and shake hands and say hello to each other. Then they go in and fight as hard as they can fight and they fight to win. As soon as that fight's over, they're shaking hands and showing each other respect again. I think that's one of the great things about the UFC and about the sport."—DANA WHITE, UFC founder

Relevant Websites:

www.ufc.com
www.tseworld.com
www.pcevents.com
www.sportstravel.com
www.gotickets.com
www.ticketmaster.com
www.premieresports.com

FROZEN FOUR

Where?
All over the country, varies from year to year. Future locations include the Verizon Center in Washington, D.C., Ford Field in Detroit, Xcel Energy Center in St. Paul, and the St. Pete Times Forum in Tampa.

When?
Beginning of April each year.

Significance:
Dubbed "the Frozen Four" (a derivation of the famed Final Four) in 1999, the Division I ice hockey tournament started in 1948 when Michigan defeated Dartmouth. Sellouts happen well in advance, making this annual tournament one of the most profitable for the NCAA and second only to the Division I men's basketball tournament.

Sixteen teams compete in the Frozen Four. Six teams automatically qualify if they win playoff championships in Atlantic Hockey, CCHA, CHA, ECAC Hockey, Hockey East, and WCHA. The semifinals are played on Thursday and the championship follows on Saturday. In addition to this significant chapter of hockey history, the Hobey Baker and Hockey Humanitarian award winners are announced. The Frozen Four tournament itself is a culmination of a weeklong celebration of all things college hockey.

Who attends?
Fans and alums from the participating schools cheer on their favorites with die-hard hockey fans from around the country. Younger hockey players pack their sticks and skates to participate in a youth clinic.

History

Michigan defeated Dartmouth in the first NCAA Division I ice hockey tournament in 1948 at the Broadmoor Arena in Colorado Springs, Colorado, which would become the home of the first ten tournaments. The "Frozen Four" was a shorter and catchier name when it became the nickname of the championship in 1999. Since that time, previous tournaments were retconned with the new name.

Records:

Frozen Four Appearances: Boston University, 20, 1950–1997; Michigan, 20, 1948–2001

Current Consecutive Frozen Four Appearances: Boston College, 4, 1998–2001

Frozen Four Wins: Michigan, 24, 1948–2001

NCAA Championships: Michigan, 9, 1948–1998

Goals: Carl Lawrence, 5, Colorado College vs. Boston College, March 16, 1950; Gil Burford, 5, Michigan vs. Boston College, March 18, 1950

Fastest Game-Opening Goal: Al Karlander, 7 seconds, Michigan Tech vs. Cornell, March 14, 1969

Fastest Consecutive Goals: Bert Dunn, 13 seconds, Michigan vs. Boston University, March 13, 1953

Fastest Hat Trick: Warren Miller, 4 minutes and 20 seconds, Minnesota vs. Harvard, March 13, 1975

Assists: Bob Poffenroth, 5, Wisconsin vs. Michigan Tech, March 21, 1970

Points: John Mayasich, 7, Minnesota vs. Boston College, March 11, 1954 (3 goals, 4 assists)

Penalties: Randy Skarda, 8, Minnesota vs. Maine, April 2, 1988

Saves: Chris Terreri, 62, Providence vs. Boston College, March 28, 1985 (3 OT)

Tickets:

For primary ticket access information, call 1-800-801-9268 for information on the NCAA lottery system.

For secondary ticket access, consider:

GoTickets, Inc.
2345 Waukegan Road, Suite 140
Bannockburn, IL 60015-1552
Toll-Free: 1-800-775-1617
Fax: (919) 481-9101
E-mail: sales@gotickets.com
www.gotickets.com

Travel Packages:

If you are going to travel to this event, I would recommend using a reliable company to work with you on making the necessary arrangements. The suppliers listed in this book have solid references and are by far the most trusted in the business. Below are some of the organizations to try for this Top 100 Must See Sporting Event.

Premiere Corporate Events
14 Penn Plaza, Suite 925
New York, NY 10122
Phone: (212) 695-9480
Fax: (212) 564-8098
Toll-Free: 1-877-621-5243
E-mail: requests@tseworld.com
www.tseworld.com
www.pcevents.com

Premiere Sports Travel
201 Shannon Oaks Circle, Suite 205
Cary, NC 27511
Phone: (919) 481-9511
Fax: (919) 481-1337
Toll-Free: 1-800-924-9993
E-mail: sales@sportstravel.com
www.sportstravel.com

Sports Travel Insider's Edge:

Best way to watch the action:
The Frozen Four Skills Challenge is an "All-

Star" type of game where fans can see the best of the senior classes that are not competing in the Frozen Four as they take the ice for the last time as college players. Competitions include puck control relay, fastest skater, hardest shot, rapid fire shooting, accuracy shooting, and penalty shot. The challenge takes place on the Friday night before the weekend games. Fans also get to witness the presentation of the Hobey Baker Award for the best college player.

Best place to get up close:
A little online research will reveal where the teams are practicing before the game. Those practices are usually open to the public and allow you an up-close preview of the upcoming action.

Looking for autographs from the college stars of today and the future NHL superstars of tomorrow? Stake out the bus loading areas where the players get dropped off and picked up.

Best travel tip:
Don't forget to pack the skates and sticks. For those families with budding hockey players and future Frozen Four participants, youth hockey clinics sponsored by the host university are sometimes held. Check schedules for availability.

Notable Quotes:

"I'm excited now and I'm not even playing. It's an exciting time, and it's just that waiting period. You can't wait for it to come, you can't wait to get on the plane to head down there and you can't wait to get started."—Josh Blackburn, Michigan goaltending coach

"Driving to the airport, nobody had any sleep, and that morning you could see all of the Rockies. We had the trophy on the bus and it was just a great feeling of accomplishment."—Head Coach Jerry

York, following Boston College's NCAA Division I hockey championship win.

Relevant Websites:
www.ncaa.com
www.tseworld.com
www.pcevents.com
www.sportstravel.com
www.gotickets.com
www.premieresports.com

WORLD FIGURE SKATING CHAMPIONSHIPS

When?
End of March every year.

Future Locations:
2009–Los Angeles, CA
2010–Turin, Italy

Significance:
Out of all the International Skating Union (ISU) championships, the World Figure Skating Championships (nicknamed the "Worlds") holds the most prestige among figure skaters and their fans. March of every year sees the best skaters in the world competing in men's singles, ladies' singles, pairs, and ice dancing. During the years of the Winter Olympics, the stakes are a bit higher as home countries vie for spots on the Olympic figure skating team.

Each member country of the ISU can enter one skater or team in each event. Exceptions are made if skaters performed exceptionally well at previous tournaments (maximum of three per category). Skaters qualify by belonging to a member nation of the ISU. Criteria to go to the "Worlds" are based on various qualifications that differ from country to country. Having the honor to compete, unknown skaters can become superstars, Olympians, or both, and join the ranks of Brian Boitano, Scott Hamilton, Michelle Kwan, and Katarina Witt.

Who attends?

Fans of figure skating and those who enjoy watching a beautiful, symphonic sport on ice. A preview of sorts to that event, each country will find out how many spots they get in the upcoming Olympic Games.

History

The year 1896 saw the establishment of the first World Championships. Men competed exclusively at the event, yet no formal rule existed preventing a woman from competing. In 1902, Madge Syers-Cave showed up most of the men by taking home the silver medal at that year's competition. World Champion Ulrich Salchow joined the chorus of complaints that Syers-Cave should have captured the gold.

In 1903, the ISU Congress took note of the accomplishment but refused to pass new rules. Syers-Cave returned to the competition in 1904, but suffered an injury, forcing her to withdraw. By 1905, the ISU decided to establish a second-class ladies competition where female skaters could compete for an ISU championship, not a world championship. In addition, the events would be held separately. Over time, the women started to compete alongside the men for their own world championship on an equal playing field… or skating rink.

Notable Athletes:

Sasha Cohen, USA
Katarina Witt, East Germany
Kristi Yamaguchi, USA
Tara Lipinski, USA
Michelle Kwan, USA
Irina Slutskaya, Russia
Scott Hamilton, USA
Brian Boitano, USA
Johnny Weir, USA

Records:

Seven Sixes, World Women's Championship:
Midori Ito (Japan), Paris, France, 1989

Seven Sixes, World Men's Championships:
Donald Jackson (Canada), Prague, Czechoslovakia, 1962

Things to know before you go:

Jumps

Waltz: The first rotational jump skaters learn as they take off from a forward outside edge, complete a half revolution in the air, and land on the back outside edge of the opposite foot.

Salchow: A skater takes off from the back inside edge of the skating foot, completes one rotation in the air, and lands on the back outside edge of the opposite foot. Variations include double, triple, quadruple, and one-foot salchow.

Toe Loop: A skater takes off from the back outside edge of the skating foot with the assistance of the toe of the free foot. The skater turns one rotation in the air, landing on the back outside edge of the take-off foot. Variations include double, triple, and quadruple toe loop.

Loop: A skater takes off from the back outside edge of the skating foot, turns one rotation in the air and lands on the back outside edge of the take-off foot. Variations include double, triple, and quadruple toe loop.

Flip: A toe jump where the skater takes off from the back inside edge of the skating foot with assistance from the toe of the free foot, turns one rotation in the air, and lands on the outside edge of the original free foot. Variations include double and triple flip.

Lutz: A toe jump with the skater taking off from the back outside edge of the skating foot with the assistance of the free foot toe, rotating in the reverse direction one rotation in the air, and landing on the back outside edge of the opposite foot. Variations include double and triple lutz.

Axel: Taking off from the forward outside edge of the skate, completing one and a half revolutions in the air, and landing on the back outside edge of the opposite foot. Variations include double, triple, inside, and one-foot axel.

Spins

Upright: A skater's body stays vertical to the ice. Includes one-foot, back, cross-foot, and lay-back spins. Variations include the Bielman position and the sideways leaning spin.

Sit: Any spin in which the skater's body is located close to the ice and the skating knee is bent to allow the skater to appear to be sitting. Variations include the flying sit, flying change sit, sit change, and sit spin.

Camel: The skater's body is horizontal to the ice, except for the leg used for spinning. Variations include flying camel or forward camel on an outside edge, or back camel on an inside edge.

Pairs

Lifts of varying degrees of difficulty include:

Armpit Lift: The male places one hand under one arm of the female armpit. The female places one hand on the male's shoulder. The male grips the female's other hand with his free hand. The arm of the male that is in the armpit position of the female is to be fully extended.

Waist Lift: The male places both hands on the female's waist and she places both hands on his wrists or shoulders. The female's head should be held high, the back should be straight, and the legs should be at a good extension.

Hand-to-Hand: Both hands of the male and female are clasped as they face each other in the closed lift position with hand-to-hand grip. Or the male is behind the female with the same grip.

Hand-to-Hand Hip: The male places one hand on the female's hip and takes her other hand in his free hand. The female's free hand is placed on the male's shoulder.

Hand-to-Hand Lasso: Different from the hand-to-hand pressure lifts in that the female rotates on her way to the top of the lift. The same is also true for the dismount.

One-Hand Lasso: Same as in hand-to-hand lasso lifts, but when the female reaches full extension, the partner releases one hand at the top of the lift and continues the lift with only one hand.

Additional pair moves include:

Twist Lifts: Thrilling, yet difficult. They include the double split twist lift, the split twist lift, and the lateral twist.

Throw Jumps: Different types of throw jumps include the throw axel, throw Salchow, throw toe loop, throw loop, throw flips, and throw Lutz jumps. Teams can execute single, double, or triple throw jumps.

Pair Spins: Depending on the position (sit, camel, upright, etc.), the direction of the partner's free legs, the skating leg, and the catching holds.

Death Spiral: The male lowers his partner to the ice in a circular rotation while she is arched backward, gliding on one foot. The female holds the male's hand while he rotates her in a circle with her head almost touching the surface of the ice. Variations include forward inside, forward outside, backward inside, and backward outside.

Tickets:

For primary ticket access information, consider: www.usfigureskating.org.

For secondary ticket access, consider:

GoTickets, Inc.

2345 Waukegan Road, Suite 140

Bannockburn, IL 60015-1552
Toll-Free: 1-800-775-1617
Fax: (919) 481-9101
E-mail: sales@gotickets.com
www.gotickets.com

Travel Packages:

If you are going to travel to this event, I would recommend using a reliable company to work with you on making the necessary arrangements. The suppliers listed in this book have solid references and are by far the most trusted in the business. Below are some of the organizations to try for this Top 100 Must See Sporting Event.

Premiere Corporate Events

14 Penn Plaza, Suite 925
New York, NY 10122
Phone: (212) 695-9480
Fax: (212) 564-8098
Toll-Free: 1-877-621-5243
E-mail: requests@tseworld.com
www.tseworld.com
www.pcevents.com

Premiere Sports Travel

201 Shannon Oaks Circle, Suite 205
Cary, NC 27511
Phone: (919) 481-9511
Fax: (919) 481-1337
Toll-Free: 1-800-924-9993
E-mail: sales@sportstravel.com
www.sportstravel.com

Notable Quotes:

"It is pretty much the same thing with every competition. Trust your training. If you work hard, then you should be okay. Just enjoy it. That is why we do the sport, because we enjoy it."—PATRICK CHAN, figure skater

"Worlds is different because you've made the team, but now the pressure of representing the entire U.S. can be overwhelming. There is more depth of skaters at Worlds, so your room for error is much smaller. One minor mistake and you could be out of the medals!"—MICHAEL WEISS, figure skater

Relevant Websites:

www.usfigureskating.org
www.tseworld.com
www.pcevents.com
www.sportstravel.com
www.gotickets.com
www.premieresports.com

X GAMES

When?

Summer X Games – Late July or early August
Winter X Games – End of January

Future Locations:

Summer X Games – Los Angles, California (2009)
Winter X Games – Aspen, Colorado (2010)

Significance:

Youthful by standards of other athletic events, the Summer and Winter X Games are recognized today as the largest action sporting event. Over 100 athletes compete in a dozen different competitions at both seasonal events. These athletic competitions involve anything but standard skateboarding, motocross, skiing, snowboarding, or snowmobiling. The stunts have names such as Tony Hawk's "900" on a skateboard or Travis Pastrana's double back flip on a motocross bike. They fly through the air, sometimes without the greatest of ease, all for prize money and medals of bronze, silver, or gold.

ESPN and ABC currently broadcast both the Summer and Winter X Games. Fans continue to pack not only the event, but also the various interactive events and concerts that run concurrently with the games.

Who attends?
Fans who enjoy watching incredible, death-defying stunts and tricks on bikes, skis, skateboards, etc.

History
The X Games made their formal debut in 1995 after extreme sports started to garner attention as a growing industry. Resistance was strong at first and the participants were considered more as stuntmen who took unreasonable risks than as true athletes. However, growing fan support won over major sponsors and television networks such as ESPN began planning the event in 1993. "EXPN" and extreme sports had come of age.

The Extreme Games debuted in Rhode Island and Vermont. The inaugural event featured nine categories that included bungee jumping, skateboarding, BMX, and street luge with competitions spanning eight days. The athletes of a new generation drew fans of all ages and backgrounds that numbered near 200,000. The sport has grown in profile and has expanded to international competitions. In 1996, Extreme Games were renamed to its current moniker, the X Games.

Today, the X Games have earned mainstream popularity, if not grudging respect from sports purists. The games are the subject of movies, commercials, and even video games. ESPN hosts an annual Action Sports and Music Awards show, a tradition that started in 2001. The following year, the U.S. Olympic Snowboard Freestyle team made a stop off at the X Games to compete weeks before the Olympics in Salt Lake City.

Notable Athletes:
Shaun White: Famed snowboarding and skateboarding trickster. Also known as "Carrot Top" and the "Flying Tomato" because of his thick locks of red hair. He has been recognized with medals, awards, and the 2008 Laureus World Sports Award for the Best Action Sportsperson of the Year.

Danny Kass: American snowboarder and U.S. Olympic Silver Medalist in 2002 and 2006 who truly embraces his punk image. Known for the difficult and eye-popping "Kassaroll."

Sarah Burke: Freestyle skier from Canada recognized as ESPN's 2001 Female Skier of the Year and 2007 Best Female Action Sports Athlete.

Tanner Hall: Free Skier from the United States who was ESPN's Best North American Free Skier in 2006. Hall also holds the record for Winter X Games gold medals with seven.

Travis Pastrana: Recognized as the first rider to achieve a double backflip in competition at X Games 12 in Los Angeles.

Jake Brown: Perhaps most famous for suffering a fractured wrist, bruised lung and liver, ruptured spleen, whiplash, and concussion after unsuccessfully attempting a Big Air stunt. He fell from over forty feet in the air and landed on his backside and back.

Records:
Youngest X Games medalist: Lacey Baker, 14, Bronze Medal, Skateboarding

Youngest X Games competitor: Allysha Bergado, 12, Skateboarding

Things to know before you go:
The X Games are more than just the games themselves, as there are many activities, concerts, and interactive fan experiences. Check out the X Games website (expn.go.com) for more information.

Tickets:
Entry to the Summer or Winter ESPN X Games is free to the public and on a first-come, first-serve basis. No tickets or passes are necessary.

Travel Packages:

If you are going to travel to this event, I would recommend using a reliable company to work with you on making the necessary arrangements. The suppliers listed in this book have solid references and are by far the most trusted in the business. Below are some of the organizations to try for this Top 100 Must See Sporting Event.

Premiere Corporate Events

14 Penn Plaza, Suite 925
New York, NY 10122
Phone: (212) 695-9480
Fax: (212) 564-8098
Toll-Free: 1-877-621-5243
E-mail: requests@tseworld.com
www.tseworld.com
www.pcevents.com

Premiere Sports Travel

201 Shannon Oaks Circle, Suite 205
Cary, NC 27511
Phone: (919) 481-9511
Fax: (919) 481-1337
Toll-Free: 1-800-924-9993
E-mail: sales@sportstravel.com
www.sportstravel.com

Sports Travel Insider's Edge:

Best way to watch the action:

In addition to being able to watch the X Games, you can become a volunteer through ESPN Event Media. Those 18 years of age or older commit to two days and attend a mandatory orientation. You get a behind-the-scenes view of the action, along with free gifts, meals, snacks, refreshments, and entries into a raffle exclusively for volunteers.

Best place to get up close:

EXPN recognizes the Interactive Village as "the designated Official Winter X Games Sponsor Booth area." The Village gives fans the chance to get autographs of their favorite X Games superstars. They can also participate in wall climbing and video game playing. There are free giveaways from sponsors and the chance to try new, upcoming products. It is usually located by the main entrance of the event and it offers fun activities for all attending fans.

X-Fest is considered the ultimate action sports and music festival. Live music plays while fans attend autograph sessions and get interactive with mini-skate and BMX parks.

Best travel tip:

They may call it extreme sports, but it is for the whole family. The X Games provide free events for the youngsters in an environment that prohibits alcohol. Several interactive activities keep your kids interested in the X Game events.

Notable Quote:

"X Games, it's an event but it's still a show. I try to put on the best show possible. I'm thrilled. This is awesome."—TRAVIS PASTRANA, motorsports competitor

Relevant Websites:

www.expn.go.com
www.tseworld.com
www.pcevents.com
www.sportstravel.com
www.premieresports.com

CHEERLEADING NATIONALS

Where?

Universal Orlando
6000 Universal Boulevard
Orlando, FL 32819

When?

Annually at the end of March.

Significance:

Once a year, cheerleading teams from elementary school to high school compete in the U.S. Spirit Nationals. Even adults get in on the action as they vie for championships in open competition. Under the auspices of the U.S. All Star Federation for Cheer and Dance Teams (USASF) and the National Federation of State High School Associations (NFHS), cheerleading teams meet every year to show off their synchronized moves and bright smiles while competing for national superiority at Universal Orlando.

The U.S. Spirit Nationals is an open competition that takes place over three days. No pre-qualification is necessary for entry or participation, which makes the competition that much more exciting and a chance to cheer for the underdog cheerleaders. Champions are crowned in various categories that include All Star & Rec Cheer Team, School Cheer Team, and Dance Team. Winners receive national championship trophies, jackets, die-cast custom medals, and a banner to proudly display in their school or other facility. In addition, six teams receive the opportunity to compete in the World Cheerleading Championship and appear on an international stage. Bring it on!

Who attends?

Aspiring cheerleaders, competing cheerleaders' family members, fans of the *Bring It On* movies, and those who enjoy people being flipped and thrown through the air with seemingly the greatest of ease.

How to get there?

From the Orlando International Airport, take SR-528 West eleven miles to I-4 East. Take I-4 East two miles to exit 75A. Follow the signs to Universal Orlando's main parking garage or to one of the three resort hotels.

Tickets:

For primary ticket access information, consider: www.usspiritopen.com/spectatortickets.html.

For secondary ticket access, consider:

GoTickets, Inc.
2345 Waukegan Road, Suite 140
Bannockburn, IL 60015-1552
Toll-Free: 1-800-775-1617
Fax: (919) 481-9101
E-mail: sales@gotickets.com
www.gotickets.com

Accommodations:

Loews Royal Pacific Resort
6300 Hollywood Way
Orlando, FL 32819
Phone: (407) 503-3000
Fax: (407) 503-3010
Toll-Free: 1-877-819-7884
www.loewshotels.com

Note: Paradise awaits you with tropical landscaping, waterfalls, and a lagoon-style pool.

Comfort Suites Orlando
9350 Turkey Lake Road
Orlando, FL 32819
Phone: (407) 351-5050
Fax: (407) 363-7953
Toll-Free: 1-800-424-6423
www.comfortsuitesorlando.com

Conveniently located just one mile from Universal Orlando.

Hilton Garden Inn
5877 American Way
Orlando, FL 32819
Phone: (407) 363-9332
Fax: (407) 363-9335
www.hiltongardeninn.com

Note: Close to many attractions and one mile from the competition at Universal Orlando. The I-Ride Trolley Stop provides transportation to local shops and restaurants.

Four Points by Sheraton Orlando Studio City
5905 International Drive
Orlando, FL 32819
Phone: (407) 351-2100
Fax: (407) 345-5249

www.fourpointsstudiocity.com

Note: All rooms boast a view of Universal Orlando Resort, International Drive, and the beautiful Orlando skyline.

Holiday Inn Express
5605 Major Boulevard
Orlando, FL 32819
Phone: (407) 363-1333
Fax: (407) 363-4510
Toll-Free: 1-800-HOLIDAY
www.hiexpress.com

Note: Twelve miles from the airport and one mile from Universal Orlando. A more afford-able option with outdoor pool, game room, and guest laundry facilities.

Holiday Inn Hotel & Suites
5905 Kirkman Road
Orlando, FL 32819
Phone: (407) 351-3333
Fax: (407) 351-3577
Toll-Free: 1-800-HOLIDAY
www.hiuniversal.com

Note: Walking distance to Universal Orlando and a fifteen-minute drive to other attractions, including Walt Disney World Resort.

On-Site Hospitality:
While there is no formal onsite hospitality, you are in the midst of Universal Studios movie theme park and Universal's Islands of Adventure.

Travel Packages:
If you are going to travel to this event, I would recommend using a reliable company to work with you on making the necessary arrangements. The suppliers listed in this book have solid references and are by far the most trusted in the business. Below are some of the organizations to try for this Top 100 Must See Sporting Event.

Premiere Corporate Events
14 Penn Plaza, Suite 925
New York, NY 10122

Phone: (212) 695-9480
Fax: (212) 564-8098
Toll-Free: 1-877-621-5243
E-mail: requests@tseworld.com
www.tseworld.com
www.pcevents.com

Premiere Sports Travel
201 Shannon Oaks Circle, Suite 205
Cary, NC 27511
Phone: (919) 481-9511
Fax: (919) 481-1337
Toll-Free: 1-800-924-9993
E-mail: sales@sportstravel.com
www.sportstravel.com

Dining:

Vito's Chop House
8633 International Drive
Orlando, FL 32819
Phone: (407) 354-2467
www.talkofthetownrestaurants.com

Note: One of Orlando's premier restaurants with sophisticated dinner options in an inti-mate atmosphere. Choose from a variety of specialty martinis, fine wines, and cigars.

NBA City
6068 Universal Boulevard
Orlando, FL 32819
Phone: (407) NBA-CITY
www.nbacity.com

Note: For the diner who loves all things bas-ketball. Sports memorabilia surrounds you as you enjoy great appetizers and entrées.

Jimmy Buffett's Margaritaville
6000 Universal Boulevard, Suite 704
Orlando, FL 32819
Phone: (407) 224-2155
www.margaritavilleorlando.com

Note: Advertises as a "cross between Key West cooking and Caribbean cuisine." A place where you can truly waste away again.

Kirkman Ale House

5573 Kirkman Road
Orlando, FL 32819
Phone: (407) 248-0000
www.millersalehouse.com
Note: Excellent food that can be washed down with a wide variety of beers.

Airport:

Orlando International Airport
1 Airport Boulevard
Orlando, FL 32827
Phone: (407) 825-2001
www.orlandoairports.net

Sports Travel Insider's Edge:

Best way to watch the action:
If you know or are related to someone in the competition, talk to the team coach about ticket orders that can be included with reservations. Not only do you get a discounted rate, but you also get the chance to get your tickets before you leave.

Best place to get up close:
Venue bracelets provide all day, unlimited access to the entire U.S. Spirit National Championships. Purchasing on Friday gives you the opportunity to buy Saturday and Sunday bracelets, avoiding the large crowds on those busier competition days. You can take advantage of all that Universal Orlando has to offer and watch the competition at your convenience.

Best travel tip:
In addition to being at Universal Orlando, you are a fifteen-minute drive to Disney World. Enjoy these and other attractions while you are in sunny Orlando.

Notable Quote:

"Quality. Honesty. Excellence.... Members of the U.S. Spirit organization remain unified in achieving these goals.... Our commitment leads to incredible competitions unlike any other in the world, original fashion and styles and top instruction from spirit industry professionals."—From the official U.S. Spirit website (www.us-spirit.com)

Relevant Websites:
www.usspiritopen.com
www.orlandoinfo.com
www.tseworld.com
www.pcevents.com
www.sportstravel.com
www.gotickets.com
www.premieresports.com

GYM DOGS

Where?
Ramsey Center
300 River Road
Athens, GA 30602

When?
From January to April during the NCAA Gymnastics season.

Significance:
When you think of the University of Georgia, you think of the Bulldogs. While higher-profile sports have reached a certain level of success, those athletes have not come close to the domination of the Georgia Gym Dogs. The successful college gymnastics program, under the tutelage of Suzanne Yoculan, have spent the better part of the last twenty years bringing home Southeastern Conference titles (sixteen to date) and NCAA National Gymnastics championships (nine to date).

Up to 10,000 fans flock to the Gym Dogs' meets at the Ramsey Center, placing them second to the football program in University of Georgia sports. They cheer on a team that brings home titles and sets records that seem impossible to break. The Gym Dogs hold the best championship team score of 198.575 from the NCAA Southeast Regional in 1998. They also boast four undefeated seasons where all other programs have yet to notch even one. Since the early nineties, it was not surprising to see a Gym Dog capture an NCAA individual title. To date, they have won twenty-nine.

Yoculan recently announced her retirement after the 2009 season. The team will be in the competent, chalked hands of long-time assistant Jay Clark.

Who attends?
University of Georgia students, aspiring gymnasts, and friends and family members of the competitors.

How to get there?
The campus and the Ramsey Center are easily accessible from I-85 North and South and I-20 West.

Tickets:
For primary ticket access information, consider: www.georgiadogs.com.

For secondary ticket access, consider:

GoTickets, Inc.
2345 Waukegan Road, Suite 140
Bannockburn, IL 60015-1552
Toll-Free: 1-800-775-1617
Fax: (919) 481-9101
E-mail: sales@gotickets.com
www.gotickets.com

Accommodations:

Holiday Inn
197 East Broad Street
Athens, GA 30601
Phone: (706) 549-4433
Fax: (706) 548-3031
Toll-Free:1-888-HOLIDAY
www.hi-athens.com
Note: Adjacent to the University of Georgia and four miles from the Ben Epps Regional Airport. Offers superior service and delicious breakfast and lunch buffets.

Holiday Inn Hotel Athens
513 West Broad Street
Athens, GA 30601
Phone: (706) 546-8122
Fax: (706) 546-1722
Toll-Free:1-888-HOLIDAY
www.hi-athens.com
Note: Located two blocks from campus. Free continental breakfast and high-speed Internet access. Onsite exercise facility, business center, and outdoor pool.

Courtyard Marriott
166 North Finley Street
Athens, GA 30601
Phone: (706) 369-7000
Fax: (706) 548-4224
Toll-Free: 1-800-MARRIOTT
www.marriott.com
Note: A hotel with a Southern rocking chair veranda and a courtyard café. Near the Classic Center, Georgia Museum of Art, and State Botanical Gardens.

Hilton Garden Inn Athens
390 East Washington Street
Athens, GA 30601
Phone: (706) 353-6800
Fax: (706) 353-6807
Toll-Free:1-888-HOLIDAY
www.hi-athens.com
Note: Walking distance from downtown and across the street from the Classic Center.

Travel Packages:
If you are going to travel to this event, I would recommend using a reliable company to work with you on making the necessary arrangements. The suppliers listed in this book have solid references and are by far the most trusted in the business. Below are some of the organizations to try for this Top 100 Must See Sporting Event.

Premiere Corporate Events
14 Penn Plaza, Suite 925
New York, NY 10122

Phone: (212) 695-9480
Fax: (212) 564-8098
Toll-Free: 1-877-621-5243
E-mail: requests@tseworld.com
www.tseworld.com
www.pcevents.com

Premiere Sports Travel
201 Shannon Oaks Circle, Suite 205
Cary, NC 27511
Phone: (919) 481-9511
Fax: (919) 481-1337
Toll-Free: 1-800-924-9993
E-mail: sales@sportstravel.com
www.sportstravel.com

Dining:

Five & Ten
1653 South Lumpkin Street
Athens, GA 30606
Phone: (706) 546-7300
www.fiveandten.com
Note: Try the Frogmore Stew (shrimp boil) and Caesar salad with apple-smoked bacon.

Grit
199 Prince Avenue
Athens, GA 30601-2400
Phone: (706) 543-6592
www.thegrit.com
Note: Vegetarian menu served in generous portions at affordable prices. Located in a historic building in Athens.

East West Bistro
351 East Broad Street
Athens, GA 30601
Phone: (706) 546-9378
www.eastwestbistro.com
Note: Diverse menu features Asian and northern Italian dishes. Also boasts an equally diverse wine list.

Last Resort Grill
174-184 West Clayton Street
Athens, GA 30601

Phone: (706) 549-0810
www.lastresortgrill.com
Note: Great Sunday brunch. Shrimp and grits are popular and come highly recommended.

Airports:

Athens Ben Epps Airport
1010 Ben Epps Drive
Athens, GA 30605
Phone: (706) 613-3420
www.athensairport.net

Hartfield-Jackson Atlanta International Airport (about sixty miles from Athens)
6000 North Terminal Parkway
Atlanta, GA 30320
Phone: (404) 209-1700
www.atlanta-airport.com

Sports Travel Insider's Edge:

Best way to watch the action:
For kids interested in gymnastics, a Gym Kids membership gives them a free t-shirt, newsletter, and the opportunity to lead the team out of the tunnel before a home meet. They also receive an invitation to attend the pre-season Sneak Peek.

Best place to get up close:
Stay after the meet to get an autograph from a Gym Dog. They love to stick around for their appreciative fans.

Best travel tip:
After an exciting experience of watching great athletes, enjoy Athens art and culture by attending the Classic Center, Georgia Museum of Art, State Botanical Gardens, or the UGA Performing Arts Center.

Notable Quotes:

"When our athletes walk on campus we tell them they have the chance to win eight championships—four NCAA titles and four SEC titles. Winning SEC

Championships are just as important to us as winning NCAA Championships. A lot of the same teams you see at SECs will be at nationals as well. With the strength of our conference, winning this meet can be just as difficult as winning a national championship. It is as competitive of an atmosphere as you'll find in all of sports."—SUZANNE YOCULAN, head coach

"I don't want to sound boastful. I understand that it's not like we're unbeatable. It's not like that. It's just that we can win and we have more than just a chance, we have a good chance."—GRACE TAYLOR, "Gym Dog"

"They are just a juggernaut right now."—GREG MARSDEN, Utah gymnastics coach

Relevant Websites:

www.georgiadogs.com
www.visitathensga.com
www.tseworld.com
www.pcevents.com
www.sportstravel.com
www.gotickets.com
www.premieresports.com

JAPAN SERIES

When?
Annually in late October.

Future Locations:
Similar to the World Series in America, the venues are decided based on the teams that make the playoffs.

Significance:
The Japan Championship Series (Nihon Senshuken Shiriizu Shiai) is the "Land of the Rising Sun's" answer to America's World Series. Champions of the Central League and Pacific League face off in a best-of-seven yakyu (Japanese for baseball) championship game. The first team to take four

games wins Japan's "October Classic." However, unlike the World Series, the season is not over for the champion. The Japan Series champion goes on to represent the country in the Asia Series.

There are differences between Japanese yakyu and American baseball. First, the ball is smaller and more tightly wound. If a game ends in a tie after nine innings, three additional innings are played. If the teams are still deadlocked, the matchup is declared a draw. General play among the athletes is less aggressive and home runs are fewer and far between. The strike zone is larger near the batter but smaller away from the batter.

Teams that go to the Japan Series are not identified completely by the city where they reside. In fact, most teams play in and around Tokyo and Osaka. Because of those clusters, Japanese professional teams are named after corporate owners and sponsors. Unlike America, baseball franchises do not have territorial requirements found in Major League Baseball. However, to gain support in the various areas, a location and the corporate sponsor identifies the team. There are only a couple of teams still solely using their sponsor's name.

Who attends?
Since baseball is the most popular sport in Japan, baseball fans from throughout the country, both casual followers and die-hard fanatics.

History
Nippon Professional Baseball (NPB) is Japan's answer to Major League Baseball (MLB). Yakyu, as they refer to it, was brought over from the United States during the Meiji Period. In 1934, the Greater Japan Tokyo Baseball Club and the original Japanese Baseball League was formed. A 1950 reorganization of the latter league resulted in the establishment of the NPB.

Baseball is the most popular sport in Japan, making the Japan Series a popular and highly watched event. Playoffs to get to the Japan Series have taken various forms since its inception. From 1973 to 1982, the Pacific League split their seasons with the first half winner playing the second half winner in a playoff to determine the team that went on to the Series. In 2004, the Pacific League changed the playoff system to have its third and second place team play in a best-of-three series and the winner would play the team ranked first in a best-of-five format. This was dubbed the "Climax Series." By 2007, both the Pacific and Central Leagues used this playoff format.

Continuing and complex financial problems continue to affect the NPB. Parent companies are subsidizing their teams to cover great losses. The only organizations that enjoy success and do not need financial assistance are the Yomiuri Giants and the Hanshin Tigers. Adding to yakyu's woes was the establishment of a professional soccer league in 1993, dividing the sports loyalties, not to mention the incoming revenues. The J. League did not cluster their soccer teams in a major city, but chose to identify their teams without any mention of a corporate sponsor. That built strong grass-roots support that continues to threaten NPB teams. The loss of popular and marketable NPB players to Major League Baseball has also affected attendance.

Current NPB Teams:

Central League
Yomiuri Giants
Hanshin Tigers
Chunichi Dragons
Yokohama BayStars
Hiroshima Toyo Carp
Tokyo Yakult Swallows

Pacific League
Hokkaido Nippon Ham Fighters
Tohoku Rakuten Golden Eagles
Chiba Lotte Marines
Saitama Seibu Lions
Orix Buffalos
Fukuoka SoftBank Hawks

Notable Athletes:
Many notable Japanese players appearing in the Japan Series have successfully made the transition to Major League Baseball, including:

Hideo Nomo
Kazuhiro Sasaki
Ichiro Suzuki
Tadahito Iguchi
Kenji Johjima
Hideki Matsui
So Taguchi
Hideki Irabu
Daisuke Matsuzaka
Kazuo Matsui
Kosuke Fukudome

Records:
Team with the most championships: Yomiuri Giants, 20 pennants

Things to know before you go:

Toshu: pitcher
Ichirui: first base
Nirui: second base
Sanrui: third base
Honrui: home
Dasha: hitter
Daseki: at bat
Anda: base hit
Naiya Anda: infield hit
Niruida: double
Sanruida: triple
Honruida: homer
Raito-mae: base hit to right
Senta-mae: base hit to center

Senta backscreen: any home run to center
Refuto-mae: base hit to left
Gisei Furai: sacrifice fly
Gida: sacrifice bunt
Streto: fastball
Kaabu: curve
Fohku: forkball
Henkakyuu: breaking ball
Suraida: slider
Dead booru: pitch that hits a batter
Kikenkyuu: brushback pitch

How to get there?
Since most teams play in or around Tokyo or Osaka, the best way to get to the park hosting the Japan Series is by subway. Parking is unavailable at most stadiums.

Tickets:
For primary ticket access information, consider: http://t.pia.jp/sports/baseball.html (website in Japanese).

For secondary ticket access, consider:

GoTickets, Inc.
2345 Waukegan Road, Suite 140
Bannockburn, IL 60015-1552
Toll-Free: 1-800-775-1617
Fax: (919) 481-9101
E-mail: sales@gotickets.com
www.gotickets.com

Travel Packages:
If you are going to travel to this event, I would recommend using a reliable company to work with you on making the necessary arrangements. The suppliers listed in this book have solid references and are by far the most trusted in the business. Below are some of the organizations to try for this Top 100 Must See Sporting Event.

Premiere Corporate Events
14 Penn Plaza, Suite 925
New York, NY 10122
Phone: (212) 695-9480
Fax: (212) 564-8098

Toll-Free: 1-877-621-5243
E-mail: requests@tseworld.com
www.tseworld.com
www.pcevents.com

Premiere Sports Travel
201 Shannon Oaks Circle, Suite 205
Cary, NC 27511
Phone: (919) 481-9511
Fax: (919) 481-1337
Toll-Free: 1-800-924-9993
E-mail: sales@sportstravel.com
www.sportstravel.com

Sports Travel Insider's Edge:

Best way to watch the action:
With the teams located in Tokyo and Osaka, you don't have to settle for just one game at one stadium. Japanese baseball provides multiple environments and ballparks for the hardcore baseball fan from America or the Land of the Rising Sun.

Best place to get up close:
If you want to immerse yourself in the entire Japanese baseball experience, pick up a pack or two of Japanese baseball cards. They are great collectibles and even better sources of information.

Best travel tip:
If you long for a different kind of baseball championship tournament, wait until October to see the best of the best Japanese teams face off for their Japan Series title.

Notable Quotes:

"There's no place like it."—TREY HILLMAN, Hokaido Nippon Ham Fighters manager

"For a Japanese player, it is not enough to win. You must win with dignity and honor."—KEN IWAMOTO, interpreter for Trey Hillman

Relevant Websites:
www.npb.or.jp

english.baseball-museum.or.jp
www.japanbaseballdaily.com
http://t.pia.jp/sports/baseball.html
www.tseworld.com

www.pcevents.com
www.sportstravel.com
www.gotickets.com
www.premieresports.com

THE TOP TEN CITIES
FOR HOSTING
A MAJOR SPORTING EVENT

There are many factors involved in choosing a top city for great sporting events worthy of inclusion in a "Top 10" list. Debating the best sports cities for having events is a discussion that many sports enthusiasts engage in, yet there is no easy answer. Every fan has an opinion. Every city will have its pros and cons, but all should fit the following qualifications:

- Locals that embrace and get behind the event.
- Support from city officials and a local organizing committee.
- Weather that provides opportunities to host outdoor activities like golf and other secondary events.
- A "central heartbeat" for the fans or an area where people are able to congregate.
- Capacity to handle an event logistically, but not so big that an event can get lost in everything else going on.
- The necessary hotel accommodations for those who travel to see the event, whether value, moderate, or luxury.
- Diverse restaurants for a variety of dining experiences.
- Quality sports facilities that can host major events.
- Status as a true "sports town." This comes from the energy and excitement that people in the town provide.
- Its own unique personality, character, and vibe.
- Airport accessibility, including flight availability and proximity to the city center.

1. Miami, Florida

PROS: South Beach is the perfect place for a central location for fans to gather. Great hotels are in abundance, as are dining options throughout south Florida. The bars stay open late for longer celebrations and revelry with celebrities in the mix. The weather is hard to beat for golf and other outdoor activities in and around the ocean. The facilities are top-notch, from tracks for NASCAR to fields for football.

CONS: Is there such a thing as too much to do while in town? The multitude of professional sporting teams and the beach thins out the sports fans and their loyalties. In addition, the city itself, and the strong vibe it provides, can overshadow any and all of the events that take place.

2. Indianapolis, Indiana

PROS: A classic sports town with great sports fans. From high school to professional athletics, the residents live and breathe sports. Hosting annual events such as the Indy 500 keeps the profile of this city on par with its East and West Coast counterparts. Sports facilities such as the new Lucas Oil Stadium and the Conseco Fieldhouse can hold their own as well. A central meeting area is prominent, and the downtown area provides a high level of excitement. The city has all necessary levels of hotel accommodations and some terrific dining options.

CONS: Really, weather is the only major con. Fortunately, it didn't stop the NFL from awarding Indianapolis the Super Bowl in 2012.

3. San Antonio, Texas

PROS: The weather usually fails to disappoint and cooperates for outdoor events. The Riverwalk and downtown area are the perfect backdrop to host high-profile sporting events. The center of the city is ideal for parties and other gatherings. The Alamodome is well suited for basketball and can house other sporting events too. With great weather comes great golfing. Also, there are plenty of quality hotels with a variety of options and pricing. Dining options are plentiful.

CONS: While the Spurs enjoy a loyal and enthusiastic following, that is really the only show in town. Lack of a variety of professional teams means a lack of opportunity to attract certain events.

4. New Orleans, Louisiana

PROS: New Orleans and hospitality go hand in hand. The French Quarter is party central and a key hub for fans to congregate. The city is known for great bars and restaurants that feature some of the best dining in the country. Hosting the Sugar Bowl for many years and providing a home for the New Orleans Saints has given the city a bevy of die-hard sports fans. Great weather makes for fantastic golfing and outdoor activities. While known for Mardi Gras, this city can host a party.

CONS: The Superdome and a basketball arena would be considered a pro, but those are the only major buildings for sporting events in the area. Limiting for any other event that wants to call the Big Easy home.

5. Dallas, Texas

PROS: Weather is great and venue space is top-shelf. Downtown is easily accessible. Many options for dining and partying into the wee hours. A large airport provides plenty of flights in and out of the city.

CONS: Like many other cities, Dallas is saddled with a lack of centralized locations for fans to meet. The city also does not have a track record of hosting major events in the past, although it will play host to the Super Bowl in 2011.

6. San Diego, California

PROS: A city filled with loyal sports fans can make any sporting event that much better. Great accommodations and resorts provide many options for an overnight stay. The weather is usually cooperative and sunny. A commitment to hospitality makes the stay that much better since the local economy relies on that industry. Die-hard golfers will love the links.

CONS: The town is very spread out, although the Gaslamp District does provide somewhat of a central meeting location. No overall vibe to speak of. Service at restaurants may be top-notch, but the cuisine itself is, at best, fair.

7. Phoenix, Arizona

PROS: You can't beat the year-round weather for outdoor events and a golf excursion at one of the outstanding courses. Indoor venue space is first-rate as well. The airport offers many flight options. This is a town that excels in the hospitality industry, providing great dining options and hotels with exceptional accommodations and service.

CONS: Being so spread out, there really is not a central location for sports fans to congregate, making it hard to feel a vibe when a major event is in town.

8. Las Vegas, Nevada

PROS: Simply put, hospitality is what Las Vegas does best. The hotels and restaurants are at the ready for major events. You are not going to find many cities with more options for lodging and dining. The Strip is the ultimate central location. Add to that the weather and the gambling.

CONS: In spite of all the hotels and casinos, major venue space is lacking. In addition, many major teams and organizations pretend not to see sports and gambling going hand in hand.

9. Tampa Bay, Florida

PROS: A great destination location with sunny weather. Perfect for playing golf or frolicking on the beach. Nearby Orlando and Ebor City (mini French Quarter area) provide even more options. Multiple restaurants to choose from throughout the area.

CONS: The area is spread out and does not have a central location for fans to congregate. Also, there is a significant lack of upscale hotel properties.

10. Atlanta, Georgia

PROS: The weather holds up well for the most part, which makes for exceptional golfing opportunities. Many hotel and dining options are enhanced by Atlanta's active nightlife. Buckhead is where the party is. Multiple sports teams making their home in the city means great space for venues.

CONS: Atlanta is a large city and a bit too spread out with no central area for fans to meet. The weather can be cooperative, but it can also turn bad quickly. A bit unpredictable; just ask those who were there the last time the Super Bowl was in town.

THE 100 SPORTING EVENTS YOU MUST SEE LIVE

1 _____ Masters

2 _____ World Cup

3 _____ Super Bowl

4 _____ Summer Olympics

5 _____ Army vs. Navy Football Game

6 _____ New York City Marathon

7 _____ World Series

8 _____ Winter Olympics

9 _____ Red Sox vs. Yankees at Yankee Stadium

10 _____ UNC vs. Duke Basketball Game at Cameron Indoor Stadium

11 _____ Wimbledon

12 _____ Stanley Cup

13 _____ Tour de France

14 _____ Cubs Game at Wrigley Field

15 _____ BCS National Championship Game in New Orleans

16 _____ Liverpool vs. Manchester United at Old Trafford

17 _____ Michigan vs. Ohio State at The Big House

18 _____ NFL Conference Championships

19 _____ Daytona 500

20 _____ Final Four—NCAA Men's Basketball

21 _____ Ryder Cup

22 _____ Baseball Hall of Fame Induction Weekend

23 _____ Harvard vs. Yale at Yale

24 _____ Kentucky Derby

25 _____ UEFA Champions League

26 _____ Rose Bowl

27 _____ British Open

28 _____ Horse Racing at Saratoga

29 _____ Late Season Green Bay Packers Game at Lambeau Field

30 _____ Canadiens vs. Maple Leafs in Toronto

31 _____ Indy 500

32 _____ Professional Bull Riders World Finals

33 _____ Dubai World Cup

34 _____ Hong Kong Sevens

35 _____ Monaco Grand Prix

36 _____ Running of the Bulls

37 _____ Rugby World Cup

38 _____ Red River Shootout

39 _____ Notre Dame Football Game

40 _____ MLB All-Star Game

41 _____ Iron Bowl at Alabama

42 _____ Epsom Derby

43 _____ Calgary Stampede

44 _____ Koshien Baseball Tournament

45 _____ Special Olympics

46 _____ Soccer Game at Maracanã Stadium in Rio

47 _____ Texas Football Friday Night Lights in Odessa

48 _____ U.S. Open Tennis Tournament

49 _____ USC vs. UCLA Basketball Game at Pauley Pavilion

50 _____ Le Mans 24

51 _____ Ironman World Championship

52 _____ Iowa vs. Iowa State Wrestling Meet at Iowa

53 _____ Golden Gloves at Madison Square Garden

54 _____ French Open

55 _____ Baseball Game at Fenway Park

56 _____ Belmont Stakes

57 _____ Kangaroos Australian Football Game

58 _____ Heavyweight Title Fight at Madison Square Garden

59 ____ All Blacks Rugby Game
60 ____ ACC Basketball Tournament
61 ____ Caribbean World Series
62 ____ FA Cup
63 ____ Indiana High School Basketball
Tournament Finals
64 ____ U.S. Open Golf Tournament
65 ____ Midnight Madness at University
of Kentucky
66 ____ Preakness Stakes
67 ____ NFL Draft
68 ____ National Finals Rodeo
69 ____ Basketball Game at Phog Allen
Fieldhouse
70 ____ Basketball Game at Madison
Square Garden
71 ____ Prefontaine Classic
72 ____ MLB Opening Day in Cincinnati
73 ____ Nathan's Hot Dog Eating
Contest
74 ____ Iditarod
75 ____ Little 500
76 ____ Basketball Game at Rucker
Park, Harlem, NY
77 ____ Boston Marathon
78 ____ Cowboys Monday Night
Football Game in Dallas
79 ____ Head of the Charles Regatta

80 ____ Florida vs. Georgia Football
Game
81 ____ Lady Vols Basketball Game
82 ____ NBA All-Star Game
83 ____ Pipeline Surfing
84 ____ Australian Open Tennis
Tournament
85 ____ Baseball Game at Rickwood
Field in Alabama
86 ____ Harlem Globetrotters
Performance
87 ____ Spring Training Game at
Tigertown
88 ____ Backyard Brawl in Morgantown
89 ____ London Marathon
90 ____ Penn Relays
91 ____ Presidents Cup
92 ____ World Junior Hockey
Championship
93 ____ Westminster Dog Show
94 ____ NFL Hall of Fame Induction
95 ____ NCAA Men's Lacrosse
Championship
96 ____ College Baseball World Series
97 ____ Beanpot Hockey Tournament
98 ____ Bayou Classic
99 ____ Little League World Series
100 ____ UFC Title Fight

ABOUT THE AUTHOR

ROBERT TUCHMAN is the founder of TSE Sports & Entertainment, a global leader in sports marketing. The company was sold in 2006 to Premiere Global Sports, a platform company of private equity firm Pfingsten Partners. Tuchman has been featured in many publications, including *The Wall Street Journal*, *USA Today*, *The New York Times*, *BusinessWeek*, and *Entrepreneur Magazine*. A frequent guest on *Your World with Neil Cavuto*, Tuchman has appeared on CNN, BET, and on the CBS Morning News. He resides in New York City.